Man Is Wolf to Man

Man Is Wolf to Man

Surviving the Gulag

Janusz Bardach
Kathleen Gleeson

UNIVERSITY OF CALIFORNIA PRESS
Berkeley · Los Angeles

University of California Press
Berkeley and Los Angeles, California

© 1998 by
Janusz Bardach and Kathleen Gleeson

Library of Congress Cataloging-in-Publication Data

Bardach, Janusz.
    Man is wolf to man : surviving the gulag / Janusz Bardach and
Kathleen Gleeson.
        p.   cm.
    ISBN 0-520-21352-1 (alk. paper)
        1. Bardach, Janusz.   2. Political prisoners—Russia (Federation)—
Kolyma Mountains Region—Biography.   3. Kolyma (Concentration
camp)—History.   4. Kolyma Mountains Region—History—20th century.
I. Gleeson, Kathleen.   II. Title.
DK771.K67B373   1998
940.54′7247′09577—dc21   98-5402
                                                                                        CIP

Printed in the United States of America
9   8   7   6   5   4   3   2

To the memory of my parents,
Ottylia and Mark Bardach.
                    JB

Contents

Foreword

The Soviet empire of Stalin's day is a world hard for most of us to imagine. Seldom has any nation endured such a massive, self-inflicted genocide. And seldom, if ever, has a major country kept so high a proportion of its own people, and those of countries it dominated, in prison. We know now that during Stalin's lifetime more than 20 million Soviets—more than one out of eight men, women, and children—were executed by firing squads or sent for long terms to the gulag. After the Soviet Union and Nazi Germany divided Eastern Europe between them in 1939 and 1940, hundreds of thousands more people from Poland, Romania, and the Baltic states found themselves in Soviet execution cellars or in the far-flung network of labor camps. A traveler today can find Polish and Lithuanian names on prisoners' graves from the Arctic Ocean to the steppes of Kazakhstan.

Few Americans are aware that the most notorious corner of the gulag, that country within a country, lay only a few hundred miles from U.S. soil. An hour or so by jet plane west of the Bering Strait, where the United States and Russia almost touch, lies the basin of the Kolyma River. For millions of older Russians, Kolyma is a shorthand word: like Auschwitz, it is the part that stands for the whole. For years, with local names changed, you could hear the same joke in every Russian city:

"What's the highest building in St. Petersburg?"

"It's St. Isaac's Cathedral."

"No, it's not. It's the Shpalerka [the former secret police prison]. Because from the top floor, you can see all the way to Kolyma."

Kolyma is where the bulk of Russia's gold is. Over a span of two decades starting in the early 1930s, more than two million prisoners were sent to mine that gold. The region quickly became legendary for its remoteness, its extreme cold, and its high death rate. Kolyma lies far beyond the reach of a railway line; getting there required crossing all of Russia on the Trans-Siberian and then traveling by ship for another week northward through the icy Sea of Okhotsk. Hundreds of thousands of underfed Kolyma prisoners perished from malnutrition, from mining accidents, and from the bitter cold. The area's record low temperature is minus 97.8 degrees F. Kolyma is the coldest inhabited region on earth.

Few prisoners returned from Kolyma to what they called "the mainland" until after Stalin's death in 1953. Those who came back, as it happened, included some of the greatest writers to survive the camps, several of whom have had their work translated into English. The most notable of these are the memoirist Eugenia Ginzburg and Varlam Shalamov, the poet and author of spare, razor-sharp short stories whom Alexander Solzhenitsyn called "the finest writer of the gulag."

For several decades, it was only through memories such as theirs that we could learn much about this place. Even long after the dismantling of the Stalin-era labor camp system, it was impossible for any Westerner to travel to Kolyma. Then, under Gorbachev, many closed doors opened. In 1991, I spent six months living in Russia studying how Russians today are trying to come to terms with the Stalin period. At the end of that time I went to Kolyma, the place I had so long read about and now at last could see.

Although I had often heard former prisoners describe Kolyma, I don't think I fully grasped the reality of the place until I stood in the ruins of a giant forced labor mining camp called Butugy-chag, still dotted with patches of snow in mid-June. Barren, rocky hills rose steeply on all sides, suddenly giving meaning to the expression prisoners had for this region: the dark side of the moon. To be imprisoned here meant not just being separated from friends and families, not just being half-starved while working twelve hours a day, not just enduring the terrible cold; it also meant being in a place of unimaginable remoteness and desolation. And even there—with nothing but snow-covered forests and mountainsides to escape to, no refuge for hundreds of miles—even there, rusted strands of barbed wire still surrounded the camp, and a group of punishment cells in the camp's internal prison had thick stone walls and heavy, cross-hatched iron bars on the windows.

In 1994 I published a book (*The Unquiet Ghost: Russians Remember Stalin*, Penguin) about my time in Russia and my visit to Kolyma. A few weeks after it appeared, the phone in my San Francisco home rang, and an unfamiliar, unmistakably Slavic voice full of wonderfully rolling "r"s, a voice that sounded as if it belonged to an energetic man of fifty or so, boomed, "I rrrrread yourrrr booooooook!"

The voice's owner, I discovered to my surprise, was not fifty; he was seventy-five. He wasn't calling from Russia or Eastern Europe but from Iowa. And he had spent five years in the labor camps of Kolyma. We chatted for a while; he was delighted to find an American who knew where Kolyma was, and he told me about the book he was beginning to write about his own experiences there. I wished him well, explained that I was moving on to write about other subjects, and said politely that it would be nice if our paths crossed someday. "Yes!" he said. "You will come to Iowa!"

I have since learned that Janusz Bardach is a force of nature; when he expresses a wish, he makes sure it is carried out. A few months later I found myself on a plane to Iowa and have returned for several more visits since. In the course of those trips, and of several that Janusz and his wife, Phyllis, have made to San Francisco, I have watched this remarkable book take shape. It is deeply satisfying to see it now in print. Indeed, to the story of a man who was forced to dig his own grave, who survived transport across Siberia in a boxcar and prison camp winters of seventy below zero, who used his wits and courage to survive again and again when so many of those around him died, and who returned to a world where his wife, parents, and sister had perished in the Holocaust, it seems superfluous to add more. The book speaks for itself.

Gripping and extraordinary as this story is, in a way I find even more moving the story of Janusz Bardach's life since the part of it told in these pages came to an end. After he was miraculously released from Kolyma, he made his way to Moscow in 1946 to live with his brother, a diplomat in the Polish embassy. He remained in the Soviet Union and studied to become a plastic and reconstructive surgeon. In 1954 he completed his surgical residency and moved back to Poland, where he had grown up. He later founded the first Department of Plastic and Reconstructive Surgery at the School of Medicine in Lodz.

An outburst of anti-Semitism in 1968 almost cost him his job, and he began to think about emigrating in order to protect himself and his family. In 1972 he became chair of the Division of Plastic Surgery of the Head and Neck at the University of Iowa Medical School. At age fifty-two he began a new life in a new country and in a tongue that was then almost totally new to him as well. But today, if you walk down the street in Iowa City with him and see the number of people to whom he booms out a jubilant greeting in a variety of languages, you would think he had lived there all his life.

The book you are about to begin reading is not the first that Janusz has written or co-authored. It is the twelfth. The others—the first written in Russian, the next half-dozen in Polish, and the remainder in English—are all in the field of plastic and reconstructive surgery. Janusz Bardach is a world-renowned specialist in congenital facial deformities. He has operated, taught, or lectured in more than twenty countries. The chances are that if you meet someone born with a cleft lip, palate, or nose within the last twenty-five years, the condition was repaired using one of the several surgical procedures that bear the name Bardach.

Few of those patients are aware that the man to whose techniques they owe a new face once endured five harrowing years in prison in the deathly, frozen moonscape of Kolyma. To have the endurance to survive what left millions dead and millions more shattered in spirit is heroic enough. To gather the strength from that experience for a life devoted to caring for others is a miracle indeed.

—Adam Hochschild

Acknowledgments

I would like to thank my daughter, Ewa Bardach, for the book's inspiration. For many years she heard parts of my story and urged me to write them down, but she had to wait a long time for this to happen. While the Communist regime reigned in Poland, I was too afraid to write about what I lived through for fear of what might happen to my brother and his family, who lived in Warsaw.

Together the authors thank Osha Gray Davidson, Richard Fenigsen, Robert Goldwyn, Marsha Nicholson, Mary Swander, and Daniel Weissbort for reading early drafts of the book and encouraging us to continue what we knew would be a long, intense cooperation.

The interest and encouragement of the following people sustained us through the months of writing and rewriting: Maiken Baird, Larry and Beverly Blades, Connie Brothers, Mary Gantz, Alison Guss, Jay Holstein, Bob Kelch, Linda Kerber, Sam and Linda Levey, Michael McNulty, and Bruce Reuter.

We are grateful to Jim Harris, Adam Hochschild, James McPherson, Gordon Mennenga, and the staff at Prairie Lights Bookstore in Iowa City for sharing their insight and professional expertise. Gordon Mennenga was especially instrumental in helping us shape the book into its final form.

Our deepest thanks go to our agent, Lynn Franklin, for her affectionate support and dedication. We also extend our thanks to her associate, Candace Rondeaux, for generously sharing her knowledge and enthusiasm. At the University of California Press, Naomi Schneider, executive editor, has given us invaluable guidance during all stages of production. Editor Scott Norton and publicity manager Amy Torack have also been wonderfully responsive and a pleasure to work with.

It would not have been possible to write this book without the warmth and understanding of our families. Phyllis Harper Bardach was not only an attentive reader and critic but also a patient listener, subjected to endless hours of book talk; Ewa Bardach, Hani Elkadi, and Suzanne Gleeson gave constructive criticism and heartfelt praise at every stage; and Frank Gleeson supported us through his unflagging interest. Our thanks would not be complete without mention of Darlene Gleeson, a dedicated supporter and reader of the early chapters who did not live to see the book's completion.

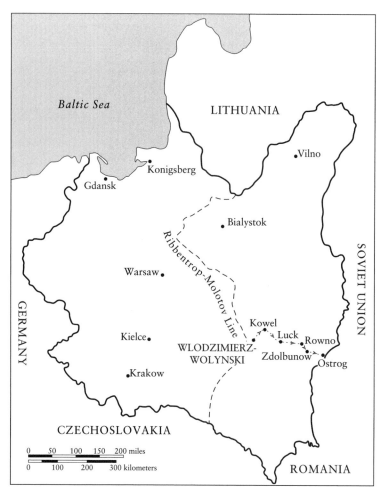

Map 1. Janusz's trip from Wlodzimierz-Wolynski to Ostrog in partitioned Poland, 1939.

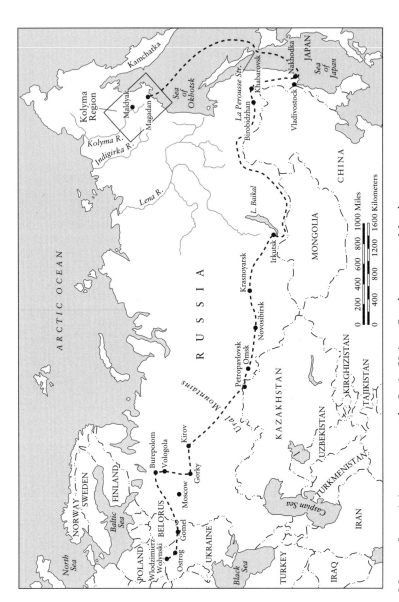

Map 2. Janusz's journey across the Soviet Union, October 1941 to March 1942.

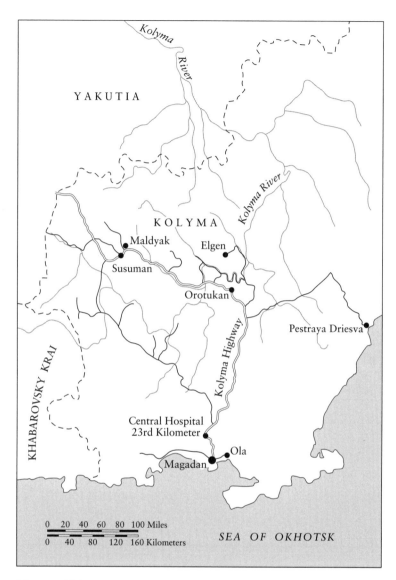

Map 3. Kolyma.

Belarussian Front Line

July 1941

The pit I was ordered to dig had the precise dimensions of a coffin. The Soviet officer carefully designed it. He measured me with a stick, made lines on the forest floor, and told me to dig. He wanted to make sure I'd fit well inside.

As I chopped up the tangled vines and hacked out the roots, the officer followed my movements with keen eyes and mounting agitation. He appeared to be about the same age as me: his face smooth and rosy in the waning light; his blond hair sticking out from his cap like flax.

"Faster!" He jabbed the stick into my ribs. "We haven't got all night!"

I tore frantically at the remaining debris, then pitched the shovel into the soft black soil. The oily earth clung to my boots and stuck to the shovel, which I beat against the ground. I imagined swinging at the officer's head, wondered if I could strike him before the pistol went off, but he seemed to know what I was thinking. The gun was pointed at my face. I thrust the shovel into the ground harder and faster, keeping the angles of the pit straight and the walls vertical, just as the officer commanded.

As the pit took shape around me, I saw myself lying face down, bound and bloody, a bullet through the base of my skull. I imagined the heavy dirt on top of me, the ants and worms eating my flesh. I didn't want to die. I didn't deserve to be shot in secrecy.

Darkness had fallen. The pit was waist deep. "Toss the shovel over there," the officer ordered.

I threw the shovel a little ways from the pit.

"Sienia, I need you for a moment." A soldier appeared from the woods. "Help me tie him up."

The soldier jumped down in the pit and pulled my arms back so tightly he nearly tore them from their sockets. He bound my wrists and ankles, told me to kneel, and pushed me into the dirt. My thoughts raced. What crime had I committed? My battalion, a heavy tank division, had been covering for other army units as they retreated, and I had accidentally rolled my tank onto its side during a river crossing. But this was a mistake, not a crime; I had repaired the tank and was ready to fight. As a Polish Jew, I hated the Nazis. Germany had invaded my homeland the previous year, and my hometown had been rescued at the last minute by the Soviet Union. Six months later I was drafted into the Red Army.

Now the Nazis were everywhere—in the air, on the roads, in the forests; invading Soviet towns with their tanks, trucks, and motorcycles. They had almost certainly taken over my hometown. I pictured my parents, my sister, and my young wife sitting on the sofa next to the wood-burning stove in the dining room, my mother's favorite place. I saw Taubcia before me, her green eyes scared and inquiring; our first anniversary was just two weeks ago. I envisioned my mother hugging her, just as she did when I left for the Red Army; my father pacing his office, trying to find a way to keep the family safe. Were they still alive? in hiding? in a Jewish ghetto?

I pressed my forehead into the soft earth. With each breath I inhaled the fragrances of the forest, aromas I had learned so well as a child, when I used to hunt for wild mushrooms. These would be my last breaths, I thought. I waited for the shot, waited to feel the cold barrel of the gun against my skull, the bullet penetrating my brain. I didn't feel sorry for myself, only sorry that my loved ones would never find my grave. I waited, waited—but there was no sound.

Night passed, with no hint of a moon or stars to brighten my dark cocoon. The night and earth and sleep and death had merged. All felt the same.

CHAPTER 1

September 1939

Early in the morning on September 1, I was drawn out of sleep by a penetrating, high-pitched whistle lasting several seconds and ending in a distant, thunderous explosion. I'd never heard such a sound and snapped upright.

Sleep and terror slowly loosened their grip, and I was able to think. I'd been up late the night before with my family; my girlfriend, Taubcia; and several friends talking and listening to the radio. My father had closed his dental office early in the afternoon and appeared, pale and nervous, to tell us that Nazi invasion was imminent. He'd heard from one of his patients that Marshal Rydz-Smigly, chief commander of the Polish armed forces, had put all units on full alert for war with Germany.

All afternoon we switched back and forth between Radio Warsaw, French Radio, Radios Kiev and Moscow, and the Polish edition of the BBC, following negotiations between the Polish and German governments. Around seven P.M. close friends came over. They were frequent guests in our home, and each brought new information about the crisis. As we ate, our attention shifted from the radio reports to a tense conversation about what we would do if the Nazis invaded.

Conflict with Germany had intensified during the summer of 1939, culminating in August, when Germany gave Poland an ultimatum to cede the city of Gdansk (Danzig in German) and the entire Danzig Corridor or face invasion. The Danzig Corridor, Polish territory along the Vistula River that separated East Prussia from Germany, had been in dispute between Germany and Poland since the Middle Ages. After World War I, under the Treaty of Versailles, Gdansk was given the status of a free city, with Poland having administrative governance over it. The legislative assembly, however, was mostly German, and with Hitler's rise to power in 1933 the assembly became more and more hostile toward Poland. In 1938 Hitler demanded that Gdansk and its region, the Danzig Corridor, be given to Germany in order to unite East Prussia with Germany.

Threatened by Hitler's increasing hostility, the Polish government signed a defense treaty with England on August 25, 1939, hoping that this agreement, in conjunction with a long-standing one with France, would discourage invasion. However, the strongly anti-Communist Polish government made no effort to establish a defense pact with the Soviet Union. By the end of August, Germany had assembled its military forces on the Polish border. In response, the Polish government secretly amassed 700,000 troops but didn't announce a general mobilization, not wanting to alarm the public or provoke Germany into war.

For Jewish people, the prospect of a Nazi takeover was particularly disturbing, though opinions varied about the likelihood of such an event. Many of our friends believed Hitler would never invade Poland, because that would mean starting a war with France and England as well. Others thought that if Hitler did invade, only wealthy Jews would be persecuted, and the rest of us would be left alone. These hopeful scenarios ignored the fact that persecution of Jews was already well underway. Since the mid-thirties, Nazi ideology had been streaming across the border and had become woven into everyday life. Jewish students at the universities were forced to sit or stand on the left side of the classroom and were often beaten and slashed with glass or razor blades. Some were thrown from second-story balconies and windows. The police and local authorities didn't intervene, nor were the culprits arrested or tried.

In 1936, harassed by my Polish classmates, I was forced to transfer from the state school to the private Jewish gymnasium. A widespread boycott in my hometown, Wlodzimierz-Wolynski,* closed many Jewish-owned stores and businesses, and in 1937 my father was requested to prove the equivalency of his Russian diploma and license to practice dentistry, something that had never been questioned since he'd begun practicing in Poland in 1921. The Polish authorities repeatedly demanded documentation from the dental school in Kharkov, even though it had been closed since the October Revolution.

My father was the first person in our family and among our friends to realize what might happen to us if Hitler invaded. During the summer of 1939, as Hitler's intentions became apparent, my father transformed from his usual upbeat, energetic, optimistic self into a solitary figure consumed by his thoughts.

On August 31, Radio Warsaw provided little information about the anticipated invasion. Instead it played bombastic military marches interspersed with official government announcements that Poland would not give in to the German ultimatum nor relinquish an acre of land and that France and England would support Poland if war did break out. But we knew that, given Germany's military might, Hitler would certainly annex Gdansk and the Danzig Corridor. As worried friends arrived at our flat and huddled in front of my parents' newly purchased Phillips radio, the only questions were these: how much more Polish territory would Hitler want; how would Poland protect itself; and how would we protect ourselves?

My father touched the end of another cigarette to the one he was smoking, then suddenly stood and walked over to the window. His hands were jittery. I'd never seen him so nervous. "What's on the radio is all propaganda," he said, puffing on the cigarette. "The government knows we can't keep Hitler from invading,

---

* Pronounced "Vlodzimirz-Volinsky" in English.

and I'm afraid to think of what will happen to us given what's already happening to the Jews in Germany." The words burst from his mouth in an angry, tense barrage. We all knew about the concentration camps and *Kristalnacht*, or "the night of broken glass." This pogrom, inspired by Hitler, took place in Germany and Austria on November 9, 1938. Jewish homes and businesses were vandalized, synagogues were burned, and nearly one hundred Jews were killed. We had read and heard about how Jews in Germany were being persecuted, their children expelled from public schools. Walking the streets had become dangerous there.

My father looked back and forth between the group and the dark, quiet street in front of our flat. Light rain hit the windowpanes. A car occasionally splashed through puddles on the deserted street. My mother suggested we listen to the Polish edition of the BBC and bent toward the radio slowly and stiffly, searching the dial. The dim light from the crystal chandelier cast a warm glow on her tired, pale face. She'd been diagnosed with colon cancer three months before and had undergone major surgery; her bobbed hair had grayed, and it pained my heart to see her so ill.

My father, bald and husky, remained standing at the window, fiddling with his black mustache. It was unusual for him to be so silent. He loved to tell stories, give advice, play cards, and talk about new business ventures. He had many friends, and our house was always full of people. My mother attracted a different group, people interested in politics and the arts. Although my father lacked the intellectual insight of my mother, he was very well known, liked, and respected. I had never seen him so full of despair, and it was more than a little unnerving.

Sioma Malski, a tall, slender law student visiting from Prague, reminded everyone of Germany's unopposed annexation of the Sudetenland, the western part of Czechoslovakia, in 1936. "The same thing can be expected here," he said sharply. "The Nazis are well organized, with modern tanks and aircraft. Poland is no match for them. And Hitler's ideas and propaganda are gaining ground in Poland. We will be in mortal danger when the Nazis invade."

"I don't think so," Mr. Bristiger interrupted. An erudite, well-dressed bachelor, he'd been a daily guest in our house for many years. He sat in his usual place, next to my mother, and leaned back in his chair, refusing to give in to the anxiety and apprehension. "Poland has the largest Jewish population in Europe, and the Jewish communities are strong here, especially in Warsaw, Lodz, and Krakow. They present a formidable force. We've got three and a half million Jews in Poland, while in Germany there's only half a million. I don't believe that in the middle of the twentieth century, three and a half million people can be exterminated like ants."

"I disagree," my cousin Lenia, a hunchback, said in a shaky voice. His intelligence and soft-spoken manner made him my mother's most favored friend. "I live in Warsaw, and I know how Poles are harassing Jews. I've been refused service in restaurants. In classes I have to sit on the left side with other Jewish students in the 'bench ghetto.' I've been shoved and hit while walking down the street. My friends have been slashed with razor blades. Never in Polish history has there been such hostility toward Jews. If the Nazis invade, every Jew in Warsaw will be in danger. There is no 'formidable Jewish force.'"

"I agree with Lenia," my mother calmly interjected, diffusing some of the tension. Although her gray-green eyes looked sad and tired, she spoke clearly, precisely, and logically about recent events. As in her friendships, she avoided superficiality in conversation. "I know anti-Semitism is strong here, but I don't think the majority of Poles are anti-Semitic. Many of my Polish friends have told me we can rely on their help if necessary. I know that some of our friends are planning to leave town when the Nazis invade, but I don't think we'll have to."

Fear washed over me. I realized that my mother, a decisive woman, had already made up her mind to stay home if the Nazis occupied our city, and I wasn't at all sure her decision was right. I had always admired my mother but was never close to her. She favored my older brother, Julek, who physically and intellectually resembled her idolized older brother, Marcel, a professor of neurology in Odessa. Left outside of her immediate attention, I developed my own interests and friendships, many of which met with her disapproval. She was an intellectual—always reading, listening to music, and analyzing politics and the arts. She had been raised in a highly accomplished family in Odessa, and she brought to our home an admiration for great poets, artists, writers, and scientists. Her uncle, two brothers, and three cousins were university professors in Odessa, Moscow, and Paris. She was fluent in four languages, having received a diploma in linguistics, and our living room served as a salon for her artistic and intellectual friends. Only now do I realize that she was never really happy in Wlodzimierz-Wolynski. Although I never heard her complain about our provincial town, she missed the intellectual environment and rhythm of big-city life and often traveled to Warsaw, Lvov, Krakow, Prague, and Paris to attend exhibitions, concerts, and plays. An atheist with strong socialist sentiments, she supported the Polish underground leftist movements and literary journals and instilled in me a sense of social justice and admiration for the Soviet Union.

Dr. Ojcer, a close family friend, shook his head as he listened to Mr. Bristiger and my mother. He had recently moved from Warsaw and was an active member of Bund, a Jewish leftist organization. He was a gynecologist in private practice, though not by choice; as a Jew, he couldn't get a position at the hospitals in Warsaw. "The situation of the Jews in Poland is hopeless," he said. "It doesn't matter if Poland gives up the Danzig Corridor or even the entire Silesia region, Hitler will not be appeased. He plans to conquer the world and exterminate Jews. Right here in Poland he has the largest Jewish population, and he won't stop until he kills us all. There are only two solutions: to emigrate as soon as possible to any of the Western countries or seek refuge in the Soviet Union. Since we're so close, I'm planning to go to the Soviet Union."

This conversation stirred up fears that had been building in me for many weeks. I'd been discussing the same issues with my friends but couldn't make up my mind about what I would do if the Nazis invaded. The question awakened me on many nights and haunted me through the days, even as I tried to distract myself by spending as much time as possible with Taubcia and our close friends.

As I walked Taubcia home that night, I was frightened in a way I never had been before—afraid of the dark, the people on the street, and a danger I couldn't see but felt swiftly approaching.

That night I fell into a deep, dreamless sleep, only to be jolted awake five hours later by the piercing whistle and its final, thunderous blast.

The watch on my nightstand read 6:30 in the morning. I heard my parents talking in sharp but hushed voices as they went into the dining room to turn on the radio. By the time the third and fourth blasts shook the building, I was dressed and running downstairs past my father. "I'll be right back. I'm going to see if Taubcia is all right."

"No! Don't go anywhere! The Nazis are bombing the city!" My father stood at the top of the stairs in his pajamas, looking lost and unsure of what to do. I ran out the door. Neighbors ran in and out of their houses, hugging and crying, still dressed in nightclothes. They picked up rubble and stared at the burning houses. I rushed blindly past them, running all the way to Taubcia's without stopping.

I had met Taubcia three years before, when I transferred to the Jewish gymnasium. Although she was two years younger than me, she helped me outgrow my childish preoccupations with raising and stealing pigeons, riding my horse, and playing hooky. She charmed me completely with her round, smiling face, long blond hair, and green eyes. I was deeply in love, spending every free moment I had with her. Under my influence she became an atheist and a member of the underground anti-fascist organization to which I belonged. She loved my mother and confided in her more than in her own parents, who, as Orthodox Jews, were initially opposed to our friendship. For a few months her parents forbade her to see me, but Taubcia persisted, and they finally gave up. The anticipation of the Nazi invasion intensified our love. We dealt with the encroaching danger not by fearing the worst but by savoring the precious hours and days we had together, planning our future as though we were destined to be free, our lives secure.

Taubcia's house had not been hit by the bombs. Her mother was in the dining room, crying, holding her face in her hands, while her father lowered his head in prayer. After a short while the bombing ceased, though for all we knew it might resume at any moment. Taubcia and I walked back to my house, holding each other closely, and talked about heading for the Soviet border.

Wladek Cukierman, a close friend and the nephew of our next-door neighbor, was waiting for us in front of my house. He lived in Warsaw but came to visit his aunt every summer, and during these vacations we became close friends. We both admired the Soviet Union and wanted to fight for social justice. In 1936 we had planned to join the Spanish International Brigade to fight Franco and his ultra-right-wing Republican Guard. My parents opposed the idea, and we never did go, but the dream stayed with us for as long as the fighting in Spain continued. We also dreamed of emigrating to France, Palestine, or South America, as many of our friends had done, and living in a commune, but our dreams crumbled under the weight of the frightening reality around us. We both applied to Polish universities but were rejected because we were Jews, and war broke out while we were still searching for what to do with our lives.

Wladek, Taubcia, and I listened to the latest communiqué by the Polish military: "At dawn, the German army crossed the Polish border at several places and is now moving east toward Warsaw. The Polish army has counterattacked on all fronts." Nearly every minute, the communiqué was interrupted by coded announcements: "TD 72 is approaching," "TK 41 and 42 passed," "TP 75, 78 are approaching." Although the phrases were cryptic, they left no doubt that a real war was in progress, and they terrified me as much as the bombs that had fallen in the morning.

Wladek and I knew that the poorly equipped Polish army, consisting mostly of cavalry, couldn't stand up to Germany's modern tanks and air force, but we both felt compelled to do something to defend ourselves and our families and agreed to volunteer for army service. We and another friend, Chaim Ochs, went to the recruitment office that afternoon. A tall, well-built captain dressed in a crisp green uniform asked us to fill out several forms. His cropped blond hair looked like beard stubble, and he was deeply tanned from his collar to his hairline. The captain slowly rubbed his square chin, as though seriously considering our applications, then looked up and glowered at us. "You're all Jews—so why are you so eager to defend Poland? Why don't you go fight in Palestine?"

Three lower-ranking officers laughed. One of them chirped, "You Jews need curved rifles so you can shoot from behind corners—that way you don't have to see the enemy!"

"Listen," the captain said, "there are enough good Polish soldiers to defend the country. We'll call on you when we need you, but for right now go home and hide with your families."

Stunned and humiliated, we didn't talk much on the way home. Feeling more vulnerable and frightened than ever, I wondered how we were supposed to protect ourselves from the Nazis and whether we could expect any help from our compatriots. Although I had grown up in a secular family in the Polish culture, as time passed I became more and more aware of my Jewishness. In school I sensed that my classmates didn't truly accept me; I felt I was a stranger among them. Some called me names and made me feel that I couldn't live happily among Poles because I was Jewish. I was welcomed in Polish homes as a "nice *Jewish* young man" because my father was a popular local dentist, but the ethnic qualifier kept me from feeling integrated and hampered my social interactions, especially with girls. Not until I transferred to the Jewish gymnasium at the age of sixteen did I feel at peace with myself and among my peers.

The Polish army's rejection of our offer to volunteer served as a stinging reminder that Jews were still outsiders. We could only sit by helplessly as the Nazis attacked our town. For the next several days the Nazis dropped bombs in the early morning or afternoon. Everyone remained tense and frightened, constantly anticipating the penetrating whine of the air-raid siren. Three large military units—two infantry regiments and one artillery regiment—were stationed in Wlodzimierz-Wolynski, and the barracks were repeated targets of bombing. Houses were destroyed, citizens were killed, and the streets were badly damaged.

As Nazi tanks and ground troops penetrated deeper into the country, throngs of Jewish refugees fled the western and central parts of Poland and began to arrive in Wlodzimierz-Wolynski. Most came from Warsaw and Lodz. Some stayed only a day or two and then moved on toward the Romanian or Soviet borders; others stayed longer, finding quarters with Jewish families in town. My parents took in several refugees; my sister, Rachel, and I moved into my parents' bedroom to let guests sleep in the rest of the house. The bedrooms were taken first, then the two couches in the waiting room of my father's office, then the Persian rugs in the dining room.

During the days the dining room became a gathering place for my family, our friends, and the refugees staying with us. With every update on the Nazis' advancement and France and England's anticipated defense, we discussed what to do next. Many refugees struggled with the harsh reality that the home they had left behind was destroyed, that the lives they'd had the week before no longer existed. The hardship of traveling in a war-torn country with no place to stay, no means of transportation, and no money to buy food led many of them to return home. My father, convinced that returning to Nazi-occupied territory was suicidal, encouraged them to persevere and offered many of them financial help.

Most of the refugees stayed with us only for a few days, long enough to rest, bathe, and prepare for the final leg of the journey to the Soviet border. A few of the wealthier ones, frightened by the Soviet Union's anti-capitalist rhetoric, chose to go to the Romanian border, even though it was twice as far away as the Russian boundary. As I passed the refugees in the hallway in the morning and listened to their stories at night, I wondered where we would go if we, too, had to leave and whether there would be anyone to take us in.

Communiqués from the front line became more and more disturbing. Poland had been left alone to defend itself; England and France, although they declared war on Germany, failed to send any troops. By September 9, Warsaw was surrounded and under siege. In many areas on the Vistula, Bug, and San Rivers, Nazi ground troops had broken through and were advancing more quickly than the Polish army could withdraw. On September 10, Marshal Rydz-Smigly attempted to coordinate the increasingly confused units east of the Vistula River, and on the same day the German Third Army breached the Bug River defenses. The Polish army quickly disintegrated, leading Marshal Rydz-Smigly to retreat toward the Romanian border. The Nazis were now at the Bug River, only twelve kilometers from Wlodzimierz-Wolynski.

One afternoon at the dinner table I suggested that we go to the Soviet Union to stay with relatives in Kiev and Odessa. We talked about how long it would take to get there and planned the best route but made no decision. A few days later, when we learned that the Germans had crossed the Bug River and were on the outskirts of town, my father asked me to take a walk with him in our backyard.

The sun was setting. A light autumn breeze brushed our cheeks and blew through my hair. We walked in silence for a while, then sat down on a bench in the dark, leafy orchard behind our house. My father put his arm around me and pulled me close. His deep brown eyes were sad and wide with worry. "Your mother is sick," he began, "and my parents are very old. None of them can survive the harsh conditions of travel. There are no trains, and although I could get horses and a wagon, the trip to the Soviet border would take several days. The roads are dangerous, filled with Polish army deserters and Ukrainian bandits. I can't leave them here alone, and I can't take them with me. When the Germans arrive, you'll be the one in the greatest danger because of your age and well-known leftist activities. I want you to leave tomorrow morning for the Soviet border. I'm sure the Soviets will open it to Jewish refugees."

My father was repeating what the Polish High Military Command had been ordering for many days—all men between the ages of eighteen and fifty-five were to leave the cities and head for the Soviet and Romanian borders. I had heard these announcements but ignored them, acting as if they didn't apply to me. I thought my family must stay together and was stunned by my father's request that I leave.

"Papa, how can I leave you alone to take care of everyone? I don't want to go alone."

"Janusz, listen to me. You must go. It can be very dangerous for you and for the whole family if you are caught."

I felt a lump in my throat and made an effort not to cry. I had never felt so close to my father. We sat for a while hugging each other. "Let's talk about this tomorrow morning," I said. "Maybe we'll come up with some other solution."

Rumors spread that Nazi tanks were heading toward town from the west and south. On September 10 and 11 the local police and civil authorities left the city, afraid of being captured by the Nazis and of being hunted down by people they had prosecuted in the past. The chief of police, who played cards with my father, came to say farewell and encouraged us to leave immediately. He was wearing civilian clothes, and I was shocked to see him and other policemen nervously trying to blend in with the local citizens.

The local officials' abrupt departure threw the town into a state of anarchy. Ukrainian nationalists with pro-Nazi sentiments wasted no time organizing a local militia to loot Jewish stores and homes. In response, my friends and I, as well as members of the Jewish sports club, Amatorzy, organized a defense group. The fear of being attacked, robbed, beaten, and killed was so overwhelming that no one could go out on the street or rest peacefully. Conflicting reports about the German army's whereabouts added to the chaos.

On the afternoon of September 12, members of the Fifth Column, Polish citizens of German ethnicity who secretly collaborated with the Nazis, donned German uniforms and strolled back and forth down Farna Street. I recognized the Schoen brothers, Bubi and Rudi, friends of my youth and sons of the local pastor.

They didn't look at me as we passed, and I ran back home. Our close friendship, which had begun in grade school, had cooled over the years as they spent their summer vacations in Germany. In one of our last conversations, nearly two years before, Bubi told me I should leave Poland with my family because bad things were going to happen to Jews.

I got home and found my mother sitting alone in the dining room. She took my hand and said, "There's nothing to discuss anymore. You must leave immediately. I don't believe they will harm women or old people. We'll survive and be together again, but you must leave town tonight."

My heart was torn, but I knew she was right. It was rumored that Nazi forces had surrounded the town and would occupy it in the morning. If I was to escape, it would have to be now. I went to say goodbye to Taubcia and stayed with her until dark. She also encouraged me to leave. We held each other, crying bitterly. I asked her to come with me, but she didn't want to leave her parents.

I returned home and began to prepare a backpack with some clothes. My father came into my room. He looked sad but smiled, patted me on the shoulder, and reassured me that we would be together again soon. He told me to be careful and to call as soon as the phone lines were back up. When I finished packing, he hugged me. "I know you can take care of yourself. I've always believed in you and am very proud of you. I know you don't want to leave, but it's better for you and for us that you not remain at home."

I could hardly hold back the tears as we hugged again and again. He gave me twenty gold coins, two rings, some Polish money, and a special belt in which to hide the coins and rings. My mother packed some food, and I took my hunting knife and the little revolver I had acquired when I'd begun to be physically harassed. I went to get Wladek, and at 2:30 in the morning we mounted my small motorcycle and rode to Kowelska Street, which led out of town. The night was pitch black—the sky was cloudy, and the streetlights were out to deter nighttime bomb-

ings—yet the thoroughfare was as busy as at midday. Throngs of
refugees on foot and in carriages and wagons had overtaken the
road and sidewalks. Everyone was heading east. It was impossible to weave through the thick crowd, so we got off and walked
the motorcycle. Bicyclists weaved between people and wagons
and cut in front of the slower travelers. Wladek and I were in a
hurry to get out of the city, hoping the crowd would thin out in
the countryside. The motorcycle's front wheel and handlebars
poked people ahead of and alongside us, and two angry men
shoved me onto a yard in front of a house. I fell down on top of
the motorcycle, and it took a minute to get back up. Wladek tried
to calm me down; my temper was raging, and my patience was
running out.

The drivers of wagons and carriages whipped their horses and
shouted for people to get out of the way. Refugees on foot
moved as fast as they could, but their bags, backpacks, and suitcases kept getting tangled and caught on wagon wheels and bi-
cycles. Women carried infants in their arms or held the hands of
young children, yanking them out of the horses' paths. A pair of
horses, spooked by the refugees running in front of them, reared
back and whinnied, their hooves clawing the air. They pulled up
short and stepped to the side; their driver whipped them repeatedly and cursed. The horses knocked over several people, then
found an opening and galloped forward, parting the throngs
with amazing speed. Behind them, a woman and her husband
searched for their daughter, who'd become separated from them.
"Hannelah! Hannelah!" the woman cried, tearing through the
crowd. It was impossible to see the ground, and the current of
traffic kept pushing them forward, farther away from the place
where they'd lost her.

Wladek and I rejoined the mainstream, walking the motorcycle with one of us on each side to keep it steady. The horses and
wagons set a brisk pace, pushing the slower travelers to the
shoulders and ditches. Parents walked with babies strapped to
their backs; men pulled carts carrying small children and elderly
people; old people pushed wheelbarrows filled with their belongings; the infirm hobbled along with canes, traveling lightly, hold-

ing on to a single bag or backpack. The refugees who had traveled the farthest were the dirtiest and most exhausted and often abandoned their bags at the side of the road. They wiped the sweat from their faces, shook out their arms, and rejoined the stream without so much as a whimper.

As we reached the outskirts of town, the sky began to lighten. Wladek and I started the motorcycle and turned onto the road that led to Kowel, fifty kilometers away. We planned to reach Ostrog on the Soviet border, going through Kowel, Rowno, and Zdolbunow.

The throngs of refugees thinned out as morning wore on. Many of them sat on the edge of the road, stretching their legs or taking off their shoes and socks to wrap blisters. Some people had spent the night in the ditches and were getting ready to resume their journey. We passed several abandoned cars that had run out of gas. Some had been stripped almost bare. Others were being pulled by horses. With little luggage and a motorcycle full of gas, Wladek and I felt light and mobile.

When we were more than halfway to Kowel, the whistling of falling bombs pierced the monotonous hum of the motorcycle engine. Wladek shouted in my ear, "Get off the road!" I drove through a ditch and into a nearby woods. We hid the motorcycle in the brush, dove under bushes, and covered our heads with our hands. Everyone else left the highway and scattered into the trees and ditches. The airplanes flew parallel to the road and blasted it with machine-gun fire, then circled back and made the same run. I had never felt more helpless. For the previous twelve days, as I listened to the sound of bombs, I always had the distinct feeling that each one would hit me, no matter where I was hiding. Now, with almost no shelter, it seemed the bombs were exploding inside my head. My temples throbbed. I had never known such terror. The thought of being maimed frightened me more than the thought of death, and I prayed that my life would end instantly if I should be hit. I lay with my face in the dirt and covered my ears as machine-gun fire rattled close to me. The barrage swept across the road and ditches, seeking out refugees, and I felt certain that my life would be over in seconds.

After two more runs the droning engines faded into the distance. Wladek and I picked up the motorcycle and headed back to the road. As we drove through the ditch we saw a group of elderly people lying in a pool of blood, their lifeless bodies riddled with bullets, their bags and backpacks strewn about them. I began to cry when I saw them because it made me think of my parents and grandparents. Timidly, survivors emerged from the woods, and the flight continued.

After the bombing, Wladek and I were terrified to drive on the open road, yet we wanted to reach the border as soon as possible. We reached Kowel and stayed with a friend until dark, resuming our journey at night, when we'd be safe from the bombing.

As the second night passed, I thought obsessively about my family. I hadn't heard whether the Nazis had occupied Wlodzimierz-Wolynski, and I struggled to control my panic and focus my thoughts on what lay ahead. I imagined that the Soviets would welcome everyone who needed protection, especially Jews, but my hopes were clouded by the memory of my first trip to the Soviet Union. When I was eight years old, my mother took Julek and me to Odessa to visit her brother. At the train station in the border city of Schepetovka, I looked with admiration at the soldiers and officers of the Soviet border guard, awed by their green uniforms and distinctive insignias. We had three suitcases (mainly filled with presents for our relatives), two handbags, and two small pillows for my mother. The guards ordered us out of the train, and we stood in line for a customs search. I remember the pillows being ripped open, the white feathers flying all over the station, and the sound of our luggage being slashed. My mother was taken to another part of the station for questioning and a personal search; Julek and I sat on a bench waiting for her, afraid we'd never see her again. Paralyzed with fear, nauseated from thirst and hunger, I fell asleep and slipped from the bench onto the floor. Some people brought me water, and when my mother came back, we collected our tattered things and got back on the train. She was worn out and had been crying.

Now, riding to Rowno under the moon and stars, I pretended I wasn't leaving home but was merely taking a pleasure ride with

Wladek. A light, refreshing breeze passed through the willow trees along the road, and it was easy to imagine that we'd soon be home and life would be as peaceful as before the war had started. Absorbed in my thoughts, I was shocked when we were stopped by flashing lights. I hadn't seen anyone on the road. I had no idea where the people had come from. Two men shined flashlights in our eyes while others surrounded us and ordered us off the motorcycle. I was astonished to see Soviet military uniforms and hear the Russian language—we were still a long way from the border. I couldn't imagine what Soviet soldiers were doing on Polish territory and could only hope that the mighty Red Army had come to fight the Nazis and expel them from Poland. I wanted to express my joy at seeing them, but someone ordered us to put up our hands. We were led into a field covered with dozens of camouflage tents. Soldiers frisked us and took away our watches and money and my hunting knife. They didn't discover my hidden belt or pistol. Even though I had a rifle pointed at my back, I wasn't afraid of being shot. I believed that the Soviet Union was a paradise for the oppressed, ruled by workers and peasants, and that the Red Army was the enforcer of social justice. I couldn't imagine them as my enemies; even at gunpoint I felt safer with the Red Army soldiers than with many of my Polish compatriots. I tried to be friendly and spoke Russian to the guard, but he only mumbled at us to walk forward and stay away from the tents.

A young officer asked who we were, where we were going, and where we were from. He ordered a soldier to take us farther into the field, away from the tents, and to watch us until morning. I stumbled over cabbage heads, so thirsty and hungry that I was ready to eat the cabbage right from the field. I asked the soldier if I could have a drink, and he said he'd bring over some water. He ordered us to lie down on our stomachs with our hands clasped behind our heads until he came back. Within minutes my position became unbearable. Very cautiously, without creating any commotion, I unclasped my hands and straightened my arms at my sides. I waited nearly an hour for the soldier to return; then, very slowly, I crawled to a nearby head of cabbage and chewed on some leaves to get the moisture. The next thing I knew, I was waking up with the sun shining brightly in my eyes. I looked around and saw Wladek sitting next to me.

"Wake up," he said. "They're gone." The soldiers and tents had disappeared as though they'd never been there. The only evidence of their presence was the fact that my motorcycle was gone.

Sitting in the field with no food or transportation, I was thankful not to be alone. I trusted Wladek. He was calm, thorough, and calculating, whereas I was quick and impulsive. Wladek was already digging beets and potatoes from the field. I ate some cabbage and dirt-crusted potatoes and was ready to move on. "Wladek," I said, "stop digging. We're not harvesting the field. Let's get out of here before we get caught by peasants."

Wladek ignored me, continuing to dig and stuffing beets and potatoes into his pack. "Cool off. We need food for later—who knows when we'll eat again." When a dog in the nearby village began barking, we grabbed the beets and potatoes and ran into the woods. We decided to stay away from the main road and walk in the forest for protection from air raids. We found some railroad tracks and silently followed them, hoping they would lead us to Rowno. The hours of walking took me back to my childhood, when I walked along the tracks at home, pretending I was on a journey to some unknown destination. I imagined a big train traveling into the exciting world that I wanted badly to know. I envisioned the beautiful sleeping and dining cars occupied by distinguished, well-dressed, French-speaking passengers. Watching the passing trains at night used to put me into a dreamy, hypnotic state. I loved to stand close to the tracks and feel the trains rush in front of me. They seemed to come from nowhere and disappear into eternity. The world of the nighttime trains was both close and far away, and I wanted to jump on and be taken away into the unknown. I always felt that the next train could be mine, taking me into the exotic, unexplored world of my dreams.

We reached Rowno in the late afternoon, hungry and exhausted, and went into town to buy something to eat. The low wail of the air-raid siren filled the air, and everyone scattered into the buildings. Wladek and I ran into a nearby park and dove under a bench. Again, I felt as if I were being hit with each explosion and hoped to die instantly. But when the bombing stopped and the air cleared, I found myself alive and unharmed. Wladek and I went back to the station, followed the tracks into the forest, and found a place to sleep.

The next morning we resumed our journey on the railroad tracks. After several hours we saw a clearing in the distance and what we thought might be the main road. As we got closer, I smelled hot oatmeal. "How could anyone be cooking hot oatmeal in the middle of the forest?" I asked Wladek. He gave me a puzzled look. As we walked out of the woods, an astonishing scene came into view: hundreds of Soviet soldiers sitting along both sides of the road, eating. Two field kitchens had been set up behind several trucks. For the second day in a row, we had run into a Red Army unit on Polish territory. I could hardly believe it.

The smell of oatmeal made Wladek and me run across the road to the kitchen. In Russian, I asked the cook if we could have some. He asked for our bowls, and I told him we had no bowls or spoons. Wladek, standing shyly behind me, took off his hat and handed it to the cook. I took off my jacket and asked the soldier to pour the thick oatmeal into the lining while I held it like a bowl. He gave me a strange look and pointed out that the oatmeal would ruin my jacket. I told him I was so hungry I didn't care. Wladek and I stayed right there at the kettle, scooping out the oatmeal with our fingers and licking them off.

Feeling full, tired, and sleepy, we sat down under a tree to rest. Someone shouted, "Hey, you over there! The officer wants to see you." I had anticipated trouble ever since we'd entered the compound. The officer looked at us inquiringly and asked if we were the young men he had seen two nights before riding a motorcycle. "How did you get here without your motorcycle? You look exhausted. Did you cover all this distance on foot?"

"Yes," I answered. "Through the forest, along the railroad tracks."

"I'll give you back the motorcycle so you can get to Ostrog this afternoon."

I was surprised by his offer and astonished that he had re-membered we were heading toward the Soviet border. We found the motorcycle on one of the trucks and sped as though we had wings to Ostrog. Encountering almost no traffic, we rode with-out stopping to Zdolbunow, a large junction with hundreds of passenger and freight cars on sprawling tracks. Many had been demolished, and the nearby station was blackened and pitted by German bombs.

An hour later we reached the outskirts of Ostrog. The area ap-peared tranquil and had not been bombed. Fall was just begin-ning; weeping willows lined the road, apples and plums were ripe on the trees, and flowers bloomed in the gardens. We followed crowds of refugees to a plaza in front of the Polish border cross-ing. Those who had traveled far on foot were tired, filthy, and sunburned. The border poles, painted in swirls of red and white, marked the Polish side of the border. The arm of the gate was lowered, and the border guards, wearing green uniforms and hel-mets, walked stiffly back and forth, their rifles held against their chest, looking serious and highly alert. The red and white Polish flag flapped on high masts next to the gate. Soft, freshly raked dirt lay in the no-man's land between the Polish and Soviet barbed-wire fences.

I was filled with awe to be standing at the border, to see the So-viet Union only fifty meters away. There, red flags with golden hammers and sickles were raised on light green and white border poles. The Soviet border guards walked leisurely back and forth. Hearing their loud laughter and occasional exclamations, I felt a kinship with them; I wanted to run through the gate and ask them to open the entrance to everyone, certain that once they knew that thousands of desperate Jewish refugees were waiting for salvation they would not make us wait a day longer.

Wladek and I waited impatiently for the historic moment. But after many hours, the gate remained closed, and we left to find the house of my former classmate, Mischa Sternberg, who lived downtown on a side street only three houses away from the main road. We parked the motorcycle behind his house, went to the front door, and knocked. Mischa answered and, although a bit surprised by our unexpected arrival, gave us a firm handshake and said he would arrange sleeping quarters for us in the basement. That night I lay down in a soft warm bed, feeling exhausted but unable to fall asleep. Now that I felt safe, I couldn't stop thinking about my family. I was frightened for them and ashamed for having left them. For a long while I lay awake, imagining my return home and my reunion with Taubcia.

When I finally did fall asleep, I was tormented by bad dreams. Again I met the Soviet officer who had given back the motorcycle, but his face was made of steel and his eyes were black slits. He shouted at me because I hadn't told him the truth about my relatives living in the Soviet Union. He bound my hands and legs, tied me to a horse, and dragged me on a long rope to the border crossing. The crowd parted, the gates opened at his order, and the officer whipped the horses into a gallop. The throng of refugees ran behind. Their contorted faces magnified as they threw rocks and stones, and every projectile, as it bounced closer and closer, turned into a person's head, its open mouth shouting at me: "Jew! Jew!"

"Stop yelling." Wladek sat on my bed shaking my arm. "What's wrong with you?" I told him about the dream. Wladek went back to sleep, but I was too lonely and frightened to sleep. All my feelings for and memories of Taubcia welled up within me. She was my first love, and I felt there was no world without her. I remembered the first secret touches of our hands, which made me feel happier than I had ever felt. I could hold her small, delicate hand all evening, feeling how close she was to me, all our tender feelings concentrated in our palms and fingers. I was mesmerized by her, finding everything about her unusual, adorable, and wonderful. Every smile, every move, every second between us was meaningful. We could talk for hours; I could listen to her, laugh with her, dance with her, and spend more time with her than the day allowed. Being in the same school, we looked for each other every break, and every day I walked her home, carrying her books. I was blind and deaf to the outside world because she filled everything that was important and dear to me. It wasn't enough that we spent all hours of the day together. During the four years of our relationship, I lay in bed at night dreaming about her and knew that she was doing the same.

At dawn a storm approached Ostrog. The thunder began far away and steadily came closer and closer, increasing in volume. Impatient to know what was going on, I awakened Wladek, and we both dressed, climbed out the window, and walked to the main street.

The thundering sound of heavy metal hitting the cobblestones was strange and new to me. The next thing I knew, a large tank with a big red star painted on the turret was coming in my direction. Soviet soldiers and officers stood on top waving at bystanders. The Red Army was crossing the border. Thousands of citizens and twice as many refugees shouted, danced, sang, and threw flowers to the soldiers on the tanks. It struck me that the Red Army soldiers we had met on our way to Ostrog were part of a reconnaissance unit exploring the country before the tanks and soldiers crossed into Polish territory.

The tanks proceeded through the gates like a chain of elephants, smashing the barbed wire fences to the ground and snapping the border posts in two. I ran alongside excitedly with many other young people, climbing on top of the tanks to talk to the soldiers, who greeted us with friendly handshakes. I was glad I could speak Russian so I could share my happiness with them. When I heard the army was proceeding west, I had no doubts that in a day or two it would reach Wlodzimierz-Wolynski, and my family would be safe. All day the Soviet units, tanks, artillery, and infantry paraded through the city. My heart was already traveling with them to Wlodzimierz-Wolynski.

The next day Wladek and I followed the army units westward, reaching Wlodzimierz-Wolynski late that night. A patrol of Soviet soldiers was walking down Kowelska Street. I felt joyous, safe, and thankful. I turned down Farna Street, dropped Wladek off at his aunt's house, and pulled into our driveway. I mounted the stairs to our flat. Not wanting to ring the bell and scare anyone, I knocked feebly and waited, each second of silence seeming to invite peril. I knocked again, more loudly. When I heard the door to the foyer open, my heart began to beat uncontrollably. My father stood in the open door dressed in his shirt and pants. He hugged and kissed me, and for the first time ever he cried in front of me. My mother, Rachel, and Taubcia came running to the door and into my arms. Even as filthy as I was, everybody wanted to hug and kiss me, and I was the happiest person in the world.

I vowed never again to leave Taubcia and my family.

CHAPTER 2

Witness

The Red Army had arrived in Wlodzimierz-Wolynski, and for the first time in several months my father was joyful and smiling. The family was together again except for Julek, who was studying in Vilnius. The next day the Soviet military command announced that our province would be incorporated into the Ukrainian Soviet Socialist Republic and called Western Ukraine. I was ecstatic. Our family no longer had to seek refuge in the Soviet Union; it had come to us. But my mother had reservations, and in her customary way she pondered the implications of occupation for our family, which by Soviet standards could be considered capitalist.

The Soviet authorities organized a local militia and city council, filling the ranks with several of my older friends who were members of the underground Communist Party. During the next several days I attended many political meetings and became a leader among young people who admired the Soviet Union. Badly wanting to be included in the avant-garde of the new society, I improvised passionate speeches and volunteered to be on committees. The Soviet authorities noticed my enthusiasm and invited me to many events, acknowledging me as a young leader.

My parents tried to cool my enthusiasm, however, warning me to stay away from politics and not to get so deeply involved with people I did not know and a system I did not understand very well. I didn't argue with them but continued my activities, believing my dreams of social justice would be fulfilled now that our city was part of the Soviet Union. I thought I would now be living in a country where all people were treated equally and without prejudice, and I was happy to discover that Soviet law punished racial and ethnic harassment with a prison term. I overlooked the fact that the new regime did not bring happiness to everyone in Wlodzimierz-Wolynski.

One of those people was my old tutor, Olga Nikolajewna Papanina. The wife of an officer in the tsarist army who had fought the Bolsheviks in the October Revolution, she came from an aristocratic Russian family. Her husband was captured by the Bolsheviks near Kiev in 1920, and she never found out what happened to him. I began to take German and French lessons from her when I was seven years old. In my young eyes she was beautiful and majestic. I imagined her in her ornate chambers, beautifully dressed, wearing many diamond rings and necklaces. The lessons with her were the only extracurricular activities that I really enjoyed. She never gave me homework, and all we ever practiced was conversation. Olga emanated inner strength and dignity. She taught me to look people straight in the eyes when talking to them, which expressed respect as well as truthfulness.

We had fierce arguments as I grew older and my attachment to leftist ideology increased. When I was fifteen I tried to discuss with her the noble ideas of Marx and Lenin. It was the only time I ever saw her angry and hateful. She didn't raise her voice but became very emotional, talking about the members of her family who were killed in cold blood. I never raised the issue again. Soon after the Soviets entered Wlodzimierz-Wolynski, she was arrested. I never found out what happened to her.

But in my youthful zeal I did not pay much attention to how the Soviet authorities took over the town. In October and November 1939, Communist Party officials, Soviet civil authorities, and the NKVD* (Narodny Kommissariat Vnutrennikh Dyel) set up headquarters in the best downtown buildings without com-

---

* In English, NKVD translates as "People's Commissariat for Internal Affairs." This organization later became known as the KGB.

pensating the previous owners and tenants. They annexed many apartments and houses for military and civilian living quarters, throwing the owners out on the street without reimbursing them or paying them rent. All possessions remained in the houses. The Polish authorities and military personnel who had remained in town were arrested, along with clergy of all denominations. Many citizens, including my parents, condemned these actions, but to me they seemed logical and necessary; the clergy and Polish authorities had strong anti-Soviet and anti-Communist sentiments.

During October and November, Wlodzimierz-Wolynski swelled with Jewish refugees returning from the former Soviet border, which never did open, and coming illegally from Nazi-occupied territory. The new Soviet-German border ran along the Bug River, only twelve kilometers west of town. The synagogues and Jewish prayer houses opened up to the refugees, and local Jews gave them food and shelter. We housed as many refugees as we could fit into our flat.

Life in Wlodzimierz-Wolynski changed swiftly. Gone was the tranquillity of a small town where everyone knew everyone and where families had lived for many years. The intrusion of Soviet indoctrination and propaganda, mandatory political meetings, Soviet control of the radio and press, and the dissolution of religious activity transformed the city. The first signs of a truly Soviet lifestyle were food shortages and long lines at the bakeries, butcher shops, and food stores, scenes never before occurring in Poland.

I absorbed the indoctrination and devoured the propaganda. As the only Communist country in the world, the Soviet Union was an island surrounded by a sea of capitalists who wanted to overrun and destroy it; therefore, strict regulation of local activity was necessary. The capitalists had to be arrested, and their property had to be confiscated and turned over to the rightful owner—the workers' state. I believed Stalin was mankind's great, progressive leader and that the social justice I had dreamed of for so long would be achieved by the new society. No one knew that the Soviet Union had become an ally of Nazi Germany or that

Poland had been secretly partitioned between the two countries through the Ribbentrop-Molotov Pact.

In late November, however, I became troubled by stories about the brutal treatment of local citizens during night searches and arrests. These operations usually focused on landowners and merchants, many of whom I had known since childhood and whose honesty and integrity had never been questioned.

One evening during dinner we had an unexpected visitor. Dr. Bubes, a rotund, jovial otolaryngologist and good friend of my parents, came to ask my father for help. The Soviet military command had given him twenty-four hours to relinquish his three houses. If he complied, he would be guaranteed his own flat and office in one of the houses and not be harassed any further. If he didn't, he would lose all of his property as well as his medical license and might even be deported. Dr. Bubes gestured helplessly, his face red with anger and despair. My mother and I remained silent, waiting for my father to respond.

"There isn't much you can do," my father said looking at the floor and running his hand over his bald head. "We have to face reality. The Communists consider us—you and me—not doctors but capitalists because we own property. Today they came to you, tomorrow they may come to me. I'm prepared to give them what they want, and I advise you to do the same." Dr. Bubes said he would bribe some patients of his who were Soviet officials so he could keep as much property as he could. "I wouldn't trust them," my father warned. "They'll take your money first, then your property."

When Dr. Bubes left, my father talked openly about our own situation. I'd never been included in such a discussion. My father and uncle owned the two-story building in which we lived. On the ground floor was the largest restaurant in town, Strzecha, owned by Mr. Pietras, and the most elegant confection shop, owned by the Hammermans. On the corner was Mr. Rodberg's barber shop. There was also a printing shop and a public health clinic.

My father said he'd give up everything so we could keep our flat and his office, as well as the flats where my uncle and grandparents lived. I was disturbed by my father's forethought. I hadn't realized that the city council officials, all of whom I knew and thought were my friends, considered my parents capitalists and therefore *vragi naroda*.* I couldn't believe that they would forcefully take my father's property and my parents' valuables. While I had been helping the Soviets establish themselves in town, my father had been planning how to defend us and our property against them.

The next morning we had more disconcerting news. During the night several of our friends' homes had been searched, and many of their valuables had been confiscated. A close friend of my father, Dr. Polanski, had been arrested. I couldn't believe what was happening and went to see Major Dmitri Roshenko of the city military command. I told him that my father, uncle, and Dr. Bubes were not capitalists and that I could guarantee their honesty and loyalty to the Soviet state. "You don't understand the essence of capitalism," he said coolly, leaning back in his chair. "Anyone who exploits other people and accumulates wealth will become, if he isn't already, a capitalist and enemy of the working class. You made the choice to support us, and we consider you one of us. But your father, uncle, and parents' friends will never be our friends. Let me warn you—don't go talking to anyone else on their behalf. The Organy** won't like it."

The threat in his voice alarmed me, as did his reference to the Organy. "Dmitri," I said, "I've supported you in every way and worked very closely with you. I thought you trusted me."

"Janusz, you know what Comrade Stalin says about trust? Trust and check. Don't trust anyone, not even yourself. This is how we must live when surrounded by enemies. You must always be on guard, even with your own family."

As the leaves of autumn blew away, the arrests of merchants and landowners continued. Each day I worried that Taubcia's father might be arrested because he owned a small fabric store. He made considerably less than a modest income, but anyone who owned a store, no matter how small; a house, no matter how

* "Enemies of the people." A term applied to political prisoners.
** The popular name for the NKVD.

shabby; or a business, no matter how unprofitable, was in great danger of being not only dispossessed but also arrested. Taubcia's father—timid, deeply religious, and soft-spoken—was unaware of the danger the new regime posed to him and his family.

I followed Dmitri's advice not to ask any more questions and not to plead on behalf of my parents and their friends, and I immersed myself even more in political activity, hoping that my devotion would save my parents from trouble. I stood up on the platform at meetings and enthusiastically gave reports. I was delegated to participate daily in local gatherings and eventually was nominated to be a designated speaker at the meetings required for all citizens. At these meetings, designed for the "political education of the masses," I presented and analyzed political and military events and explained the role of the Red Army, which was to save the eastern part of Poland from the capitalists by incorporating it into Ukraine. In late November, the Soviets prepared a referendum to make official the incorporation of Western Ukraine into the Ukraine Soviet Socialist Republic, and I was one of the few local citizens appointed to the election committee. Working during all my spare time on the committee, I became friends with two young Soviet officers, one of whom, Yuri Savchenko, became a frequent guest in our home.

During the first week of December a curfew was imposed on the city. An increased number of soldiers patrolled the streets, and rumors spread that dozens of cattle cars were arriving at the train station. I went with my friends to the station to see what was going on. Red boxcars were lined up by the hundreds and hooked to coal-burning locomotives. Their presence indicated that deportations were being planned, but no one knew exactly when they would take place or who would be deported. I tried to find out from my Soviet friends what was going on, but they hadn't been given any information. They only knew that the NKVD was in charge of the operation, and I didn't know anyone in this secretive organization.

Late in the afternoon on December 5, Yuri Savchenko came to my house, out of breath, and told me that mass arrests and deportations would take place that night. He thought my parents might be on the list. I dashed through the waiting room of my father's office, something I never did, and found him working. He raised his head in surprise. "I need to talk to you," I said, squeezing his shoulder. "I'll get mother and we'll wait for you in the bedroom. Please come as soon as you can." My father showed up immediately. I told my parents with great shame and dread about the danger we were in.

"I expected something like this," my mother said. "I'm not surprised. My only hope is that they leave the permanent citizens alone."

My father paced nervously across the bedroom. He stopped next to the chair where my mother was sitting. "I was prepared to give up properties so we could keep our flat, but I didn't think we'd be deported." His nervousness filled the room.

My mother looked at me inquisitively. "What do you think? You know them. What should we do?" It was the first time my parents had asked for my advice. I felt more frightened than ever.

"Go into hiding, either in Spielberg's shelter or in Ostrowek at Mr. Vorbrot's estate."

"But how can we get there?" asked my father, his brown eyes wide with fear. "I don't think we have time to hitch up the wagon and leave town before curfew."

"Let's go to the shelter," my mother said. "I'll ask Nuchem to prepare it for us."

I ran to get Taubcia and warn her family.

The sun had dropped below the horizon, and I felt a chill despite my sweater and coat. The plaza in front of the train station was swarming with curious townspeople and refugees, the latter huddled together in groups. The months of being without homes had taken their toll: the refugees appeared frail, dirty, and disheveled. Many wore only light jackets, sweaters, or torn, filthy clothing that neither matched nor fit properly. The din in the streets seemed to increase as word about the special action spread. Twilight found more Soviet soldiers on the streets. They walked quickly in and out of the train station and shouted at the refugees and civilians: "Go home! Disperse! Get out of here!" I felt trapped. The military patrols, trucks, cattle cars, and machine guns positioned at each corner convinced me that no one was safe. Hiding was our only salvation.

Abe, Taubcia's brother, answered my loud knocks. Taubcia and her parents were praying at the dining room table. Taubcia came up to greet me, but her parents didn't move or say anything. I respected Taubcia's parents, but her father didn't like my secular ideas or my influence on his daughter. I was about to say something when Mr. Stern put a finger to his lips. I waited another minute, then interrupted their prayers. "Mr. Stern, we don't have much time. The Soviets are going to arrest and deport people tonight. No one knows for sure who will be arrested, but I'm worried that you may be on the list since you own the fabric store. Please, come into hiding with my family for the night."

Mr. Stern's heavy brows nearly covered his pupils. After a long pause he said angrily, "What else have you heard? All I see are refugees running back and forth. They don't have jobs or any place to stay. We're not refugees. We've lived here for twenty years. We're not going to leave."

"Mr. Stern, with all due respect, you and your family are in danger. There are hundreds of cattle cars at the station. People will be deported tonight. Not only refugees, but merchants and property owners. I'm sure you're on the blacklist."

Mr. Stern pushed himself away from the table and stood up. "Stop trying to frighten my family and me. This is nonsense. You're too young to understand what's going on. Some crazy refugees are running around spreading panic, and everyone is responding to this. No one knows better than God what is going to happen. He leads us and protects us in moments of danger, and He will take care of us. We've survived all these years, and we'll survive this night and many nights ahead if it is God's will."

Mrs. Stern had been sitting at the table with her head lowered while her husband spoke, but now she rose from her chair and walked over to him. She rarely addressed her husband directly in the presence of guests, but this time she interrupted him.

"Shimon, this isn't right. Abe and Taubcia have a right to decide what they want to do. If they want to leave with Janusz, they should go. I believe God will take care of them." She looked at

Taubcia and me until she began to sob, then abruptly left the room.

I squeezed Taubcia's hand, encouraging her to come with me. Her gray-green eyes were full of tears, and her blond hair was in tangles. "Papa, I'm going with Janusz. I'll be back as soon as things quiet down." Her voice was tearful, but her grip was strong and reassuring. I felt that we trusted each other, and it made me feel better. "I wish you, Mama, and Abe would come with us. I think Janusz knows what he's talking about." Abe sat motionless and speechless. He was still sitting like this when we left.

Taubcia and I ran as fast as we could to my house. Kolejowa Street was crowded with military patrols and pedestrians, so we took the back alleys, climbing fences and running through backyards. Farna Street looked like it did on Sunday after Mass. We were out of breath when we reached the back of my building. Light was coming through the entrance. I didn't know why the doors would be open. As we got closer I saw that the doors to the entryway had been broken and were hanging from their upper hinges. Pieces of splintered wood lay on the floor. Panic set in. Had the arrests already begun? On the spacious landing outside our flat, all was silent except for the pounding of my heart. I pulled the key out of my pocket and slowly unlocked the door. The lights in the dining room were dim, but as we walked in I heard hushed voices and saw my parents, grandparents, sister, and uncle's family gathered around the dining room table listening to the BBC. My mother asked in a quiet, frightened voice if we'd seen any soldiers around the building. Half an hour earlier a group of them had broken down the door but had not entered the building. I told her that on Farna Street, groups of soldiers were randomly pounding on doors, smashing windows, and breaking down gates.

My parents were ready with food and blankets. Spielberg lived next door, and we went to his house through our backyard. When the war started, he and his brothers had built a shelter next to his home. The outside entrance was covered with bushes. The inside entrance was in the cellar and could be reached through the house. The dirt walls were reinforced with logs and moss, and the hard dirt floor was covered with a patchwork of wolf hides and deerskin rugs. A kerosene lamp sat on a tree stump. The ceiling, supported by logs, was high enough that we could stand up and walk around. Several chairs were in the room, but everyone decided that lying down would be more comfortable. My mother was in pain. I told my father I was going home to bring more blankets and pillows for her and my grandmother and asked him to stay near the door to let me back in.

He stepped near the door as if trying to block it, looked me in the eye, and said, "I want you back in fifteen minutes."

Outside everything was quiet. The streets were empty. It was past curfew. I hid behind a bush to give my eyes time to adjust to the dark. The night was windy. Heavy clouds moved quickly across the sky. The moon flickered between them, giving me just enough light to survey the alley. I slipped to the back of the building, walked lightly past the hanging doors, and bounded up the stairs to the landing outside the three flats. I paused a moment, searching for my keys.

"Stop right there," a voice said in Russian. "Get your hands up and move over to the wall." My heart beat furiously. Someone roughly grabbed my shoulder and turned me around. Two others were behind him. A flashlight shone in my face. "What's your name and what are you doing here?"

I looked at my interrogator. He was much taller and bigger than me, with Mongolian features and a slight accent. He had tiny black eyes and no lips, just two thin parted lines and large yellow teeth. I couldn't see his rank in the dark, but I saw the pistol in his hand. The second man was almost as tall as the first but had blond bushy hair and a youthful, freckled face. The third man was short and stocky. With his thick neck, flat ears, and crooked nose, he looked like a boxer or wrestler. All three wore long wool coats and Soviet army hats with the earflaps turned up. I didn't think they were regulars of the Red Army; they acted more like members of the NKVD.

I answered in Russian, "My name is Janusz Bardach. I work with Major Roshenko. I'm vice-chairman of the city election committee."

"Where did you learn such fluent Russian?"

"My mother is from Odessa, and we speak Russian at home."

"Is this your flat?" He banged on the door.

"Yes."

"Do you have the key?"

I reached into my jacket and was suddenly hit on the neck. My head fell forward.

"Nobody said you could move!" shouted the Mongolian. "I just asked if you had the key. Answer the question and don't move unless I say so. Now, do you have the key?"

"Yes, I have the key. I'll open the door and let you in."

"Go ahead, but slowly."

I tried to figure out what they were looking for—apartments to loot, families to arrest, or people out after curfew. We stepped into the waiting room of my father's office, and I turned on the lights. Magazines were displayed on a large table surrounded by a semicircle of green and beige upholstered chairs.

The Mongolian looked around. "What the hell is this? Who lives here?" He looked from chair to chair and walked up to the plants next to the window. "No tables, no beds . . . who lives here?"

"This is the waiting room for my father's patients."

"What are all these paintings for if your father is a doctor?" He ran his hand over a vase. "The people who come to see your father are sick—why do they need all this luxury? Paintings, plants, mirrors—I wouldn't mind living in this room."

"We like to have a nice waiting room to make the patients feel comfortable before they enter my father's office. They can relax, read, or talk here, and this makes them feel better."

"What do you mean, 'feel better'? When I go to the doctor I don't feel good. And I wait two or three hours in a dirty hall with a hundred other people no matter how sick I am. In the Soviet Union, the doctors are for everyone. Your doctors are only for those who can afford shit like this." He picked up an ashtray and held it in the palm of his hand. "Your father must be grabbing up money right and left. I bet he won't treat a person if he doesn't have money. So," he looked at me sharply, "where is the man who owns all these paintings and chairs? I'd like to meet him. Where is he?"

"He's with my mother in Odessa."

"Why did they go to Odessa?"

"Because my mother had surgery. They went to visit her brother, who is a professor in the medical school there."

"Oh, so none of your family works. They're all doctors and professors—bloodsuckers!" He walked into the hallway and went into the dining room. I followed behind him while the two other men looked at the rest of the flat. "And when do they come back?" He ran his hand over the glass of my mother's china cabinet and fiddled with the wooden latch.

"I expect them back next week or the week after." I felt light-headed.

He held the pistol against my chin. "If you're lying, you and your family will pay for it." His black eyes bore into mine. "I'm a captain of the NKVD stationed here in town. I'll be back to check on you." He stepped back and turned to one of the officers. "Kostia, he works for Roshenko. Think he can be trusted? Should we take him as a *ponyatoy** for the night?"

A witness? For what? I didn't know what he was talking about.

Kostia nodded with approval. The Mongolian turned to me and said, "I'm in charge of cleaning the city of our enemies. According to the law, we need a civilian witness to accompany us on our searches and arrests. I order you to come with us. In the morning, after you sign the documents, you can go home."

I looked at his flat nose, yellow teeth, and beady eyes. I'd never been close to anyone from the NKVD, but I knew their reputation of terrorizing people in town.

"Comrade captain," I said, "I'll be your witness, but please explain what I have to do."

"What you have to do!" he snorted. "You don't have to *do* anything except witness our activities and sign the documents in

* A civilian required by law to assist in and witness searches and arrests, legitimizing the activities of the NKVD.

the morning. Since this is a socialist state, we do everything required by law, and the law states that a civilian witness is necessary for all searches, arrests, and executions to make sure the procedures are performed properly. Now, do you understand?" He squinted at me. "And one more thing: don't even think of deceiving us." He tapped his finger on my chest.

The longer he talked, the more nauseated I became, afraid that my father would come looking for me.

"Kostia!" the captain shouted. The blond-haired soldier appeared from the other room with a fistful of my mother's silver spoons. He was smiling, as though he were at a party and having a good time. "You're responsible for the witness. Don't let him out of your sight." The captain reached into his coat pocket and pulled out a list. "Andrei, here's the list of names, addresses, and numbers of people in each household. Do you know the route?"

"I think I know the general layout, and we have him to help us."

Andrei handed me the list. I recognized many names—friends of mine and of my parents. I flipped to the second page and froze: "Shimon Stern—4." Taubcia's father. My father's name was also on the list, but for some reason it had been crossed off. Perhaps I would be able to scratch off other names when no one was looking.

The captain, whose name was Gennady, explained that the operation would last until six or seven in the morning. After we finished, the city would be declared a frontier zone with restricted housing and travel privileges. He emphasized that only those considered loyal to the Soviet Union would be allowed to live in the city or travel through it. "Let's move," Gennady said, placing his hand on my arm and directing me toward the door. "You lead us. When we approach the house, you ring the bell or knock on the door. In Polish, you announce that the NKVD is conducting a search for refugees."

We left through the kitchen and went to the backyard, where the truck was parked. We drove down Farna Street, passing the cathedral and the only movie theater in town. In the small park behind the theater, military trucks were parked haphazardly. As the truck rattled over the uneven stones, I thought that it wasn't only I who was trapped but also all the people on the list. Frantically, I tried to think of a way to warn them that we were coming.

The wind ripped through my coat and hair. On Lucka Street we passed the newly built Lutheran church, where Mr. Schoen was pastor. The family had crossed to the German side when the Soviets arrived. Farther down the street we reached the poor Jewish section. A few houses had straw roofs; some had barns attached, with a cow or a couple of goats in the yard. Most of the houses had only two rooms, a kitchen, and a cellar or an attic. I had some friends who lived in this section. The street lamps were dim, and there were no lights on in any of the houses.

At the end of the street, Andrei slammed on the brakes. A broken wooden fence lined the property of the house. Gennady checked the number on the gate to see if it matched the one on the list, then walked briskly toward the house. Andrei, Kostia, and I followed. The yard was full of weeds. The wooden walls had begun to rot, and the whole house looked as though it were sinking into the earth. Gennady told me to knock and speak to the tenants in Polish. Though he could understand Polish quite well and could speak a little of it, he wanted me to communicate with the citizens during the searches because I would be less intimidating than an NKVD officer.

The door opened into darkness. I couldn't see anybody but sensed the presence of people in the room. "Is anybody here?" I called out. A woman's voice with a thick Jewish accent replied, "What do you want?"

"I want nothing. I'm with the NKVD, and they're looking for refugees. If you're housing any, they must come forward. The officer wants to check everyone's papers. Refugees will be deported to the Soviet Union, and if the owners of the house try to hide them, they too will be deported." I felt a blow in the ribs.

"This is not a place to give speeches," Gennady shouted. "Don't say more than I tell you."

Dazed, I sat down in the closest chair, bent forward, and held my head in my hands. Somebody lit a kerosene lamp. There were three people in the room, two men and a woman, all in their thir-

ties. They were well dressed and appeared to be urban and educated.

"We don't live here," said a tall dark-haired man. "We came
from Warsaw. We belong to Bund, the Jewish leftist organization,
and we have great admiration for your country and leadership."
The man spoke nervously but seemed confident that his message
would please Gennady.

Gennady was annoyed but didn't interrupt the man. He asked
me for a translation. When I told him what the man said, he
smiled and put his hand on my shoulder as though he were dis-
closing some fatherly advice. "Well, we'll send them someplace
safe and where they'll have an opportunity to work for the sake
of our country." He turned to the three people and said sharply
in broken Polish, "You have ten minutes to pack and get on the
truck!" They looked at each other with surprise. The tall dark-
haired man tried to say something else, but Gennady turned
around, grabbed him by the arm, and escorted him outside. The
other man picked up their bags, and everyone followed Gennady
out to the truck. With his shotgun, Kostia directed the woman
and two men to climb over the sideboards. The two men got in
first, then pulled up their female companion. Kostia ordered
them to sit down on the floor next to the cab with their legs
crossed and told them not to get up.

Kostia and I leaned against the gate and faced the deportees
while we drove down the street to the next several houses on the
list. With the same arrogance and indifference, Gennady, Andrei,
and Kostia picked up several more families of refugees and two
local families who were hiding them. Thirty-some people sat
cross-legged on the floor of the truck clutching the few belongings they managed to carry with them.

We pulled up to a two-story house in a more affluent neigh-
borhood. Gennady pounded on the door. When no one answered, he kicked it in. He called Andrei and Kostia to help him
search the house. I followed. No one seemed to care that the
truck was left unguarded. I had never been told to guard the deportees, and I hoped that while we were gone some of them
would escape.

Walking from room to room, Gennady shouted for people to come out. We walked to the back of the house and saw that the door leading to the backyard was open. In a voice vibrating with anger, Gennady bellowed, "If anyone is hiding back there, you'd better come out. If you don't, I'll search the bushes and shoot anyone I find." There was silence for a moment while Gennady strained to see in the dark. When his eyes adjusted, he fired three shots randomly into the bushes.

"Stop firing!" a man screamed. "We're coming out." Five adults, including an old woman, and two children came out of the bushes with their hands up. Gennady went up to the first man and hit him in the face with his pistol, bloodying the man's nose and splitting his lip. Kostia and Andrei herded them onto the truck. No one bothered to ask their names, where they were from, or what their occupation was. Hiding in the bushes was criminal enough.

"Move over!" Kostia shouted. "Make a place!"

None of the deportees had moved while we were gone. A few of the women cried softly to themselves. The men stared at the floor. None of them looked capable of lifting their heads, let alone jumping off the truck and running, although it would have been easy for them to hide in someone's backyard. Gennady and his men didn't know the names of the refugees, and I was certain that the next day no one would bother to look for them. I tried to make eye contact with some of them to transmit the idea of escape, but the few who looked at me didn't understand my hint. They all seemed paralyzed by fear. I realized they were afraid of me, too. I felt worn out and deeply ashamed.

As we got closer to the train station, shouting, wailing, and crying pierced the air, punctuated by gruff Russian commands. Hundreds of deportees were gathered on the plaza and guarded by soldiers. Several trucks were parked on the circle in front of the station, a place usually reserved for carriages. We pulled up behind the last truck and watched those ahead of us unload. Soldiers with bayonets surrounded the trucks, taking every opportunity to threaten, kick, shove, and swear at the captives. One old man in a black suit and yellow shirt had trouble walking, and a guard shoved him to the ground and tore a gold watch from the man's pocket. He kicked and swore at the terrified man, calling him a capitalist pig.

Gennady disappeared and came back with two other NKVD officers, stammering to each other and staggering from side to side. "We're next in line to unload," Gennady slurred. "Get these fucking parasites off the truck." A group of soldiers surrounded the truck, ordered the deportees to get down, and led them inside the station. Kostia and I followed. A soldier ordered our group to sit on one of the platforms. NKVD guards and soldiers walked among the throngs, kicking and cursing at anyone who got up or moved. People shouted names, trying to find family members or friends. Hungry children cried in their mothers' arms. Parents and children looking for each other clawed at the soldiers and darted about. The soldiers threw them against the floor and beat them until they lay quietly or moaned. Pleas for water were ignored. People who had fainted were dragged into the station. The cattle cars were filling up. The bars were bolted shut. Muffled, anguished cries escaped through the grated windows.

I lost Kostia in the train station and looked around to find my way out. In one of the open cars I noticed one of my classmates and his father. Without thinking, I weaved between soldiers and their captives and walked up to the car. A field with bushes and trees lay on the other side of the tracks, and when I peered around the car I saw that the area wasn't guarded. I went up to my friend and told him I would open the door on the other side so he and his family could hide in the nearby woods. Without thinking, I slipped under the bumpers and came out on the other side of the car. I pulled the bar and opened the door wide enough for a person to get out. My friend, Silik Shternfeld, his family, and four other people jumped out and disappeared in the night.

Although freedom was waiting in the woods, no one else had the will or courage to leave the car. The Soviets had been in town only a few months, but they knew how to turn people into sheep, how to take away their will and dignity and make them obey orders, even if the orders led to their own destruction. The NKVD knew that fear was the best guardian; they didn't need to bother with securing the other side of the tracks.

When I returned to the truck, I found Gennady completely drunk. He stared at me with blurry eyes: "Where've you been? I was looking for you." He hadn't been looking for me. He didn't care. He was dead drunk.

"I was here. What do you want me to do?"

"Get me a bottle of vodka in the restaurant—or maybe two." He reached into his pocket and gave me a wad of rubles.

We drove downtown again and turned at the cathedral onto Kowelska Street. Gennady continued to drink from the bottle, passing it back and forth with Andrei. Through the cab window I could hear his loud, crude curses as he talked about the upcoming searches and arrests. I didn't know whether his cruelty and righteousness were caused by his drunkenness or whether it was simply typical of NKVD officers.

I don't remember how many houses we went through before we arrived at tenement number 294, but I remember the people at this house as vividly as I remember the number. The middle-aged woman who answered the door was tall and lanky, with beautiful dark eyes, gray hair, and a fair complexion. She looked frightened but not surprised. Her husband remained seated at the dining room table, looking sick. His face showed no alarm or fear when Gennady entered the room. There was also a young girl who looked about Rachel's age, thirteen or fourteen years old, and a young man of about twenty-five who had a small reddish beard. I thought I had seen him before, but I wasn't sure where and I didn't know his name. He looked at me for a clue about what was going to happen.

One large room served as a kitchen and dining room. The wooden floor was painted red, and a small glass chandelier hung above a large rectangular table. The dinner dishes were still on the table.

"Where's your cellar and attic?" Gennady asked perfunctorily in his broken Polish. He tried to be intimidating, but the vodka kept him from pronouncing the words clearly.

"The cellar entrance is over here," replied the woman, pointing to a trapdoor with a ring in the floor next to the stove. "The stairs to the attic are over there."

"Kostia, you and Andrei go to the cellar, we'll go upstairs." He turned to me. "Lead the way." I looked at the woman and caught her frightened expression; her husband and children looked silently at the floor.

Gennady and I climbed a narrow ladder to the attic. I pushed open the trapdoor and stepped into the darkness. "We need a light," Gennady shouted. "Is anyone here?" He raised his voice impatiently, but nobody answered. The woman climbed the ladder with a kerosene lamp in her hand. As light filled the attic, I saw them huddled together, clinging to each other with terrified expressions. There was a young couple with two small children, no more than five or six years of age. A little girl with large dark eyes was covered with a scarf. Her mother held her close as though she were lulling her to sleep and protecting her at the same time. Her brother, a year or two older, sat next to her with his father's hand around his waist. He wore a white shirt and black jacket that was too big for him. His face looked pale next to his dark curly hair. With his free arm, the father hugged his wife, pulling her close in a simple, protective gesture.

"Who are these people?" Gennady asked. I translated his question into Polish for the woman with the lamp.

"Our relatives. They live with us."

"Let me see their documents, and your family's, too," Gennady barked.

The young couple sat motionless. The woman gave me the lamp and left the attic. Gennady told me to ask the couple their names and where they were from. "Rosen," the man answered. "We came to visit our aunt, Madame Schwartz. The war started when we were here visiting her, so we couldn't go back to Lublin, where we live."

"Lublin?" Gennady inquired. Suddenly he grabbed Mr. Rosen by the hair, pulled him to his feet, and hit him in the stomach. "You filthy refugees! Nazi spies!" The children began to cry, which further irritated Gennady. "Make them shut up! Or do you want me to take care of them?"

The mother pulled them close to her, but they couldn't stop crying. Gennady grabbed the little boy's hands, jerked him loose from his mother's arms, and threw him against the floor. "Shut up, I said!" The mother screamed. The father tried to say something but could only gasp for air. Gennady picked up the boy and held him for a second, looking closely at his face, then threw him forcefully against the wall. The boy screamed in pain and terror. He got up and walked over to his mother, holding his shoulder with his hand. It had been dislocated.

"Get them downstairs, all of them!" Gennady barked at me. "And round up the people who hid them. They can't be trusted." I held the lamp while the family descended the ladder. I wanted to convey my guilt and sorrow but was too ashamed to look into their eyes.

"Mr. Commander," Madame Schwartz said, "we are poor working people. We're happy you've come to liberate us from the Nazis. Please leave us alone. My husband is dying of cancer and won't survive the travel. If you need to take anyone, please take me." She looked straight in his eyes and took a step closer to him. "I will go and work for you as you wish, but please, leave my husband and daughter." With all her will and dignity, she told him how she and her family had often been hungry, had no work, were a real proletarian family. I looked at Gennady. He wasn't listening. His porcine eyes moved around the room from the old man to his son and daughter and to the young family standing together holding their belongings. Gennady ordered them out to the truck. Kostia herded them together and poked them with his shotgun as they struggled to climb over the sideboard.

We repeated the same procedure at several more houses. Between arrests, Gennady guzzled vodka from the bottle he had brought with him and became more and more drunk. He passed the bottle to Kostia and Andrei, and the three of them talked about hunting for refugees as if they were speaking of wild ducks or jackrabbits. Gennady, however, professed to be bored, complaining of the ready submission of the deportees. He wanted more of a challenge.

After we had "cleaned up" the poorer districts, Andrei announced that we would be searching houses in one of the wealthiest sections of town. Gennady talked excitedly about all the goods they would take. We drove halfway down Kowelska Street and stopped in front of one of the newest houses, that belonging to Dr. Schechter. His children, Dalek and Marusia, were close friends of mine. Gennady's mouth gaped open when he saw the magnificent facade. His excitement seemed to sober him.

My stomach churned. We stood at the door for several minutes without getting an answer. There were no lights on in the house. Gennady cursed and held his thumb on the doorbell. He pulled the bottle of vodka from his coat pocket, took a long swig and handed it to Kostia. Kostia and Andrei took smaller swigs and handed the bottle to me. I'd never drunk liquor before, so I handed it back. Kostia sneered, "I suppose you're a virgin, too. Hey Gennady, this little prick's never had a good drink or a good fuck!"

"What's the matter with you?" Gennady grabbed my arm. Vodka drooled down his chin. "Don't you drink with simple people?" He grabbed my jacket with one hand and put the bottle to my mouth with the other. I twisted away, but Kostia hit me in the stomach. "Drink!" I took two sips. The alcohol burned my throat and stomach.

Gennady ordered Andrei to break down the door, and after several blows with the crowbar the handle broke. We stepped into the front hallway. Gennady turned on the lights and looked around in stupefied silence. A majestic marble hallway stretched out in front of us. Off to the side was Dr. Schechter's office. His dark mahogany desk stood in the middle, and Gennady walked straight to it. He ran his hand over the smooth wood and then, in a moment of unexpected rage, smashed it with the crowbar. "Capitalist swine! Motherfucking parasites! We need to find these bourgeois exploiters!" He smashed harder and harder without pause, making several holes in the wood. He then ran back into the hallway and smashed the paintings and chandelier. In the living room he stopped abruptly when he saw the magnificent ceiling, tall windows, concert piano, table, and chairs. He smashed the piano and ordered Kostia and Andrei to destroy everything in the room. Each strike fell on my heart as Gennady stormed through the house, swinging randomly at the furniture, paintings, and candelabras, destroying the home where I had spent a great part of my childhood. He ordered the house to be searched from the attic to the cellar, every room and every closet, including the servants' quarters. Kostia and Andrei emptied drawers, closets, and cabinets and packed suitcases they'd found with clothing, jewels, dishes, vases, and figurines. Gennady ordered Andrei and Kostia to destroy everything in the house they couldn't take with them and to meet us in the backyard. He was determined to find the Schechter family.

In the backyard there was a large brick barn. The gardener, his wife, and the night watchman lived in the three attached rooms, and Gennady thought the Schechters might be hiding there. He pounded on the wooden door until the gardener and his wife, dressed in nightclothes, answered.

"Where's the Schechter family?"

"They're at home," the gardener murmured.

His soft, sleepy reply further enraged Gennady. "You son of a whore!" He grabbed the gardener by his nightshirt and pulled him close. "Find them or I'll kill you!" Spit sprayed in the gardener's face. Gennady pulled the gardener outside and threw him on the ground. The man stood up, wiped the spit off his face, and ran toward the house.

The gardener's wife began to wail. "Holy Mary! Holy Jesus! Please, I beg you, leave us in peace. Oh God! Holy Mary! Save us!" This was too much for Gennady. Although he barely understood Polish, he understood her religious invocation.

He grabbed her by the robe, which opened, exposing her breasts. "Filthy whore. I'll teach you a lesson." He began to kiss and fondle the woman. Her screams pierced my heart.

The gardener came running back to the barn. "Sir, please stop. Leave my wife alone. I'll do whatever you want, but please, leave her alone!"

"Did you bring your master and his family?" Gennady shouted.

"I don't know where the Schechter family is. I went through the entire house and checked the backyard. I couldn't find them anywhere." He had barely finished the sentence when Gennady punched him in the face.

The gardener's nose bled profusely. He put both hands to his face, still pleading with Gennady to leave his wife alone.

Gennady let go of the woman. "Liar!" he said. He pointed his pistol at the man's face and fired. The gardener's wife jumped on Gennady, scratching him. He flung her to the ground and drew his pistol.

The night watchman appeared, and when he saw the gun pointed at the woman, he ran up to Gennady and pushed him, throwing him off balance. Kostia and Andrei cocked their pistols, ready to shoot, when Gennady shouted, "Leave him for me! I'll teach him what it means to attack an officer of the NKVD. He's going to lick my boots and beg to die quickly." Gennady smashed the pistol across his face and tried to kick him in the groin but missed, landing his foot on the watchman's stomach. The watchman doubled forward. Gennady smashed the pistol on the back of his head.

As Gennady beat the watchman, I walked away and looked at the orchard of cherry and plum trees, where the Schechter family was hiding. The summer before, Dalek had shown me an underground shelter at the end of the neighbor's lot, behind the shrubbery. I couldn't stop thinking how close they were to being found and killed. Afraid that my intense thoughts might somehow transmit the knowledge of the shelter to Gennady, I went back to the barn.

The watchman's face had puffed up. His eyes were closed, his nose was bleeding, and his upper lip was split in half. Gennady straightened up and backed away from him. He looked exhausted, and I thought he had finished, but then he lunged at the watchman again, grabbed him by both ears, and tore them out. Blood spurted onto the ground. I went back outside and vomited.

As Gennady started to kick the watchman again, my peripheral vision caught a movement in the back of the barn; Kostia and Andrei were dragging the gardener's wife into a corner. She screamed and twisted, trying to free her limbs. Andrei pinned down her arms while Kostia spread her legs. She screamed wildly, and Kostia slapped her across the face and cursed. When Gennady stumbled over, Kostia got up and pulled up his pants.

"How was it?" Gennady asked. "Did you give her a good Russian fuck?"

He breathed hard. "The bitch loved it."

"Is she still alive?"

"I think so. You go next, boss." But Andrei was already on top of her.

Gennady took two big swigs of vodka, then handed what little was left to Kostia. They both laughed wildly and slurred obscenities while Andrei raped the woman. She didn't scream anymore, and I didn't think she was moving. Gennady couldn't stand straight and hung on to Kostia to keep his balance. "Hurry up, Andrei, I can't wait any longer." I thought the woman was dead. "Andrei, did you finish her off?" Gennady asked.

"No, she's just pretending. Go ahead."

I slipped outside and walked around in the cold air. A few minutes later, I heard two more shots.

Gennady, Kostia, and Andrei emerged from the barn. "Where's the little Polish prick? Why didn't he have a good time with us?"

I was trembling, afraid of giving him the wrong answer. "I've been outside waiting for you, Gennady."

"Well, we did fine without you, didn't we?" he said to Kostia and Andrei.

"Yes sir. We did quite well. It's a pity this little Polish shit couldn't learn something from us. Well, there'll be other chances. Then we can teach him how the NKVD treats enemies of the people. Let's go."

We got in the truck and headed toward the center of town, where several trucks like ours were crisscrossing the city, and from time to time we stopped so Gennady could exchange information with officers in the other trucks. After one of the stops, Gennady asked me if I knew a family by the name of Ozerow. I knew both sons very well; one of them had been a classmate. "They are members of the Ukrainian Nationalist underground. They aren't home. Let's try their friends' houses," Gennady said.

Gennady's order surprised me. By now I was exhausted physically and had trouble concentrating. I was anticipating the end of the arrests and had trouble thinking of someone who wouldn't be endangered by our visit. Jurek Olesiuk, a Ukrainian, was a well-known Communist. I thought it would be safe to lead Gennady to his house.

The house was close to the Luga River, where I had spent many summer days. We drove down bumpy Vodopojna Street. All the houses were dark. There was no light in Olesiuk's house, and as we approached dogs began barking. Gennady was already tense, and the barking upset him even more. Two large German shepherds ran back and forth on long leashes attached to a wire. I'd forgotten about them, and when I saw this unexpected obstacle I regretted my choice. The dogs barked viciously and ran back and forth, rattling the wire with their chains. "Shut these dogs up." Gennady drew his pistol and was trying to aim at one of the dogs when the front door opened.

Jurek appeared in his shorts. He told the dogs to be quiet and then called across the fence. "Who are you and what do you want?" He asked first in Polish and then repeated the question in Russian.

"We want to talk to you about your friends, the Ozerow brothers," Gennady said. "We've been told they're here and we need to talk to them."

"There's no one else here, just me and my parents. Why did you come here to look for them?" The dogs were still barking.

"I'm gonna shoot these bastards!"

"You don't need to do that, comrade." Jurek unhooked their chains from the wire and led them to a shed. He then opened the gate and let us in. In the darkness he probably couldn't see the blue insignia of the NKVD, but he saw me. "What are you doing here?"

"Jurek, the comrades are looking for the Ozerow brothers. They aren't home. I thought you might know where they are."

Jurek looked confused. "You know as well as I do where they might be hiding. For the last month I haven't had anything to do with them. You know the sort they are."

Gennady pushed me roughly aside. "Enough of this talk. I need to find out about the Ozerows and their group of Ukrainian nationalists and counterrevolutionaries. Since you know them, give me their names and addresses so we can find them. Let's go inside." Gennady stepped into the house without waiting for Jurek. "Andrei, you come with me and we'll talk to this man. Kostia, take him," he pointed to me, "and wait outside. Stop anyone who tries to come to the house."

I didn't like what was happening. I knew Jurek would try to press his affiliation with the underground communist movement instead of directly answering Gennady's questions. I also knew that Gennady wouldn't tolerate it. Now he had a chance to arrest not only the Ozerow brothers but also an entire group of counterrevolutionaries, and he wouldn't stop until they were found.

We'd been waiting for half an hour or more when the front door banged open and Jurek stumbled out. Blood dripped from his face, and his shirt was torn. He covered his face with his hands and pleaded with Gennady, "Please, comrade, call Rosia Rubenstein or Olek Maksimiuk. I worked with them for years. We're all members of the same underground Polish Communist Party. Please believe me. I told you everything I know."

"Don't lie to me. The Polish Communist Party doesn't exist. Your Politburo members were found to be traitors and were executed in Moscow in 1937. Your party was disbanded on Stalin's personal order. If you're still a member of the Polish Communist Party, then you're also a traitor. I'm going to find out all you know about the other members of your party and the Ozerow's Ukrainian terrorist group. You'd better start talking now or you'll be singing when I interrogate you in my quarters. This is the last time I'm going to ask you. What are the names of the people in both groups, and where do they live?"

Jurek repeated that he was a Party member, but this made Gennady more suspicious and hostile; he was convinced that Jurek could lead him to a large counterrevolutionary group.

"Let's go," Gennady said to Kostia and me. "There's nothing more to do here. Andrei, take him to headquarters. Tomorrow I'll talk to him, and maybe then he'll understand me better. I don't think he can hear me right now." Gennady laughed loudly and looked at all of us for signs of admiration.

Jurek couldn't walk by himself. He limped, dragging his bare and bloody left foot. Kostia and Andrei lifted him up and shoved him onto the back of the truck.

Gennady took out the last bottle of vodka from his coat and told Kostia and me to come with him to the riverbank. He lay down on the grass. We sat next to him. He took several swigs from the bottle and passed it to Kostia.

"Look at the trees and sky. Everything is so beautiful in the moonlight. At your age I entered the NKVD school in Kiev. I loved to go to the Dnieper River and sing on the riverbank with my friends." Gennady continued his drunken reverie, with Kostia looking at him attentively. I lay on my stomach in the cool grass and closed my eyes, trying to separate myself from the horror around me.

Andrei returned with the truck, and we searched the first two houses on Kolejowa Street. We then headed toward the train station. After unloading the captives, Andrei parked the truck in front of Taubcia's house.

It was daybreak. I felt frozen in my place, unable to speak or move, filled with dread and shame. How would I be able to face Taubcia if I participated in the deportation of her family? How could I stand in front of Mr. Stern, who had never had a high regard for me? I wouldn't be able to restrain myself if Gennady attacked the Sterns; I'd rather die than witness their being beaten and tortured. Before jumping out of the truck, I grabbed the crowbar and told Kostia we might need it to break in. He nodded but didn't say anything.

I stood back as Kostia pounded on the door. Gennady and Andrei were tired, and Gennady seemed to have lost interest. He yawned repeatedly and kept checking his watch. No one answered our knocks. Kostia turned the doorknob and the door opened. The four of us went into the kitchen. Gennady ordered me to tell everyone to come out and gather in the dining room.

I could barely squeeze a sound from my convulsed throat. I said in Polish, "Please, anybody who is home, don't be afraid. Come out to the dining room." There was silence.

"Louder," Gennady said. "Nobody can hear you."

"Please, come out to the dining room."

There wasn't a sound in the house.

"Search the premises." Gennady said. I led everyone from the dining room to the living room and into both bedrooms, but no one was there. In the parents' bedroom a closet was open. The luggage was gone. My heart was pounding so hard I was afraid everyone could sense my fear.

After walking through all the rooms, Gennady smashed a vase on the living room table. "To hell with them. We'll get them some other time. I'm tired. Let's go."

Gennady released me but said I had to come to his office in the afternoon to sign the papers.

The sun was up as I walked home. I had no idea if my family and Taubcia had made it safely through the night. I worried that someone might have left the shelter to come look for me and had been caught. Or perhaps the shelter had been discovered. Although extremely tired, I became frantic and began to run.

The broken doors in the entryway looked the same as they had the night before. I climbed the stairs and opened the door to our flat. No one was there. I ran out to the backyard of Spielberg's house and knocked frantically on the door leading to the shelter. Nuchem Spielberg answered. Everyone was there, worried and tired but unharmed. My mother and Taubcia started to cry when they saw me, and everyone hugged me and asked where I'd been. I told them what had happened and that we had searched Taubcia's house but no one was there. Taubcia began to cry and wanted to find out what had happened to her family.

Her house was still empty. A neighbor, Madame Eschner, called us to come over. She told us Taubcia's parents and brother had gone to the train station early in the morning with their suitcases and had volunteered to be deported. We figured that living so close to the train station, the Sterns had witnessed the deportations all night and heard the prisoners' screams. Taubcia's parents probably decided to give themselves up voluntarily to avoid forceful arrest.

In the afternoon I went to Gennady's office. His eyes were bloodshot, and he didn't say a word, just handed me two sheets of paper. I signed a report of the searches and arrests and a statement that I would never tell anyone what I witnessed that night.

CHAPTER 3

Red Army Soldier

One bright morning in the summer of 1940, six months after the night I witnessed the deportations, my father came with the morning paper in his hand and showed us the front page. The headline read: "Red Army Draft July 5." All men born between 1918 and 1922 were to report to their district's registration site for a medical examination.

My mother, Taubcia, Rachel, and I were sitting at the dining room table. "What are we going to do?" my mother asked in a breaking voice. She set down the silver samovar and put her arm around me. "I don't want you to go into the army." Her eyes were full of tears, making me feel that something terrible had already happened. My father pulled up a chair next to me. Taubcia went into the kitchen and sat at the small table next to the stove. Rachel followed. Taubcia had been living with us since her family was deported, and she and Rachel had become as close as sisters.

The sadness on my parents' faces made them look old; I felt more sorry for them than for myself, and I felt guilty, as though I had brought this pain upon them. I didn't know what to say. I stared at the black, white, and silver geometrical pattern on the oilcloth. The dishes and silverware, scattered haphazardly on the table, became suddenly dear. I thought about how much I would miss the white china I had loved since childhood, with the black and gold pattern of a knight on a horse spearing a dragon. Gennady and his men had stolen the china that was most precious to my mother, that which she had brought from Odessa.

The thought of being drafted into the Red Army had never occurred to me. In the Soviet Union, only eighteen-year-olds were drafted, and I assumed the same rule would apply in the Western Ukraine. I had always been frightened of the military, with its authoritarian orders and rigid indoctrination. My temper and impulsiveness had gotten me into trouble all my life, and I could hardly keep silent with my opinions. I didn't think I could ever be an obedient soldier.

But I would've been happy to join the Polish army to fight the Germans in 1939. I would've joined the Red Army to defend the socialist state if it were attacked by capitalist countries. I still believed in fighting for social justice, but I was no longer sure the Soviets were working toward that end, at least not in Wlodzimierz-Wolynski. I still believed in Stalin, the Politburo, and the principles of communism—I had even thought of appealing to Stalin when my friends' families were arrested. But living under the Soviet regime for eight months had diminished my enthusiasm and devotion. I was less active in politics and instead worked full-time as the director of the sports club Spartak.

From a friend I found out that Niunia Zeger, my brother's former girlfriend, would be one of the medical examiners in my district. I told my father, and it didn't take him long to come up with a plan to keep me from being drafted.

Over the next few weeks my father and I consulted with Niunia and agreed that I would claim to have a severe hearing impairment, a disability that could be easily faked. With my father, I practiced pretending I couldn't hear and asked him to repeat questions louder and louder. Although I practiced frequently, it was very difficult to pretend to be someone I wasn't.

The examination took place on the Ostrowski estate, across the Luga River. Fog snaked between the banks. As the sun burned off the haze, a pale blue sky emerged. I saw several former Polish classmates and young men from town amid the hundreds of draftees from nearby villages. I could find only two other Jewish friends. Most of the Jews lived in a different part of town and therefore went to another area for their examinations.

Four tables were set up on the grass in front of the barn. Two doctors in white coats sat at each table, and officers checked the files and talked among themselves. A bald, skinny, chinless Soviet officer stood up on a ladder and, speaking through a megaphone, ordered us to strip naked and form four lines alphabetically. I took off my shorts, shirt, and, with a pang of self-consciousness, my underpants. Standing naked with my Polish peers, a situation I had always taken great pains to avoid, made me feel extremely uncomfortable. Although my Jewishness was known to everyone, the mark of circumcision had always been a cause of embarrassment and ridicule during my years in the Polish gymnasium.

Upset by my nakedness, I succumbed to a wave of nauseating doubt. My plan to fake a hearing impairment began to seem dangerous. I'd never attempted such a fraud before. I stared at the dew in the grass, losing myself in the hundreds of tiny prisms. It was so hard to believe it was me standing naked waiting to be drafted into the Red Army.

When the officer's blue eyes met mine, I thought he looked at me strangely, as if he suspected me of something. He asked my name and date and place of birth. I spoke hoarsely. "Young man," he responded with an unexpected burst of enthusiasm, "you look fit and healthy. Your tan is remarkable." He smiled broadly. "But you should probably take off your trunks when you go swimming so you'll be tan all over." He smiled at me again and turned to the doctor. "He's in excellent condition."

The remark about my tan and his unexpectedly pleasant manner surprised me. The lie about my hearing seemed more and more preposterous. When Niunia asked about my complaints, all I could say was that I'd had pneumonia several times and contracted bronchitis easily. Niunia looked at me discreetly. She put a stethoscope to my chest and asked me to inhale and exhale. In between commands she mumbled something, but I was too frightened to listen closely or respond.

Another officer sitting at the table said to the officer in charge, "I wish all my children were as healthy as this young man." He stepped over to Niunia, who was still listening to my heart, and said, "'A' category, doctor?"

"I think so," she said softly.

"So what's your choice—the navy, air force, or tank units? The navy and air force service is five years, the tank units are four. Which do you prefer?"

Four years, five years—both sounded like prison terms. I didn't think it would make much difference. I'd never flown in my life and had never been on a ship, and it occurred to me in a split second that being on the ground would offer not only the shortest but also the safest term. I surely would be well protected in a tank on the battlefield in case there was war. "Tanks," I responded.

I was ordered to appear at the train station on July 28, 1940, my twenty-first birthday.

I walked home slowly through streets where I knew every house, every stone on the sidewalk, every tree, bush, fence, and gate. I was overcome by the feeling that this would be the last time I would ever see these things, as if I had been struck by a fatal, incurable disease. I couldn't escape my fate. But what upset me most was the fact that the fates of my parents, sister, grandparents, and Taubcia also hung in the balance. Why did all these lives have to be affected? It was like a prison sentence to me—four years away from my family, my life. I couldn't imagine how my father alone could take care of my mother and aged grandparents, Rachel, and Taubcia. I was afraid for myself, but I was more afraid for them—gentle, wonderful people who didn't understand how brutal and inhuman the Soviet authorities could be. I tried to shake off the shock and anger—anger toward a world that had allowed the occupation of a free country in the middle of Europe; the harassment and persecution of Jews; the destruction of my life and of my family. Rage gripped me, and despair lodged itself in me like a rock. I knew it would stay for a long, long time.

I climbed the hill behind our home, a favorite sledding spot, opened the gate that led to the backyard, and walked up the back stairs and into the kitchen. Everyone was waiting for me in the dining room, silent, anxious, and hopeful.

"Papa, I couldn't do it. I was put in the 'A' category."

"I was hoping so much Niunia could keep you from the service," my mother said tearfully.

Taubcia squeezed my hand.

"It's not Niunia's fault. I couldn't pretend. I just couldn't do it." I bent over and hugged my mother, feeling her tears on my cheek.

"Which branch are you assigned to?" my father asked flatly. He was upset with the outcome but tried to hide his emotions.

"I'm in the tank units. I'll be attending a school for heavy tank drivers and mechanics in Orel. I leave with the other recruits on my birthday."

I wanted Taubcia to be a member of my family before I left, and we decided to get married before my departure.

The preparation for the wedding didn't take long. My parents took care of the arrangements with the rabbi who was still in town. The Soviets had already closed the churches and synagogues, and most of the priests had been arrested and deported. But old Rabbi Meyer Finkelhorn had not been harmed and was still performing religious ceremonies in private homes.

The wedding took place in the waiting room of my father's dental office. We wore our ordinary good clothing, making no attempt to employ the usual nuptial costumes or decor; my mother and Taubcia arranged some plants under the window and on the window sill. Only my parents, sister, grandparents, uncle, and cousins attended the wedding. They sat on the waiting room chairs, still arranged in a semicircle. We said our vows under the *hupa* in the middle of the room, and I stomped on the glass, but there was no festivity. The fact that I would be leaving in three weeks dominated the thoughts and feelings of everyone, stripping the marriage ritual to its most basic elements. Taubcia cried bitterly because she didn't know the fate of her parents. We were still overwhelmed by the fear of the NKVD, which continued to conduct searches, loot homes and stores, and arrest wealthy citizens.

From time to time rumors of rape and murder surfaced, but nothing appeared in the newspapers, which had been taken over by the Party and NKVD. There was no law in this scary time because there was no Poland.

Everyone stayed up late the night before my departure, sitting outside in the garden. Taubcia and I sat on our favorite bench under the large apple tree, its branches heavy with red fruit. The thick foliage of the acacias blocked out the street below and enclosed us. We continued talking after everyone went to bed. We held each other, kissed, and cried. Few words of love and devotion were left unsaid between us.

The next morning I blended in with the other somber young soldiers flocking to the train platform. All of us wore casual, old clothing, knowing we would be wearing military uniforms for four years. Everyone lugged a wooden suitcase painted red, yellow, or black, some looking more worn than others. Small trunks with dangling locks—the customary luggage for departing soldiers—always made me think of miniature coffins within which the remains of the dead could be placed and returned home.

There was nothing left to say to Taubcia or my family while we waited for the train. Ever since the draft had been announced, I had felt as though I were standing on a plank, hovering over the black open sea, and I wanted the final moment to pass as quickly as possible. I remember the sounds of the locomotive on that early morning, the taste of coal dust in my mouth, and the cool metal railing against my hands as I watched my family get smaller and smaller and finally disappear in the distance. I remained in the corridor for several hours watching the landscape change. I recognized every station and building, every creek and river, as I had taken this train many times. The station signs read Iwanicze, Sokal, Maniewicze, and finally Lvov-Podzamcze, where we remained on the sidetracks for several hours.

I thought about Julek. He lived here, but I hadn't seen him for several months. Julek was prominent in the Polish Socialist Party; Lenin and Stalin considered socialists and social democrats more dangerous than capitalists and severely persecuted them. Julek had gone into hiding when a classmate of his, Rosia Rubenstein, denounced him at a Komsomol meeting. I froze in my seat as I heard, "Juliusz Bardach is a sellout socialist who must be found, arrested, and eliminated." I was asked to leave the meeting as Julek's case was discussed. Deeply frightened, I warned Julek, and he and his wife, Fruma, moved to Lvov to hide among the thousands of Jewish refugees. I visited him several times, staying for a day or two.

The train continued its monotonous journey. It was a sunny summer day. The wildflowers were in full bloom. Everything was fresh and green, perfect for a picnic or a mushroom hunt in the forest. This countryside was something I belonged to, and as long as I stood at the open window I had the feeling of still being at home, not yet parted from my family and the town where I'd lived all my life.

The hours stretched on and on. Two and a half days later, we arrived at our final destination, Orel. Military personnel in green uniforms greeted us at the station. A captain ordered us to throw our bags onto a tarp-covered truck, form a column four men abreast, and march to the barracks. An hour later we arrived at four red brick buildings surrounded by a high, spiked iron fence. Each barracks housed thirty new recruits. I had a lower bunk next to a Russian named Ivan Kravetz. He was handsome, tall, and muscular, with a scar above one eye that made half his face look very serious. The other half looked friendly and inquisitive, and we quickly became friends.

For the next three months we trained for the harsh conditions of combat. Reveille was at five in the morning. Regardless of the temperature, we were permitted to wear only our undershirts, pants, and boots during the morning exercise routine, which lasted forty-five minutes and included a two- or three-mile run. A half-hour was given to wash our face and hands, brush our teeth, and use the latrine. We all put on new uniforms, wrapped cloth around our feet, pulled on stiff, black army boots, and marched to the main building. I liked the morning exercises, and the cold didn't bother me, but the washing routine and latrine were almost unbearable. There were no showers or hot water, and the sinks, floors, doorknobs, and faucets were filthy.

The combat drills were evil-spirited, however, and I hated them with all my heart. There were days when we hiked ten to fifteen miles with fifteen kilograms of gear on our backs. We walked, ran, jogged, crawled, and hit the ground on order. Five miles was difficult; ten was backbreaking; and anything more, torture. Many soldiers could barely finish, but there was no excuse unless someone fainted. All were obligated to finish no matter how weak, ill, or exhausted they were, even if it meant finishing three, four, or five hours later than the group, and all exercises were performed without a drop of water, which made them even more cruel. I was lucky to be in good physical shape, but it was difficult to see the drill officers humiliate the weak, clumsy soldiers. They delighted in degrading several overweight, poorly coordinated Ukrainians and Russians, along with a Pole who had the unfortunate name of Mikolajczyk—the name of the prime minister of the Polish government in exile in London.

I was a diligent student of deprivation. In less than a month I'd transformed into a rugged Soviet soldier, quickly realizing that the only way to tolerate the conditions was to wipe out of my mind any thoughts of the warm, fresh sheets and hot showers of home. I could get used to life without these conveniences, but adjusting to life without my loved ones was far more difficult. I lived for writing letters to Taubcia. Every Sunday I wrote to her and my parents, my only link to the outside world. While writing I escaped the inhospitable compound and felt close to Taubcia, as if I were sending a part of myself in each letter. It took three weeks for the first letters to arrive from home, and I was crazy with fear that something bad had happened. The envelope had been resealed, which disturbed me, but I didn't mention it to anyone. I saved the letters and reread them several times, memorizing parts of them. Reading was like seeing, hearing, and even touching Taubcia and my family. I kept the letters in my wooden suitcase under my bed.

One day during monthly inspection I was ordered to open the suitcase and remove the contents. An officer took the letters I had tied with a ribbon and asked me in what language they were written. When I told him they were in Polish, he said he would have them translated and that from now on I could no longer write or receive letters in foreign languages. Ivan whispered to me late that night that the officer was from military intelligence. As a former Polish citizen, I was still considered foreign and therefore suspected of political illiteracy and unreliability—this much was made clear on a daily basis. But I don't know how much effect my parents' comparative wealth or my running political commentaries had on how I was perceived.

Two hours of every day were devoted to political education. Our *politruk*,* Senior Lieutenant Abrasimov, was filled with the pomp of his position. He tried to be congenial with us, tried to fit in, but he hopelessly lacked humor and charm. He spent hours reading from propaganda booklets and praising Stalin's wisdom, leadership, and genius in all spheres of human activities. Reciting often from the *Book of Propagandists*, he required that our answers be given word for word from the same book. We also studied *The Short Course of the Bolshevik Party*, written by Stalin and considered to be sacred and infallible. There was no room for personal interpretation, no room for questions or clarification, and no room for commentary. During one of the first political sessions, I asked who was in charge of the Red Army, Marshal Voroshilov or Marshal Timoshenko. The *politruk* spent ten minutes condemning me as an ignorant, illiterate bourgeois, which ended in his pronouncement that the Red Army, the nation, and progressive mankind was led by Comrade Stalin.

In the grandiose main building of the Tank Academy, with its spacious, polished hallways and large classrooms, hung massive red banners:

LONG LIVE STALIN, GENIUS OF MANKIND.
LONG LIVE STALIN, THE GREATEST MILITARY LEADER OF ALL TIMES.
LONG LIVE STALIN, THE GREATEST LEADER OF THE WORLD PROLETARIAT, WHO LEADS US TO THE VICTORY OF COMMUNISM.
LONG LIVE STALIN, THE GREATEST TEACHER AND SCIENTIST OF THE WORLD.
LONG LIVE STALIN, THE BEST FRIEND OF ALL SOVIET CHILDREN.

---

* Political leader.

Portraits of Marshal Timoshenko, the defense minister, and Marshal Voroshilov, the Politburo member responsible for the military, were displayed in some isolated hallways, but they did not compare to the icons of Stalin.

I found it impossible to take our *politruk* seriously. The adulation of Stalin and exaggeration of his abilities were ridiculous, and I couldn't believe that anyone could possibly believe the verbiage. But to my horror I discovered that, without exception, my peers took the slogans, banners, portraits, and lectures extremely seriously. The little jokes I made about our *politruk* frightened my classmates; they admonished me that not only jokes but even honest questions could get a person investigated by military intelligence.

The first time I tried to share my criticism with Witold Strzelecki, a classmate from the Polish gymnasium and a devout Catholic, he rebuked me gravely, declaring that he never wanted to hear me talk like that again. He said we both were honored to be able to serve in the Red Army and that the Soviet system was the best for the people. He had foresworn his Catholic beliefs and planned to join the Komsomol to demonstrate his devotion to the Communist Party. He was one of the first soldiers from Western Ukraine to be promoted to the rank of corporal.

Boot camp lasted three months, after which we spent less time doing heavy field exercises and began training to become tank drivers and mechanics. The rooms with special tank equipment were guarded by armed soldiers. In the military, everything was secret—the construction of the tank, the cannons, machine guns, periscopes, and hatch mechanisms, as well as all the written rules, regulations, codes, transcripts, books, and journals. We weren't allowed to take anything out of the classrooms. I joked that only the toilet paper wasn't secret, but no one laughed. There was no room for humor when it came to the Party leadership, the state, or the military command. The only jokes permissible were those dealing with sex and drunkenness.

I belonged to a group of high school graduates with good grades who were selected to become drivers and mechanics of the most modern Soviet tank, the T-34. We spent hours learning about the smallest details of the motor, equipment, and maintenance procedures. I liked learning how to operate the tank. Driving fifty tons of metal gave me a sense of immense power. The T-34 could plow through concrete buildings, uproot large trees, and cross riverbeds.

But life as a soldier was mundane. After a long day of lectures, exercises, and political indoctrination, I was too tired to talk to anyone, and I didn't have anything in common with most of my fellow soldiers anyway. Strzelecki and Mikolajczyk didn't get too close to me because I was Jewish. Joel Jucht, the only other Jew in the unit, kept to himself and befriended some Ukrainians from Wlodzimierz-Wolynski. It was strange to find myself so alone. Only Ivan Kravetz, who slept next to me on the bottom bunk and was on my tank crew, became a real friend. We talked at night, whispering back and forth about our lives prior to the army. He was better educated than the other soldiers, and we helped each other during the exercises. But my friendship with him was unlike any I had had before. Every conversation came to an abrupt end, as if it were hitting an invisible wall. For the most part Ivan was open and sincere, but part of him was closed off, and I couldn't figure out why.

I spent some of my free time with a few soldiers from Leningrad. Petrov, Fyodorov, and Sackun had been friends in school, and they were always teasing each other and telling stories. They welcomed me into their circle, and one Sunday they invited me to spend the whole day with them on leave. As soon as we left the compound we went to a kiosk, bought two large flasks of eau de cologne, and mixed them with lemonade in a glass Fyodorov had brought with him. With mischievous excitement, I joined the others in gulping down the concoction. To this day I remember the taste and smell of white lilac cologne, because I spent the afternoon vomiting in the park where we had gone to find amorous adventures. I was sitting on a bench belching cologne when Fyodorov introduced me to two middle-aged women whom he had met weeks before. I wasn't interested in any adventures, and I was too sick to go and eat with the group. The three remaining hours I sat on the bench breathing fresh air and drinking water from the fountain. I didn't go out with them again.

After six months I began to feel better adjusted to military life. By now I was corresponding with my family in Russian, as ordered by my superiors, but Taubcia couldn't write or read Russian, so our correspondence was conducted through my mother. My father continued his practice and hadn't been harassed, but there was no word from Julek. Taubcia was working as a clerk in a store, while Rachel attended a Russian school.

I hadn't had any conflict with my superiors and thought I was doing a good job of demonstrating my dedication to the Red Army by excelling in my classes. Our *politruk*, whom I considered to be close-minded and of mediocre intelligence, started to call on me during every class to discuss the international situation, about which I knew much more than he. Impressed with my knowledge, one day he asked me to see him in his office after class. He offered me a cigarette and cordially asked me about my home, my family, and my plans for the future. I felt that I had nothing to hide and told him about my parents, my wife, and my plans to become a physician.

"I'm impressed by your knowledge of world history and geography. We need people like you. I'd like to recommend you to the Komsomol."

The Komsomol—I was surprised to be asked to join this organization so soon. It was a step short of joining the Party. Most Soviet soldiers already belonged, having joined during high school, but it was rare for former Polish citizens to be invited to join.

The idea did not appeal to me. I was doing okay within the confines of a soldier's life, but I didn't think I could handle the rigors of the Komsomol in addition. Its mandatory weekly meetings included self-examination and a sort of penance where one confessed one's political sins—such as my father's owning our house and my brother's membership in the socialist party. Interrogation followed in the form of an inquisition, and I didn't want to subject myself to any of it.

"I don't feel that I'm politically educated enough to receive such an honor," I said. "I need to study more and read more of the classic works of Lenin and Stalin to be prepared."

"I disagree." He looked at me sharply. "If I want to recommend you, it means you are already in good political standing. I'll give you another six months to get ready, and then I'll introduce you to the Komsomol."

It was difficult for me to keep this incident to myself, and late one night I told Ivan what had happened. He listened attentively but barely responded, making me wonder what to think of him. He'd been acting strangely around me, and I thought perhaps I had misjudged his friendship. He would cut me off abruptly in the middle of a sentence, change the subject, or walk away when I talked about our *politruk*, the senseless exercises, and the cruelty of the junior officers. I asked him what was going on between us, and in the darkness of the barracks, he spoke in the gravest tone. "You must learn to keep your mouth shut. Former Polish citizens are automatically suspected of being untrustworthy and hostile to the Soviet state. You shouldn't be talking to anyone about anything political, even if what you have to say is positive. I don't want to have any more discussions about politics or the army."

I was deeply confused and a little frightened. I thought I'd been monitoring myself pretty well, refraining from making sarcastic comments about the political education and praise of Stalin. But not to be able to talk about joining the Komsomol with my closest friend? The boundaries of safe conversation were far too narrow. I started to feel claustrophobic, as if everything were a trap and I would have to be on guard at all times, a stance that was completely foreign to me. For the first time I realized that I didn't understand Soviet thinking and probably never would. This was the beginning of a long, arduous struggle to examine my socialist ideals, to think about the Soviet Union as it was and not as I had imagined it to be.

Months later, when Ivan and I were alone inside the tank, he told me he had thought a great deal about that late-night talk. He didn't know if I had been trying to provoke him or if he could trust me, but after observing and talking to me over the ensuing months he decided I was trustworthy. He asked me to keep secret everything he was about to tell me. "I don't know if you understand this, but if a single word of this conversation gets back to our superiors, especially to military intelligence, we both will be in deep trouble. My father and his brother were struggling with the same disillusionment you're struggling with now before they were arrested in 1937. I haven't heard from them since. My mother has been in exile for ten years, and I spent the last three years with my grandparents. When I was drafted, military intelligence interrogated me at length about my family and my allegiance to the Soviet state. A few months ago I was called again to their quarters. They asked me to inform on you. Don't talk to anyone about anything political. Talk about sports, girls, drinking, but politics is off limits to everyone, especially to you. Don't trust anybody, *anybody*—not even me."

"But I have nothing to hide," I protested. "I'm not going to betray the Soviet Union. I don't know why I would be watched—I don't know why anyone has to inform on me. I'm certainly not an enemy of the people."

"This is the way of life, Janusz. Get used to it. Watch yourself. And above all, don't forget what I'm telling you. There are probably others who are watching you."

Although I still didn't understand why I would be watched or informed on, I did finally understand Ivan. He was a true and trusted friend. I no longer went out with other soldiers or talked much about my life in Poland or my thoughts, hopes, and worries. Instead I threw myself into the political education classes, doing whatever I could to prove my allegiance to the Soviet state.

One morning I was told to report after breakfast to the officer on duty in the main building. There, a junior officer led me to a room on the second floor. Two other officers were sitting at their desks typing on old typewriters. A large portrait of Stalin and smaller portraits of Voroshilov and Timoshenko hung on the walls. After several minutes I was invited into a private office by a well-groomed, middle-aged captain.

A mahogany desk took up half of the small room. Bookshelves packed with files lined the walls.

The captain motioned for me to sit in an armchair. "Tell me about yourself. Where are you from? What do your parents do?" His voice was calm, his manner friendly and patient. I thought he was going to invite me formally to join the Komsomol, and it was hard to hide my nervousness.

"I was born in Odessa, but I lived all my life in Wlodzimierz-Wolynski, where my father is from. My mother and her family are from Odessa. I was raised bilingual. She's always admired the Soviet Union. Her family still lives here. I was raised with the belief that only communism could bring happiness to all people. I helped the Red Army establish themselves in our town and promoted the ideals of communism. Before I was drafted, I was nominated by the military command to be director of the sports club Spartak."

I watched him closely during my soliloquy. His lack of expression made me stop.

"So, this is about you. What about your parents, brothers, and sisters—do you have any?" He sat back in his chair, stretched his arms, and pulled out a white pack of cigarettes with the blue Belomor insignia on the front. He looked as though he'd never produced a bead of sweat in his life. He held out the cigarettes and offered me one.

"Thank you, sir, but I don't smoke."

"You drink?"

"No sir."

"You don't fuck either?" He raised his thin eyebrows in mock astonishment.

I blushed. In Poland, no adult ever talked like this. "I'm married."

"That's too bad. You'll be here for four years. Who's taking care of your wife?"

"My parents."

"So, tell me about your parents," he said with interest, sitting up in his chair.

"My father is a dentist. My mother is a homemaker."

"Doctors and dentists were rich in Poland, weren't they?" he asked.

"We lived quite well."

"Would you consider them capitalists? Did they own property—buildings, land, woods?"

"I would never call my father a capitalist. He works very hard, from early morning until late evening. He does own a building, even two. But he bought it with hard-earned money."

"So this is your perception. You still don't understand the essence of capitalism, but you'll get educated. Tell me about your siblings." His languid pace continued. I was getting extremely nervous. I didn't know who he was or why he was asking such personal questions.

"My brother is finishing law school in Vilnius. I haven't seen him in a long time."

"Yes, we know all about your brother. What I need to know is where he is now. We'd like to talk to him."

My mouth was parched. "I don't know. He left Vilnius in 1940, spent a few weeks at home, and left again. I've been here eight months. I don't know where he is."

"Your parents must know. I'd like you to find out from them so you can give us his address next time. I want you to be here next month, the same day and time, with information about your brother. I'm Captain Grenko. You know how to find me.

"I'd also like you to get to know your two Polish friends, Strzelecki and Mikolajczyk. Tell me what you find out about them." He smiled as though we were friends. "You can go now." He didn't shake my hand, just looked at the door.

I was paralyzed with fear. I couldn't believe that Rosia Rubenstein's comment at the Komsomol meeting in Wlodzimierz-Wolynski would evolve into a search conducted through intelligence channels, as though Julek were a convicted enemy of the state. I wondered how I could warn Julek of the danger he was in and tell him to stop contacting my parents. I knew his address but was afraid of sending a letter. I decided to tell my father when he came to visit.

I was perplexed by Grenko's demand to divulge information about Strzelecki and Mikolajczyk. Ivan had been ordered to inform on me; it made no sense that they would trust me to inform

on others. I deliberated over how to give Grenko benign information, make him lose interest in the suspects and decide I was a
worthless informer.

At the next meeting I tried to behave and appear ignorant, emphasizing my interest in sports, but Grenko was less congenial.

"Cut the bullshit. Do you have the material?"

"What material?"

"Your brother's address and information about your Polish
friends."

His rough, direct tone caught me off guard. "I can't provide
you with my brother's whereabouts. I have no idea where he is."

"Don't your parents know where he is?"

"I don't know. They haven't written me anything about him."

"Did you ask them in your letter to provide his address?"

I stuttered again. "I didn't do it yet. But I'll ask in my next letter and we'll see what happens."

"Don't play cat and mouse with me!" He slammed his fist on
the desk. I jolted back in the armchair. He leaned over and held
his face close to mine, his thin lips tight and glistening, and said,
"I told you to write to your parents, and you didn't do it because
they know where your brother is and you're trying to protect
him. Don't come to me next time without this information. We
still trust you, but it isn't going to last forever. You must prove
your loyalty to the Organy. Get me this information."

He leaned back in the chair and played with a pencil on the
desk. His tone shifted again, and he became surprisingly friendly.

"So let me ask you: whom do you consider more loyal, Mikolajczyk or Strzelecki?"

In the same parched voice, I told him I didn't know them very
well. I'd only gotten to know them in Orel.

He smiled ironically. "You never met either of them?"

I was afraid he sensed the lie. "Actually, I knew Strzelecki as a
young child, but we lost touch over the years. I never met Mikolajczyk until the army."

"Right. I know you knew Strzelecki in school, but then you
moved to another school—correct? We know everything; we

even know what you think. Let me give you some advice: these meetings will go much better if you don't try to hide anything."

Smug and self-satisfied, Grenko continued the interrogation. I was sweating through my tunic and had to keep wiping my face.

"What do you know about Mikolajczyk and his family? How'd they get to Wlodzimierz-Wolynski?"

"He never talks about his family or his past. He's well educated and well mannered, probably raised in an upper-class family. He's a diligent and dedicated soldier."

Grenko scribbled on a tablet long after I had finished. Finally he asked, "So there's nothing suspicious about him?"

"In what respect?" I was truly confused, although I knew Grenko would interpret my question as evasive.

"Did he ever make critical remarks about Comrade Stalin, the Party, or Voroshilov, Timoshenko, or members of the Politburo? Was he ever critical of the Organy?" Exasperation escaped with every word.

"We don't discuss these things," I said firmly.

"Well, find out! We need to know what he thinks."

After two hours I was exhausted. I needed to talk to Ivan.

That night I moved close to him, woke him up, and whispered in his ear about the two meetings. "Just tell me what I'm supposed to do. How do you deal with this?"

He remained groggy and spoke slowly and calmly. "Stretch out the information for as long as you can. They'll ride you pretty hard, but it's the only way to deal with them. Don't sign anything. Just talk rubbish. That's all I'm doing."

His advice did nothing to relieve my anxiety, which was perpetual. I thought constantly about what I could tell them at the next meeting, fabricating better and better stories that wouldn't get me or anyone else in trouble.

A few days later I had some good news for a change. My father was going to visit me in two weeks, not the next month, as originally planned. My mother, Rachel, and Taubcia would visit me during the summer. I couldn't wait for the day of his arrival. I asked my commanding officer for half a day off on Saturday to greet my father at the train station.

I arrived at the train station an hour early and was struck by the appearance of the disembarking passengers. The burden of daily living—waiting in long lines to get food, living with three other families in a two-bedroom apartment, working ten-hour days, barely having enough money to buy clothing—showed in their hunched shoulders, stooped backs, and drawn, unsmiling faces. Irritation, rudeness, and hostility emanated from the crowd.

My father appeared at last, carrying a simple suitcase and wearing a hat. He was no longer the figure he had always been in my mind, walking straight, tall, and lively, greeting everyone he passed with a smile. His face was as gloomy as the dark gray raincoat he wore. His handsome features had faded into a set expression of worry, fatigue, and despair.

I ran up to him, hugged and kissed him warmly, and picked up his heavy suitcase. It was so wonderful to have him close, to make contact with the world I had left behind. The shabby hotel room he checked into was the best we could find. Neither of us was aware that in the Soviet Union, to obtain a hotel room, one needed a *komandirovka*, a special requisition that verified one was visiting on business. The few hotels near the train station had filthy lobbies and abrupt, arrogant clerks. Exhausted from the travel and the search for a room, he finally did what I thought he should have done from the beginning: he slipped a fifty-ruble bill to the clerk.

The room was dirty, smelly, and decaying, but we enjoyed each other's company and were happy to sit down and rest. Sitting next to my father on the bed in my soldier's uniform, I felt a wave of warmth and tenderness that I had rarely experienced with him. He livened up as he told me about things at home. My mother was doing slightly better but remained frail; Taubcia and Rachel were running the household for her. Between my mother's poor health, the closing of my uncle's glassware store, and the slowing of my father's practice, life had become difficult. He missed my brother and me and was deeply worried about both of us. The NKVD had come to our home twice looking for Julek. I told him the NKVD was pressuring me for Julek's address and warned him to tell Julek not to contact anyone in Wlodzimierz-Wolynski and to move from his present address. I also told him about Grenko's demand that I inform on my peers and about the NKVD's attempts to get my peers to inform on me.

I had to be back at the barracks before ten o'clock. I lay awake thinking about my father, so close and so far away. I had a permit to spend Sunday and Monday with him and joined him for breakfast on Sunday instead of eating at the barracks. I felt his warmth and love in the way he looked at me, touched my hand, and talked about my future. He was worried about the possibility of German invasion and said that, if my mother's health improved, he wanted to move away from the Nazi border, only twelve kilometers away, to Kiev or Odessa, where our relatives were.

We spent that day at the park and talked for hours, then went to dinner, trying to make it special despite the stained linen, the poorly washed dishes, and the flies that kept landing on the food. Everything smelled like cabbage soup. I asked the same questions over and over, listening to my father's answers as though for the first time. His presence diminished the distance between me and the rest of my family, and I cherished every moment between us. Suddenly it was late, and I had to get back to the barracks.

Sunday was a visiting day for parents at the Tank Academy. I was planning to take my father to see the buildings, but he said he didn't feel like going. He didn't want to meet any of the commanding officers; he was from a different world, he said, and had nothing in common with them. I was crushed when he decided to leave on Monday rather than spend three more days in Orel, as he had initially planned. He said he was worried about my mother's health. I understood and didn't question his departure.

The train was to leave at four P.M., and he asked me not to come with him to the station. He said he was tired and needed to rest. He got on the streetcar that took him to the station and waved goodbye, but I jumped on with him. He embraced and hugged me but asked me firmly to get off at the next stop. I did, but the moment the streetcar moved away I had a premonition that this would be the last time I would ever see my father. I ran after the car, but it was gaining speed and I couldn't catch up. I looked at the lonely figure standing on the back deck, waving at me with hat in hand, until the car disappeared. With a heavy heart I returned to the barracks, and for the next several days I avoided any conversation about his visit. Every minute I berated myself for having listened to him and gotten off the streetcar. It wasn't until many weeks later that Joel Jucht told me that he had been interrogated by military intelligence about my father and his visit and that they had ordered my father to stay away from the Tank Academy and leave the city.

At the end of May, two weeks after my father's visit, I was again invited to join the Komsomol, this time by the political chief of the Tank Academy, Colonel Sidorenko. I met him in his plush chambers. A robust man, graying at the temples, he met me with a warm smile and handshake. His uniform was perfectly tailored, and his movements were slow and mannered. Although he tried to make me feel relaxed, his controlled, commanding behavior intimidated me.

"I know you were reluctant to join the Komsomol back in the fall," he said in a voice fit for a tearoom. "But what about now? To be asked to join the League of Young Communists is a very special honor. We rarely extend this invitation to our own young people, and almost never to anyone raised and educated abroad." He stopped and looked at me with his lamb-like eyes.

I couldn't use the same excuse I'd used with my *politruk* and so I decided to join, thinking I would be protected from further suspicions and harassment. Colonel Sidorenko proposed that I become a career officer at the Tank Academy, an offer I definitely didn't want to accept. I told him about my desire to return to my family and become a doctor. Sidorenko didn't try to hide his disappointment and suggested I think it over. "A medical career in the Soviet Union isn't the same as in a capitalist country, where doctors make a good living. You'll never be as rich as your father. In this country you'll earn less than a trolley-bus driver, and much less than a coal miner."

On June 1 the Tank Academy moved to a summer camp about eighty kilometers from Orel. The camp was hidden in a dense forest and surrounded by hills, bluffs, and rivers. We camouflaged the tents and tanks with branches. Rigorous exercises lasted all day, and lengthy political lectures took place every evening. But I was relieved to have moved far away from Orel and the meetings with Grenko and Sidorenko. Summer camp was to last until September, by which time I hoped they would forget about me.

A few weeks into the summer we were awakened at five o'clock in the morning and ordered to assemble in the main area. The commander, a general from the old guard with silver hair and shimmering medals, announced that war had broken out with Germany. It was June 22, 1941, eleven months after I had been drafted and nearly two years after the signing of the Ribbentrop-Molotov Pact. Nazi air and land attacks had come without warning. I was shocked more than frightened, believing like everyone else that the Ribbentrop-Molotov Pact assured a lasting peace.

The commander delivered a grave but obsequious speech full of devotion and subservience to Stalin. There was talk among the soldiers that he had once been Stalin's close ally but that lately he'd fallen out of favor. Although I sensed the falsehood and hypocrisy in his speech, I was too inexperienced to make deeper judgments. Although I scorned the military and NKVD, in my eyes Stalin remained a great leader. I didn't think he was aware of the mindless indoctrination, suspiciousness, and senseless interrogations that went on in the military.

German invasion meant that my family was in mortal danger; Wlodzimierz-Wolynski had probably been captured on the first day of war. I wanted to be sent to the front immediately, thinking I would be closer to them and would be able to fight for them. I reported to Major Poltorak, the commander of our unit, and asked to be sent to the front line with the first wave of tanks. I was filled with emotion, ready to go immediately to fight the Nazis, to do everything possible and impossible to save my family.

"Sir, I am originally from the Western Ukraine, from Wlodzimierz-Wolynski. The Nazis have just invaded the area. I was raised there. I want to go there on a mission. I know every river and every road. I know the people I grew up with. I can demolish the railway tracks. I can find them with the help of my friends who still live there and who can organize. . . . " I was so emotionally charged, so eager to do heroic things that I missed the way the commander was looking at me. Suddenly I stopped talking because I couldn't find his eyes. His face was a cold mask.

"How do you know all these things? Where did you learn to demolish trains and perform other tricks of sabotage? You're just a young soldier. Wait for your orders like everybody else. You're dismissed."

The atmosphere of the camp was expectant, with rumors flying that we'd be heading back to Orel. We hung around the tents waiting for orders, but none were given. Officers ran back and forth, unsure of what to do. The daily routine was abandoned. The guard posts were reinforced. Our superiors gave us no information about the situation at the front, and we were forbidden to listen to the radio or read the newspaper. Four days passed before we went back to Orel. The morning after our return, we headed for the front line.

We reached the railroad station before dawn. The new tanks, the T-34s, were lined up on the train platforms. They'd been shipped straight from the factory, and factory instructors had come along to prepare them for combat and update us on mechanical and operational changes. Our battalion was part of the 99th Tank Division of the 25th Mechanized Corps. Trained as both driver and mechanic of the T-34 tank, I was proud to receive the tank and be instructed in its new technology.

We left the Orel station at dawn and headed west. I worked alone with the instructor inside the tank. As a security precaution, no operating manuals had been printed, so I had to memorize everything he told me. Around ten o'clock in the morning, the train suddenly came to a halt. I opened the front hatch and looked out. Soldiers were jumping out of the cars and running into a nearby field, trying to reach the woods. As the soldiers ran, I heard the whistling sound of falling bombs.

The instructor told me to follow him through the hatch. He ran across the field and caught up with several other people. The German planes dipped down and flew low, spraying the field with machine-gun fire. I couldn't catch up to him. Right before the next round of fire, I dove to the ground and covered my head with my hands. The German planes dropped more bombs and sprayed the tracks with bullets. I lay on the ground paralyzed with fear, terrified they would come back. I knew I wouldn't survive long in the open field.

When the whistling bombs, buzzing engines, and crackling machine-gun fire stopped, I raised my head and looked toward the train. The engine and two cars behind it were derailed and burning. The rest of the train, which carried tanks on the platforms, was intact. I stood on my trembling legs. At least fifty people lay scattered in the field. The two people closest to me lay face down with bullet holes across their backs. I moved away from them to the group that had been running ahead of me. All seven of them lay motionless, among them my tank instructor. Nearly everyone who reached the woods before the gunfire had broken survived, while nearly all of those caught running across the open field had been killed. I survived, but I did not feel relieved or happy. I was shocked, grieved, and terrified that the next time it would be me.

CHAPTER 4

Court-martial

Survivors crawled and limped out of the woods. I hadn't realized how many soldiers were on the train; aside from our tank battalion, hundreds of infantrymen had also been part of the transport. We didn't know for certain if the raid was over, so no one would go near the train. I was ready to run into the woods at the slightest sound, and I listened deeply for the distant droning of a propeller.

Major Poltorak was among the last to come out of the woods, accompanied by two junior officers. He walked directly up to the train, climbed up on a platform, and called for everyone to gather close.

"Listen up," he hollered. His voice was tense, angry, and shaken. "As of this moment, I'm in charge of the tank battalion and military men. I order all members of the tank battalion to return to their tanks and check the instruments and fuel levels. Turn on the tanks and let the motors run. We'll be assembling ramps at each platform and taking the tanks down. Drivers, take your tank immediately into the woods and camouflage it." He pointed to a trail leading into the forest. "Pull off to the side of the trail and wait for further orders.

"Infantry, bring the injured to the train, remove the dogtags from the dead, and bury the bodies."

My crew—Ivan Kravetz, Vladimir Nikitin, and Mischa Fyodorov—was alive and unharmed. Fyodorov was the tank commander; Ivan, the gunner in the turret; Vladimir, or Volodia, the
machine-gun and radio operator. We got to our tank and checked
it over; all systems worked fine. I maneuvered it down the ramp
without falling off the edge—a grave danger because I couldn't
see the ramp and had to rely on hand signals. The crew got in,
and we drove into the woods. Parked under the trees, hidden by
bushes, we climbed out of the tank and gathered around Major
Poltorak and the other officers, who were examining a map trying to figure out our location. We didn't know how far we were
from the front line or what direction to take to find the rest of our
division.

Late in the afternoon Poltorak ordered everyone to drive to the
road that led to Bobrujsk, which, according to their calculations,
was approximately one hundred and fifty kilometers away.
Poltorak didn't know where the front line was but assumed that
Bobrujsk was the gathering point for our tank division.

After driving continuously for two days and nights, we came
to a bridge that was too weak to carry the tanks. Major Poltorak
ordered me to take my tank and try to find a shoal where we
could drive across the river. My crewmates crossed the bridge on
foot, while I drove the tank carefully down the steep embankment. I took off my clothes, jumped into the river, and searched
for a shallow place. I found a sandbar at the widest point of the
small but winding river and walked across. It seemed like a safe
place to drive the tank through, so I marked the sandbar with
sticks and climbed back into the tank.

I accelerated gently, trying to inch the tracks over the riverbed.
They dug into the silt, and after a long moment I felt the tank
creep forward. I continued to accelerate slowly. Halfway across
the river the tank leaned a little to the left. Twenty yards or so
from the far shore the tank tipped a little more, and I accelerated
harder. Just then I realized I had left the hatch open, but it was
too late: water had already begun to seep in. The bank was now
only five yards away; I pushed the accelerator to the floor, but the
tank tipped over on its left side, hoisting the other track up in the

air. Water cascaded through the hatch. I climbed out and swam to the bank.

As I walked up to the road, Poltorak waved his pistol at me. "You imbecile! Are you so stupid you didn't think to shut the hatch? Savich, Milutin, Perdzynski, get your tanks and see if you can pull this bastard out!" They spent nearly an hour trying to pull the swamped tank from the riverbed, but it was no use. The tank was deeply entrenched in the mud. Meanwhile, the other vehicles followed the marked sandbar and, with their hatches down, crossed the river safely. Poltorak ordered me and Nikitin to stay put while he and the rest of the battalion moved on to join the army unit.

For one day and two nights Nikitin and I stayed with the tank. We cleared a little space for ourselves and hid among the tall reeds and cattails, took the machine gun and grenades from the tank, and kept our eyes on the road, about five hundred yards away. From our hiding place we watched an unending procession of Nazi motorcycles, trucks, and light tanks speeding deeper into Russian territory. Our tank, almost completely submerged in the water, looked like a fragment from one of the many vehicles that lay abandoned, broken, or burned out on the roadside. The German motorized corps moved down the road while a chaotic flock of civilians scurried along the shoulders in the same direction, burdened by knapsacks, suitcases, or small pushcarts. Families herded their cows and goats. Barking dogs ran up and down the embankments. I couldn't imagine where they all were going. The refugees sloughed off their possessions as they went—a winter coat, a knapsack, pieces of china, toys, boots, clothing. I could tell how far many of them had traveled by how much stuff they still carried. Scavengers roamed the ditches picking up after them. I admired the drivers of the horse-pulled wagons, who competed with the Germans to keep their wagon wheels on the road. If the wagon was in good condition and not too heavily loaded, the driver could maintain position among the trucks and light tanks, but most of the wooden vehicles had broken apart or were in the process of doing so and as such were relegated to the bumpy shoulders. Many were abandoned altogether. I lay on the warm, sandy earth behind the machine gun and kept my eye on the black swastikas, ready to shoot.

We weren't far from the old Polish border, and I was tempted to run home. I shared this thought with Nikitin, but he didn't respond.

At the end of the first day we were very hungry. Our food rations, soaked in the river, had dissolved, and we were afraid to use firearms lest we reveal our hiding place, so we tried unsuccessfully to kill wild ducks with stones. Late that night, when there was no movement on the road, I threw a grenade in the river. We waited nearly half an hour before we had the courage to move, but no one came. We gathered about two dozen fish, cleaned off the scales, and cooked them.

In the middle of the second night, two Soviet officers kicked us awake. "Is this how you guard a tank?" one of them mocked. "If we were Nazis you'd both be dead. Whose turn is it to be on guard?"

"Mine," I said.

He grabbed me by the tunic. I thought he'd strangle me. "Is this any way to guard a tank? Now, tell me exactly what happened."

"Comrade commander," I said, unable to distinguish his rank in the dark, "we came to this river after two days and three nights of driving with little rest and very little food. We fought Nazis along the way. I was very tired and lost my concentration when driving the tank across the river."

"We're all tired, but you're the only one who didn't make it with the battalion. Are you waiting here for the Nazis so you can give them your tank?"

I was astonished. "I'm a Jew. I hate the Nazis. My family is under Nazi occupation. I want to fight them. I want to prove my devotion to the Soviet state."

The officer looked at me steadily. "Well, that's your story." He then turned to Nikitin. "Let's see what your friend has to say. What's your name?"

Tall, blond, freckle-faced Nikitin stood at attention, clearly frightened.

"My name is Vladimir Alekseyevich Nikitin. I'm the gunner in this tank. I've nothing to do with Bardach. He caused all this trouble, and I'm simply here to watch him."

I was stunned. All the time Nikitin and I had spent together, he'd seemed friendly. He'd told me about his parents, factory workers in Leningrad who worked long hours but could barely feed him and his siblings. He told me how he often stole food from the marketplace. Now I realized he had only pretended to be friendly. "Volodia," I said, "what do you mean you've nothing to do with me? We've known each other almost a year. We've been in the same tank for seven months. I thought we were good friends?"

Quiet, shy Nikitin glared at me. "Your friends are Siberian wolves. I've never been your friend. Yesterday you asked me to abandon the tank and run away with you to Nazi-occupied territory, to your hometown in Western Ukraine. You are Polish. You aren't one of us. You're a traitor!" He spat on the ground.

The commander shook his head, pulled out a pack of cigarettes, and offered one to his companion. He lit the cigarette, shielding the flame with his hand. "I get the picture. In two hours, two heavy tractors will come to pull out the tank, and you," he pointed his finger at me, "will be responsible for returning the tank to operable condition." He put his hand on Nikitin's shoulder. "Bardach will stay here with Lieutenant Sedov. You come back to camp with me to file a report."

I wasn't surprised by the officers' gruff manner toward me. Letting a tank fall into German hands would be a disastrous tactical error, as it would give the Nazis knowledge about the Red Army's newest and most powerful weapon. There was no choice but to retrieve the tank from the river, as all information regarding it was to be kept top secret.

The tractors arrived and pulled the waterlogged tank out of the river. I installed the machine gun, climbed into the tank, and was hauled to my unit miles away in the forest. I worked on the tank the rest of that day and well into the night. When I finished, I joined my crew in the tent.

The next morning I awakened early to check the tank engines and instruments one more time. While walking to the tank, I was stopped by two officers on the narrow footpath. "Please, step over here." One officer walked in front of me and the other walked behind. I heard him cock his pistol. They took me deep into the woods.

The leading officer suddenly stopped, asked my name, place and date of birth, and the names of my parents. I answered, wondering frantically what was going on. He ordered me to drop my belt, give up my pistol, and empty all my pockets.

"Am I being arrested?" I could hardly form the words. The officers ignored the question and continued to frisk me. "What have I been accused of? Why are you taking everything from me?"

"Shut your fucking mouth. We ask the questions, not you." One officer punched me in the stomach.

In the breast pocket of my shirt I kept photographs of my parents, my sister, and Taubcia. When I caught my breath, I asked if I could keep them.

"You'll get them back," one of them said as he snatched them away. "Now you'll come with us to the division headquarters."

Without being allowed to go back to the tent and retrieve my things, I was led away, ordered onto a truck with a number of other soldiers, and taken deeper in the forest. Several hours later the truck stopped at a camp. Several guards surrounded the truck and led the other soldiers and me far into the woods. Daylight was fading. An officer dismissed my guards, picked up a stick, and made lines on the forest floor. He handed me a shovel and told me to dig.

I dozed in the pit, waiting to die. I heard leaves crunching. Clumps of dirt fell on my head.

"It's midnight," a new voice said. "Go and rest."

"He's asleep." It was the officer who had watched me dig. "Early morning he'll be court-martialed. He's a *zapadnik*—one of those Polish traitors."*

"Are many other prisoners to be court-martialed?"

"Several. Siemion and Tolia are guarding them nearby."

* The term *zapadnik* applied to Ukrainian, Polish, and Jewish prisoners who had lived in the Polish territories seized by the Soviet Union in 1939.

The officer walked off. I dozed again.

The sound of birds chirping high in the trees brought me back from sleep. I could no longer feel my arms or legs. I tried to move my fingers to test whether I was still on earth or floating somewhere above the trees and clouds. Then a pain seared through my neck, and I felt my pulse throbbing in my temples.

The guard jumped into the pit and untied me. "Get up."

The pain in my body was so great that I fell when I tried to stand. Along with the pain came a surge of dread that I would be ripped away from the warm, fresh morning. The guard hit me in the back with the butt of his rifle and said, "To the left." My legs felt like pieces of wood as I stumbled on the uneven ground. I rubbed my wrists and squeezed my hands to revive them. We followed a path through the dense forest and came upon a small clearing. The grass was trampled. A table and chair had been set up in the middle. Cut branches and sliced tree trunks were scattered everywhere. The table and chair looked ridiculous in the clearing. I couldn't believe anyone would bring such accoutrements to the front line when the Red Army was in full retreat. Behind the trees soldiers were talking, and I thought about my crewmates, who were just waking up to eat their dry ration. Ivan probably wondered what had happened to me.

"Sit down," the guard ordered. I sat about twenty feet from the table, positioning my legs carefully to keep them from cramping, and looked around. The breeze blew across my face, and the scent of fresh soil and fallen leaves rose from the ground. I could smell mushrooms in the vicinity. The sun began to glow through the heavy branches of the old deciduous forest, its rays gleaming through the red and gold leaves, dispersing light in colored fragments. The phrase "the sun rises in the east and sets in the west" ran through my mind. I remembered my mother's fascination with the East, which for her and for other Jewish intellectuals in Poland meant the Soviet Union. All her life she was homesick for Odessa, on the Black Sea, fondly known throughout the Soviet Union as "Odessa-Mama"—the capital of artists, writers, crooks, and thieves.

Several files, stacked one on top of the other, lay on the table next to a fresh pad of paper. Two quill pens lay neatly beside an inkwell just like the one I had used in school. My mind raced: Why am I being court-martialed? The accident with my tank? My hesitation to join the Komsomol? The interrogations with Grenko? Critical comments made about Stalin? What crime did I commit?

The four officers in charge of the court-martial emerged from the woods and sauntered onto the stage—for that was how it appeared to me: the table, wooden chair, the stumps in the clearing. It was all a dream, make-believe, a play, and very soon it would all be clear that I was only hallucinating or acting. One officer stood behind the table and held on to the back of the chair with both hands, rocking it back and forth. His narrow cheeks and high forehead were pale, his blond wavy hair receding. His white hands and long fingers were like those of a pianist or writer—definitely, I thought, not the hands of a court-martial official. He reminded me of the Catholic priest who played bridge with my father. Although he wore the green insignia of the judiciary service, he seemed not to belong to the military. For some lunatic reason, I felt close to him.

He looked through the stack of files, then turned to another officer sitting on a stump: "Comrade Colonel, we've got seven cases today. Do you think we'll finish before the Nazis start flying?"

"It's mostly up to you, Captain. Keep the cases short and to the point."

The man sitting hunched over on the stump had a meaty, pockmarked face with sagging jowls and dark circles under the eyes. His double chin hung loosely. He, too, wore the green marks of the judiciary service on his collar. The four rectangular badges indicated his rank as full colonel; but even without them, his manner left no doubt that he was in charge. For a second his deep-set eyes looked through me as though I weren't there. He then blew his nose into a dirty piece of cloth, pulled out his pistol, and polished it with the same cloth.

The captain pointed a long white finger at me and said to the colonel, "I hope you shoot the bastards. They're all guilty of high treason against our Beloved Motherland and Comrade Stalin." He was in a hurry to get the trial over with, as they all were, anticipating early morning Nazi air raids.

"Let's go chief," said one of the other officers. "The faster the better. I want to have breakfast before we move, and I don't know if we'll have time before the bombing starts."

The colonel blew his nose loudly, spat, and said to the captain, "Are we starting with him? Let's not waste time. Read his file, but only what matters." Nobody looked at me except the captain—coldly, indifferently, and only for a few seconds.

"You're a Jew, aren't you?" The captain's lip curled in a one-sided smile. "So why do you work for the Nazis? Why did you want to betray your tank unit and cross over to the German side?" He spoke louder as he read questions from a note in my file. "Why did you try to persuade your crew member to join you in betraying your Motherland? Oh, but you're from *Poland*. This isn't *your* Motherland. Why did you try to talk Vladimir Nikitin into deserting and driving with you over to the German side? He wrote two pages about you. He described the kind of person you are, what kind of monster, how you hate our great Soviet Union. He said you 'blasphemed our Beloved and Revered Genius of Humanity, the Greatest of Leaders, the Wisest of Teachers, our Dear Comrade Stalin.'"

He turned to the other three officers. "Comrades, I cannot bring myself to read the testimony of an honest and devoted Soviet soldier who paints the true picture of this traitor standing in front of you, expecting mercy from the heaven in which he believes. I cannot read these pages because I don't want to soil my lips with the filthy expressions this man used to describe our great Soviet state and our Beloved Leader and Teacher. He doesn't deserve to walk the same earth, breathe the same air, or live another day among us."

His thin face faded before my eyes. The tree stumps blurred. I heard only a voice droning in the distance. The brightening sky filled with small clouds, the wildflowers, the leaves changing color, the birds talking to each other in the early morning all seemed beautiful and horrible and absurd.

The fourth officer walked up to the table and looked at the paper. "I'm not going to read this shit. Just looking at this traitor, I want to shoot him myself without bothering with a sentence. I know how he was raised. I know the hostility he has toward the Soviet people who brought freedom to the Polish peasants and workers. I was in the army that liberated the Western Ukraine in 1939. I remember entering Wlodzimierz-Wolynski, where he lived. They all hated us. I propose that we end our deliberations and take a vote. I vote for execution."

The young major with the high cheekbones spoke. "I'd like to hear what he has to say. Then I'll vote."

Without raising his head, the colonel extended his left arm and pointed his index finger at me. "Say what you have to say in your defense. You have five minutes."

I wasn't sure I could pronounce a word. A spasm moved from my stomach to my throat; I choked, and my thoughts whirled: I'm a Jew; I hate the Nazis; I volunteered to fight them on their own territory; I would sacrifice my life fighting the Nazis. But I couldn't make a sound. I stumbled to my feet and turned to the colonel. I tried to focus my mind, to select the most important and convincing words. But before I could open my mouth, the colonel looked up.

"Do you want to say something, or is there nothing to say in your defense?"

"I'm Jewish."

"Speak louder. And tell us something we don't already know. Being Jewish doesn't mean anything to me. I know many Jews who were executed for high treason, and there are probably many more who would love to serve the Nazis the way you do."

"But I'm Jewish! My family is in Nazi-occupied territory. Perhaps they've already been killed. All I ask the court is to let me fight the Nazis on the front line, to serve the Red Army any way I can. I never tried to sabotage my tank. I didn't sink it so I could wait for Germans, and I never said any of the words you read from the testimony of Nikitin. I'm innocent, and I don't want to die now."

I was empty and exhausted. I thought about jumping the guard or colonel to bring the torture to a quick end. My words had been incoherent, illogical. I felt ashamed, beyond salvation, as if something precious were gone forever. I closed my eyes.

The colonel spoke: " . . . and be executed today by the order of the court-martial of the 99th Tank Division of the 25th Mechanized Corps. The verdict is unanimous, and there will be no appeal. It will be read to all units of the 25th Army as an example of what happens to those who engage in anti-Soviet activities."

I sat with my face in my hands, stunned by how quickly and easily the death sentence was pronounced. Waiting for the trial to begin, I had believed deep down that someone would carefully review my case and listen to my story. But I was only a grain of sand, minuscule, weightless, and destined for oblivion.

Then an NKVD officer I hadn't seen before walked up to the colonel. He glanced at me in a curious way. "Bring the prisoner to my tent," he said to the guard.

The tent was concealed in the woods by bushes and birch trees just fifty yards from the clearing. For the first time since my arrest, I walked without being tied, blindfolded, or prodded by a gun at my back. I could easily escape, I thought. I could hide in the forests and make it back to Wlodzimierz-Wolynski. I was tense, ready to act, yet somehow paralyzed. I stepped into the officer's tent.

"Sit down, please." He offered me a wooden chair next to a table and dismissed the guard. The officer paced back and forth, hands clenched behind his back. His thin, delicate frame, eyeglasses, and neatly combed hair set him far apart from the military officers. He cleaned his round glasses with a handkerchief and put them back on. His nose was long and curled under slightly at the tip, and his round shoulders reminded me of my brother, who was more comfortable in the library than on the soccer field. I waited impatiently for him to talk, wondering desperately why he had taken an interest in me.

The captain stopped pacing, sat on the cot, and looked at me closely. He seemed nervous. "Don't be afraid," he said. How could I not be afraid? Was this just another kind of torture? I couldn't say anything. I began to cry silently and covered my eyes with my hands. I hadn't cried when I was arrested, nor when I was lying in the pit, nor when I was sentenced to death. But this officer's kind voice made me relax a little; his words made me feel again.

"Are you hungry?"

I nodded, and he gave me a couple of biscuits and a piece of dry sausage from his duffel bag. I was very hungry, but when I swallowed, my throat went into a spasm and I almost vomited. I asked for a glass of water and drank it in one gulp.

"My name is Efim Polzun. I'm the NKVD officer here to supervise the procedures of this court-martial. I need to ask you some additional questions that were not clarified at the hearing." He looked at me intently. "Repeat once again your name, the name of your parents, and the place and date of your birth."

"My name is Janusz Bardach. My father's name is Mark, and my mother's name Ottylia. Her maiden name was Neuding. I was born in Odessa on July 28, 1919."

"Do you have relatives in Odessa?"

"My mother's brother is a professor of neurology at the College of Medicine at Odessa University. His name is Marcel Neuding. His wife is Rosalie Neuding, a famous painter. My father's relatives also live in Odessa."

"Tell me the names of your father's relatives, what they do, and where they live."

A new wave of panic gripped me. The NKVD frequently arrested the relatives of convicted enemies of the Soviet state, and I realized I was putting my relatives in grave danger. But I was too drained to resist. "My father's side of the family lives on Alexei Tolstoy Street, number 16. My great uncle Bardach organized the emergency service at the University Hospital in Odessa. This service bears his name. He has three sons. The oldest, Alexander, is a microbiologist working at the Pasteur Institute in Paris. The middle son, Misha, finished law school and is an attorney in Odessa. The youngest son, Sioma, was a university student when the war started." As I talked about my relatives, I remembered all the details my parents had told me about these people whom I had never met, having left Odessa when I was only six months old.

The officer rose from the cot and smiled at me. A strange sadness filled his eyes. I started to say something, but he put his hand out to stop me.

"I know you're telling the truth. I live on Alexei Tolstoy Street in Odessa. I know the Bardach family—I grew up next to them. Misha, your cousin, was my classmate in law school. I'll do my best to save you, but I don't know if I'll be able to keep you from going to prison. I'll ask for a short term, no more than ten years. I know it's very long, but it's the best I can do."

He looked at me warmly for a moment, then glanced through the flaps of the tent. "You probably know that a court-martial has only two sentences: guilty, which means execution, or not guilty, which means being sent to the front, where you will have nearly a 100 percent chance of being killed by the Nazis. Perhaps going to prison will save your life." He looked at the ground and said in a softer voice, more to himself than to me, "I doubt I'll survive much longer here in freedom." He put his hands on my shoulders. "Remember my name and address, and maybe after the war we'll meet again. At least let's try."

He took money from his billfold, stuck it in my shirt pocket, and gave me a big chunk of dark chocolate and all the biscuits from his bag. He hugged me and asked me to wait there in his tent. In ten minutes he was back. "On account of your youth and honesty, your sentence has been commuted to ten years in the hard labor camps. It's already been signed. The guard will take you to the truck and you'll be transported to Gomel."

We hugged and kissed, and I cried bitterly.

The next moment the guard took me to join dozens of other military prisoners in a clearing close to the pit I had dug the previous night. Several guards armed with rifles paced the periphery of the group, their steel bayonets glistening in the morning sun.

Everything was singing inside of me. My lucky stars had sent me this young Jewish man from Odessa, this close friend of my cousin, who took such a great risk in saving me. Only later did I understand the heavy price he could have paid, or perhaps did pay, for changing the sentence. During the years of the great purges, no one was above suspicion of collaborating with the enemies of the Stalinist regime.

CHAPTER 5

Cattle Car

In the early afternoon a truck took me and several other military men to the prison in Gomel. Nazi bombs were exploding everywhere—some far in the distance, others so close I could feel the vibrations through the wooden bed of the truck. I didn't know why we were going to Gomel instead of moving farther east into safer territory.

We stopped at a heavy wooden gate. Four NKVD guards in green uniforms stepped up to the cab. A portly, red-headed officer with a piggish face shouted at the army lieutenant in charge of us, "You can't stop here. Our orders are not to accept any more prisoners. Turn this truck around and get out of here." His angry words barely covered his panic.

The lieutenant climbed out of the cab and slammed the truck door. "Your NKVD comrades ordered me to bring these prisoners here. There's a war going on, and I'm not about to drive around looking for another prison."

The NKVD guard stuck his bayonet out in front of him as if he would use it. His three comrades—rifles slung over their shoulders—appeared heartless and arrogant, accustomed to their special power and impunity. "No need to fight over this scum," the guard said, looking nervously in the direction of the bombing.

"Dump them any place you want and shoot the bastards. Just don't leave 'em here."

The army lieutenant replied coldly, "Your superiors ordered me to bring these prisoners here. If your men weren't arresting so many soldiers, maybe we'd have more men to fight this war."

I'd never seen such hostility between the Red Army and NKVD; as soldiers, we were given the impression that they always worked together.

"What if the prison doesn't take us?" someone whispered.

"They'll probably shoot us."

"What if the Nazis get much closer?"

"They'll lock us in the cells and run. They don't care what happens to us."

The lieutenant told the driver to turn off the engine. The soldiers guarding us jumped off, pulled out their pistols, and joined the lieutenant. For a moment it looked as if they would shoot, but the NKVD guard, glancing once more toward the sound of artillery fire, broke his stance and unlatched the gate. The lieutenant got back in the cab, the engine fired up, and the truck jerked forward.

Inside the compound, the lieutenant ordered us off the truck. We stood meekly in the prison yard, squinting in the setting sun. Some of my fellow prisoners had to hold up their pants to keep them from falling, but I'd tied mine with a string before getting on the truck and was able to stand straight. A guard with greasy black hair and pimples read our last names and told us to respond with our first and patronymic names; date and place of birth; and sentence, code, and term.

"Bardach," he shouted.

"Janusz Markovitch," I shouted back. "Odessa, July 28, 1919. 193.15, section D. Ten years." I stepped back in line.

When the count was finished, two guards escorted us rapidly into the prison. We felt our way along the walls of the dark corridors and were shoved by twos and threes into the cells. When my turn came, the guard opened a door and pushed me and two others inside. Hot reeking air blasted in my face; the acrid smells of sweat and urine stung my eyes and nose. I felt pinned at the door by the insolent gazes of dozens of prisoners already crowded into the cell. A mass of half-naked men sprawled across the floors and bed boards, sleeping, smoking, talking, and playing cards, all sweating profusely and wiping their faces. A tiny square window in the corner had been barred and partially boarded up.

"How close are the Nazis?" several men asked. "What's happening on the front?" The news that the Red Army was retreating rapidly ignited an ongoing argument. One faction wanted the Nazis to come, believing the NKVD guards would run and we'd have a chance to escape; the other faction argued that the NKVD would kill us all before fleeing. The Nazis were coming, of that I was certain, and I knew there'd be no escape for me.

When the argument died down, a pale, scrawny young man on one of the upper bed boards said loudly to his friends, "Maybe these warriors got some smoke."

His elaborately tattooed neighbor pointed to me and said coolly, "Bet his boots'll fit me."

They looked like a bunch of small-town hoodlums, probably petty thieves, not hardened criminals as they would have liked everyone to think. They talked as though they were alone in the cell, letting the rest of us know who was in charge.

The prisoners who had arrived with me found places to sit, but I stayed near the latrine barrel, where there was just enough space to lean against the door, the only spot where I wouldn't be pressing against the slimy, stinking flesh of other men. A steady stream of prisoners suffering from diarrhea waded between bodies and lined up to use the barrel. One of the young hoodlums jerked my head toward him. His hand was filthy, and his outstretched arm was blackened with tattoos.

"Bet you'd like one like this." He pulled his penis out of his pants and held it in both hands, pointing it toward me. "Take a good look. You're gonna suck a lot of 'em." He jutted his broken front teeth and pointy chin into the air and laughed. His matted black hair fell over his forehead, partially obscuring his large black eyes. I kept my head down and hugged my knees to my chest. He squatted and peered at my face. "You look at me when I piss, but don't open your mouth or I'll piss in it." He let out a high-pitched snort and looked at his friends back on the bed board. I tried to ignore him but was growing tenser by the moment, afraid of what I might do if he hit or touched me.

The young thugs turned their attention to a prisoner who was rolling a cigarette. "Hey soldier, you'd better give us some tobacco." The man licked the edge of the paper and ran his finger along the length of the cigarette, pretending not to hear anything. He sat cross-legged on his neatly folded military tunic. His bare arms and chest were large and muscular. The fellow who had harassed me shouted for the man to roll a cigarette for his friends, too. No response. Two other prisoners jumped down and held a hand out in front of the man, who now had a burning cigarette between his lips. "This one's for us," one of them said. The man paid no attention. One of the youngsters tried to grab the cigarette, but the man turned away. Everyone was watching. Then, without any warning, he leaned back, bent his knees, and kicked one of his harassers in the genitals. Screaming in pain, the boy fell to the floor, holding his crotch with both hands.

"I don't want to fight," the man said to no one in particular, "but I don't give anyone anything unless I want to." He spoke clearly and with authority. No one made a move to help the youth groaning on the floor. His friend climbed back on the bed board, and the other prisoners looked away as though nothing had happened.

I tried to avoid touching the soiled floor with my hands, wanting to preserve whatever cleanliness I could for as long as possible, but my pants stuck to the wooden floor, and the stench was poisoning me. Periodically I was splashed by urine or liquid feces from the barrel, but I didn't have the courage to move away.

As the cell darkened, snoring filled the air. Some prisoners moaned and mumbled in their sleep. There were twenty-four places in the cell but more than a hundred stinking, sweating, twisting men on the bed boards and floor. When someone changed position, the whole row turned over as if on command, rolling slowly, precisely, into new positions. I stared out the partially boarded-up window, watching the sky turn black as I wrestled with shock, sadness, and despair. I couldn't stretch out, but I dozed on and off, escaping for a few minutes into sleep. When I awoke, I ruminated obsessively over the fate of Taubcia and my family. By now the Nazis probably had occupied Wlodzimierz-Wolynski. Was my family still alive, hiding somewhere, or had they already been killed? I hoped that my father, with his professional and social connections, would find a way to keep them safe.

I berated myself for not going home when I was alone with the tank. I could have made my way back—I knew the rivers I would cross, the forests I would hide in, the paths that would take me back home. I knew the terrain, the people, and the languages. I could have made it. I hoped my friends—Chaim, Dalek, Bubek, Mosha, Izia—were still alive. Perhaps they could help my family.

The sound of moaning interrupted my musings. An emaciated, hunched-over figure was trying to balance on the edge of the barrel. He looked at me but didn't seem to see me. His military shirt was black with filth, and his pants lying on the floor were soaked and crusted. He grimaced as cramping racked his body.

The next time I woke to shouting. The explosions were so close it seemed the building was being hit. Like everybody else, I hoped the bombing would bring us freedom; if our guards fled, maybe we could break out and hide before the Nazis arrived. Several prisoners pounded on the door for the guards to remove the barrel. I was hungry and thirsty; judging from my cellmates' complaints, the time for feeding must have passed some time ago.

For an hour or more there was no sound from the corridor. Word spread that the guards had gone, leaving us without food or water, locked in the cell to be bombed or shot by Nazis.

"Open the door, you bloody motherfuckers!"

"Where's our food?"

"Let us out, you fucking bastards!"

"Murderers! Fascists! Let us out!"

Still no response. The young hoodlums shouted the loudest and began breaking up the bed boards. Several of the young soldiers joined them, and together they rocked the bunks back and forth until they came apart. They picked up the heavy pieces of wood and attempted to pry loose the boards covering the window. They dismantled the bars and broke the window, but we were on the third floor—too high to jump out. I shouted and pounded, too. We kept it up for a few hours, but the iron door did not give an inch. Abruptly, the mood changed from furious but fruitless activity to fatigue and resignation. There was no way to break out. We lay listlessly amid the dismantled beds, broken beams, and seepage from the barrel. We feared dying of thirst and hunger as much as we dreaded the arrival of the Nazis.

In the early afternoon, with no warning, the door opened. The guard announced that we were moving to another prison and that we'd be fed when we embarked on the train. We filed out of the prison and formed a long column, four men abreast. Surrounded by guards with bayonets and barking dogs, we walked to the train station.

"Keep in line!"

"Pull in tight!"

"A step to the left or right will be considered an attempt to escape, and you'll be shot without warning!"

Sharp hunger pains pierced my stomach. I had no saliva. My taste buds were so swollen they felt like bristles on a brush. I felt completely empty, aware only of the hollow feeling in my legs and the guards' commands to pick up the pace. We dragged ourselves as fast as we could past wooden houses with broken windows and peeling paint. Their dark green window frames and shutters were broken, their doors wide open or missing completely. Rotting food and reeking sewage filled the gullies on both sides of the street; a row of street-level market stalls were boarded up. The place seemed deserted, yet I spotted two men watching us from an upstairs window, probably Nazi collaborators.

As we approached the train station, army vehicles and infantry units passed us in a hurry. At some intersections, cannons on stationary tanks were pointed in the direction from which we had come. The guards prodded lagging prisoners with their rifle butts, and I struggled to keep pace. Near the station, they marched us down a short side street and ordered us to crouch. My thighs and calves ached. I feared I'd get a cramp and fall over. Two rows in front of me, a large middle-aged man did go down.

A rattling sound escaped from his throat with each slow breath. White foam seeped from the side of his mouth. His neighbors tried to hold his head, but he threw it back, and in an instant the guards were there hitting everyone who tried to help him. "Leave him alone! Get back in the column!" they bellowed. Two guards grabbed the fallen man's arms and dragged him to a ditch. Two more prisoners fell, and the whole column began clamoring for rest and food and water. The guards put a quick end to that with shots from their rifles.

A lanky dark-haired boy about sixteen years old remained next to one of the fallen prisoners. "It's my father! He's dying! Help him!" He looked around with wild eyes.

A Mongolian guard struck the boy in the head with the butt of his pistol. "Get up and get back in the column!"

The bleeding youngster lay next to his father, hugging him tightly. The guard kicked the boy repeatedly, but he didn't move. As the guard leaned over them, the boy turned and spat in his face. Two shots rang out, and the two bodies were dragged to the side of the road.

In the late afternoon we went to the train station, where we were ordered to crouch next to an iron fence along the sidetracks. I held onto the bars and looked out at the railroad yard. It looked as if the entire city had come to the train station. Men, women, and small children loaded with satchels and suitcases ran frantically back and forth between the trains, trying to get into one of the green passenger cars. A few coal-burning locomotives hissed and puffed smoke. People sat on the roofs, dangled from windows, hung onto ladders, and jammed themselves in the corridors. A mob of crying, screaming, cursing civilians and military officers fought to get near the doors of the cars. They shoved, kicked, and pushed each other down without mercy. Those already on the steps, most of them men, ferociously beat back the rest of the crowd, which tried to pull them down. Men already in the cars pulled women and children through the windows. Those who couldn't get onto a train ran along the platforms or crawled under the trains to look for places elsewhere. Everywhere people were calling out names, torn between trying to find their families and getting on a train to save themselves. Women with babies in their arms were stranded on the quays and between the trains. No one bothered to help them. Newly arriving officers and civilians shouted that the Nazis had broken through the city's defenses, increasing the panic even more. A few officers even drew their pistols to get through the crowd and onto a train. The people in this mob looked and sounded like wild beasts caught in a fire, trampling over the weak in a desperate attempt to reach safety.

The guards told us to run across several tracks and platforms to a train of red cattle cars. The doors were open. I climbed into a car. On either side of the door were three tiers of unfinished wooden boards. The force of incoming prisoners pushed me to the far side, and I crawled onto the lowest tier and lay down with my head toward the front of the train. Over a dozen others slid onto the same shelf. Space became tight. With every move, splinters from the raw wood pierced my palms and fingers. Several poked through my pants and shirt into my skin. The door rolled shut. The sliding metal bar screeched across and locked us in. The shooting and artillery barrage got closer. We shouted vainly for water and bread as the train screeched and clattered, moving forward and backward as cars were connected. We heard explosions nearby, footsteps running along the platform, and guards shouting at civilians to stay away. As the train pulled out, the wail of a siren announced an air raid.

In my dark, narrow berth, I could neither lie on my back nor turn around. My neighbor breathed down my neck and pushed me with his knees, and involuntarily I pressed my knees and face against the person in front. Weak with hunger and thirst, I drifted into unconsciousness.

Some time later the screeching and grinding of the train jolted me awake. We slowed to a halt, and I crawled off the bed board and looked out the grated window. The train had stopped on a curve. I could see that it was a long, long train, with passenger, freight, and cattle cars. We had stopped in a forest, and it was wonderful to smell the damp leaves and breathe the fresh air. A thick underbrush came right up to the dirt road next to the railroad tracks, and puddles had formed from the previous night's rain. Two elderly peasants passed by in a horse-drawn wagon piled with hay. They looked curiously at the train, paused, and exchanged some words. Then the driver jiggled the reins and quickly drove off. I watched them for as long as I could, but as the sound of trotting horses faded into the distance I realized I was no longer a part of the outside world. The air, forest, peasants, horses, and puddles were no longer a part of my life.

The door slid open and a bright flashlight illuminated the car. "Get your water and bread." We sat hunched over on the edge of the bed boards while small loaves of dark bread were cut into pieces and passed out. I held my bread ration (*paika*) in both hands and rubbed it against my lips and nose. It was smooth and heavy like clay and smelled of a sharp freshness I had never noticed before. I bit into it with a rush of excitement and devoured the whole thing. When it was gone, I was as hungry as before.

An unfamiliar fatigue stole over me. I wanted only to sleep. For the next two days I got up only for my *paika* in the morning and a bowl of coarse oatmeal in the evening. I used the barrel and got a drink of water, if there was any. My thoughts entangled like vines, running in all directions, crossing each other in time and place, bringing to the surface memories I had long forgotten. My neighbors paid no attention to me, and I had no interest in them.

In the middle of the third night a gang of hideous-looking men tried to strangle me. I couldn't breathe. I tried to fight them off, kicking and pushing; suddenly I felt a sharp pain in the stomach. "Stop it, goddamn it! Wake up!" The prisoner in front of me jabbed me with his elbow. Covered with sweat and gasping for air, I slid off the board to get a drink of water. When I returned, the same neighbor moved over slightly to let me in. The moonlight seeping through the tiny window illuminated his thin pale face and sympathetic smile. His name was Anatoly, and he asked what I had done in the military. I told him I'd been a tank driver and mechanic but had had some bad luck with my tank and was accused of sabotage.

"We've all had bad luck," he replied. "My family is in Nazi-occupied territory in Western Ukraine, and I'm afraid they might be in more danger than we're in. I had to leave them behind when my unit moved on. I never guessed I'd end up here." He turned over again, and we both fell asleep.

On the fourth morning on the train I got up and joined the prisoners walking back and forth across the cattle car for exercise. I counted my steps across the car, and with every lap I touched the wall as if I were swimming in a pool. Five or six military prisoners, all in green army pants and black boots, sat bare-chested on the edge of the bed boards, their chests, backs, and arms covered with welts. They were picking off bugs and squashing them between their thumbnails. I had never seen lice before and watched with fascinated horror as the men cursed and counted out loud, competing with each other. Listening to them speak about their arrests and trials, I felt more contempt toward the Soviet military than I had while in the Red Army. Some of the men addressed each other by rank, even in the conditions of the cattle car. Their reeking breath made me turn my head away.

Anatoly leaned against the wall on his pale, muscular arm. He was taller than I had thought, and thinner and paler. His gray hair and unshaven face were dirty. He had told me how, as a major in an engineering battalion, he had blown up a bridge to stop advancing Nazi troops. He had acted without a direct order, however, and was arrested for sabotage and given ten years in the camps. Several other prisoners had been convicted of treason for retreating when their orders were not to give up an inch of land. "No stepping back" was the slogan coined by Stalin, meaning defend and die but do not retreat.

A bushy-haired military man was seething with anger. Heavy bags under the eyes made him look about fifty years old. He wore an unbuttoned military jacket, baring a dirty undershirt and dark, hairy chest. Despite his filthy attire, his age and dominant bearing let everyone know he was a high-ranking officer. His lower jaw protruded slightly. He licked his chapped lips. With an extended hand, he silenced the group.

"I can't believe that only days ago you all were proud Communists and members of the glorious Red Army. I remain an officer devoted to the Army I have served since the Revolution. I trust in the wisdom of our commander-in-chief, Comrade Stalin, the Politburo, and our marshals. Yes, we've all been arrested. But on the front line there is no time to sort things out." He chopped the air with his hand as he spoke. "When we're away from the front line, we'll be judged again and fairly."

At first everyone was stunned by his speech, but as he droned on, contempt crept across the men's faces. When he finished, the listeners grumbled disgustedly. Another military prisoner, a lanky, red-headed, freckle-faced man slid down from the bed board and said, "General, I agree with you completely." He looked defiantly at the group. "I'm sure our great leader has carried out a secret plan to defeat Germany. We are only small pieces in the big war machine which he directs. We cannot know what he is planning, but we must trust that it is for the good of the country."

Listening to these phony speeches, I thought about what I had learned from my Soviet friends in the Red Army. NKVD informers were everywhere, and I had the feeling that the general and his subordinate were talking with this in mind. During Stalin's purges of the military in 1937–1939, many heroes of the October Revolution and the Civil War had been accused of participating in anti-Soviet conspiracies. Marshals Tukhachevsky and Blyukher, army commander Yakir, and many others loved by the civilians and admired by the military were accused of being German, Japanese, and English spies. The general must have survived the great purges himself by making loud, obsequious declarations such as the one he had just delivered to us. Perhaps he was smarter than he seemed.

"Major Hefnel, you always were an ass-licking son-of-a-bitch." A middle-aged officer who had been smiling ironically leaned toward the red-haired man, trembling with anger. "Didn't you learn anything in these last two months? Are you blind as a kitten or just stupid like your general here? If there is a secret plan, I fuck this plan and both of you. You think we're at a Party meeting? You think this war is going as planned? No, we're here in this filthy, stinking, motherfucking cattle car, while thousands and thousands of our people have been killed and the Nazis have taken over vast areas of our country. You think this is the plan? Which plan? Whose plan? You're both a pair of liars spouting this nonsense, and I hope you both die at the first camp." He climbed onto an upper bed board and spat down loudly in the direction of the officers.

Another military prisoner who looked relatively clean ended the conversation with a pointed anecdote. "I'll tell you about Soviet justice. I was in Brest when the Germans attacked. Three-quarters of the men in my unit were killed. I barely escaped with a few of my officers and soldiers. When we joined the Red Army in Mogilev, we were all arrested. We'd spent several days in Nazi-occupied territory, and military intelligence accused us of being spies and traitors. Is arresting our own people the secret plan of Comrade Stalin or of the NKVD? I cannot listen to people like you, General, and your ass-licking major. You should both be shot."

Most of the prisoners in the car laughed and clapped. I was glad to know I had company.

Our train did not move very quickly. We were often diverted to a siding, sometimes for two or three days, because the stations were overwhelmed with other trains carrying soldiers, tanks, and cannons. Through the small grated window of the cattle car, I heard a good deal of what was going on outside—soldiers marching and guards shouting orders to hurry; the screeching of heavy tanks and cannons as they were loaded onto transport cars; bombs bursting and machine guns firing in the distance. Smoke and falling ash burned my eyes. The station names told us we had gone from Belarus to northern Ukraine and then northeast into the Russian republic. No one in the car knew our destination, but many guessed we were heading northeast, toward the Komi labor camps.

After ten days, everyone and everything was filthy. We only got water to drink twice a day, and all had to drink from a single cup chained to the wall. With no water for washing and no toilet paper, everything we touched caused diarrhea. Anatoly was one of the first to be hit, but then more and more prisoners fell ill. Soon, three or four of them were sitting on the edge of the barrel at the same time. Just when I didn't think it was possible to become any filthier, I discovered I was infested with lice. For several days I pretended not to notice the itching and refused to take off my shirt, feeling degraded, as though I had personally failed in some way. The lice violated the sense of decency I had grown up with; to be filthy was to be vulgar, ignorant, the scum of the earth. The bugs must have been incubating since shortly after I'd been on the cattle car, because they were everywhere—my body was covered with welts. I looked with horror at the crawling seams of my undershirt. I picked out the lice as best I could and squashed them against my thumbnail, just as the other prisoners did. But I still felt them crawling all over—on my stomach and chest and in my hair, pubic area, and armpits. They were all along the seams of my underpants. My horror intensified when I discovered them in my eyebrows. At first I tried to wipe them away, but then I took to my task with vengeance, relishing the hunt for my own lice. They varied in size and color. Nits preceded the smallest lice. Some lice were flat and opaque, others swollen and gray or tinged with red. They became more aggressive in hot temperatures, and body heat excited them. Killing them soon gave me special pleasure; I inspected every one of them pinned on my thumbnail and grunted with pleasure at the sound of their bursting bodies.

The only time anyone interrupted the hunt for lice was when food was distributed. During the second week of the journey we got an extra portion of salt herring. Sometimes it was the whole herring, other times only half. We fought over who got the half with the head, because the brain contained phosphorus, which was supposed to be nutritious. When I grabbed a herring head, I sucked everything from it and then chewed on the bones, crushing them into a paste that could be safely swallowed. Afterwards I was sick from thirst and waited for hours until the guards brought water, of which there was never enough.

By the second week Anatoly had lost all his strength. He crawled between the barrel and bed board, and his pale, wasted body smelled of feces and decay. With sick, watery blue eyes and outstretched hands, he begged me for additional pieces of bread or herring. "Janus," he called one morning, pronouncing my name in Russian. "Please, if they're giving out herring, save me a piece, a head or a tail, anything you can get."

"Anatoly, why don't I report you sick? You need to be in a hospital. I don't think herring is going to do you any good."

"No!" He grabbed onto me. "Don't tell anyone I'm sick. You know what they do to sick people. They'll shoot me, throw me in a ditch. They don't need sick people in the camps."

I assured him I would say nothing and promised him half of my herring. I couldn't help him with anything else. About half the prisoners in our car were sick, some too weak to move on their own, even to the barrel.

One afternoon I looked into Anatoly's glassy eyes and realized he was dying. I didn't know what to do about it, but I knew it would happen very soon. His heavy wheezing kept me awake at night, and when it suddenly stopped I knew it was over. I took his hand and squeezed it tightly, but he didn't squeeze back. Many other prisoners also died. The guards removed the corpses in the mornings with the same disinterest and detachment they showed when delivering our rations. I didn't know what was done with the corpses, and I spent long nights worrying that I too would end up sick and helpless on the bed board with no hope that anyone would care what was happening to me.

One night when the heat and smell kept me from sleeping, I sensed that my neighbor in front of me—an *urka**—was also awake. I tapped him on the back and asked his name. "Fima," he said flatly. After a whispered exchange, I realized he was one of the thousands and thousands of *bezprizorniki*, children abandoned when their parents had been arrested or killed during the Soviet Union's Civil War.

The next morning he invited me to meet the other *urkas* on one of the upper bed boards. There were over twenty of them, all elaborately tattooed on their torsos, backs, and arms. The emblems of naked women, striking snakes, soaring eagles, vodka bottles, machetes, and playing cards identified these men as members of the underworld. Although I had difficulty understanding their jargon, they were more congenial than the military prison-

* Professional criminal.

ers, and I began to spend most of the days with them. They wanted to hear in great detail about my life in Poland; in turn, they told me about the different labor camps, especially those in the far northeast, Kolyma and Chukotka, which were rumored to be the worst. There, it was said, the guards shot prisoners for sport or sent them to work without coats or boots and placed bets on how long it would take them to freeze to death. I had never done hard physical work, and the thought of spending ten years at it was terrifying. No matter what my destination, I had little chance of surviving, and these ever-present fears gave rise to thoughts of escape.

The presence of my fellow prisoners was a great deterrent. They would notice anything I did and inform the guards, because if anyone escaped, the prisoners in the escapee's car would be held responsible for not reporting it. My clothing was another problem. Even if by some miracle I were to get free of the cattle car, my tattered military tunic, pants, and boots would clearly mark me as a deserter. I had only the vaguest idea in which direction to run and would receive no help from the local population; I envisioned Russian peasants surrounding me, wielding pitchforks and scythes. Crossing the front line into Nazi-occupied territory would be suicidal; I imagined quick, clean shots hitting my back when I was discovered.

But ten years in the labor camps amounted to a long, slow death sentence. It had sounded good when it was substituted for execution, but one night in prison and twelve days in the train had shown me what the next ten years would be like, and I didn't want any part of it.

I began searching along the horizontal planks at the front of the car for a loose end or protruding nail. During the day, when most of the prisoners were up and engaged in lice hunting, I pushed against the boards, looking for a loose spot. At night I moved as close as possible to the wall and searched quietly so as not to awaken anyone. Finally, I felt a board give a little. The loose board was near Fima's bunk, and the next day I worked on it while he visited his friends on the upper bed board. With only my fingers to work the nail, the task was slow and painful. After two days it had loosened only slightly, and my fingers were raw. I was going to abandon the idea when I spotted some pieces of wood on the floor. I told the curious prisoners who saw me grab them that I was going to use them as a pillow. One of them made a good lever, and I quickly weakened both the board I had been working on and the one below it. I could push them open at any time, and I knew that the coming night would be the night of my escape.

That evening I closed my eyes but lay wide awake, my heart pounding furiously. I pictured myself squeezing through the opening, standing on the buffer between the cars, getting a good footing, and pushing off the train. I would roll onto the ground and hide in the shrubs surrounding the tracks. The best time would be just before dawn, when I'd be able to see forms in the emerging light. I'd have to wait until the train slowed down on the curves, however. I hoped it would stop on the outskirts of a town so I could seek cover quickly. My doubts had evaporated. It was my only chance. I was both afraid and not afraid of dying. Throughout the night the train rushed through the fields and forests, taking me as far away from freedom as possible. Heavy with anxiety and despair, I fell asleep.

I was awakened in the predawn hours by the screeching of the train's brakes. As soon as the train stopped, two guards slid the door open and distributed *paika* and herring. It was unusual to be fed so early, but I moved to the edge of the bed board and waited. Through the open door I saw branches and leaves silhouetted against the sky and heard the chortles of birds. Two prisoners behind me, too ill to move, seemed unaware of the feeding frenzy around them. The train was stopped, and it would be easy to slip out while everyone was concentrating on the food.

I put the last of the herring in my mouth and scooted backward. As I leaned against the wall, the two broken planks began to give way. The breeze slipped in through the opening, and I heard cicadas clicking urgently. With a pounding heart, I pressed harder against the planks and slipped my arm and shoulder through the hole. I grabbed onto the rough vertical beam, brought my knees to my chest, and slipped out. My dangling feet found the buffer, and I slid down onto the track and lay under the train between the rails.

I breathed deeply for a moment to calm my shaking body. To my left the guards were still delivering rations; the sound of their boots scraping against gravel traveled directly in my ear. Flashlights swept the area between the cars and guards. About four feet away was a field of tall golden grass.

Very slowly I crawled over the rail and into the grass. When I glanced back at the train, my heart sank. I'd forgotten to push the boards back, and the breeze blowing through such a large hole would certainly attract attention. I wanted to rush back and fix it, but I was too frightened to move. Every minute the sky became a lighter shade of gray, and the trees gained a sharper contour. It would only be a matter of minutes before I was discovered.

Two guards stood on top of the train smoking and casually looking around. While they oversaw the food distribution, I inched through the grass, stopping several times near shrubs to avoid drawing attention. As soon as I made it to the first trees, I started running.

CHAPTER 6

Retribution

Twigs, dry leaves, and pine needles crunched underfoot, sounding to my frightened ears like thunder that could be heard for miles around. The edge of the forest was sparsely covered, and as I jumped over small bushes and fallen trees I was certain my running figure could be spotted from far away. My back burned as I imagined the guards aiming and taking fire. I ran straight ahead into the densest part of the forest, hoping to hide in the thick greenery. I breathed deeply for the first time in weeks; the morning air, so fresh and crisp, rushed across my face like ice-cold water.

I breathed to the rhythm of my thoughts, running faster than ever before, my heart thumping wildly. I forgot my hunger and weakness, the filth and death of the prison transport, and sprang over vines and tree trunks feeling strong and fleet. My mind raced like a fast-moving stream. Where am I? Which way should I run? Where does the forest stop? I mustn't get trapped in a thicket. Find the edge of the forest and stay close to it. Stay away from villages; stay away from people. Peasants are dangerous. I'll have to do it alone. I must get to a big city, but I don't know where I am. What was the last city we passed? I can't remember. How do I get out of this forest? What if I get lost here? What will I eat? Is there food in the forest? Are there fields I can eat from? I mustn't panic. Calm down. If I could make it out of the train, I can make it out of the forest.

The more lost I became in the forest, the more lost I became in myself. My panting filled my ears; the green leaves and dark trees blurred in my sight. My legs quivered and finally gave out as I jumped over a fallen tree. My hands sank into the soft wood with a hollow thud, and I lay across the rotted trunk with my face in the damp moss. White worms and beetles scurried over my hands. Everything came to a sudden halt—my thoughts, my legs, my heart. I rose to my knees and frantically brushed off the crawling specks. The impervious canopy of maples and oaks kept the morning light from penetrating to the damp forest floor. I couldn't make out any natural paths or distinguish small details. Sweat fell in my eyes; blood pounded in my temples. I remained kneeling, trying to focus. How far am I from a town? Which direction? I don't have money to pay for a room or food or clothing. I don't have a single piece of paper to identify myself. Food, I can steal— but documents? Without those, I don't exist. They'll throw me in prison right away. I'll never make it. Maybe I should go back, turn myself in, rather than be hunted like a wild boar. Eventually I'll be caught. The train is probably still there. The guards will kill me for sure. I'm dead either way.

I began looking for some kind of trail, scanning for places where the vines and trees thinned. When I came upon a creek with tall grass growing alongside it, I started to run. Fear drove me on- ward. No matter how dark my thoughts became or how lost I felt, I ran. Thorns tore into my hands and arms as I parted the brush; sweat streamed down my face and back. The forest, which had al- ways been my haven, closed in around me; I felt consumed by it. My chest heaved from shortness of breath, and I stopped running, leaned over a log, and threw up. If I ran much farther, I'd collapse. I was a good sprinter but couldn't run a long way without getting exhausted. The more nervous I became, the worse my breathing got. I had to lie down to keep from passing out.

After resting, I got up and walked slowly through tiny open- ings between the shrubs. In the distance I heard the faint sound of dogs barking. I thought it must be coming from a nearby village and strained to discern the exact direction. My legs were numb from the cold, yet I was sweating profusely. Streaks of blood appeared on my slashed hands and arms, but I felt no pain. I had no idea how far away I was or how much time had passed, but it didn't matter. I was driven by only one thought: to get away as fast and as far as possible.

I moved ahead in the thick cover, feeling somewhat safer, until I heard the dogs barking again. This time they were closer, and I realized they and their masters were searching for me. I pictured the German shepherds with their panting, parted mouths full of fangs and heard the angry, cursing guards. Fear spurred me on again. I swam through the brush, throwing my arms forward and parting the sea of bushes in front of me. Suddenly I came to a clearing and broke free, running as fast as I could to reach the brush at the other end, surprised by how much strength I still had. On the other side of the clearing I searched for open spaces between the trees. The barking sounded again, and now I heard voices. I crashed through a rotten tree trunk and fell spread-eagled into lush ferns. Hysterical, and certain the hunters had heard the noise, I got back up. Run, run, run, I commanded my body, but running was impossible. The voices and barking were very close.

*"Davay! Davay! V peryod!"**

My chest was so tight I could hardly inhale, but I tried to run, terrified of being mauled by the dogs. I grabbed a stick to fight them off. I just wanted to be shot. My pursuers came closer; I could hear distinctly the obscenities they shouted at me. I looked frantically for a place to hide, knowing I'd be caught momentarily but hoping against hope that the dogs would miss me. Shielding my face with my forearms, I rushed into the densest brush and huddled close to the ground.

As the dogs bore down upon me, I jumped up and turned toward them, wielding the stick high in the air. They leapt and pinned me to the ground, their hot breath in my face, their fangs poised to slash into my flesh.

---

* "Let's go! Move it!"

*"Ne tron!"** The dogs froze, holding me under their heavy paws. I tried to stop trembling, afraid that any movement would make them tear into my throat. I couldn't see the guards anywhere but heard them repeatedly calling to the dogs. *"Ne tron! Ne tron! Sadis."*** The dogs sat down next to me. I opened my eyes and saw them panting, drooling, and watching me closely.

"Crawl out of there, motherfucker."

On all fours, I inched out of my hiding place. With a sharp blow, my head snapped backward, and my ears rang. Another kick, and my cheekbone emitted a sickening crack.

"You cocksucker! You're going to die for this. These dogs will eat you alive."

As I struggled to stand, the same guard spat in my face and punched me in the gut, doubling me over. His knee caught me on the chin. "You were strong enough to run away; you ought to be strong enough to pay for it." The guard was hulking and blond with wide cheekbones. His forehead and cheek were bleeding. "You'll beg to suck my cock. You'll beg to die quickly. But you'll die a hundred times before you're out of your misery." He unleashed his heavy hand on my face, his knuckles cracking my bones, my mouth and nose full of blood. Through blurry eyes, I saw the other guard: short, dark-haired, barrel-chested, his eyes gleaming with hatred. He said nothing as he walked behind me and viciously bound my wrists. Then he clubbed me on the back of the neck with his pistol. I felt as if my head were flying away.

As we walked to the train, we were joined by more guards and dogs. "I knew we'd get him," the blond brute panted jubilantly. "No one can run away from these dogs. One day I'd like to let them feast, see how they rip the bastard apart."

My captors took me to the guards' compartment, a passenger car that had been converted into one large room. There was a table and several chairs at one end and ten or more neatly made cots at the other. The middle of the room was empty.

---

* "Don't touch!"
** "Sit!"

The blond guard grabbed me on the neck with a strong grip and pushed me face down on the floor in the middle of the compartment. He stepped on my back as though I were his trophy.

"Here he is, Commander. It's up to you to decide what to do with him, but I'd let the dogs work on him. They deserve it." He pushed me with his boot toward a bench along the front wall of the cabin and ordered me to lie under it and face the wall. I rolled onto my side, my wrists still tied behind my back, and crawled like a worm across the dirty floor. The space beneath the bench was very tight, and I could barely squeeze in.

"So what are we going to do with him?" The blond guard asked.

"We should be reaching Vologda soon. We'll leave him there to stand trial," someone calmly replied. I assumed this was the commander. I tried to turn and see the person who wanted to spare my life, but I couldn't budge.

"I think we need to teach the *ze-ka** a lesson so no one else tries to escape. Let's bloody him up and parade him in front of the prisoners."

Someone else concurred. "We need to teach them how to love our country and respect our laws."

Steps approached. A boot kicked me repeatedly in the back and buttocks. "Crawl out of there," my captor snarled.

"Cool off," said the commander in a low voice.

"Right," someone else joined in. "You don't need to kill him. Just make it so he'll never want to fuck again." The compartment filled with laughter.

I tried to crawl out but wasn't making much progress. Someone tugged on my shirt and pants and dragged me to the middle of the floor. A guard untied me and tore off my shirt. Someone rolled me onto my back and pinned my head down; someone else held down my legs. I couldn't see anything but heard several people walk across the floor—a circle of spectators.

"You fucking slime!" A belt buckle smashed across my stomach.

I screamed. My muscles contracted fiercely. I thought I would vomit and soil my pants.

---

* Prisoner. Though short for *zakluchoney,* the term *ze-ka* was the official form of address to prisoners.

"Give me the belt! I'll castrate him for life."

"Smash his balls."

"Beat his face to a pulp!"

"Hit him again! Harder!"

The buckle smashed across my ribs and abdomen again and again; I howled in pain. One blow struck deeply in the groin, and I felt warm urine in my pants. The belt was being passed around the circle. Before every strike, there was an agonizing pause as the torturer wound up to release the hardest blow he could. Before long I couldn't get enough breath to scream and simply moaned. Every soft part felt ruptured, and every bone felt cracked. After a particularly hard blow to the chest I thought my heart would stop. I could barely get any air and became dizzy. After another couple of blows I lost consciousness.

Drifting in and out of this state, I heard someone say, "Maybe that's enough. Let him catch his breath."

Cold water splashed on my face. The slightest movement of my head made it spin, and I lost consciousness again.

"Is he still breathing?"

"I think he's all right," said the guard at my head. "Just turn him over."

Pressed against the floor, the raw flesh of my stomach and chest burned. The blows continued, landing on my back and buttocks, but these were less painful than the strikes to my stomach and chest. As the beating continued, my head felt shrouded. Darkness descended, closing me off from everything and everyone. Pain drifted away; I didn't feel a thing.

Cold water splashed again and again on my face. Someone slapped my cheeks. As I regained consciousness, I heard the familiar voice of my captor. "Wake up! Wake up! We're not finished yet." They rolled me back over, and through the cigarette smoke I saw several guards standing over me. Several others sat on the benches and chairs, smoking and drinking vodka. "Here's to you, Commander," one of them toasted, "for your leadership and service to the Motherland." Everyone stood up and clinked glasses.

"This is to our Leader, Beloved Comrade Stalin." It was all I heard before being struck and fainting again.

When I woke up, I heard someone say, "Let's tie his balls."
Everyone laughed loudly. The *urkas* had told me this was what
they did to traitors. I didn't think I could survive the pain from
this gruesome torture.

"I think he needs more blood on his face," someone commented. "Then he'll be ready for the *ze-ka*." The blond guard
raised my face and punched, cutting my lip and nose. Blood
dripped from my nostrils, staining my shirt.

"Show him to the *ze-ka*," the commander ordered.

I couldn't stand on my own, so two guards lifted me by the
arms and dragged me out of the car. The searing, throbbing pain
came alive. I fainted.

In front of the first car the commander shouted, "This man
tried to escape this morning. I want everyone to look at him. The
next person who tries to escape will be shot."

In front of each open car the warning was repeated. I could
barely see well enough to know when we had reached my former
car, but I heard someone shout, "It's him! I knew he was a traitor. I
knew he was an enemy of the people!" I didn't recognize the voice,
nor did I care whose it was.

Back in the guard's compartment, I was shoved again under
the bench and told not to move.

"Get him some water," the commander said in a thick, intoxi-
cated voice. "I don't give a shit if he dies, but I don't want him to
die here. I'm not going to write an explanation as to how or why
he died in this car. We caught him. We made a good example out
of him. And now I want to deliver him alive to the NKVD. Let
them try and shoot him, but I'm not going to hold a trial here.
It'll be my ass if he dies in our quarters."

I didn't care what happened. Nothing mattered anymore, neither life nor death. I just didn't want to be beaten again.

Some time later, I was awakened by a strong kick in the buttocks. The car was dark, illuminated only by a lamp. I lay on my
side, my knees bent as much as possible in the tight space. It felt
as though I were in a coffin. My head seemed to be floating above
my body; I could hear what the guards were saying but couldn't
make a sound of my own. With the slightest movement, pain

flamed through my body. I tasted the salty blood on my lip and sniffed it through my fractured nose. The guards were eating, and the smell of pea soup with bacon made me aware that I hadn't eaten for a long time, but I didn't feel hungry. I didn't want to be bothered by anyone; I just wanted to lay undisturbed and wait for my end. I was fairly certain I wouldn't make it out alive. "Let's change guards and feed the parasites," someone shouted. Men clomped in and out of the car. Those who remained were toasting each other.

"I felt highly honored when I was invited to join the NKVD. Although guarding these scum wasn't what I had expected, I'm proud to be with this unit and want to toast all my friends with whom I've spent the last two years."

"To you!" the others shouted. The chairs scraped against the floor. Guards asked for more soup and canned pork.

"You know what I like most about my service with the Organy?" another guard said. "This is the most elite service. We are the most trusted and most competent defenders of our Beloved Motherland. From my class only two people were offered to join the NKVD. My career and my life is with the NKVD." His speech was punctuated with loud belches and hiccoughs.

"So let's toast our outstanding leader, Lavrenti Pavlovich Beria, the closest and most loyal friend of our Great Leader, Comrade Stalin."

Everyone stood up, pushed aside the chairs, and shuffled across the floor.

"Grisha," someone shouted. "Check the bastard to see if he's still alive."

"Yes, Commander. But if he's alive, I hope he chokes when I feed him."

The guard dragged me out from beneath the bench, and I lay in the middle of the floor, unable even to sit up. A tin cup with water was handed to me, but I couldn't raise my arm to take it.

"If he doesn't want to drink, let him go back under the bench," Grisha responded. The commander told him to put the water in a shallow dish next to me on the floor. I lapped at it like a dog, with my face half-immersed. I drank slowly, trying to keep down every gulp. My stomach still hurt and was cramping. The smell of the soup nauseated me.

"Maybe he'll eat something," the commander said. "I don't want him to die. I already told you I don't want to write a report on him."

One of the guards stuffed a piece of bread in my mouth. My stomach lurched, and I spit the bread out. The punch in the face came so rapidly that it threw me backward. My head hit the floor, and blood began running from my nose again. "This fucking scum doesn't want to be taken care of. Let's just throw him off the train and leave him to die and rot."

I broke completely, soiling and wetting my pants, which infuriated the guards. A hundred jeering faces blurred in and out of focus.

"Get rid of the stinking swine!"

"Throw him off the train."

"Feed him to the dogs."

The commander shouted above the other voices, "Put him in the storage closet behind the toilet. We'll decide what to do with him in the morning. But he'd better be alive when we get to Vologda."

The storage closet was packed with bags, brooms, buckets, mattresses, and dirty rags. Guards pushed me in and shut the door. In the pitch-dark enclosure, I slumped to the floor and tried to clear a place for myself. There wasn't enough room to lie down, so I assumed a half-sitting position, stuffing some rags under my aching body.

I couldn't tell how long I remained there, but time didn't matter. I didn't want to live but wasn't strong enough to end my life. Darkness played with me. I couldn't see my own hand stretched in front of me, but I saw vividly Grisha, dogs, and the cattle car. I wasn't sure if I was asleep or awake, my imagination took such strange turns. At first my thoughts had some logic to them; my failed escape held some meaning. I wanted to get home. That was why I had jumped off the train. I wanted to get back to Taubcia and my parents. But why didn't I try to get home when the tank was in the river? I had told myself then that I had to stay and fight the Nazis, but deep down I had been afraid of running. But after my arrest and my confinement on the cattle car, fear gave way to anger and determination. I didn't deserve to waste my life in the filth and stench of prisons and camps. I deserved to live. I hadn't committed any crime. I had to try to get out of the train. I had to try to slip out of the injustice that prevailed upon me, enraged me, and blinded me to everything else. I felt myself drifting away, a dark current mixing everything together. I wasn't asleep, but I wasn't in charge of my thoughts; the current was taking me away from myself like a lapping tide, the waves black, the sea unknown.

"Stalin, the Greatest Leader. Stalin, the Genius of Mankind. Here's to Comrade Beria. To the NKVD. To the proletariat." Through the door I heard the same slogans I had shouted in the Red Army. But what I saw were the heads of vipers, their eyes black and beady, their fists striking my body. My flesh was on fire; my stomach ruptured; my head exploding. The smell of my own shit was stifling. "Is this death?" I wondered. "Is this what my comrades felt as they lay sprayed with bullets in the marsh?" I leaned against a bucket with my face in my hands and cried softly, unable to stop the tears or the thoughts that propelled them. I had deserted my family. Not voluntarily, but I had left them. Maybe I did deserve to die, to be killed. I wanted to die. Silently, I prayed: Please, God, if You exist, take me now. I don't want to live. But please save my family. Keep them from being tortured and killed. There is no one else I can ask for help. I never believed in You. I thought You were only the goodness in my heart, the goodness inside a person. But now I know that wasn't right. There is no goodness in people's hearts. People are cruel, vicious, full of hate. I don't know if You exist, but if you do please save my family.

I feel sick and dizzy. I'm sweating. The dark horse of sleep wants to take me away. I don't know who I am anymore. I climb on the horse. I hear its galloping hooves. It is running away inside me.

The door opened. I sensed light on the other side of my eyes.

"He stinks like fucking shit," Grisha said to someone in the corridor. "I can hardly breathe. Go to the toilet and clean yourself." He held a shirt and underpants in his hands. "Throw out your clothes and put these on."

I was so stiff, swollen, and bruised that I couldn't get up. Grisha leaned over and yanked me up by the arm. I screamed, then fainted from the exploding pain. I awakened to cold water being splashed on my face. I was lying next to the toilet.

"Get cleaned up."

With every breath a thousand needles pierced my lungs. My abdomen was distended. I was afraid something was damaged inside, because I felt full but hadn't eaten.

It took a long time to take off my dirty shirt and soiled underwear because they stuck to my blood-crusted skin. Pulling away the clothing not only was painful but also started the bleeding again. I splashed water on the scabs, but it wasn't enough to soften them, and so I ripped off a piece of my shirt, soaked it in water, and held it against the sores, working the rag over my body inch by inch and pulling the clothing off slowly and diligently. I couldn't reach my back or buttocks, and tearing the shirt away was excruciatingly painful. My back started bleeding again. The gruesome sight of my body nearly made me faint. Every inch of skin was red and blue, and places on my chest, arms, and abdomen were raw. My urine was red.

The guard played with his pistol while he watched me through the open door. He saw the bloody urine but made no comment. He wouldn't let me near the open window, and so he took the soiled clothes with disgust and threw them out of the train. He disappeared for a while and came back with a pair of green military pants, the same color as those of the guards. I put on the clean underwear and shirt. The pants were at least two sizes too big, and my feet were too swollen to pull the boots on. The guard helped me back to the compartment, ordered me to sit on the floor, and gave me water and oatmeal. Too bruised to sit, I leaned over on my side and scooped out the oatmeal with my hand, but after several mouthfuls I vomited and was pushed back under the bench.

"He won't eat," Grisha said. "He wants to die, Commander. Let me help him off the train."

The commander spoke with irritation. "I told you already, I want to transfer him to the local NKVD alive. He can die there the very next minute, but it will save me a lot of trouble if he doesn't die here. I have to report each *che-pe*,* and I don't want to explain why he died in our compartment. You missed your chance to kill him in the forest. Now he's under my supervision, and if he's killed in this compartment and someone reports it, it will be my ass. So shut up and quit talking about killing him. I've had enough."

After a long while I felt thirsty again and needed to use the toilet. It was late in the afternoon when, for the first time, I asked for water.

"I'll get you some food and water," someone said. "We'll be reaching our destination soon."

This was the first time I had heard or seen this guard. He helped me to the toilet and waited at the open door. My urine was still bloody. "You need to go to the hospital," he said. "It's bad when you piss blood."

He helped me move out into the middle of the floor, where I gulped down two full tins of water without feeling any pain in my stomach. He handed me a bowl of cold oatmeal, which I ate with my fingers. I licked the bowl to get every bit. Right away I felt dizzy and sleepy. I wanted to go back under the bench, but the outside door opened and three guards entered. In the presence of his comrades, the guard who had fed me suddenly became impatient and in an angry voice ordered me back under the bench. He kicked me as I crawled, landing the heel of his boot on my back. "Go! Hurry up! Disappear!"

I spent another night under the bench. The train was moving very slowly, stopping for hours at a time. I wasn't sure where we were going or when we'd arrive, and I was afraid that any place I'd be transferred, the local NKVD would interrogate and torture me. But staying longer in the compartment would result in more beatings. I didn't think they'd kill me, but the beating I had endured was worse than death.

---

* Unusual incident; short for *cherezvichainoye proishestvye.*

Guards walked in and out of the car, scraped the chairs against the floor as they moved up to the table. They began singing military songs that I had sung and knew well. I stayed awake through the changing of shifts and the late meal of the new guards. "Is he still under the bench or did you get rid of him?" the commander asked.

"What do you mean? You ordered us to keep him alive."

"I mean did you transfer him back to his car? We're not going to bother with him anymore. We taught him a lesson; I'm sure he'll never attempt another escape. Put him in the car next to us and let's forget about him."

The commander was drunk, tired, and irritated. I wasn't sure if it was true or a joke. For the first time in three days, I thought again of living. Most of all I thought about my family, whose fate I wouldn't know for a long time.

The commander ordered me out of my shelter and gave me a piece of bread, a bowl of hot bean soup with bacon, and a wooden spoon. I ate sitting on the floor with my back to the bench. I was still severely bruised, my face swollen all over. A piercing pain shot through my chest when I inhaled deeply.

I was ordered to stand up and follow the guards off the train. With the first breath of fresh air, I felt that I had regained part of my freedom, something that couldn't be taken away no matter how oppressive the conditions were in the labor camps. I knew that a hard life lay ahead of me, but I also knew I had survived something extraordinary.

CHAPTER 7

Burepolom

The morning remained darkened by a fleet of gray, churning clouds. Thunder cracked, and the wind blew through the massive pines. Tiny spears of rain pelted my wounds, and in minutes I was drenched, shivering, and splattered with mud. As the truck rattled over cobblestones and bounced over holes in the dirt road, I felt as though I were being beaten all over again. We were driving deep into the forest, far away from any city, far away, I thought, toward a place where I could only expect to be treated with harshness and total indifference.

Around midday we pulled into a large settlement encircled by a tall wooden fence and several coils of barbed wire. We had arrived at a prison camp called Burepolom, which meant "fallen forest destroyed by storm." The truck lurched to a stop in front of a large log cabin. Guards herded us with their rifle butts into a spacious hall. A prisoner with a pot belly and rosy cheeks stood up on a bench and bellowed, "Everyone undress and turn in your clothing to be steamed." For the first time since my arrest six weeks before, I was going to bathe. The man could barely be heard above the din of excited prisoners. The anticipation of bathing, the absence of guards, and the space to move around galvanized everyone, making us raucous and giddy.

"Look at this fucking *predurok*,"* shouted a tall, slender, gray-haired man with sunken cheeks, his voice trembling with hatred. He pointed toward the eunuchoid man still standing on the bench. "He grew his fat on our misery and by stealing our food." The gray-haired man moved through the crowd to get closer to the *predurok*. "Do you remember me, you dog's prick? You're the motherfucking Party secretary who had me expelled and signed the order for my and my wife's arrests. You sent my children to an orphanage. You took our apartment." The hall quieted down, and the man addressed the prisoners. "I know him from Omsk. I remember what a big Party dignitary he was and how he treated simple people. He may look like a prisoner, but he's not one of us." He turned back toward the man, pointed his finger, and shouted with hatred, "I hope you die here with your balls cut off and your eyes dug out."

The hall erupted with cursing about the Party and NKVD. I was astounded by the open remarks. Outside of prison, this blasphemy would certainly end in a long prison sentence.

While most of the prisoners quickly undressed, I labored to take off my boots and socks. I could raise my leg without too much effort, but trying to pull off the boots strained my lower abdomen and cut my breath short. It took me a long time to wiggle off my damp footwear and peel my T-shirt and underwear away from the oozing sores. Many of the naked prisoners looked fit and healthy, but just as many had little flesh covering their bones; their ribs stuck out and little pouches of skin hung from their buttocks. These men had the wild, wandering eyes of beaten dogs, ever vigilant, trying to escape the next blow. In contrast, tattoos, predatory gazes, and loud conversation distinguished the *urkas*.

While standing naked, I tried to hide my circumcised penis by pulling it in, but concealment wasn't necessary; the cuts and bruises on my chest, stomach, and thighs drew much more attention. The rectangular belt buckle had left its imprint on several places across my belly and chest. Scabs had formed, and the deep

---

* A prisoner of high status who worked for the administration.

purple bruises were turning blue and red. None of the cuts or scratches were infected, but lice were crawling everywhere. Naked prisoners brushed up against me and jostled me around, inflicting more pain on my ruptured, bleeding body and making me tense and irritable. I felt their lice being wiped off on me.

Before entering the bathhouse, we received crude haircuts. Three barbers snipped and flicked clumps of oily, matted hair onto the floor without changing or wiping off the clippers, and this made me feel even more hostile. On top of my own filth, I would be contaminated by other peoples' crusting scalps and hair. The barber was fast and rough. He grabbed and snipped fistfuls of hair from the middle of my head, and before I knew it he had clipped my sparse beard, armpits, chest, and pubic hair.

I headed for the bathhouse. Steam rolled out from between the wooden doors, smelling like dirty water. I walked into a hot, dense fog. The putrid smell of urine rose from the floor. It took a few minutes to adjust to the hazy conditions and to distinguish people, the faucets, and benches. To my deep disappointment, there were no showers, only several faucets of hot and cold water. I grabbed a small abandoned barrel that had been cut in half and equipped with a handle. Scum floated on top of the water; I worried that I'd never get clean. I made several trips to the faucet. Again and again I washed my bald head, face, and ears, rubbing off little coils of dirty skin. The grayish brown soap smelled like an old dirty rag, but when it disintegrated I scrounged for little pieces lying on the benches and floor and used them.

The prisoners had spread themselves out evenly on several rows of long wooden benches, washing themselves and each other. Some soaked their feet in wooden buckets. Naked bodies glided across the soapy floor between the faucets and benches, and condensation dripped from the walls and ceiling. Only after sitting for a few minutes on the bench, refreshed and relaxed, did I notice shouting and laughter not far from me. Through the steam I saw two young men, both *urkas*, standing together. They held each other at the waist and brushed their erect penises over each other's bodies. Sitting on a bench, another skinny fellow masturbated a friend, who held him in return. I glanced around to see if anyone else had noticed and became aware of several other couples in intimate positions. A middle-aged man lay on a bench masturbating in front of everyone. He ejaculated and smeared semen all over his body. No one reacted. I knew almost nothing about homosexuality except that in the Soviet Union it was punishable by at least five years in prison, a fact stressed repeatedly in the Red Army. I could hardly believe that prisoners had any sexual desire. Mine had disappeared the moment I was arrested, and I thought it was gone forever.

I went again to the faucets and passed an excited group of prisoners gathered around a bench next to the wall. Those in the back row were jumping up, trying to see over the heads and shoulders of those in front, who were shouting obscenities and holding their penises.

"Go!"

"Faster!"

"Hurry up!"

A young man lay on his stomach, and another man lay on top of him, embracing him around the chest and moving his hips back and forth. His back was tattooed with shackles, chains, and the popular Soviet slogan "Work is an act of honor, courage, and heroism." On both sides were trumpeting angels. He breathed heavily, while the young man underneath moaned and cried out. The spectators shouted. I caught sight of the young man's grimacing face.

Chelovek cheloveku volk—"man is wolf to man." My mother had taught me this phrase when I was a child. Now it bore into my heart every day, every hour, as I saw prisoners fight each other savagely for *paika* or a puff of a cigarette; heard them curse, cry, and moan; smelled their decaying, rotting bodies; saw them die. I could be forced to lie on a bench in this or in another bathhouse and be repeatedly raped not by my oppressors—whom I considered to be the NKVD guards—but by my fellow prisoners. For the first time I realized how vulnerable I was—only twenty-two, alone, and still too weak to resist an assault.

I was granted a week of rest in a barracks for convalescents to recover from my injuries, and at the end of the week I was summoned to the guard's shack for *etap*.*

Our *etap* was on foot and lasted for two days. We followed a dirt road through a forest and arrived at a small camp affiliated with Burepolom. The compound, smaller than a school yard, contained two barracks, one log cabin, and an iron hand pump in the middle. Both barracks were windowless and made of rotting boards. The roofs were coated with tar and topped by several rusty smoke pipes. One barracks was half the size of the other and was situated against the barbed-wire fence. A *predurok* led a group of us to this barracks and told us to find a place on the bed boards.

Three continuous tiers of rough, warped boards lined the long sides of the barracks, which appeared to sleep several hundred prisoners. As in the cattle car, there were no mattresses, pillows, or blankets. The floor was nothing but damp, packed dirt, which, along with the moldy wooden walls and bed boards, suffused the barracks with a musty smell. The stale air was made thicker by the heavy odors of sweat, urine, and excrement. A breeze came through gaps in the wooden walls, but it wasn't enough to circulate and freshen the air.

Dozens of prisoners lay on the bed boards in their clothes, some stretched out like logs, others curled up like worms. Their fetid bodies and pale, translucent skin and sunken eyes made me think of Anatoly. I wondered how ill they were and how long they'd gone unfed and uncared for. Most of all, I wondered how quickly they had deteriorated to this state. It appeared as though nothing was being done to help them. One of them begged repeatedly for water, and I filled a dirty tin cup and gave it to him. Out of his rags, the man extended a skeletal hand with long nails caked with dirt. He turned his head to look at me and tried to say something but started to hiccough. He drank the water and asked for more, and I brought him another cup. Other prisoners moaned or mumbled over and over. I bent over a young man and tried to understand what he was saying, but his disjointed words made no sense.

* Transport; shipment of prisoners.

His skin was yellow, his face covered with sweat; he was shivering, and his teeth chattered. His putrid breath seemed to emanate from his bowels. I thought it was the smell of death.

My heart grew heavy as I looked around at the dying prisoners, my new living quarters, and the tiny compound in which my every move would be monitored by armed guards. I had believed there would be a base level of humanity in the camps—a regard for human life to keep prisoners from dying unnecessarily—but no one cared.

The door banged open, and a crowd of coughing, sniffling, spitting prisoners crept into the barracks. Like their ill counterparts, these moving figures appeared ravaged and log-like, barely able to raise their eyes or lift their legs as they shuffled across the room and hoisted themselves onto the boards. The arrogance and crudeness of the *urkas* had vanished; only their tattoos set them apart. The prisoners' hands were bent, as though around an ax or saw handle. They looked menacing but were dead tired, falling asleep the moment they lay down.

What sounded like a church bell rang in the courtyard to announce *poverka*.* Everyone who could rolled promptly off the boards and shuffled outside, grumbling and cursing. The brigades lined up in blocks, five people deep. Guards with German shepherds patrolled the periphery. A man named Kovalov was in charge of the brigade to which I had been assigned. He was a bulky man with large, tough hands, Slavic cheekbones, and a gruff manner. He had no tattoos, so I knew he wasn't an *urka*, but he wasn't a political prisoner, either. From his crude manners and language, I gathered he'd probably worked in a factory or in construction. He picked out the newcomers to his unit and put our names on the list.

Despite the cool autumn weather, many prisoners—including me—wore only light clothing: tattered civilian shirts, army or prison tunics, ill-fitting army or prison pants. Those without jackets pulled their arms in close to their bodies and squeezed their hands between their thighs to keep warm. A few of the new arrivals and *predurkis* were dressed well, wearing winter jackets,

---

* Roll call. Head count.

warm hats, gloves, and boots. There was a great assortment of footwear—boots, galoshes, wooden clogs, and *laptys*.*

Darkness had fallen, but there was no sign of the camp commander. Floodlights shone down from the towers, illuminating a sea of pale, lifeless faces. Nearly an hour later the camp commander, accompanied by several guards and *predurkis*, stomped onto the porch. Stout and red-faced, he held an NKVD cap in his hand and tried to steady himself on a guard's shoulder. His long military coat of gray-green wool flapped open, and his green scarf hung unevenly outside the collar of his coat. One of the guards shouted, "Attention! The camp commander will receive the reports."

One by one the brigadiers stepped up to the porch and, in military fashion, loudly reported the count of the brigade. Each report included the same formula, reminding me of roll call in the Red Army. Kovalov remained at attention, looking straight at the commander. He read from his clipboard in a raspy voice, loudly articulating every word. "Citizen Commander. Brigadier Kovalov reports the state of the seventh brigade. There were thirty-seven prisoners at work. Three members of the brigade were sick and remained in the barracks. One of them died. Two prisoners died at work. One was severely injured. Another committed the crime of self-injury. There are four new prisoners in the brigade. The total count at this time is forty-one. Two people are still sick in the barracks. The injured prisoner was sent to the hospital. The self-injured prisoner was arrested and is in the isolator. Tomorrow's work force will be thirty-seven." I couldn't imagine the kind of labor that would result in so many deaths and injuries.

As the reports droned on, the commander's head bobbed from side to side. "That's enough," he interrupted. "Go on," he said to several brigadiers after they had barely spoken. At the end of the reports, the drunk, impatient commander and his entourage stepped off the porch and staggered along the line of prisoners. The commander looked into the faces of the men, stepping

---

* Makeshift shoes consisting of leather, canvas, wood, tire tread, or any other material bound to the foot with string.

deeply into the formation as though he were looking for someone special. No one met the commander's gaze.

"You," he shouted, poking a prisoner in the chest. "Speak."

A thin, graying man responded with his name, code, and sentence.

"Speak up. What's your code?"

"KRTD. Fifteen and five." He nervously tugged at the bottom of his dirty jacket.

"Trotskyite," the commander slurred, slapping a baton into his gloved hand. The man seemed to step back in formation, but the commander nodded at two guards, and they pulled the prisoner out into the middle of the courtyard.

"You," he shouted. A prisoner who appeared to be about my age and fresh from freedom stepped boldly up to the commander and recited his code.

The commander walked on. When he came to my row, he chose a young man in the back. "You. Code and term."

The man whimpered the letters more than he spoke them. "KRTD. Ten."

The commander gestured with his baton for the man to step into the middle of the courtyard.

During the two-hour ordeal, the commander chose about ten more prisoners, all with the code KRD or KRTD. KRD signified counterrevolutionary activity; KRTD stood for counterrevolutionary Trotskyite activity. Several guards, restraining dogs on silver choke-chains, led them through the gate and outside the zone. They appeared to be heading toward the commander's and guards' quarters.

No one said a word until we were back in the barracks, where tense but hushed conversations erupted. I crawled onto the bed board and lay on my side with my arm under my head as a pillow. Two prisoners lay down next to me, whispering anxiously to each other.

"I feel like I'm losing my mind. I tremble so hard when I see this animal."

"What are we going to do? I'd rather be shot than go through this everyday."

"I can't stop thinking of killing myself. Only you and Sergei gave me the strength to go on. Now I have only you."

"He was so devoted, a real Bolshevik. What's happening to us, Viktor? What's happened to the ideals we fought for? I'll go crazy unless we make *etap* soon."

At four A.M. the ringing rail sounded for us to get up. Despite my fatigue and the cold, I kept the exercise routine I had followed at home and in the Red Army, washing my face and hands at the hand pump. I wanted to retain as much pride in myself as I could, separate myself from the many prisoners I had seen give up day by day. They'd stop caring first about their hygiene or appearance, then about their fellow prisoners, and finally about their own lives. If I had control over nothing else, I had control over this ritual, which I believed would keep me from degradation and certain death.

Each morning four searchlights lit up the courtyard, shining on the procession of prisoners shuffling between the barracks and outhouse. The evening before I had visited the latrine and, seeing the overflowing holes and the thousands of maggots, decided to wait until we left the camp to relieve myself. The ten or so holes were hardly enough to accommodate the nearly one thousand prisoners in the camp. Prisoners stricken with diarrhea relieved themselves while waiting in line.

I went to the kettles and lined up for my morning ration, which consisted of a ladle full of coarse oatmeal and *paika* weighing five hundred grams. Accusations and cursing burst out behind me: "You steal my bread, you steal my life! I'll kill you! I'll dig your eyes out!"

I heard the beatings and the cries of the accused, but no one paid attention. Another group surrounded a man lying on the ground and kicked him repeatedly—in the head, face, back, stomach. One man aimed for his genitals. The prisoner lay motionless while they shouted, "To a thief, a thief's death. To a dog, a dog's death! You'll die for this, motherfucker!"

A man with feral eyes held his bread in his brigadier's face. "Is this my five hundred grams? Is this my whole portion for the day's work? I want to weigh it. I want to know who's stealing from me. I saw how you gave bigger portions to your friends."

The brigadier pushed him away. "The prick is always thicker in someone else's hand." He turned back toward the loaves of bread.

The prisoner tried to grab the knife, but the brigadier cuffed him hard. The man stopped arguing and walked away, cursing the brigadier, the commander, all of life.

The brigades left the courtyard in numerical order. Outside the camp we stopped by a wooden building to pick up tools, then walked down a newly cleared path into the forest, each of us carrying shovels, handsaws, iron wedges, and sledgehammers. I slipped on the clay and sank into the mud, even though I was wearing my military boots. The stragglers greatly irritated the guards and their barking dogs. *"Davay! Davay! Podtyanis!"** The guards stood on the sides of the path on firmer ground, kicking and hitting with their rifle butts those who slipped and fell. The snapping dogs and shouting guards made us scramble forward. On a hill, an older man slipped and slid backward, taking down three other men. Guards kicked them hard and threatened to shoot them if they didn't hurry up.

I was able to keep pace fairly easily despite my convalescing limbs. After walking for about an hour, we reached a newly paved road. The partially dug ditches were filled with rainwater. My brigade moved on. Where the pavement stopped, wooden planks began. Footprints and wheelbarrow marks meandered in all directions. Pyramids of sand and gravel were piled next to the road. We continued deeper into the forest, the brigades behind ours dropping off at their work sites. The wooden planks stopped where the road was still being cleared of rocks and branches, and logs of equal length were piled high. Several brigades extracted the stumps and roots of the newly felled trees. I was amazed to see that the roots of trees could extend so far out and be so enormous, some of them as thick as tree trunks themselves.

Our work site was at the end of the road, deep in the woods, and we had the longest way to walk. My brigade was assigned to cut down trees and clear out brush; small yellow flags indicated

* "Let's go! Catch up!"

where the trees were to be cut down. The brigades behind ours stripped the trees of their branches and sawed the branches and trunks into pieces. Kovalov told two prisoners to build a fire and gave the rest of us our assignments. I was paired with another young prisoner who looked pale and exhausted. He appeared to be nearsighted, squinting when Kovalov showed us which trees we had to cut down to fulfill the norm for the day. Upon closer inspection, my partner, whom Kovalov called Pike, appeared gangly and childlike, and I was disappointed to have such a weak work mate.

"Get the saw," Pike flatly commanded. I grabbed a saw, and we took up positions around the first tree. The rusted teeth pierced the bark, releasing a bitter scent. I pushed and pulled with all my strength, thinking that the faster we worked, the sooner we'd be done.

"Slow down, idiot!" Pike yelled. His hostility startled me. "Do you want to kill both of us before noon? We work for twelve hours, and we don't eat until we return to camp. Now, follow my rhythm."

Pike knew a lot about cutting down trees. He knew not to cut too deeply into one side but to cut evenly from three sides and to cut so that the tree would fall into an open space. As we got closer to the center of the trunk, the saw became stuck. We pulled it out, and Pike hacked out a wedge with the ax to clear a deeper path.

The most dangerous moment in tree felling came when the trunk lost its connection with the stump. When this happened, the base of the tree often jumped sideways, and you never knew which way it would go. This was riskier than the actual falling of the tree. The thundering and cracking sounded like an approaching storm, and the tree would crash down and strike the forest floor like a bolt of lightning—fast and final.

At noon we had a half-hour *perekur*, or smoke break. Prisoners clustered in groups and smoked *makhorka*, the cheapest, crudest tobacco rolled in newspaper. Others dried ash leaves or weeds in the fire and rolled and smoked them. I never smoked and wasn't about to start. The noon tea was nothing but *kipya-*

tok, boiled water with leaves of various trees added for taste. The dirty brown concoction tasted bitter, but everyone said it had vitamin C, which would prevent scurvy, and I gulped it down.

After a full day of labor I was exhausted, and we still had to make the long march back to the barracks. The route seemed longer and more difficult than in the morning. The light rain that had started in the afternoon was still sprinkling, and the mud and clay were deeper. Each step of my leaden boots sent a searing pain through my twisted back. At the barracks everyone hurried to lie down and rest until the evening meal. Then we had another head count. The commander, drunk as the night before, slapped and hit prisoners at random and selected another dozen or so men to leave with him and his entourage. The fear and anxiety among the prisoners as we walked to the head count filled me with terror. Everyone kept to himself, and I realized something horrible was going on in the camp.

In the darkness of the barracks, a political prisoner lying next to me explained that the commander sought to purge the camp of political prisoners—Trotskyites, Bukharinites, and Zinovievites, all of whom were given the code KRD or KRTD. These acronyms stood for counterrevolutionary activity or counterrevolutionary Troskyite activity. The camp commander felt it was his obligation to finish Stalin's extermination of these traitors, and he made it into a game, trying to distinguish the political prisoners by their faces and leading them off to their deaths outside the camp. No one ever returned, and it was rumored that he didn't simply shoot them.

I soon learned that this was one of the worst camps in the Soviet Union. The hard labor and sadistic commander earned it the nickname *dokhodilovka*.*

Starvation was routine. We weren't given enough food to sustain us throughout one day of hard work, let alone weeks and months. Starving prisoners hunted for mice and rats with sticks and stones. They cooked them on the wood-burning stove and

---

* The place where one reaches the edge. A killer camp.

peeled off the fur before engulfing them. It made me sick to
watch, despite the emptiness in my own stomach. At times I felt I
could eat anything, and I learned from experienced prisoners
how to ease this intense hunger. They pulled out certain weeds
and chewed on their roots, washing them with their saliva and
spitting out the dirt until the grit was gone. I found a few small
roots and chewed on them. Most were tasteless, but some were
so bitter I couldn't swallow them. I found a few wormy mushrooms. They weren't poisonous, and the impulse to eat them was
great, but I couldn't stomach them. Some prisoners ate them anyway, saying the worms provided protein. Gradually I learned that
anything I could chew—even a leaf or fresh twig—gave the illusion of eating.

The evening meal was generally watery soup with pieces of
rotten potatoes, beets, and cabbage. Everyone watched everyone else, hoping to grab something left by a neighbor. I couldn't
help but drink the watery soup in big gulps, but the thick harsh
oats I chewed carefully, pushing them with my tongue between
my clenched teeth before swallowing. I frequently recalled an
image from my childhood: the large garbage bins filled with dis-
carded food from the restaurant below our flat in Wlodzimierz-
Wolynski. The garbage was removed daily by pig farmers, but at
dawn I sometimes spotted vagrants digging through the refuse
and eating it. The first time I saw them I couldn't believe that a
human being could fall so low as to eat garbage. I asked my
mother how this could be, and she told me about the many hungry and homeless people in the world. But, she added, the Communists in the Soviet Union were building a new society where no
one would starve or be homeless.

The rich garbage pile from the restaurant now seemed like a
feast. The camp kitchen lay outside the zone, so the garbage
wasn't available for foraging, but I knew that if I could reach it, I
would dig right in.

Although I became more efficient with the saw, ax, and wedge, the
pain in my back became excruciating. The muscles cramped frequently and unexpectedly, and pain shot through my legs with

every movement. The pads on my palms and fingers blistered and broke; finally thick, tough calluses formed, and I developed the same frozen, claw-like grip I'd seen on the prisoners the first day in the camp. I was frightened that I was approaching the state of exhaustion reached by many other prisoners, who were no longer able to walk. As Pike and I grew weaker, we fulfilled less and less of our norm and received less and less to eat. One afternoon Kovalov took me aside and said, "Let me have your boots. Then I'll put you back on full rations. I'll also give you an extra *paika*, or even two."

My boots were my only treasure. But the sucking in my intestines nearly drove me to eat boiled shoe leather or the bark from a tree, and in the evening I gave Kovalov my boots. In return he gave me extra rations and camp shoes made out of worn leather, with tire tread for the soles.

The weather turned colder and wetter, but no additional clothing or footwear was issued. I still wore the green tunic and pants the NKVD guards had given me, plus the shoes from Kovalov. Coughing, hacking, and sneezing filled the barracks. The only medical care in the camp was provided by the camp's *feldsher*.* This man, also a prisoner, was crude and frequently drunk, with a pockmarked face and bloodshot eyes. It was rumored that he drank the disinfectant alcohol called "Blue Night." When ingested in large doses it supposedly caused blindness or even death, but the *feldsher* seemed to suffer no ill effects. He was the only one who could excuse someone from work; under extraordinary circumstances he could send someone to the hospital at the central camp. There was a limit on how many prisoners he could keep from work or send to the hospital each day, so he essentially had the power to decide life or death.

Many prisoners mutilated themselves in order to escape from the camp and be sent to the hospital. This usually happened at the work site; the ax came in handy not only for cutting wood. One man smashed the bones in his hand with a heavy stone. Another chopped off his toes and half of his foot. A prisoner in my brigade asked another prisoner to cut off all four fingers on his

* Medical assistant.

right hand. Such injuries were considered criminal acts of sabotage, and those who committed them were sentenced to additional time.

For the first two weeks I was in camp I slept next to Stepan Kulikov, a history student from Leningrad. He was infected with tuberculosis, and although he was spitting blood, he wasn't released from work. His eye sockets and cheeks grew more hollow each day. He was aware of what was happening and talked to me with great sadness and despair. Every morning he said as in prayer that maybe he would be called to *etap*. Stepan went to see the *feldsher* twice but was never sent to the hospital, and one day he didn't appear in the evening. I was told that while walking to work, he had stepped out of the column and walked slowly into a nearby field. The guards barked out several warnings, then fired several shots.

During my fifth week I was paired with Vasia, a man about ten years older than me. We worked together for three weeks, and I got to know him quite well. He was tall and muscular and had a pleasant smile on his broad Slavic face. His humped nose and protruding ears made me feel sympathetic toward him.

In 1938 he had been arrested with a group of other students and several professors, all of whom were accused of organizing a Trotskyite cell aimed at overthrowing the government and assassinating members of the Politburo and even Stalin himself. He told me part of his story during breaks, but most of our conversation was carried on at night, when we lay whispering next to each other on the bed board.

Vasia had spent two months in Lefortovo prison in Moscow, where he was beaten daily and denied sleep for weeks. For two months he wouldn't sign a confession, because the entire case had been fabricated. Then his interrogators told him that his parents and younger sister would be arrested as accomplices. Although this was a common practice, Vasia couldn't believe that his father, a leading aviation engineer and devoted member of the Communist Party, would be arrested and falsely accused as he himself had been, and so he didn't relent. But two months later he was shown confessions signed by his fiancée, two close friends, and one of his professors. He signed the confession and was given a KRTD sentence with fifteen years in the camps and five in exile. Forbidden correspondence and contact with the outside world, he didn't know what had happened to those arrested with him.

When we met, he was in good physical condition and had an optimistic outlook on life. He believed he would be out before his sentence was up, repeating again and again that the day Stalin died, all political prisoners would be rehabilitated and freed. I did not share this view. Even though I was beginning to think that many of Stalin's opinions were extreme, I still thought the NKVD and lower-level Party leaders were responsible for the mass arrests, sentences, and executions. And I thought that if only this information could reach Stalin or his close associates—Molotov, Kalinin, or any other Politburo member—the false accusations, arrests, interrogations, and executions would be stopped and many prisoners, including me, would be released.

At noon break one cool autumn day, Vasia and I went to the edge of the clearing with a cup of hot tea to talk in privacy. The ash and maple trees had shed their red and gold leaves, which blew across the dry, hardened ground. My body had conformed to the demands of tree-felling; my chest and arms bulged, my coarse hands had stiffened, my back was permanently bent. My neck and lower back ached persistently, but I no longer experienced excruciating pain.

In the distance a whistle shrieked. Then other whistles blew repeatedly. The guards ordered us to gather immediately near the kettle for a head count. Kovalov bounded into the nearby brush to retrieve anyone wandering out there. Everyone was present in our brigade, but two prisoners from another brigade had escaped. One of our guards took two dogs and joined the search team as they ran past our brigade and into the woods. The other guard aimed his cocked rifle at the lineup and ordered everyone to sit down. We weren't allowed to return to work until further orders were issued from the commander. The guard boasted, "It won't take long before they drag these sons of bitches back, if our dogs don't tear 'em apart first."

The manhunt made me think how desperate my own escape attempt had been. It was painful to wait for the prisoners' capture—the only outcome possible. We were so deep in the forest and so far from any city that they'd never get away. I could almost feel their bursting hearts as they stumbled over bushes and fallen trees. As we sat around the kettle drinking *kipyatok*, no one talked very much. Everyone was silently cheering on the escapees, hoping by some miracle they would succeed, but three hours later whistles blew in the distance, announcing the return of the search party. "I told you," the guard smiled triumphantly. "They got 'em."

Several guards dragged in the two limp bodies. The escapees' faces were unrecognizable, bloody pulps with hanging bits of flesh and hair. The German shepherds had shredded their shirts and pants and limbs. Blood was everywhere on their bodies. The guards threw them on the ground and kicked them repeatedly. One of them still moaned and cried loudly. The other made no sound. Each nerve in my body throbbed, as though I were being beaten all over again.

All brigades were summoned to witness the consequences of trying to escape. The commander got up on a stump and waved his pistol recklessly. "Guards, assemble your brigades. I want an exact count of all the prisoners. Defiance, insubordination, or attempted escapes are punished by the worst possible means—"

A prisoner holding an ax stepped up on a stump and called out, "You cock-sucking murderer! Motherfucking fascist! You've killed so many of us! I'm not going to wait for you!" He swung the ax over his head and rushed toward the commander, scattering prisoners as he went. Several guards fired on him. The commander raised his pistol and shot him in the face. No one moved toward him; the commander walked slowly up to the prisoner, murmuring something, and fired several more times at the man's head. Not a word or breath could be heard. The commander ordered everyone to form a column and return to camp.

That night *poverka* was more terrifying than ever. The commander fired shots randomly into the air. Everyone could feel his murderous craving. Nearby, a prisoner sobbed quietly; the rest of us were quiet, hanging our heads, closing our eyes, trying to travel far away. The commander shot three prisoners in the formation and chose another group to be led outside the gate. Vasia and I linked arms as we walked back to the barracks.

Talk about *etap* with Vasia was never-ending. Every day we both became more exhausted, and the hunger that consumed us grew greater. Days extended into weeks, and still neither of us was called. Every night at *poverka* I worried about him; his political sentence put him in mortal danger, making me feel more desperate for his departure than for mine. But I sensed the limits of my own reserve approaching and was becoming extremely anxious for myself. Then, one morning, my name was called for *etap*.

CHAPTER 8

Siberian Trail

From October 1941 to March 1942 I crossed the Soviet Union, staying in transit prisons along the way for days and weeks at a time, never knowing how long I'd stay or where I'd end up. I memorized the names of the stations we passed or stopped at: Gorky, Kirov, Sverdlovsk, Petropavlosk in Kazakhstan, Novosibirsk, Krasnoyarsk, Irkutsk, Chita, Blagoveshchensk, Khabarovsk, and finally Buchta Nakhodka on the Sea of Japan. I watched the steppes, mountains, and deep forests glide by, trying to absorb as much as I could of a continent I had never dreamed of seeing and feared I would never pass through again.

A dark green Stolypin car, especially constructed for the transport of prisoners, replaced the cattle car of my initial journey. It was attached to a regular commercial train carrying passengers and freight. Compared to the flimsy, vermin-infested barracks at Burepolom, the Stolypin was a royal chamber. It was clean, and every day we swept and dusted it by order of the guards. There was no latrine barrel in the compartment. The Stolypin retained the structure of a passenger cabin, with benches that seated four people and two upper bed boards on each side. The paneled walls were varnished, and each compartment was heated. The only emblems of prison life were the barred windows and barred inner door.

I got a berth on the upper shelf, where I had the luxury of stretching, rolling over, and lying in whatever position I wanted, even when the compartment was packed with ten to fourteen prisoners. The lower two-thirds of the window was painted white so that no one could see in or out, but the upper third, which could be opened for ventilation, wasn't. I could see the countryside and breathe the fresh air when the small hinged window was open. The only discomfort was the heat, but I didn't mind; I stripped down to my underwear.

At the beginning I traveled luxuriously; with only five other prisoners in the compartment, everyone had enough space to lie down. A startling thing happened the first morning. With no explanation or ceremony, we were each given two days' rations of bread and herring and one can of horse meat. As a prisoner I'd never had so much food in my possession, and I divided the loaf of bread and herring into four portions, two for each day. Just smelling and touching the food was an enormous pleasure. The juices in my stomach flowed; I salivated copiously. The temptation to eat everything at once was great. I divided and redivided the food, putting the bread and can of horse meat in my shirt, taking them out, and reexamining them again. When I didn't have food, I thought constantly about how to get it; now that I had it, I thought constantly about how I was going to eat it.

I wanted to prove to myself that I had the willpower to save the food for later. But what was I to do with the herring? Leave it out on the table, where someone could steal it? Prisoners stole other prisoner's food with their eyes, watched it vigilantly to see if someone else got more *paika* or herring. I didn't know what kind of prisoners were with me. They had divided their rations and hid what they didn't eat in small string purses under their shirts. But I didn't have such a purse, and I couldn't keep the herring in the pouch of my shirt. I decided that for my first meal, it would be better to eat the whole herring along with one portion of bread. I began with the head—masticating slowly, sucking out the juice, licking the oil off my fingers. With my tongue I cleaned the flesh off the bones, then ground them into a paste and fervently swallowed.

My hunger hadn't subsided a bit. At Burepolom I would have been more than satisfied with the meal, but the novelty of the horse meat and the heavy clump of bread against my skin made my hunger run wild. I took out the *paika*, smelled it, and put it back. I climbed to the upper bed board and looked out the window, but I hadn't had a full stomach in so long that I couldn't get my mind off the food. "Don't touch it. You need food for tomorrow. Think how you'll feel the next day," I told myself. But how could I think about the next day with the warm bread clinging to my body? I couldn't. I pulled out the can of horse meat and scooped out several chunks with my fingers. The meat and dark brown gravy mixing with the bread inside my mouth assuaged my hunger for the first time in months.

When I got down to half a can of horse meat and two portions of bread, I scolded myself and resolved to wait until noon to eat again. But why should I have to wait? I didn't know if it was better to eat quickly and feel full or expand the time of the feast and let every bite of food linger in my mouth. When you are thirsty, you don't know when to stop drinking; when hungry, you don't know when to stop eating. If I ate everything now, would my stomach realize I had stocked up for the next day and be satisfied? Or would I feel just as wild with hunger tomorrow? I wasn't ready for this trial. After an hour of deliberation, I pinched off a tiny piece of bread and put it in my mouth. Then I pinched off another. It went down much better soaked in the horse meat gravy. When I finished gorging myself, I searched through my tunic for crumbs as though they were diamonds, then curled up on the bed board. The blood flowed to my stomach, and my thoughts scattered like clouds into nowhere.

The next day the hunger returned, but without the sucking feeling. I felt peaceful and secure, something I hadn't felt in months. I was happy not to be working in the forest. Alone on the top shelf, I lay comfortably on my stomach, resting my chin on my hands, and watched the scenery. The train cut across many flowing creeks and rivers, and I imagined how good fishing would be in these uninhabited places. Every year since my eighth birthday, my father had taken me fishing on the Luga River. The trips became a ritual: my mother would prepare eight ham and cheese sandwiches and four hard-boiled eggs and pack two bottles of lemonade and several single-shot bottles of vodka for my father. There had to be a full moon so we could see (for some reason my father thought the best fishing was at night), and we always went to the same place upstream, where the river widened. We'd hide the boat in reeds and cattails, eat the sandwiches, and drink our drinks; then my father would hook the night crawlers, spit on them three times for good luck, and cast the lines as far as he could. He taught me how to hook the night crawlers, but the slimy, writhing bodies gave me shivers. He got me excited by talking about catching northern pike, although I later learned they didn't bite night crawlers.

When I would try to start a conversation, my father would put his finger to his lips and look out at the water. I was forbidden to talk, he'd say, because if the fish heard our voices they would swim away. I used to doze off on the quilt we had laid out on the bottom of the boat while my father smoked and drank the vodka. When I awakened I would look at the stars and the reflection of the moon on the river and listen to the mysterious sounds of the night, feeling both secure and adventurous. We never did catch a northern pike, but the morning after our outings we sometimes went to the local fish market and bought some to take home to my mother.

When we reached the foothills of the Ural Mountains, the train slowed and sputtered, hissed and chugged. I thought we'd have to get out and push. It was late October, and the dark clouds lay so low they nearly touched the treetops. When it wasn't raining I could identify the trees: white birch, elm, acacia, fir, spruce, mountain ash. Fields suddenly appeared through my window, bare and ravaged after harvest or undulating with wild, uncut grasses. Sometimes I could discern a wooden or clay shack built into a crevice. All had straw roofs, and there was no evidence of electricity. Many houses had been boarded up and lay in various stages of decay. I tried to guess which ones had been abandoned and often was startled to discover a shred of clothing or roaming chickens near shacks I'd considered deserted.

How could people live in this wilderness? Rarely did I hear a dog bark or see cows, ducks, or geese. The train swung close to a village of five or six connected shacks. Filthy, coatless, barefoot children, their bellies distended from hunger, threw stones at the ducks and geese. Peasants working in the fields looked as derelict as the hovels in which they lived. On their feet were *laptys*. Their coats were torn and dirty, and they wore shaggy scarves tied under the chin. Two cadaverous oxen foraged alongside the road in the mud. A horse pulling a cart seemed to sink into its own cavernous ribcage.

How different the Soviet countryside was from that in Poland. There the food was plentiful, the wagons sturdy, the horses fit and strong, and the cows plump and numerous. The peasants coming into town for church on Sundays were clean, nicely dressed, and well mannered.

I had thought a socialist state would take care of everyone, that there would be no poverty, that all would have enough to eat, a good place to live, and decent clothes. The land now belonged to the workers and peasants—so why was the countryside so poverty-stricken? The *politruks* had preached in the Red Army that the *kulaks*, well-off peasants who exploited the landless, were considered bourgeois and were therefore exiled or imprisoned. With the peasants now owning the land, why wasn't the countryside thriving? Why weren't the fields burgeoning with oats, rye, barley, and buckwheat? Where were the cattle? Why were the few oxen and horses starving? Perhaps the villages were so isolated that the modern socialist changes hadn't yet reached them.

We were fed two large crackers twice a day and sometimes half a herring. I remained perpetually hungry, but it didn't spoil the journey. Not having to work a single day, I could relax on my bed board, thinking and rethinking my thoughts, or sit on the bench talking to other prisoners. As more prisoners filled the compartment, I became possessive of my place on the top shelf. I got down only to use the bathroom and came back as quickly as possible. Most of the men sat on the benches, immersed in their tales of sorrow, nearly all of them having been recently arrested. The compartment buzzed with nervous questions, speculation, and bravado, but I wasn't interested. It made no difference to me whether I would be mining coal or gold, cutting down trees, or building roads. After Burepolom I'd become fatalistic, living one day at a time. Escape was the farthest thing from my mind. I thought only in terms of what I could do now to strengthen myself mentally and physically. On the upper shelf I did push-ups, pedaled my legs, and flexed different groups of muscles throughout the day. To keep from getting bored and to discipline my mind, I told myself stories. More precisely, I wrote them in my mind, as though I could store them and retrieve them later when I had the resources to write.

Since adolescence I had wanted to become a writer, philosopher, or explorer—anything that would get me out of Wlodzimierz-Wolynski and bring me fame. My peers looked up to me as a leader, affirming my belief that I would achieve great things. I was very ambitious and liked to take charge, and all of this made me feel special. But feeling special came with a price: I felt responsible for taking care of other people. I felt that my friends and family needed me, and as I learned about the poor citizens of Wlodzimierz-Wolynski, I felt obligated to learn how they lived and to help them, too.

The poorest people in my hometown lived in the Jewish district, only one block away from the center of the city. The winding streets leading to the big synagogue were unpaved, and during the rains the gullies overflowed with raw sewage. The stench overwhelmed the Jewish district and permeated my friends' homes, and the waterlogged boards thrown down as sidewalks sank into the muck when walked on. Families of eight, ten, twelve, or more people—usually three generations—lived crammed together in two or three rooms. There was no running water. Sometimes the kitchen, living area, and bedrooms were all in one room.

Some of my friends from the soccer club and the riverbank lived in this area, and I thought it was important to visit them and see how they lived. I found an authenticity in the slums, sensing that I was seen for the kind of person I was, not for the family I came from. I had become an idealist without knowing it; in

communism, I found answers to the troubling differences between rich and poor. I daydreamed that I could help these families by inventing something and becoming a millionaire and giving the money to them. I often imagined myself a hero in different
places and incarnations, making sure that justice came to the
good and needy.

Falling in love with Taubcia added a new dimension to my
views on happiness: in addition to the socialist ideals I was raised
with, I believed love was necessary. If everyone could immerse
themselves in the spiritual life rather than in the material, the
problems of the world would be solved. People would stop
killing each other. Human life would be cherished. There would
be no more crime or war. Taubcia and I and our friends dreamed
of living in a self-sufficient commune where all believed in the
goodness of the heart and helped one another. But now, lying on
the upper shelf of the Stolypin car, I no longer daydreamed of aid-
ing the poor or creating a just world. The object no longer was to
eradicate poverty but rather to survive, to keep the vulnerable—
including me and my family—from being persecuted, tortured,
and killed. I had given up all hope of trying to achieve social justice for all.

Instead, I dreamed of adventure. I decided to begin my writing
career in the Stolypin car, composing the stories in my head and
memorizing them from beginning to end. In most of my plots, I
was an international spy. Disguised as a journalist, I traveled the
world, met politicians and movie stars, mixed with wealthy aris-
tocrats, and uncovered scandals, injustice, and persecution. I
wrote reports for foreign newspapers, drove large automobiles,
sailed in luxury yachts on the high sea, and was surrounded by
beautiful women who fell in love with me. My nickname was
Gray Wolf, and my port of call was Odessa. In other stories I was
an explorer. I mapped the Arctic, explored the jungles of the
Amazon, rode a horse through the American West. Many dangers befell me, but I always escaped because of my charm, clever-
ness, and knowledge of the natural world.

Initially I found inscribing the stories in my mind extremely
difficult. It was hard to keep the twists in the plot straight, espe-

cially the farther along I got. But in the process of creating these tales I often recalled people and moments I had long forgotten. The past became sharper and more meaningful—my relationship with my older brother, for instance. Although I was five years younger than Julek, I felt that he needed my protection. When he was seventeen, a group of Polish Nationalist thugs harassed him in the school yard, and he was ineffectual at warding off their blows. I grabbed a stick and charged at the group, swinging wildly and shouting like a maniac. They backed off and left Julek alone after that. I saw him so clearly now. I had no idea where he was but hoped he was making it through the war.

The more I thought about the characters in my stories, the more I came to understand the restlessness that lay deep in their wandering hearts. The heroes of my stories lived lives of freedom. There were no barriers, no limits, no constraints. Their restlessness kept them moving. But for me, a prisoner, freedom lay on the other side of the grated window, a perpetual reminder of all I had lost and might never get to experience. I rebelled bitterly against being locked in the Stolypin, and I tried to find comfort in the thought that there was some fate I was destined to live out, one that I could influence by using my intellectual, physical, and personal skills. This was the only way I could contain my bitter sorrow.

Early one morning the train blew its horn and began slowing down. Signs on the station buildings read Sverdlovsk. Guards trotted along the platform, and I thought they were getting ready to feed us. A guard unlatched the glass door, slid it open, and bellowed through the bars, *"Gotovsya k vikhodu!"** Ten minutes later the barred doors slid open in the compartments around us and further orders were barked: *"Davay, davay! Shevelis!"*** Out into the cold gray morning, sleet spitting in our faces, we were ordered to squat close to the ground. We remained there for over an hour, being counted again and again. My legs became

---

* "Get ready to leave!"
** "Let's go! Move!"

weak and quivering; my coat got drenched, my body shook, and my fingers, ears, and toes grew numb. Several trucks arrived. Built especially to transport prisoners, they were painted black and called Black Ravens (*chorny voron*). The guards packed in as many of us as possible and slammed shut the iron-barred door, separating themselves from us. Squeezed together in such a small, stifling space, with everyone breathing in each other's faces, the prisoners were volatile. The guards, protected by the iron bars, smoked cigarettes and ignored the fights.

In the Sverdlovsk transit prison, a large brick building overlooking the city, I got a place on an upper bed board and waited to be called for another *etap*. Across from me on the lower bed board, a group of young *urkas* played blackjack. I used to skip school and play poker or blackjack with friends on the riverbank and considered myself a skilled gambler. The *urkas* were playing for food and clothing, and I thought it would be good to try to stock up on some of these things. They talked constantly and didn't seem like they were paying much attention to the game.

I addressed the dealer, a young man with a shaved head, a red bandana tied around his forehead, and two gold crowns on his front teeth—considered chic among the *urkas*. He told dirty jokes and stories as he dealt and smiled incessantly. "Can I play?" I asked.

"Let him in. There will be more at stake," one of the players commented.

Two young men made room for me, and the dealer handed me twenty wooden matches. "Five matches is your sugar or soup. Ten matches is your *paika*. The value of your clothing will be assessed by the condition of each piece," the dealer explained. "Everyone starts with twenty matches. You can buy more from the person who is winning."

The dealer, Vanya, started dealing the cards, which were so flimsy they felt like well-used paper rubles. The red designs were smudged and worn off. The corners were bent, peeling, or missing entirely. My first card was an ace. I was going to be lucky. I could feel it. I put the card down nonchalantly, put five matches in the pot, and extended my hand for the second card. No blackjack—instead, a four. I ended up losing the hand.

In the next several games I was more cautious, betting only a few matches. I won a few hands but lost more. Caught in the heat of gambling, I paid little attention to how much I was losing. My tunic, pants, and boots were gone, along with my next two days' rations, and suddenly the *urkas* demanded that I give up the items right then. Sitting in my underwear, I became angry and even more determined to win. I paid scrupulous attention to the dealer. I didn't notice any tricks, but whoever was dealing always beat me. And anytime I got an ace, the next card was sure to be low. I was down to two matches. At that point I won a small pot. I bought back my shoes and pants from the dealer. I wanted to get everything back from these hoodlums and take away more if possible.

In the next game my first card was ten. My intuition told me I'd get an ace for my next card, so I bet the rest of my matches. The dealer's first card was also ten. My next card was nine. This was my great chance. The dealer, however, came up with an ace of hearts for his second card. As he reached for the matches, I threw my cards down and swept up the pot.

"You cheat!" I roared. I'd drawn the ace of hearts two games before, and it should have been on the bottom of the deck.

One of the *urkas* slammed his fist into my arm, and I let go of the matches. The dealer leaned back and kicked me in the genitals. "Give me back the boots and pants, you little prick." Enraged, I struck the dealer and swung my arms to keep everyone away. Someone came up from behind and threw me between the bunks. The *urkas* pinned me down and pulled off the boots and pants, then kicked me on the back and buttocks.

"Get this dog's prick out of here. And don't forget, you owe us your *paika* today and tomorrow, and your soup and sugar. If you don't pay up, you'll never eat again." I furiously spit the dirt out of my mouth and crawled back up to the bed board.

That evening walking back from headcount, I heard two prisoners behind me speaking Polish, and I asked what was going on in Poland. They were from Lodz and had traveled through Wlodzimierz-Wolynski on their way to the Soviet Union to escape the Nazis. They'd destroyed their documents while traveling through Nazi-occupied territory and were arrested at the Soviet border. But that was all the information I could get before we parted.

Back in the cell, I felt a heavy hand on my shoulder. "What language were you speaking out there?"

I turned around, startled. "Polish."

"Come up to my bed board and let's talk." The man's face was red and pitted, and a deep scar ran down his forehead. He was bald and had a little white mustache just under his nose and wide blue eyes. He pulled himself up to the upper bed board in one swift move, next to the hoodlums, and said, "Come on. They won't bother you." I obeyed. Five other *urkas*, older than the blackjack players, leaned against the wall, waiting to dig into the evening meal.

"What are you looking at? Haven't you seen food before?"

I didn't realize I was staring, begging with my eyes. Wary of getting mixed up with another group of criminals, I wasn't sure how to respond. "I'm coming from Burepolom," I said, hoping to change the subject.

"So you survived with your skin but not your clothes," one of them piped up.

"Where are you heading?" the bald man asked.

"I don't know. Doesn't make much difference."

"You'll care when you get there," said a wild-haired man in a brusque voice. "You might've survived Burepolom, but there are far worse places. Pray you never get sent to Kolyma."

"Never heard of it, and I've got ten years ahead of me, so I don't really care where I end up."

"You'll care when you get there."

"You must be a university student to be spouting shit like that," a young *urka* said.

The bald man took off his shirt. Tattoos covered his pale but muscular arms, back, and chest. A ring of braided snakes was tattooed around his neck, hanging down toward his nipples like a mink stole. "Give him a piece of bread and some lard. Misha, move, make room for him."

Why was this man—the apparent leader of the group—acting so friendly toward me? I felt unsettled, but Misha gave me the bread and lard, and I ate greedily. *Urkas* usually didn't break bread with outsiders. Meals were an important *urka* ritual, and I had heard that allowing someone to eat from the same bowl, or sharing a piece of *paika*, was a rite of initiation into the group. In the barracks and prisons, they kept to themselves, staying close to one another, eating together, playing cards, and telling jokes. There was an established hierarchy. The *pakhan* was the pack leader; his orders meant more than the orders given by the guards. Obviously the bald man with the white mustache was the *pakhan*, but why he'd invited me to eat with them was beyond me.

"Those young thugs worked you over pretty well. They were cheating the whole time, you know that?"

"I thought it was fair and honest—until the end."

A burst of laughter escaped from deep in his chest. His pals laughed just as loudly. "Honesty and fairness don't apply to a pigeon like you. You looked like a sissy sitting in your underwear, but you took it like a man. They got your clothes and food, but you kept going. You would've played until they'd taken your skin. You're hard inside—I like that. But you'd better be careful with *urkas*, especially the young, cocky ones."

He crossed his legs and leaned forward, grabbing a piece of bread and smearing it with lard. When he finished eating, he lit a cigarette with a military lighter, took a few drags, and looked at me inquisitively. "Tell me about the life of capitalists. I've never been abroad. All I've heard and read is that ordinary people are starving while the bourgeois live well. I can see you don't come from a poor family—you've probably been to the university."

They were obviously impressed by the idea, so I went along with it. "I went to the university in Warsaw," I said confidently. "Two years. I wanted to be a writer."

"So tell us how you lived in the great capital of Poland," the *pakhan* prodded.

"In Warsaw I was a student, so I didn't live in opulence. But my family lived well. I wouldn't consider us rich, but we had seven rooms with two porches, a stable, a large garden with fruit trees, and two dogs."

"What are you talking about?" a jowly man asked with his mouth full. "Seven rooms for one family?"

"My father had his office there, and my brother, sister, and I each had our own room. I also had a horse, and when I was fifteen my father bought me a motorcycle."

"Bullshit," the men leaning against the wall grumbled. "Nobody lives like that."

"Your father was a millionaire," said the *pakhan*, who was called Riaboj, or "Pockmarked."

"No, he was a simple dentist in Wlodzimierz-Wolynski. We lived ordinary lives."

"Tell us more about your 'ordinary life,'" another *urka* joined in.

"Every year we went on vacation in the mountains or on the seashore."

"This is a life you see in movies," one man said. "I don't believe a word of it."

"No, I believe him." Pockmarked studied me and thought carefully about what I was saying. "But I'm sure his father was a millionaire."

"Not everyone lived like we did. But hardly anyone was starving." I paused for a moment, not wanting to stir up envy in the group. "There was poverty. There were rich and poor. But I've seen the same or worse in this country."

"There is never justice for all," Pockmarked said knowingly.

"What about the food in Poland? I bet you had really good food." The jowly *urka* was intensely interested and still eating.

If I had learned anything from my previous interactions with criminals, it was that I had to downplay the food we ate in Poland. These descriptions raised the most disbelief, ignited heated discussions, and turned their curiosity into hostility and contempt. Instead I decided to tell them about the social life of an imaginary restaurant in Warsaw, where I'd always hoped to live one day. I dreamed of going to elegant restaurants, wearing a custom-made gray suit with a yellow rose in my boutonniere. I'd drink French champagne and light cigarettes with paper rubles.

In reality, the only nightlife I knew of went on at the restaurant below our flat. But that was enough for me to start talking.

"There was a restaurant in the old city of Warsaw called Blue Velvet," I began. "I'd go there every night to listen to music and dance. There was a special table of women who could be invited to dance, have a drink, or eat a meal with you. They were young and beautiful—"

"These women were whores!" one of the *urkas* exclaimed. "Can't you tell the difference between a lady and a whore? Well, you obviously haven't fucked much."

"I swear, it was perfectly respectable. They were nice girls."

"Right, strange beautiful women you could invite for a drink—"

"Or a fuck!"

"What do you think, we don't know life?"

"I'm sure you know what you're talking about," I said, not wanting to start a fight. "All I'm saying is that their job was to keep single men company at the restaurant. I don't know what they did afterward."

"How young were they?"

"Twenty, twenty-five years old. I don't know. They were young, slender, and had graceful gestures and inviting smiles. They wore long, close-fitting gowns made of silk with low-cut necklines. But they were very mannered and gracious, like they came from good homes."

"I bet if I paid them enough, they'd fuck me."

"None of them would fuck you," Pockmarked retorted. "You have to have style to get a woman like that, and you don't have it."

I watched the men's eyes as I talked. Buoyed by their interest, I fabricated a tragic story about a young dancer who got pregnant, was cast out of her family, and ended up alone in the city. As I spun my tale, the cell became quiet. The crude conversations and arguments subsided. Even the *urkas* who had cheated me had crowded around the bunk to listen. I dragged the plot out for as long as I could, careful not to give too much scenic detail or use too many artful phrases, as these made the *urkas'* attention wane.

At the end of the story Pockmarked slapped me on the back. "You're a great writer! A real *chelovek*.* From now on you are my personal guest at every meal. Vanya," he called to the young *urka* who had cheated me, "get this man's stuff and give it back to him. Everything. And don't touch his food."

The next morning Pockmarked bellowed, "Where's my story-teller?" I climbed up to the bed board and was greeted by the group as an old friend; Pockmarked even shook my hand.

I started another story about my imaginary adventures in the Wild West. I took the plots from some books by Carl May, who wrote while in prison in Germany about Old Shutterhand, Old Surehand, and the Indian chief Winnetou. He'd never been to America. Nor had I. But I talked on and on about the cowboys, In-dians, and women; the desert, mountains, and ghost towns, em-bellishing the stories with all I could make up. Everyone in the cell was interested. Romances, westerns, and spy stories had been banned in the Soviet Union because they didn't contribute to rais-ing social consciousness. The new heroes in Soviet novels were so-cialist revolutionaries, devoted Communists, and, of course, work-ers and peasants. I told story after story, and Pockmarked made sure I was well rewarded with food. I felt like a king with his court.

When it was announced I'd be leaving the Sverdlovsk prison, Pockmarked gave me some advice. "Don't get mixed up with fuckheads." He gripped my shoulder. "If you do get in trouble, use my name. The criminals know who I am, and it might help you. But you'll also need to know my occupation to prove you re-ally know me. I'm a bank robber, and my specialty is in safe-cracking."

Riding in the cramped Black Raven, I felt confident and secure, feelings I'd thought were gone forever. Pockmarked's name was a ticket to security in the *urka* world, and my talent as a storyteller was as valuable as any tool or weapon.

The train snaked back and forth as we descended the Ural Moun-tains. Dense pine forests covered most of the slopes, although a

---

* A real man.

few of the rounded summits were barren. I had looked forward
to going through the large cities of Chelyabinsk and Kurgan, but
they were as dirty and lifeless as the mountain villages. The hundreds of smokestacks in Chelyabinsk churned out a dirty brown
residue that colored the air and stained the buildings.

At the station in Kurgan, as at all the stations, dozens of
women, young and old, sold boiled eggs, raw potatoes, and
chunks of lard to the regular passengers through the train windows. Their faces were lined and deeply tanned, their teeth missing, their coats and shawls shaggy and torn. None of them approached the prisoners' car, except for a group of children who
threw stones and rotten apples at us. It was as if we were invisible.

Leaving the city, I noticed that the pedestrians were as drab as
their surroundings. The women kept their heads and faces covered with shawls, and men walked about in worn-out coats and
hats, hardly looking up or noticing one another as they scurried
down the street. The place hardly resembled what I had imagined
a Soviet city to be—vital and clean with durable buildings and
clothing. After all, wealth was being distributed equally; the
workers were in power; they were in charge of their lives. The
cities were so different from the picture that had been painted by
the *politruks* and propaganda in the Red Army.

Two Pentecostals, a father and son, had joined the compartment. I observed them murmuring prayers together and crossing
their lips before they ate. I asked if they were Catholic. Quietly
and somewhat reluctantly, they replied they were Pentecostal, a
denomination of which I had never heard. I wasn't the only one
to observe their behavior. Two other prisoners sitting on the opposite bench mocked them, calling them "Jesus freaks" and
"little Christs." The praying men ignored the taunts, but the ring-
leaders continued their antics, imitating the Pentecostals' prayer-
ful poses and crossing themselves in obscene places. Then an argument ignited. A military prisoner, who had been silent, accused
the Pentecostals of being cowardly and unpatriotic because they
refused to fight in the war.

In transit prisons, as well as on the train, conversation revolved
mainly around food and women. Arguments and fights erupted

over petty issues because of the limited space—only when sleeping could a person enjoy solitude. Opinions constantly conflicted. Exaggerated claims about one's life and status before prison frequently caused arguments or fights; sometimes it took the entire compartment to separate the combatants. When there were two or three *urkas* in the compartment, they immediately tried to take over. Five or more and the rest of us were under their complete tyranny.

When the name Petropavlovsk appeared on the station buildings, the compartment became agitated. The so-called Petropavlovskyj Isolator was one of the most feared maximum-security prisons in the country. Several seasoned prisoners assumed we'd spend the whole winter here and were frightened of the freely imposed punishments. I didn't know the difference between a maximum-security prison and the transit prisons I had been through, but the nervous talk of my travel companions was contagious; I, too, feared what lay ahead.

A cold wind blew snow into my unshielded face as we walked from the train station to the prison. The streets and rooftops were covered with drifts. Surrounded by robust German shepherds and fur-cloaked guards, the column looked piteous and bedraggled. I'd heard Petropavlovsk was a large city, but the buildings were shabby and only one story high. There were no cars or carriages at the station, not even Black Ravens to transport us.

The cold and the raw wind were crippling. The rubber tire tread on my shoes conducted the cold through my feet and into my legs. My calves cramped, nearly forcing me to walk on all fours. The wind sliced through my tunic and numbed my ears, nose, chin, and fingers. I was nervous about getting frostbite and tried to wiggle my toes even though I couldn't feel them.

As we moved down the street, townspeople started to follow us. It was an odd feeling to have civilians take notice. Most in the entourage were women wrapped in shawls and long heavy coats made out of felt. To my amazement, they began shouting at the guards.

"Fascists!"

"Murderers!"

"Why don't you go and fight on the front!"

"Lazy cowards. Leave these innocent men alone!"

The guards tried to push them away with their rifles. "Fuck off, you old whores! These men are traitors, enemies of the people. They deserve to be shot. Have no mercy on them!"

This enraged the women even more. Most of them were Kazaks—I could tell by their Mongolian features. Raising their fists, they jeered, "Liars! Bastards! Everyone of these men is innocent, just like our husbands and sons!" They began throwing snowballs at the guards. Several shots were fired into the air, and the women backed off several paces but continued cursing and following us. They tossed parcels, bread loaves, and potatoes and bacon wrapped in cloth into the column. One woman removed her shawl and winter coat and gave them to a man who had none. I caught a pair of woven woolen mittens. As we climbed the steep hill to the prison, the women remained at the bottom, shouting, until we had passed through the gate.

The prison was an enormous stone and concrete structure with thick walls and a twenty-foot-high brick outer wall with barbed wire and broken glass on top. The watchtowers overlooking the grounds stood close together. Inside, the cell was packed with prisoners. There were no bed boards, mattresses, or benches—just a cement floor and four walls made of stone. The grated window was partially boarded up on the outside, allowing a narrow beam of light into the cell. A latrine barrel stood next to the door.

I found a spot where I could lean sideways against the wall. The peephole in the door, called the Judas, flipped open, and the guard shouted, "Everyone up. No lying down during the day." Several prisoners lying on the floor, freshly bruised and bloodied, moaned and slowly sat up. I looked around to see if there was a gang of criminals in the cell, but it was nearly impossible to distinguish the various different types of prisoners.

I picked up parts of a nearby discussion about the situation on the front. The Red Army had been retreating during most of the war, and Moscow was surrounded. The war seemed so far away now. Part of me didn't think it mattered anymore, I felt so isolated. Then I thought of my family, caught in the crossfire between Germans and Russians.

An older man wearing an open gray shirt leaned against the wall. His broad shoulders, straight back, and loud voice marked him as a former officer. "I don't think we can defend Moscow," he said. "If the German tanks use the pincer tactic, Moscow will be surrounded on all sides. There will be no way to break through the blockade. Their air force and tanks are more advanced than ours. I'm afraid we let them in too quickly and too deeply."

A young military man stepped toward the officer. He was still in uniform, which meant that this was one of his first prisons. He argued with force. "Napoleon also penetrated quickly and deeply in 1812. He got as far as Moscow. But General Kutuzov and the winter brought him down. Hitler, like Napoleon, has no idea what a Russian winter can do or what the Russian people can endure. We may not have all the modern technology, but we have the fighting spirit and love for the Motherland. I'm sure Stalin's strategy is to lure the Nazis deep inside the country, cut them off, and then watch them die in the winter."

The older man at the window and two others next to him laughed mockingly. "What are you talking about, 'Stalin's strategy'? When did he become a great military leader? He killed our best marshals and generals. Now, with the threat of losing the war, he's finally resurrecting the old cadre from the camps."

The military men argued about the German advance into Soviet territory and the continuing retreat of the Soviet army on all fronts. Despite their arrests, some of them remained staunch Communists and praised Stalin as a genius of military strategy. Others were critical of Stalin but still believed in Communist ideals. The remaining prisoners openly criticized Stalin, his close supporters, and the Politburo.

It was hard for me to understand why, under such grave conditions, so many high-ranking commanders and ordinary military men had been arrested. Were there really so many traitors and spies? At first I thought the NKVD was solely responsible for the arrests of innocent people, but I couldn't imagine the NKVD would arrest high commanders of the military without Stalin's approval. The more I listened to the military prisoners, the more I doubted that Stalin was ignorant of the ongoing mass arrests, especially as we continued to lose the war.

The other thing that puzzled me was how the military commanders could continue to believe that their arrests were mistakes. Was my arrest a mistake? No. The court-martial officials knew what they were doing; they acted with a purpose. They arrested me to set an example for the other soldiers of what happens to anyone who speaks out against the regime. Did these military men really believe in Stalin's goodness, or were they just pretending? I'm sure they had learned that in a large group like ours there would be informers.

I no longer felt a thread of connection with the other military prisoners. I was not a professional military man, and I never fell for the indoctrination and imbecilic propaganda taught in the political education classes. To the contrary, the heavy indoctrination made me despise the military. I despised it even more as I watched these former officers continue to act with smug superiority toward ordinary prisoners, as though they were still of high rank and in commanding positions.

One day a stooped gray-haired man with wire glasses was brought in. He twitched and trembled continuously, and no one could help but notice him. He spent the days roaming from group to group, listening intently to discussions but never participating. One afternoon I found him leaning against the wall next to me. His hands shook, and he constantly scratched his body, ran his hand over his hair, and blinked his eyes. Although he stood beside me, he didn't talk. Of all the prisoners in the cell, he was the only one who appeared to be Jewish.

I could spot a Jew anyplace. I had learned to do so in Poland, where Jews had to recognize each other as a matter of security and survival. I looked not for the stereotypical dark hair and eyes but rather for a discerning, inquisitive look and an outwardly calm appearance mixed with an inner nervousness. When I encountered these qualities, I knew I could approach the person and get a response. My father made me aware of this affinity among Jews, and it was reinforced when I transferred from the Polish to the Jewish gymnasium at the age of sixteen.

After looking me over furtively, he whispered, "Are you Jewish?" I nodded. "You know, it's best not to make it known that you are Jewish," he said. I already knew this. Many guards and prisoners were anti-Semitic, and the *urkas* loved to intimidate the physically inferior Jewish intellectuals. As for myself, my dark hair, long face and nose, and narrow-set gray eyes made my Jewishness easily recognizable, and my whole life I'd been on the lookout for trouble by anti-Semites.

"Are you political?" he asked. I briefly told him my story, then listened to his. "I spent five years building the Belomor Canal. But I was an actor in the Jewish theater in Moscow. One night we were all a little drunk, telling stories and joking, and I told a joke about Beria. I thought it was a good one. But the investigator didn't think so." He talked rapidly and smiled, as if he enjoyed telling a good story. He mimicked Beria's heavy Georgian accent and did an impersonation of him.

Elia was one of the large number of political prisoners known as "jokers." All had been sentenced for one thing—telling a political joke. Jokes about Stalin or any other member of the Politburo were considered subversive and punished with three- to ten-year sentences.

"I finished my five-year term four months ago," Elia continued, "but now I'm being investigated again. My poetry got me in trouble. Several of my poems were stolen. The next time I saw them they were on the interrogator's desk." He continued talking in the same swift, rambling manner. There was nothing I could say, as his fear of interrogation ignited my own irrational fears of being interrogated.

The nights at Petropavlovsk reminded me of the night in the prison in Gomel, lying on the bare floor, swathed in the body heat and communal odor of my cellmates, smelling the putrid breath of the person behind me and feeling the sweat, hair, and dirt of the prisoner in front. I felt weary and hostile. Gone were my timidity and revulsion.

That night Elia squeezed in next to me to sleep. His body was trembling. In the middle of the night I awakened to a guard's voice calling out names. Elia's was among them. The men were ordered to go into the corridor. Elia went stiff, then got up. It was just as he had anticipated. I began shaking, as though I had been ordered to rise myself. In the morning the door opened, and Elia and another prisoner were shoved into the cell and crumpled to the floor. Their eyes were bruised and swollen. Blood stained their shirts. "I signed everything," Elia whispered as I tried to make a place for him next to the wall. "And they still wouldn't let up on me." His voice sounded as though it came through a tunnel—hollow, faint, far off.

The NKVD had elevated beating to an art. If political prisoners didn't confess quickly enough to suit the interrogators, guards burned them with cigarettes, inserted needles under their nails, or pulled their nails out altogether. Those who resisted were clubbed, kicked in the genitals, or beaten until their bones were broken. Interrogations could last for days and nights without end, with bright lamps shining in the prisoners' eyes to keep them awake. Some said that the sleepless nights, when they were forced repeatedly to tell their story, were as torturous as the savage beatings. Any mistake or inconsistency was followed by an interrogator's rage. "You're lying! Yesterday, you told me you met Jakovlev in December 1935. Now you tell me you knew him since September 1933. So you were already plotting for two years, and now you're trying to deceive me."

Sometimes prisoners I hadn't seen before entered the cell alone and at odd hours. They looked half-alive and could hardly walk. Weak, emaciated, mumbling nonsense, sometimes crying, they were returning from the isolator, a special punishment chamber reserved for serious crimes and infractions.

I'd never forget the beatings I received after my attempted escape. The experience was so fresh in my mind, I was afraid the authorities would find some reason—or no reason—to do it again. I became obsessed with the thought that with every opening of the door, my name would be called. I tried to reason with myself that since I had already been sentenced and that unless I did something wrong, I wouldn't be interrogated. But it was impossible to rid myself of the fear, especially hearing the muffled screams in the corridor. I obsessed that somehow my attempted escape would be brought to someone's attention and interrogation would begin. I'd be accused again of treason and sentenced to death.

Each day after breakfast we were taken for a walk in the inner yard. We walked briskly in single file with our hands clasped behind our backs, our heads hanging to avoid looking at the watchtowers, guards, and German shepherds. Talking was forbidden during the two laps around the yard and in the corridor. Sometimes after the walk prisoners didn't return to the cell. For a while the disappearances were a mystery. Then one day a rumor circulated that there were informers.

Three times a day we were taken to the bathroom, a large room at the end of the corridor. It had an antechamber with ten sinks and faucets. The inner sanctum had ten holes in the cement floor. The guards remained outside, and so the bathroom became the social hub and market for the prisoners. In the cell we could not talk too loudly for fear of being overheard. But in the unsupervised toilet prisoners could talk, scheme, trade food and tobacco, and plot or take out revenge.

The very day that the rumor circulated about the informers, a group of *urkas* surrounded a military prisoner, literally catching him with his pants down. *"Stukach!"* they yelled in his face.* The *urkas* grabbed the man by the arms, turned him upside down, and dunked his head in the hole. "Admit it, or you'll go in again!" The man didn't say a word. After several dunkings, they let him go. Back in the cell, he was still arguing his innocence. The next day he disappeared after the courtyard walk.

For days arguments flared: was he an informer or not? I never found out. I was called for *etap* at the end of November.

* "Informant!"

CHAPTER 9

Buchta Nakhodka

My next stop was Novosibirsk. One of the busiest transit prisons, it held several thousand men. From here prisoners were sent north by boat up the Ob or Yenisey rivers to uninhabited areas, land rich with natural resources. Labor camps were scattered throughout the wilderness; one of them was in Kolpashevo, Narym, the area where Stalin had been in exile.

My barracks housed at least five hundred prisoners and had no windows; the air was stale and heavy, and the chatter deafening. I couldn't find a place to sit or lie down, which drew the attention of the *urkas* and irritated the prisoners sitting on the floor. "The only space left is under the bed boards!" they hollered, kicking me as I passed. I tried to keep my gaze averted but attracted more and more hostile stares, any one of which could lead to a beating.

At last I heard two men speaking Polish. Their legs dangled down from the second tier, and I introduced myself, saying I was a newcomer looking for a place. The men let me slip in. They'd been in Novosibirsk for three weeks and were still waiting to hear their final destination.

Josef was the uncle of the younger man, Bruno. They'd both been in the publishing business in Krakow, but after the Nazi invasion they fled to Lvov. In 1941, when the Nazis took over the city, they followed the retreating Red Army all the way to Kiev. There they were arrested for counterrevolutionary propaganda and given ten-year sentences.

"We weren't used to keeping our mouths shut," Bruno explained. "We talked all the time—about the miseries under Soviet occupation, the persecution of Jews, the special privileges enjoyed by the Party and NKVD."

As we sat in our underwear in the hot, reeking barracks, I listened to my new friends discuss translations of Anatole France into Polish and Meterlinck's book *The Life of Ants*, in which he makes analogies between insect and human societies. I was enthralled. Not a single word was wasted on frivolous talk or bravado; not once did they complain about the miserable conditions. In their presence, my storytelling skills seemed trivial.

A few days later they were gone, both called for *etap*. We hugged and wished each other luck, and then they disappeared into the throngs of ragged men. All leave-takings were that way, no matter how well you'd gotten to know the other person: abrupt and unemotional.

My turn for *etap* came a little while later, and I was on my way again. The train chugged slowly eastward, and into my view from the top bed board came a beautiful hilly landscape and a deep blue lake. It lay in the deepest valley, and I brightened with the recognition that it was Lake Baikal, the deepest lake on earth, more than a mile deep. As we got closer I saw ships and fishing boats on the lake and people on sandy beaches. My heart ached at the sight.

By the time we reached Irkutsk, the possible destinations were dwindling, and by Khabarovsk we who remained in the car knew we were destined for Kolyma. Although I'd heard enough frightening things about the camps in the region, I still didn't know what to expect, other than the fact that it was cold. I remained strangely calm.

Imprinted in my memory are the buildings and names of train stations. The most memorable—and the only one that brought me delight—was that in Birobidzhan, the main city of the Jewish Autonomous Region. A sign called out the name in both Cyrillic

and Yiddish. The train station was small and shabby, which surprised me. Although Birobidzhan had been carved out of virgin
jungle on the Bira River, I had imagined it to be a burgeoning industrial and cultural center. The Jewish Autonomous Region,
created in 1934, had been praised as a solution to Jewish independence outside of Palestine, and during the Soviet occupation
of Wlodzimierz-Wolynski I toyed with the idea of going there to
help build a Jewish socialist state. I felt sad to be so close to what
could have been my future and couldn't stop thinking about what
my life would have been like had I gone.

With the steppes far behind, the hills became mountains and
the fields became forests. The train cut across large, nameless
rivers carrying chunks of ice and snow from distant locations. We
spent long intervals on the sidetracks in Chita, Blagoveshchensk,
and Khabarovsk. Over the days and nights I began to see the Soviet Union through the eyes of the many people I had met. The
stories of false accusations and arrests of family members—including children, aging parents, distant relatives, and friends and
acquaintances—forced me to reassess my youthful impressions of
the Soviet state, the Communist Party, and most of all the Soviet
system of justice.

The prisoner lying across from me on the other shelf, Aleksy
Mitrofanov, a native of Novosibirsk, had been a chairman of a
collective farm and a member of the regional party executive
committee. The Party was his religion; Stalin, his god. Mystified
by his arrest, he talked to himself out loud, asking questions to
the walls, puzzling out the sequence of events. He'd been given a
twenty-year sentence for conspiring to overthrow the state and
for economic sabotage, the meaning of which he could barely understand. The NKVD official who arrested him, his wife, and son
had been a friend for many years.

"I swear I had no enemies," he said. "Everyone was my friend.
For years I fed the Party and NKVD officials with farm products
when the stores were empty."

"So what happened?" I prompted.

"Well, the farm didn't fulfill the plan. But on the books," he
shook his finger excitedly, "the plan was fulfilled over 100 per-

cent." He snorted. "And each inspector from the regional center was treated very well."

He rambled about fishing trips and parties he'd been invited to by the high regional officials. The only conclusion he could come to was that two student interns from Moscow—"brainwashed zealots," he called them—believed the propaganda in the newspapers and radio and denounced the leadership of the collective farm, including himself. "I know they were Jewish. I could smell them."

"*Smell* them?"

"Well, they didn't have humped noses or Yiddish accents. Moscow wouldn't send one of them here. They looked normal, but I knew they were Jews because of what they did to me. When they arrived, I treated them like my own children. Then they betrayed me. Only a Jew would do that."

Although Aleksy bragged about being a political prisoner, trying to impress me with his code of 58.8 and 11, he knew nothing about politics. He was a simple-minded fraud.

Political prisoners were not simply arrested and sentenced as individuals but were usually alleged to be members of some organized counterrevolutionary group. I learned that investigators fabricated not only individual cases but group conspiracies; Stalin's belief that no enemy of the people acted alone was well known. "Where there is one, there are many," he was fond of saying. "Conspiracies must continually be exposed."

Changing from one transit prison to another, I encountered prisoners of all ages, nationalities, professions, and beliefs. In the process, I began to learn the articles and sections of the criminal code. A prisoner's code could provide important information about the type of person he was. Someone with a code of 59 had been found guilty of committing murder or causing great bodily harm; a person sentenced under code 72 was a petty thief or burglar. Of course, the prisoner was not necessarily guilty of the crime indicated by his sentence and code.

The most common code among political prisoners was 58, with numerous subsections referring to everything from counterrevolutionary agitation and propaganda to espionage, sabotage, assassination, and group conspiracy. My code, 193.1.B, stood for wartime treason while serving in the military.

Depending on the code, the sentence might include additional articles granting or denying various privileges, such as visitation or receipt of mail, food, and clothing. Prisoners sentenced under article 58 were usually denied privileges, while criminals (except for murderers, rapists, and counterfeiters) were usually granted all privileges save visitation.

Most political prisoners were not criminals at all but rather were people like my brother, whose political and philosophical views marked them as enemies of Stalin's regime. Strangely, socialists were more despised than members of right-wing parties; Stalin feared they would sway the proletariat away from communism. Many people blindly dedicated to the regime, as well as people who knew nothing about politics, were randomly arrested and sentenced simply to perpetuate terror and paranoia. This was Stalin's primary means of keeping the citizens under control.

The train unloaded at Buchta Nakhodka, the holding pen for the thousands and thousands of prisoners awaiting the last leg of their journey north—through the Sea of Okhotsk to the labor camps in Kolyma. The voyage could only be undertaken when the ice had thawed on the sea. I arrived in Buchta Nakhodka in March. The next ship going north wouldn't be until May.

I was assigned to the Polish barracks, which were encircled by a barbed-wire fence, creating a prison within the prison. My joy at hearing the Polish language quickly turned sour, however, as I lay on the lower bed board next to the door listening to my fellow prisoners.

"Captain Wygodzki, may I borrow your tin can? I'm thirsty."

"Colonel, it would be an honor to share the same can with you." Several men hunched over the stove, clutching beat-up tin cans and looking hungrily at a pot of boiling water.

"Governor Stepniewski! Your tea is ready. Shall I bring it to you?"

"Mr. Jasinski, you needn't bother yourself with my tea. I'll be with you as soon as I find my scarf." The governor rummaged through his rags and produced a filthy piece of cloth. He wrapped it carefully around his neck and tucked the dangling ends under his tunic.

Although I was accustomed to the social formality of my culture, I found this pretentious display disgusting. That my compatriots continued to ape the exaggerated manners of Polish society in the stinking barracks, where all of us lived worse than animals, was ridiculous and idiotic, symptomatic of all that was wrong with the culture I had come from. I wanted to remain as far away as possible from these self-important prisoners, but I was freezing in my place by the door. Every time it opened a draft blew in, and after a couple of hours I couldn't take it anymore. I got up and walked over to the stove. The conversation I wandered upon there made me want to turn and run, but curiosity got the better of me.

"Mr. Bogucki," said a man with greasy gray hair and beard stubble. He had a high forehead, long face, and intelligent blue eyes. His woolen suit coat, now stained and threadbare, still held its shape and conveyed its former elegance. "I wonder how, as a member of parliament, you could have allowed such a strong Nazi influence in the press and universities? I think the students' behavior toward Jews in the universities was excessive and improper. The police didn't intervene, as you know, and I was one of the few professors to defend the students."

Mr. Bogucki twiddled his fingers continually while looking at the floor. On occasion he looked up, glared sidelong at his opponent, and checked the faces of the people listening.

"Professor Jaworski," Bogucki responded, "your name is very well recognized all over Poland. I'm highly honored to meet you in person. I like your ideas, but I don't like all the things you've done. As an active member of the National Democratic Party, I supported close ties with Germany. In essence it was an anti-Semitic party, but I was always against physical assault. My idea was to demonstrate our superiority over the Jews by economic sanctions and success in business and industry. This is why I liked your ideas of industrializing the country. But I did not approve of your getting up in the Auditorium Maximum at Warsaw Univer-

sity and defending Jews and Communists. The reprimand you delivered to our patriotic students was against the best interests of
our country."

A tall blond man wearing military fatigues laid his hand on
Bogucki's shoulder. "As a merchant and factory owner, I couldn't
agree with you more. The first step toward the destruction of our
country was giving equal rights to Jews. If they come into power,
we'll be the first to be dispossessed and thrown into prison. I
hope the professor now realizes the cancer this group is to our
society. We've got three and a half million Jews in Poland—more
than in any other country in Europe. We gave them too much
freedom. We were too tolerant of their scheming and cronyism.
No wonder so few banks and businesses are in Polish hands."

The others nodded or mumbled in agreement.

What a shock to be in the same barracks with the very people
who had encouraged anti-Semitism in Poland, even before the
Nazis arrived. These men were pleased when Jewish businesses
were destroyed, when Jewish students were beaten, when synagogues were burnt.

"So what do you want?" The professor glared at Bogucki and
his blond military supporter. "What do you want—to exterminate the Jews? To support the Nazi policy? What's your idea?
Throwing Jewish students off the balconies at the universities
didn't teach our students Christian morality or ethics. I consider
myself a good Christian," he said, straightening up, "and I believe that a human being is a human being no matter what his religion, skin color, or heritage."

An emaciated prisoner joined the circle. He wore the remnants
of a Polish officer's uniform. "Professor, your idea of treating
Jews the same way we treat every other citizen in the country is
preposterous. I commanded a large army unit, and I can tell you
that Jews are totally unfit for the military. They lack the bravery
of the Polish officers. I did everything I could to keep them out of
my battalion. They never would have sacrificed their lives for our
country."

"What about you?" the professor retorted. "You didn't sacrifice your life—if you did, you wouldn't be here, along with thou-

sands of other Polish soldiers and officers. It's not only Jews who didn't sacrifice their lives but many Poles as well."

"I beg your pardon." The words exploded from the officer's mouth. "Are you accusing me of cowardice? Are you saying I left my soldiers and gave up voluntarily? Are you? I fought for as long as I could, and I retreated according to the orders of the Polish High Command."

"Don't talk about the orders of the High Command," a newcomer joined in. He wore a dirty gray uniform, the color of the Polish air force. "The High Command stopped acting the second week of the war. It was in total disarray, everyone running away to Romania to save his skin. And Marshal Rydz-Smigly led the pack of cowards, and he made sure they didn't leave without first stealing the national treasury."

"Who are you to offend the honor of the Polish soldiers whose bravery is known all over the world?" the army officer shouted. "If we were in Poland, you would pay with your life for this slander."

"Shut up," the air force member said, exasperated. "I'm sick of listening to well-groomed officers whose bravery is only with women. Shut up and stop making threats. This isn't an army barracks, and we aren't your soldiers." He got close to the officer's face. "If you want to fight, fight me. Leave the old professor alone. He's the only one who makes any sense."

The professor slipped between the two men. "Let's stop arguing. This isn't the time or place." His low-key voice calmed the group. The men drifted back to their bed boards or over to the water barrel.

I went back to my place on the bed board and lay down. Before the war started, I had believed in the myth of Polish heroism. I thought Poland would defend itself admirably against the Nazis and put up a good fight, if not prevent the invasion. But to my surprise the Polish army folded in three weeks. There was no national uprising, no coming together to defend the country. The Poles liked to boast about what proud, fierce fighters they were, but after listening to the talk in the barracks I doubted their heroism and nobility more than ever. The anti-Semitism I had tried to understand for so long began to make sense as I lay on the bed board thinking. Rather than discuss what was happening to their beloved homeland and what could be done to save it, the Poles continued to seethe and sneer at the Jews. Their patriotism was based on glories of the past; the only battle that consumed them was the easy, harmless one against Jews.

I felt more vulnerable than ever. Although I tried not to meet anyone's eyes, I caught a few cold stares while standing in line to get my *paika*. I was sure other prisoners suspected that I was Jewish. My hair was dark, my nose rather long, my eyebrows a bit bushy. But I was raised in an assimilated family. We considered ourselves to be as Polish as our neighbors. I didn't know if there were any other Jews in the barracks—I didn't have the courage to walk around and find out—but I worried about being harassed or attacked by some lunatic anti-Semite. Everyone was on edge just looking for a fight. I felt like a hunted animal. Wanting desperately to get out of the Polish zone, I faked stomach cramps one morning and asked the guard to let me go to the ambulatory clinic.

A counter divided the large clinic in half. Behind it was a desk, several small tables bearing an array of flasks, and shelves filled with crucibles of all different sizes. The smell of drugs and disinfectants brought back memories of my father's office.

The doctor sitting behind the desk had thin white hair and appeared to be my father's age. He looked healthy, smiled pleasantly, and asked about my complaints. I told him I had severe stomach pain, which I knew was from hunger, and asked for tincture belladonna or tincture opium.

"So you already know the diagnosis and the treatment?" He seemed pleasantly surprised. He invited me to lie down on the couch and examined my stomach.

"I'm full of lice," I warned him.

He paid no attention and pressed on my abdomen. "How do you know this terminology?"

"I was a medical student before the war."

"Really? Where?"

"In Poland, at the Warsaw University."

"How far did you advance—the first or second year?"

Afraid of exaggerating too much, I said, "Only the first. I was ready to begin the second when the war started."

He finished examining me, but the conversation continued.

"What were you sentenced for?" I told him my article and code. Prisoners waiting in line opened the door to see what was going on. "Go to the back behind the storage shelves," the doctor said. "There's some soup you can eat. We'll talk later."

Beside myself with gratitude, I grabbed his hand and tried to kiss it. He pulled it back. "Don't ever grovel," he said.

"Doctor, I'm in the Polish zone. It's terrible there. Please, help me get out."

He patted my arm and sent me to the storage room.

I filled my stomach, then fell asleep on the floor. I was awakened some time later by an older man. "Dr. Semyonov wants to talk to you."

The doctor greeted me in his office and asked, "How would you like to be my night watchman? Our watchman left yesterday on *etap*, and I'm looking for a replacement." I nodded enthusiastically. "Good. I'll inform the guards that you won't be returning to your barracks. The job requires that you stay awake all night to make sure no one breaks in to steal medicine. If there is an emergency, you must wake me up. You'll be assigned to sleep in a nearby barracks for workers. My *feldsher*, Osipov, will take you to the bathhouse for delousing."

My new job brought a degree of security and luxury I hadn't known since before my arrest. For the first several days no amount of food was brought from the kitchen that I couldn't engulf at once—a loaf of bread, half of a bucket of beet and potato soup, a bowl full of coarse oats with pieces of shredded whale meat. In no time at all I gained weight and regained my strength. On occasion Dr. Semyonov asked me to test the food in the kitchen. The tester was to write an evaluation of the food and the performance of the cooks in a special book. The cooks were *urkas*, Dr. Semyonov warned me, so I had to choose my words carefully.

1. Ottylia and Mark Bardach with Natan Neuding, my maternal grandfather. Odessa, 1919. Author's collection.

2. Ottylia and Mark Bardach with Julek, age nine, and Janusz, age four. Wlodzimierz-Wolynski, 1923. Author's collection.

3. Rachel Bardach, my sister, age fifteen. Wlodzimierz-Wolynski, 1939. Author's collection.

4. This memorial plaque, dedicated to Professor Jakov Julievich Bardach, my father's uncle, hangs at the entrance to the emergency service at the teaching hospital in Odessa. 1970. Author's collection.

5. With Taubcia Stern on Farna Street. Wlodzimierz-Wolynski,
1937. Author's collection.

6. With Taubcia on the riverbank during the summer of 1938.
Author's collection.

7. Skating with friends in Wlodzimierz-Wolynski during the
winter of 1939. Author's collection.

8. Billy, my German shepherd, in the garden of my home in
Wlodzimierz-Wolynski. Author's collection.

9. Ruins of Urchan labor camp, Kolyma. Isolator at lower left.
1991. Courtesy Alexander Togolev.

10. Ruins of the isolator at Butugychag labor camp, Kolyma.
1991. Courtesy Alexander Togolev.

11. Watchtower and remains of the barbed-wire fence at Urchan
labor camp, Kolyma. 1991. Courtesy Alexander Togolev.

12. View from isolator cell window at Butugychag labor camp,
Kolyma. 1991. Courtesy Alexander Togolev.

13. The remains of a uranium mine in the mountains of Butugy-chag near the Yst' Omchug labor camp, Kolyma. 1995. Courtesy Tomasz Kizny.

14. Remains of the barbed-wire fence at the Yst' Omchug labor camp, Kolyma. 1995. Courtesy Tomasz Kizny.

15. Remains of uranium and stenum mines at the Yst' Omchug labor camp, Kolyma. 1995. Courtesy Tomasz Kizny.

16. Prisoners at a logging camp retrieving logs from the river. 1933. Courtesy Tomasz Kizny.

17. Prisoners transporting gold ore. Note the wheelbarrow run-
ners. 1995. Courtesy Tomasz Kizny.

18. Remains of Sopka gold mining camp in Butugychag, Kolyma.
1995. Courtesy Tomasz Kizny.

19. Prisoners building the Belomor Canal. 1931–1933. Courtesy
Tomasz Kizny.

20–21. Release document dated June 9, 1945. Author's collection.

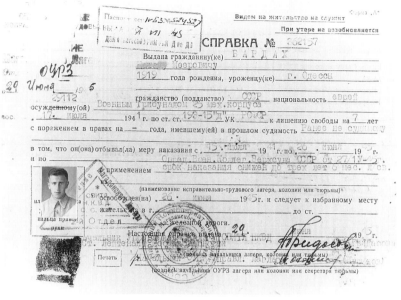

Форма "А"

Паспорт се... №... №...
Выдан ... 7 VI 45
Док о ... Дно дз

Видом на жительство не служит

При утере не возобновляется

СПРАВКА № 362157

Выдана гражданину(ке) _____ Мееровичу _____ БАРДАХ

1919 года рождения, уроженцу(ке) г. Одессы

гражданство (подданство) СССР национальность еврей

осужденному(ой) Военным трибуналом 25 мех.корпуса

17 июля 194 1 г. по ст. 193-15"д" УК РСФР к лишению свободы на 7 лет

с поражением в правах на — года, имевшему(ей) в прошлом судимость Ранее не судимую

в том, что он(она) отбывал(ла) меру наказания с 15 июля 19 41 г.по 20 июня 19 г.

и по Опред.Воен.Коллег.Верхсуда СССР от 27/IV-

с применением срок наказания снижен до трех лет 6 мес. л.св.

(наименование исправительно-трудового лагеря, колонии или тюрьмы)

освобожден(на) 20 июня 1945 г. и следует к избранному месту

жительства в г. _____ до ст.

Отдел _____ железной дороги. 20

Настоящая справка выдана _____ июня 19 г.

Печать

(подпись начальника лагеря, колонии или тюрьмы)

(подпись начальника ОУРЗ лагеря или колонии или секретаря тюрьмы)

Выдано продовольствие на _____ суток с _____ 194 год

Выдано денежное пособие в сумме рублей _____

(прописью)

Выдано денег на питание в пути рублей _____

(прописью)

Выдан билет на проезд от ст. _____

до ст. _____ железной дороги

стоимостью рублей _____ или деньгами на билет в сумме _____

Возвращено личных денег в сумме р 3000 = две тысячи два

07/08

(подпись начальника ОУРЗ или секретаря тюрьмы)

Начальник финчасти _____

Подпись освобожденного Бардах

выдаче продуктов и денег в пути следования

Штаб ВОХР
СВИТЛ НКВД
Принят 5/III 1945 г.
Подпись Агаф...

Штаб ВОХР
СВИТЛ НКВД
Пакет 194 г.

Штаб ВОХР
СВИТЛ НКВД
3/III 1945 г.
Подпись Агаф...

Дата и подпись лица, производившего выдачу _____

Расписка освобожденного _____

1620

Дорогой любимый братик!

Письмо твое получил которое ты выслал 6/VIII. Очень рад, что и тебя уже все в порядке. Я хлопотал по твоему делу в Москве и думаю, что это тоже помогло.

Получаешь ли ты переводы денег, которые я тебе посылаю через родных? Теперь я посылаю тебе справку на основании которой ты должен заявить о желании перехода в польское поддансьво. Я очень хотел-бы, что бы ты возможно скорее переехал в Лодзь, где у меня хорошая квартира и где ты мог бы учиться в стоматологическом институте, но открылся в Лодзи. Надеюсь, что смогу тебе помочь приодеться и устроиться на учебу или работу.

И так прошу сделай все для приезда. Жду тебя единственный мой с нетерпением. Крепко целую тебя Юлик

22. A letter from Julek. December 1945. Author's collection. It reads as follows:

Dear Beloved Brother,

I received your letter which you sent on 6/XI/45. I am very happy that everything is all right with you. I have intervened on your behalf in Moscow, and I think that maybe this will help [you to leave Kolyma].

Did you receive the money I sent to you through our relatives? Now I am sending you a document which will be the basis for making an immediate request to change your citizenship back to Polish. I would like very much for you to come as soon as possible to Lodz where I have a good apartment and where you could attend the Stomotological Institute, which opened recently. I hope I will be able to help you get some clothes and help you study or find a job.

And so I am asking you, do everything you can for a speedy arrival. I am waiting for you, my only one, impatiently.

Kiss you very much,

Julek

23. Julek Bardach as a colonel in the Polish army. 1945.
Author's collection.

24. With Julek, a colonel in the Polish army and military attaché, at the Polish embassy. Moscow, 1947. Author's collection.

25. Nikolai Rafaelovich Piasetsky. Moscow, 1947. Author's collection.

26. In one of Julek's uniforms altered for civilian purposes.
Moscow, 1947. Author's collection.

It wasn't difficult to write a good report, though. The food served to the tester was of a much higher quality than that given to the prisoners—freshly baked rolls with raisins, scrambled eggs, fried sausage, sugar, and jam. The table was laid with a white tablecloth, clean napkin, and silverware. The manners I'd been raised with came back naturally; I felt like a judge in a gourmet contest.

Dr. Semyonov and I lapsed into conversation whenever we were together, never running out of things to talk about. He never complained about his sentence or the charges brought against him, which were completely fabricated, but instead pondered the essence of human nature. "How can people become so indoctrinated and deprived of humanity that they advance their own career by ruining the lives of innocent people?" he asked again and again. He was interested in my father's practice in Poland, and he gave me advice on how to survive in Kolyma. "You must avoid work in the mines," he warned. "Try to get a job in the hospital as a *feldsher* or an orderly. Use my name. Some doctors up there might know me, since everyone passes through Buchta Nakhodka."

Dr. Semyonov taught me the basics of medicine so I could pretend to be at least a third-year medical student and maybe get work as a *feldsher*. He gave a great deal of his time and patience to his most desperate patients, saying he was happy to be a doctor so he could help those who suffer. "A good word, a warm touch, a piece of bread, a cup of soup, a day free of work—these little things may allow a person to live one more day. This is how I was saved when I was building a road in the taiga, and I'll do the same for others for as long as I can."

When Osipov was transferred to another camp, I took over his responsibilities, becoming Dr. Semyonov's righthand man. I changed dressings, distributed medicine, and gave subcutaneous injections. I also took over Osipov's cot in the supply room. From there I witnessed how Dr. Semyonov dealt with the *urkas* who demanded narcotics. "Live and let live," he said when I asked him why he gave them drugs. "Never take advantage of a fellow prisoner no matter what you can gain or how insignificant it might seem. If you let the people below you live, the people above you will let you live."

Before meeting Dr. Semyonov, I had forgotten how it felt to be warm, to shave, to be free of lice, to have decent clothes, to have enough to eat. He made sure I got new and clean prison garb, camp shoes, and a warm, quilted jacket, and he gave me a civilian shirt, which I thought was elegant and which I wore in the evenings. Meeting him changed everything.

One day, out of the blue, I was assigned to work as a night *feldsher* in the hospital zone. I reported to the doctor in charge, a plump, smiling, round-faced young woman named Valentina Sergeyevna Popugayeva, a graduate from the Moscow Medical Institute. She volunteered to work in the system of northwestern labor camps on a contract for Dalstroy, the state-owned company in charge of the natural resources and free laborers in the region. This was her first job.

The barracks contained thirty-six beds, all for patients with chronic illnesses. The prevailing diagnoses were malnutrition, scurvy, pellagra, diabetes, tuberculosis, and chronic ulcers. I worked from seven in the evening until seven in the morning. During the days I slept in the barracks for workers.

I became good friends with Dusya, a housekeeper and food distributor. She was a well-educated, sophisticated woman with raven black hair, fair skin, and dark eyes. It was her fifth year in the camps, and now she was heading along with everyone else to Kolyma.

Dusya was the wife of a Central Committee official who was arrested in 1937. She and her two children, both students, were arrested four months later under the article ChSIR.*

I don't know how Dusya maintained her high spirits; I don't know where she kept her sorrow hidden. I never saw her despair. She hated Stalin and the NKVD, but the hate didn't take over her life. I think I reminded her of one of her sons, who was the same age as me. She didn't know where he was, and she would always

---

* *Chlen semyi izmennika rodiny*—a family member of a traitor of the Motherland.

say that perhaps there was someone taking care of him just as she was taking care of me.

One night while I was sleeping in the nursing station, Dusya burst in and woke me up. "Janusz, I must stay with you until morning. Two men are after me. They came to my barracks, and I recognized one of them as an interrogator at Lubyanka. He was an NKVD colonel, and now he's a *predurok* in the camp. He tried to rape me during interrogation, but I spit in his face and he beat me into unconsciousness." She climbed under the blanket next to me, shivering with fear.

For the next several days Dusya remained frightened. "Why are you so afraid of him?" I asked. "He's a prisoner like you. He has no power over you now. Here, you can really spit in his face."

"The man was a colonel in the NKVD. Despite his being a prisoner, the NKVD guards and officers still support their own men. He can do whatever he wants here. He'll never pay for it."

One night I was summoned to treat a young *urka* who'd been severely beaten. The red-haired man's face was smashed, and blood was spattered all over his civilian shirt and jacket. His eyes were so swollen he couldn't see, and I was sure he had several broken bones in his face. I cleaned the blood off his face and helped him get to the hospital, where I visited him every day. His name was Jora, and he thanked me for taking care of him. He said he hoped he could help me one day.

The prisoners returning from Kolyma, all chronically ill, talked endlessly about the place, trying to prepare me as best they could. They said the winters lasted nine months and that it was so cold that spit turned into ice before hitting the ground. Frostbite took fingers, toes, ears, and noses. The winds knocked you off your feet, and the only way to walk was to hold onto ropes that went from building to building. The snow was blinding. Prisoners got lost during storms and weren't found until spring; during the night, snow drifted over the barracks and buried the roads. Worst of all was the work—twelve hours a day of digging gold in the permafrost.

These tales were told to me by toothless, limbless, emaciated men in the last stages of disease. They'd been "commissioned" to go back to the mainland (as northern exiles referred to the Soviet Union), one of the most sinister administrative procedures in Kolyma. Decided by a group of free doctors and NKVD officials, "commission" meant that a prisoner was too sick to recover and work. It was cheaper to release him than to continue feeding him until his death. Every prisoner in the camps dreamed of being commissioned. What they didn't realize was that release only came when there was little hope of recovery.

Rudolph Andreijevich Stolpe was one of these men. His deeply frightening appearance remains in my memory. Though only thirty-eight years old, he looked at least sixty. A poet and writer, he had been publishing since the age of twenty-four, and he read me some of his poetry and writing, which he had memorized.

Stolpe couldn't walk. The skin around his thin bones had transformed into yellowish leather—in some places it was translucent. His ulcerated legs and buttocks wouldn't heal. When I changed his dressings, he asked optimistically if the ulcers were healing. I always lied. Pellagra had damaged the nerves of the skin, so he couldn't tell if the sores were healing or not. He had lost nearly all his teeth, his cheeks were sunken, and his facial features sharpened like a bird's, but his eyes shone with intelligence and happiness. He had no doubt that he would soon be free and head home to complete his recovery. His parents had been shot as German spies, and he knew they were gone, but he had this eerie optimism that he would be returning to a better life.

Many patients with advanced stages of pellagra were disoriented and confused; some were demented. The three main symptoms of the disease were known as the "three Ds"—dermatitis, diarrhea, and dementia. Dr. Popugayeva told me that the cause of pellagra—a deficiency of niacin—and its cure—yeast suspended in a water solution—had just been discovered. But it was too late for Stolpe—he died in our sick ward.

More than half of the prisoners in the ward were in the advanced stages of scurvy, which did different things to the mind and body. Bleeding gums, loss of teeth, weakening and hemorrhaging of the blood vessels, soreness and stiffness of the joints, and severe anemia were the primary symptoms. Hemorrhaging in the muscles, skin, and internal organs caused so many ailments that treating advanced cases was almost impossible. Essentially, the patients bled to death internally.

Patients with open tuberculosis were separated from the other patients by hanging sheets. Before they became too weak, they were animated and coherent. I was drawn to them, even though I was afraid of contracting the disease.

Dr. Popugayeva was concerned about my going to Kolyma, and I was terrified, seeing the commissioned prisoners who had returned from there. I asked if she could think of anything we could do to keep me from going up north. She said she'd see what could be done.

I saw Dr. Semyonov three or four times a week to talk or play chess. One evening I shared with him my anxiety about Kolyma and my hope that Dr. Popugayeva would come up with something to save me from the *etap*. Dr. Semyonov was disturbed. "For your own sake and for Dr. Popugayeva's, you mustn't tell anyone else that she's trying to help you. If anyone finds out about your connection, she could be arrested and sentenced for helping a prisoner. If you are on the list for *etap*, you'll be shipped. Prepare yourself to leave any day. It's easier that way. Life in the camps is run by forces outside our control. Whatever happens to us, we have nothing to say and no way to change the turn of events. But our will to survive will help us make it through. Let's look for each other over there. A mountain cannot meet a mountain, but a man can meet a man at any place and at any time."

One evening I got a message to visit Jora in his barracks. In the dim light I saw something going on in a corner. Prisoners were crowded around, and I heard moaning, groaning, sharp cries of pain. I moved closer. My eyes adjusted, and at the end of the barracks I saw a man hanging on a rope, his hands and legs bent behind his back and tied together. The rope was looped over a rafter, and two prisoners were pulling him up in the air and lowering him on top of a bed board. His cries were excruciating.

"Don't worry about him," Jora said, glancing at the hanging prisoner, "he's getting what he deserves. He had his word in court. He's lucky to stay alive."

Jora didn't look at all sick. His red hair looked bushier than ever; he was rosy-cheeked and smiling. Dressed in civilian clothing, he didn't remind me at all of the person I had seen so savagely beaten. He was only a little taller than me, but his broad chest and shoulders made him look massive.

"I'll tell you why I asked you to come over. I'm going to be sent to Kolyma on this or on the next ship. I'd rather go sooner than later. I don't want to get on the same ship as those guys who beat me up. They'll try to finish me for sure on the ship. I need to talk to Dr. Semyonov. He can get me on the next ship with my friends."

I was confused. Underneath his cool, controlled behavior, I could tell Jora was scared. He looked to me like a nice Jewish boy from a well-to-do Moscow family. With his guitar, red jacket, and ruffled shirt, he made the impression that he was on vacation and not in prison. I couldn't imagine what was going on with him.

"Why are they after you?" I asked.

Jora took a deep breath and held my arm. "I guess if we're friends, I should tell you. In Moscow I stole suitcases at the train stations. I'd leave my apartment in the morning with two empty suitcases loaded with newspapers and rags to give them weight. Every day I went to a different station—there are five huge stations in Moscow—and when I spotted a suitcase that looked like one I had, I stood next to the person and inconspicuously moved my suitcase closer to theirs. When they were ready to leave, I picked up theirs and walked away, fast. Soon I organized a small group who did the work for me. But then another group started operating in our territory. At first I tried to make peace with Arcady and his people, but they didn't want to share anything. They were older and more experienced. Fights broke out, and we all landed in Butyrki prison. Instead of making peace, we're still fighting. I just want to get away from them. Maybe you can help me."

We went to see Dr. Semyonov. It wasn't easy for me to explain Jora's problem, but Dr. Semyonov caught on right away. He said he'd try to put Jora on the next ship.

Meanwhile, a plan was hatched to keep me from being sent north. I was admitted to the hospital with a high fever and severe abdominal pain, symptoms that could pass for inflammation of an undisclosed origin requiring bed rest and intensive treatment. Lying in bed, I felt both strange and restless. I hadn't been healthier since my arrest, yet I was pretending to be sick and debilitated. The chart that hung at the foot of the bed read, "peritonitis?" Dr. Popugayeva was in grave danger for putting me on the list of sick patients. I felt terribly guilty.

On the third night of my convalescence three NKVD officers walked into the barracks. The lights flickered on. I looked toward the entrance, and when I saw them I knew without any doubt why they were there. They strode up to my bed and pulled down the blanket. "Dress immediately, you faker!" one of them bellowed. Slowly, I sat up in bed. One of the officers stepped between the beds and slapped me in the face. "We told you to get up. Move!"

In a minute I was dressed. The two officers took me to another barracks for the night.

The next morning dozens of trucks transported us to the harbor. The guards herded us as close to the water as possible. Someone said seven thousand prisoners were on the transport.

A refreshing breeze blew off the sea, and the salt tingled on my skin. The sun shone brightly. I looked at the sky with hope and sadness. Like Jack London's hero Martin Eden, I wanted to jump into the water, to swim away from the guards, prison, Kolyma, my life. Prisoners swarmed around me. I felt lonelier than ever, not knowing a single person in the crowd. Watching the sea was soothing and disturbing. I became mesmerized by rippling waves. Thoughts of suicide drifted away, replaced by a calm resolve to survive. I didn't know when or how my life would end, but I was determined not to give up easily.

"Janusz," someone called out. Jora ran through the throngs of prisoners, pushing people aside, holding his guitar over his head. His bright jacket and fancy ruffled shirt were gone, however, and he was dressed like every other prisoner. "It's so good to see you. Let's sit away from the crowd." We moved as close to the shore

as possible and lay on the grass on our stomachs. It was warm
and peaceful. I was relieved to find someone I trusted, someone I
considered a friend. The sun shining on my back and the rhythm
of the waves relaxed me. I dozed in and out of sleep.

A hot, piercing pain awakened me. I screamed. Jora was
screaming, too. Blood gushed from his neck. I felt a sharp pain in
my lower back and felt paralyzed from the waist down. It was the
last thing I felt before fainting.

CHAPTER 10

Slave Ship

I regained consciousness in a tightly sealed space—dark, coffin-like. The raw wood beneath my cheek smelled of mildew, sweat, and urine. Obscenities echoed through the dank wooden chamber. The small of my back throbbed, and when I reached around I discovered a bandage extending all the way around my waist. Then it came back to me—the port in Buchta Nakhodka; lying on the grass with Jora; Jora screaming, blood streaming from his neck. He'd been stabbed; I must have been, too.

I had no idea how I'd gotten on the ship or who had bandaged me up. Once the prisoners had been assembled at the dock, there was no turning back. The sick and injured were packed into the holds along with everybody else. If we died, nobody cared.

After a while I could make out people walking by and a bed board above my head. A dim light came in from the far end of the quarters. I was on the transport ship.

"I saw you two cock-suckers bleeding on the grass like pigs," my neighbor piped up. "What happened?"

Although I couldn't see his face, I could tell his teeth were broken or missing by his lisp.

"None of your business."

"Look motherfucker, I'm just asking, *kindly*, what's your problem."

I didn't respond. I propped myself up on my elbows and felt around the bed board for my *paika*. Pain seared from my back into my legs. I lay back down and wiggled my toes. At least I wasn't paralyzed.

"You missed your ration," my neighbor commented. "The *predurkis* tried to wake you and your friend, but you were out of it. Your bread is gone."

Jora lay next to me, moaning in his sleep. His hand and forehead were hot, and he didn't answer when I tried to wake him. He needed a doctor. I slid off the bed board and tottered toward the dim light. The narrow passageway intersected with other passageways, which all looked the same. Afraid of getting lost, I counted the number of blocks and kept track of the turns I made. Staggering from post to post, I came to a wider passageway and saw a staircase at the end. The stench of the latrine reached my nose. A ray of light seeped through the opening at the top of the stairs, and through the smoky haze red, blue, and black tattoos swam before me. On every bare back, chest, and arm were elaborate images of bottles, knives, pistols, soaring eagles, Soviet stars, running horses, gallows with swinging bodies, male and female genitalia, and bold claims of personal endowment: "My prick is thicker than my fist." "Tanya loves my cock."

The wide iron staircase, overrun by chattering *urkas*, resembled a tree full of grackles. A young *urka* on one of the upper steps shouted and waved a shirt to a friend. "Fiedia, come here, you dog's prick! We've been waiting for you."

Large, sleepy-eyed Fiedia, with a red handkerchief around his neck, lumbered up the steps between bodies that parted to make room for him. "Watch it, motherfucker!" an older man said. "You nearly stepped on my hand. Don't you have eyes? Or are they in your ass?" His buddies laughed.

Leaning against a nearby post, I surveyed the situation and waited for an opening to climb the stairs. The *urkas* smoked and laughed, talked loudly, slapped one another on the back, groped and insulted each other as though they were on a holiday cruise.

Skinny youngsters ran wildly up and down the stairs looking for friends.

On the bottom step, five middle-aged men leaned against the railings, puffing on cigarette stubs and talking seriously. "I got word from Magadan," one of them said tersely. "You can fuck my mother if I'm lying." He glanced quickly from face to face to see if he'd gotten the other men's attention. With his retracted chin and protruding nose, he reminded me of a stork. "My friends from Odessa are *predurkis* at the transit camp in Magadan. We won't be freezing our asses in the mines. They'll take care of us."

One of the men cut in. "Who the fuck are you, Rat? You think you're a big man? You think you can keep us from digging gold?" He squeezed his lips together and got close to Rat's face. "Give me the names of your friends who are so important they can take care of us. I don't want to rely on a shit like you to save me." He climbed the steps.

I saw my chance and darted in behind him. The *urkas* made room for him but closed back up and stared hard at me. Impatient to get a doctor, I barged through. I got halfway up, but someone grabbed my shoulder, squeezed it forcefully, and turned me around. I screamed as my back twisted. "Look at this sissy!" The older *urka's* face lit up, amused. He gripped my lower jaw with iron fingers and thrust my face toward his friends.

I tore his hand away from my face and shouted, "Fuck off!" I tried to release my arm, but his grip was firm. His round black eyes bore through mine. "Don't fuck with me," he hissed.

The *urkas* around us were suddenly silent, staring. All the faces looked the same—coarse, mocking, hostile. Blood rushed to my head and throbbed in my temples. The brutish faces blurred into one.

"I hope you choke on your own cocks! My friend is dying. I need to get a doctor."

He let go of my arm and stepped back. "Slow down, man. Don't get so hot. We thought you were a mama's boy." He grinned and patted me cautiously on the shoulder. "It's a long way to the hatch, and you don't look so good. I'll go with you."

He introduced himself as Igor. He had white teeth, a rarity among *urkas*. He was tall—I only came up to his chin—and he grasped my arm firmly to guide me to the upper hold. I felt stumps where his first two fingers had been. A cobra was coiled around a naked woman on the middle of his chest, and beneath it was the phrase "Love Kills."

I needed to rest in the upper hold before climbing the steep staircase to the hatch. Igor peered closely at my face. "Where you from?" I told him my name and said I was from Poland. "Poland!" he blurted out. "How the hell did you end up here?" I told him my story.

Igor pulled a cigarette rolled in newsprint from his breast pocket and lit it with an army lighter, highly valued among prisoners because of the high metal sides, which shielded the flame from the wind. His face glowed. A ragged scar marked his forehead and chin. "So, who's your friend?" I told him about Jora. "Jora the Dandy—I know him! We were together at the Kotlas camp. A real *chelovek*. It's good to have such a friend. What happened to you two?"

I told him about the stabbing.

"You're lucky you ran into me and not Arcady and his men. Back at the port, Jora got crazy with an ax. Chopped off the head of Arcady's number-two man. Arcady's on the ship. I'm sure he's looking for Jora. We're still in the harbor, so they're laying low, but out at sea they'll come looking for you, that's for sure. They'll scour both decks to find Jora."

Igor glanced around the hold the whole time he talked. I figured he had his enemies, too. "After we get Jora to the deck, you'd better come hang out with me." He stomped out his cigarette, grabbed me under the armpits, and lifted me up to the hatch. He banged on the steel door with his fist.

The hatch opened, and rifles were thrust in our faces. "We need a doctor," Igor declared. "A man in the lower hold was badly stabbed. He's got a high fever. This one here was also stabbed and needs a doctor."

"Bring the sick one to the hatch," one of them said. "You," he added, pointing his gun at me, "crawl out and lay on the deck."

The sunlight pierced my eyes as I pulled myself through the opening and eased myself down to the deck—the hatch was elevated about three feet. The final hop jarred my injured vertebrae, and I fell to the deck in agony. Oblivious to my cries, the two guards went about closing the hatch and replacing the iron lever and crossbar, safely sealing themselves and their comrades off from the mayhem below. Two machine guns mounted high on stands were aimed at the hatch. Next to the hatch, two firehoses were wound around giant wooden spindles. The briny air smelled of freedom, of the endless space of the sea and sky. I breathed deeply, imagining I could take the air with me when I returned to the suffocating hold. I watched the seagulls circling the ship and dreamed of flying away with them into oblivion. The sun-drenched deck warmed my body, and I rolled onto my side and propped my head up to see the water. Waves crested, broke, and disappeared into the green sea, the whitecaps glimmering like miniature flashes of lightning.

As an adolescent I'd dreamed of sailing these far eastern and northern seas. I had imagined myself an explorer, sailing on long voyages to unknown places. The strange names captured my imagination, and I liked to say them out loud: the Sea of Okhotsk, Sakhalin, Chukotka, Kamchatka, Kolyma, the Kuril Islands, the Arctic Circle, the Arctic Ocean. I dreamed of bathing in the hot springs in Kamchatka, imagined the steaming volcanoes covered with snow. I wanted to dig for gold in Chukotka and Kolyma; to go to the coldest place on earth, Verkhoyansk; to sail the Kolyma and Indigirka rivers to the Arctic Ocean; to meet the Eskimo tribes—the Evenks and Youkagirs. I wanted to live with them and learn their languages, religions, and cultures; to kayak on the open ocean, hunt for seals, sleep in tents, and snowshoe in the taiga to hunt for bears. I wanted not only to explore these places but also to write about them. And here I was. But I was no explorer. I was a slave, and this was my slave ship.

Igor and another prisoner emerged from the hatch carrying Jora. He was unconscious. The guards put him on a stretcher and took him into the cabin. I followed. The doctor stitched my wound as though he were repairing a shoe, and I tried to comport myself as such. I clenched my teeth as the needle pierced the inflamed flesh and the raw thread burned through the skin. The pain was unbearable as he tightened the knots, but I didn't flinch or make a sound.

When I was dismissed, the guards removed the iron lever and crossbar and opened the hatch. I obediently climbed in and descended into the nest of ants. The hatch slammed shut. I clung to the nearest pole until my eyes adjusted, then went to find Igor. He welcomed me like a younger brother and announced to his men, "This is Jora's Polish friend." They made a space for me on the bed boards, and I took it.

In the middle of the night I woke to the rocking of the ship and the grinding of the engines. The loud penetrating noise made me think the engine room was right behind my head. As the engines vibrated rhythmically, the temperature rose by incremental degrees. Igor and his men took off their shirts and rolled them under their heads as pillows. I did the same.

The next morning Igor's men began arguing about the route we would take to get to Kolyma. One man asserted convincingly that we would sail through the Pacific Ocean. Another worried about the icebergs should we travel through the Arctic Ocean.

At the age of fourteen, my classmate Shimek Polakowski and I began to quiz each other on all aspects of geography. We memorized cities, capitals, languages, rivers, mountains, natural resources, climates, and cultures, and we challenged each other frequently for several years. I saw the map of Kolyma clearly before my eyes and reproduced it on the bed board using undershirts and splinters of wood. Igor's men gathered around. The more places I could identify, the more interested they became. I told them about the Japanese island of Hokkaido and the island of Sakhalin. They'd heard of Sakhalin but had never heard of Hokkaido or La Perouse Strait, which ran between the two islands. "Where do we go after we pass through La Perouse Strait?" they wanted to know. I named all the islands of the Kuril Archipelago—Kunashir, Iturup, Urup, Sinushir, Onekotan, Taramushir—islands that separated the Sea of Okhotsk from the Pacific Ocean.

Everyone was quiet, listening to every word. Then the questions started rolling: Who lived on the islands? What did they do? Did the islands belong to the Soviet Union? Were there any camps? I was surprised by their genuine interest and by the sudden absence of arrogance, vulgarity, and bravado.

Nighttime galvanized the *urkas;* they moved in the darkness like cats. One night I was awakened by an excited discussion among Igor, his men, and a group of newcomers. I sat up and leaned next to the wall. Igor was talking to a man sitting opposite him on the crowded bed board. He looked straight into the man's eyes, and I sensed he was firmly in command. "Find out exactly where the food is. We can't afford to break into some other quarters. Leonid said there's a double wooden wall between our hold and the storage room. The same wall extends to other quarters—the engine room, tool room, sleeping quarters for the mechanics. Let's not hurry. We won't do anything tonight. We've got to explore this wall first. We might have to take out two or three boards to crawl into the space to see what's there."

The next morning, *predurkis* armed with clubs wandered through the hold to deliver *paika* and herring. They walked in groups of six to eight, watching each other's backs. Most of them were hardened criminals, but some had been NKVD and Party officials. *Predurkis* were selected on the basis of their physical power, brutality, and disregard for other human beings. They were especially cruel to political prisoners, the majority of the prison and camp population. Politicals, inexperienced in street fighting and often tortured and weakened during interrogation, were easy prey. There was an unwritten pact between the *predurkis* and *urkas*—"live and let live." The two groups coexisted and tried to avoid conflict. The NKVD guards never came down to the hold for fear they would be overpowered by the prisoners.

Soon after we finished the morning ration, a storm came up. Everyone clung to the bed boards as the ship pitched and fell. The sharp smell of vomit was added to the stock of other human odors. The violent rocking made it almost impossible to walk, and so the ill and incontinent relieved themselves right where they were. The healthy threw them out into the passageway. I held tightly to the bed board and tried to keep from hitting my head on the one above. I was terrified the ship would hit a rock and overturn or become inundated. I couldn't help imagining that we would all drown in the sea prison, with no way to swim and no way to get out.

When the violent rocking stopped, Igor announced we were moving to another place. His men had located the food storage, and we were moving to a bunk next to that wall. The floor was slippery and blocked with retching prisoners. My stomach went into my throat every few minutes, but I breathed deeply to keep from getting sick. Men lay on the bed boards and in the passageways, whimpering and crying between heaves. Helping each other along, we reached a vacant bunk next to the wall. We occupied both levels, and the men who had visited Igor during the night settled in next to us.

The excitement of the upcoming break-in charged two scrawny fellows sitting next to me. "I've been dreaming for a year to eat smoked pork, the kind in the big cans they sell in the food stores before Christmas. Canned meat is the best. I can just smell it. I don't care about anything else. You can have the rest, but I'm eating a can a day."

A pimple-faced boy reminisced, "Yeah, I had smoked pork in a can a long time ago. But mostly I gathered empty cans in the streets. In the orphanage, we didn't get smoked pork. We had meat only two, maybe three times a year. It was kasha and soup and soup and kasha. I'm hungry for a good meal. Every night I dream about it."

Throughout that day, a hollow, repetitive pounding sound came from the bed board below and continued into the night. I awakened to excited voices. Igor whispered loudly, "Get everything onto the upper bed board. Be sure to put the boards back in place."

Canned food and burlap bags surrounded me. Hands continued reaching up to put more and more food on the bed board. Round loaves of bread flew through the air.

"Stop it!" Igor said. "Don't get greedy. We'll go back in two or three days."

Cans upon cans of smoked pork, mackerel, condensed milk, beans, and peas were spread out on the upper bed board. Igor sliced open the loaves of dark bread with a handmade pocket knife. Everyone leaned in close, stared hungrily, and waited for the word to start. "Open the cans," Igor said. Two *urkas* whipped out spoons with sharpened handles and went to work puncturing and prying off the lids. After several cans were opened and their contents emptied onto a shirt, Igor gave the word to dig in.

What followed was a feeding frenzy. Everyone grabbed pieces of bread, tore off pieces of rolled meat with their fingers, scooped out beans and peas with their hands, or ate straight from the cans. Smacking, grunting, belching, licking, and chewing replaced the bragging and cursing. No one argued or fought.

"Igor, are you sure we won't get in trouble when the guards find out the food is missing?" I asked.

Igor looked at me with disgust. "What's the matter with you? Didn't they ever teach you to have a good time in Poland? We'll be on our way to a gold mine when they discover the food is missing. Stop worrying. Eat up."

The aroma of smoked pork made me salivate. I spread it on a piece of black bread and chewed slowly and deliberately to retain the flavor as long as possible. It smelled and tasted better than anything I'd ever eaten in an exquisite restaurant.

An *urka* poked at a bag. "Macaroni!" he shouted.

"We need to cook it," his buddy said.

"Don't bother. I love it just the way it is." He grabbed a fistful of the hollow pieces, stuffed them in his mouth, and chewed deliriously for a long time. With his eyes closed and his chin tilted upward, he ground down the mixture with his teeth, his Adam's apple bobbing up and down with each swallow.

After an hour of eating, the *urkas* shoved the leftover food next to the wall and covered it with shirts. Then everyone lay down in a great heap, belching, passing gas, and sleeping. Next to me was Pietia, a tall blond youth with a sweet face and engaging smile. I wanted to sleep, but he had the urge to talk.

"I never knew my parents," he said. "I grew up with other kids on the beaches in the Crimea and in Odessa. Some older kids took care of me. They taught me to steal and beg. I wish I had a mother somewhere, some place, to write letters to and maybe to see sometimes. I try to remember her, but my earliest memory is of lying on the beach in the sun, a campfire burning.

"I saw my mother so many times in so many different ladies while walking the beaches. I always looked closely at them, hoping one of them would recognize me and tell me I was her son. They were all young and pretty. I don't really care about girls. I've had plenty of them. But I dream about my mother."

Pietia propped himself on his elbow. His voice got softer, slower. I thought he had tears in his eyes. I had spotted Pietia the first day I joined Igor's group. His affiliation with the underworld was evident in his tattoos, vocabulary, and behavior. But the civility of his expression and gestures, his dreamy eyes and tears, suggested something soft and cultured in him. I immediately liked him. The fact that he confided in me made me want to be his friend, something that didn't happen every day.

The *urkas* broke into the food storage room again two days later. This time they found a box of crude tobacco, worth gold to prisoners, and enough food to sate everyone's appetite. They even shared the bounty with strangers from other blocks. I'd never seen such generosity among prisoners.

Though I continued to keep company with Igor, I felt out of place hanging around with criminals. Their only conversations were about crimes they had committed in the past, crimes they intended to commit in the future, women, booze, and food. But I was pleased that they had accepted me and let me stay with them during the journey. They liked having a foreigner among them. In spite of their arrogance and self-centeredness, they craved to know more about the outside world. In addition to telling them about my life in Poland, I told them stories—some that I'd read, others that I made up. *The Count of Monte Cristo* and *The Three Musketeers* won me many listeners, and I felt my status rise with every twist of the plot. Real storytelling was rare and highly valued among the *urkas;* most of them were illiterate, and their crude, primitive way of thinking was more suitable to bragging and insulting than to sustaining a plot.

After the second break-in, *urkas* I'd never seen came to the upper bed board to talk to Igor. It became crowded, and I was pushed into a far corner. They talked late into the night, and I realized they were planning some other action. It was hard to make out the details of what the men were saying, but they seemed greatly agitated. Accusations and curses took over the discussion. "Are you with us or not?" one of the men said angrily to Igor. Whatever he wanted, he wanted it now.

"You're on your own. You have to go through the food storage to get there, and if the guards or *predurkis* find out, we'll all be in deep shit. Be patient. Wait a few more days until we get to the zone."

"I thought you were a real man. You're just a cock-sucker."

The newcomers jumped down from the bed board.

Igor was disturbed. He got up on his knees and addressed his men. "I've lived through things like this before. It never ends well. Stay right here with me." One of Igor's men offered him a cigarette. Igor held it tightly between his lips and inhaled deeply. No one spoke. I fell back to sleep.

In the middle of the night, high-pitched screaming jolted me awake. It came from below the bed board. Women's voices. I crawled toward the edge of the bed board. Igor's men lay on their stomachs, heads hanging over the edge, looking into the passageway. "The bastards did it. No one move," Igor commanded.

I looked down into the passageway. Men were clustered around a hole in the wall, pulling women through the opening like bags of flour and carrying them away. I didn't know women prisoners were on the ship; they must have been loaded on after we'd been locked in the holds. As soon as the women appeared through the hole, the men tore off their clothing. Several men attacked each woman at once. I could see the victims' white bodies twisting, their legs kicking forcefully, their hands clawing the men's faces. The women bit, cried, and wailed. The rapists smacked them back.

A sharp ripping sound directly across the passageway caught my attention. A piece of material—white with red and orange flowers—was dashed to the floor. Another sharp rip; another swath of material was torn away. The dark-haired woman lay pinned to the bed board, a man anchoring each limb. Other men tore at their pants and climbed on top of her in succession. She never stopped thrashing her head from side to side.

"Lay still, bitch. You'll choke on my cock if you don't stop yelling."

I lost count of how many women had been captured. Screaming could be heard farther and farther away in the hold. When the rapists ran out of women, some of the bulkier men turned to the bed boards and hunted for young men. These adolescents were added to the carnage, lying still on their stomachs, bleeding and crying on the floor. Hundreds of men hung from the bed boards to view the scene, but not a single one tried to intervene. The passage was jammed with bodies. Shrill cries and whimpers pierced the grunts and bellows.

I stared at the flowery dress lying in the passageway, so much like a dress my mother, sister, or Taubcia would wear. I couldn't stop thinking of them. Images of Nazis in tall black boots intruded: their confident march; pale, muscular bodies; swastika armbands. I could see them tearing the dresses of my mother, sister, and Taubcia, shouting obscenities at them. I could hear Taubcia's cries, hear her calling after me. I shook with rage, revulsion, and fear, unable to help the women, unable to tear myself away from the horror, the Goya painting come to life—the open mouths, streaming blood, contorted bodies.

I crawled across the bed board to find Igor. He and several others sat against the wall, smoking. "Don't get worked up," Igor said.

"Why doesn't anyone stop them? They're torturing—killing these women! Can't you do something, Igor? They'll listen to you. Your men will obey you."

"Sit down. Those aren't men, they're animals. Violent brutes. My men here, we're criminals, but we aren't killers. I've never raped a woman. Never raised a fist at a woman. Those beasts won't listen to anyone, only to their cocks. Get away from there. Sit with us."

But I couldn't sit quietly. I went back to the edge of the bed board. The men had begun clearing out. On the bed board across from me, a very young woman, her long blond hair in matted tangles above her head, her breasts unrecognizable, lay in a pool of blood. Her body lay perfectly still; her eyes were softly closed. But her faced twitched involuntarily, like the wing of a dying bird.

A sudden burst of freezing water came from both ends of the hold, knocking down everyone in its path. The high-powered stream was sprayed along the passageways, clearing them completely. Water burst across our bed board, soaking my clothing. I lay down flat, but it was impossible to escape the torrent, which came on and off, seeking out every prisoner. Igor, with water dripping from his head and clothing, bellowed, "Get that hole boarded up!" He jumped down and continued yelling and gesturing, his face contorted with fury. Several of his men followed and helped him cover the hole. The shower continued. When it stopped, an announcement came through a bullhorn, "All prisoners remain in your places."

Floodlights from both ends moved slowly toward the middle of the hold, illuminating the passageways and creating deep shadows. Flashlight beams skittered around the bed boards and floor. The pack of *predurkis* reached the woman who lay naked and motionless across from our bed board. She hadn't changed position, even when the water was turned on.

"Fucking bastards! Here's another one," a *predurok* shouted. "Bring the stretcher. Get a *feldsher*." He felt for a pulse. "She's gone." His voice faltered. "There's so much blood." He crawled off the bed board and moved on.

Another voice came over the bullhorn. "I need another stretcher! We've got a mess down here."

Soaked and shivering, our group was ordered down from the bed boards. The ice-cold water came above the ankles. My feet went numb. The *predurok* in charge asked if we knew who was responsible for the dead woman. No one knew any names.

For the next three days I didn't move from the bed board except to go to the latrine and to get water. Prisoners were coughing and sneezing, and many went to see the doctor. The whole atmosphere remained subdued. By the end of the voyage, my pants still hadn't dried out completely.

One morning I was roused by silence. The engines had stopped. Several hours later, our hold was called to disembark. We were the last to leave the ship. No one knew for sure how many prisoners had arrived—estimates ranged between six and ten thousand.

A cold wind blew in through the hatch. "Hurry up!" a guard spat into my ear. I pulled myself up and climbed out into the jarring daylight. The guards prodded us with the butts of their rifles. I yelped when one of them hit my back, but the moving column carried me forward, down the ramp, and onto the quay.

The sun was low on the horizon. I saw snow-capped hills in the distance and welcomed myself to another world.

"Kolyma, Kolyma
wonderful planet.
Twelve months are winter—
the rest, summer."

CHAPTER 11

Welcome to Kolyma

Stalin's face was plastered everywhere—on billboards, warehouse buildings, even the cliff sides. His deep-set eyes, bushy eyebrows, mustache, and gray army tunic appeared wherever I turned. I had the feeling I was back in Orel at the Tank Academy, where Stalin's portrait hung in every hall, office, and classroom. Along with the portraits, red banners were posted on the buildings and emblazoned on the cliffs around the port:

GLORY TO STALIN, THE GREATEST GENIUS OF MANKIND.
GLORY TO STALIN, THE GREATEST MILITARY LEADER.
GLORY TO STALIN, THE GREATEST LEADER OF THE INTERNATIONAL PROLETARIAT.
GLORY TO STALIN, THE BEST FRIEND OF WORKERS AND PEASANTS.
GLORY TO STALIN, THE FATHER, TEACHER, AND BEST FRIEND OF ALL SOVIET PEOPLE.
UNDER STALIN'S LEADERSHIP, ONWARD TO THE VICTORY OF COMMUNISM.
UNDER STALIN'S LEADERSHIP WE WILL DEFEAT THE NAZI HYDRA.
DEATH TO HITLER AND HIS HENCHMEN.
WATCH WHAT YOU SAY, SPIES ARE EVERYWHERE.
DEATH TO THE SPIES.
MORE GOLD FOR OUR COUNTRY, MORE GOLD FOR OUR VICTORY!
KOLYMA WELCOMES YOU!

I read the slogans with utter distaste. If there was one liberating aspect to being a prisoner, it was the escape from the daily barrage of Stalinist indoctrination. The *urkas* ignored all things political, and in some ways I admired them for it. Though arrogant and vulgar, they displayed a sense of honesty and dignity I had rarely seen in the Soviet military.

The port of Magadan lay nestled in the Bay of Nagayevo, sheltered from the choppy waves of the Sea of Okhotsk. The wharf and a single road had been carved out of the hills, exposing yellowish clay walls that towered above the port. The thousands of prisoners trudging up the road looked like a giant gray and black millipede.

"Davay! Davay! Podtyanis!" I could barely hear the guards' commands in the roaring wind, which wailed from all directions like a circle of vociferous wolves; it bit at my face, blew dirt in my eyes, and beat against my ears and head. A sagging charcoal sky grazed the peaks of the surrounding hills. The thick air coated my face and clothing and left a lacy white residue on the shrubs near the bay. I rubbed my arms and licked the salt off my lips. Some prisoners had hats; others bound their heads with scarves. I tucked my chin down, raised my shoulders, and covered my ears with my hands.

The guards divided the prisoners into groups. I found myself corralled into a column of three hundred or so men, and we marched up the road, four abreast. Walking up the steep hill after eight days on the ship strained my badly weakened muscles. Not many walked upright. The majority shuffled, hauling their bodies up the hill, each prisoner following his own rhythm, unaffected by the shouts and blows of the guards. My soaked shoes and foot rags were falling apart. I had taken out the shoestrings and wrapped them around each foot to keep the soles from flapping open, but the gravel cut through the laces in no time. The soles flapped back open, and rocks got trapped inside. Every step was like walking on a bed of nails. I stopped to pull out the pebbles. "Move!" someone shouted. "Do you want us all to get shot?" I hastily dumped out the stones and scrambled back into place.

Small single-story wooden houses lined both sides of the street with wooden fences demarcating the front yards. A horseshoe, a Russian symbol of good luck, was nailed to every front door. As we got closer to the city, the wooden houses were replaced by two- and three-story apartment complexes. The storefronts boasted elegant displays of bread, cheese, fish, ham, and flowers, much like those I'd seen in Orel. There the displays had been made of wood—the stores actually carried only a few basic staples, far less than the window displays promised, and I wondered if these displays were also made out of wood.

The locals walked quickly past us with their heads down, showing no alarm or curiosity. No one stopped to watch. No one shouted angrily at the guards or raised a single fist of protest on our behalf. No bread or clothing was thrown to us. The men wore dark jackets and pants and tall black army boots. I spotted only a few men in shirts and ties. The women's skirts and coats were made of dark flannel or wool. Even though it was early spring, many people still wore heavy coats. Everyone appeared preoccupied, rushed, and slightly on edge. Women clutched net bags called *avoska*, or "maybe"—shorthand for the hope that maybe there would be something to buy.

The huge territory of Kolyma had only one highway. It began in the center of Magadan and extended hundreds of kilometers into the interior of Siberia. Every place along the Kolyma Highway was named according to its distance from Magadan.

The first transit camp we came to was called the Fourth Kilometer. We went through the ritual of shaving, bathing, and delousing. The heat from the delousing destroyed my undergarments and shoes, and the *predurok* in charge issued me new undergarments and a pair of used boots and dry foot rags. Although the boots were too big, I got them to fit by stuffing in extra foot rags, and they were only slightly worn.

Three weeks later, my barracks was summoned to the administration building for a medical examination. An emaciated prisoner swept the bare ground outside the entrance. Tall, thin, and unshaven, with opaque eyes and deep creases in his face, he appeared half dead. His clothing looked and smelled as if it hadn't been changed for a long time. He wore a red scarf around his neck and had a good winter hat, which he wore with earflaps down despite the balmy weather. Was this the fate that awaited us?

The walls and ceiling of the examining room were painted white; the wooden floors had been scrubbed clean. A breeze blew through a large window, rustling the white curtains. On each desk and on the window sills were healthy green plants. On one, the red fuchsia buds were just opening. A stack of brown, green, and white files lay on a desk, all tied with shoelaces. When the doctor handed mine to the nurse, I saw that it was relatively thin. I wanted to know what was inside—the transcripts from my trial? the attempted escape? the time I faked being sick in Buchta Nakhodka? I wondered if there were any notes about the changing of my sentence. I couldn't help but worry that Efim Polzun, Dr. Popugayeva, or Dr. Semyonov might have been written up for trying to help me. I thought about how my file had traveled all the way across the Soviet Union on a parallel journey, how it had followed me without getting lost among the thousands and thousands of other files. My fate was in that file.

The officer looked at me, checked something in the file, and closed it. On the front page was a large stamp—"KOLYMA-TFT." The last three letters stood for *tyazoly fezichesky trud*, or "hard physical labor." I was paraded in front of the doctors—one male, the other female. By now I felt none of the shame that had so troubled me at the beginning of my imprisonment. The female doctor carefully inspected my eyes, ears, teeth, tongue, and throat as if she were examining a horse on the market. She ordered me to breathe deeply, cough, exhale loudly, and cough again. I held my breath when she listened to my heart. She roughly palpated my liver and intestines and thumped each kidney, which was painful. I flexed my biceps, quadriceps, and pectoral muscles, demonstrated twenty-five situps and pushups, and ran in place for five minutes, then bent over on command for an anal inspection, which startled and embarrassed me. The male doctor declared me healthy and said to the nurse and to the NKVD officer, "First labor category. No restrictions."

Nearly all of the men who arrived with me were put in the same category, even those who were middle-aged or older. New arrivals were always the top choice for heavy labor because they were usually healthier and stronger.

The results of the examination produced a chaos of feelings. I was terrified of the hard labor but relieved to know I was in good physical condition. The stab wound in my back had healed perfectly. I thought about trying to fake an illness, but I also knew it probably wouldn't have worked.

Strangely, I wasn't afraid of the gold mines. I thought I was strong enough to sustain the physical effort and smart enough to figure out how to survive. In fact, the North attracted me. I had read and reread Jack London's stories as an adolescent and dreamed of following his heroes to Alaska and to the gold mines of Klondike; running dogsleds through the mountains and over ice-covered rivers and lakes; paddling a canoe in dangerous rapids; hunting bears and wolves; living in a log cabin; and, most of all, digging and panning for gold in mountain streams. These images formed my picture of Kolyma, despite what I had heard from and saw in the faces of the returning prisoners.

Before *etap*, everyone tried to find information on the various gold mining camps. When someone had news, we all gathered around, united in a way we never had been. Speculation rocked the barracks. Pestraya Driesva was considered to be one of the worst places, with winds strong enough to knock a man over. Even during the summer prisoners had to hold onto ropes when they walked. Ojmiakon was reputed to be one of the coldest places on earth. Kadykczan and Sejmczan, both of which had multiple subdivisions, were renowned for their terrible treatment of prisoners. I avoided thinking too much about what lay ahead and tried to bask in the relative comfort of the transit camp. We didn't have to work; the air was fresh; the food was decent; and I was free to walk around and talk to people.

By chance I met a professor of ethnography from the University of Omsk, Georgi Kabanov. His left ear was folded in, and he had a bulbous nose and a turned-up lip. He possessed a degree of tranquillity rarely encountered in the prison system. I had long, leisurely conversations with him, and he told me about the history of Kolyma, something no one else knew or cared to know.

Kolyma was accessible only by plane or boat, making it far removed from the civilized part of the Soviet Union. The people who lived there referred to the rest of the Soviet Union as the "mainland" and thought of themselves as living on an island, even in a separate country. The government enticed free people to work in Kolyma by doubling their salaries, giving them earlier and better pensions, and allowing them six months of vacation every two years. Although Kolyma was one of the richest places in the world for natural resources, especially gold, the harsh environment and weather discouraged any organized exploration or settlement until 1931. That year the Central Committee of the Communist Party issued a decree to begin industrial development of Northeast Siberia, then known as Lower Kolyma. Edward Berzin was appointed the first director of Dalstroy, the state-owned company in charge of developing the region. He had high credentials, as he had been in charge of building the large paper mills at the Wishera labor camps. Dalstroy consisted of two major directorates: the NKVD, which administered the labor camp system; and the Industrial Directorate, which oversaw industrial production and development. As chief of both directorates, Berzin was the undisputed governor of the entire region.

Beginning in the mid-thirties, and especially at the time of the great purges of 1937–1939, hundreds of thousands of prisoners were pipelined to Kolyma. A special fleet was created to ship thousands of prisoners at a time. Buchta Nakhodka, the largest transit camp in the area, warehoused between twenty thousand and thirty thousand prisoners at a time. In 1936 the territory under the Dalstroy governance was enlarged to include the entire Kolyma River basin, as well as the Indigirka, Nera, and Moma river basins. Dalstroy's labor camps and organized mining operations expanded northeast into the territory of Chukotka and westward into the basin of the Jana River. The camps went as far south as Okhotsk.

In 1935 criminals accounted for more than 50 percent of the prisoners in the Kolyma labor camps. However, the mass arrests of 1937–1939 radically changed the composition of the camps; political prisoners now made up more than 90 percent of the camp population. In the early 1930s, a shortage of guards forced the camp commanders to use criminals in that capacity, and the precedent remained in place. Criminals now ruled over the political prisoners; they could be counted on to intimidate, harass, and brutalize as severely as the NKVD did.

As the territorial expansion of Dalstroy continued, the number of prisoners grew geometrically. New waves of internal terror created a perpetual supply of new convicts to replace the thousands and thousands of prisoners who perished in the gold mines. Untold numbers of Politburo, Central Committee, and NKVD officials fell victim to the mass arrests and executions in Moscow; and Berzin and his crew met the same fate in Magadan. In 1937 he and his top men were arrested, shipped to Moscow for trial, and executed. The chief of the labor camps of the Northeastern Directorate, Vaskov, hung himself in the Magadan prison, which he had ordered to be built and had personally supervised. The prison is still known today as Vaskov's House.

Berzin's successor, Garanin, went down as the cruelest, most sadistic NKVD chief in Kolyma history. A friend I met at the Central Hospital on the Twenty-third Kilometer told me Garanin had once visited the hospital. At roll call, he asked the prisoners if they had any complaints. When one of them asked for better clothing and food, Garanin shot him on the spot.

Another Garanin story comes from the camp on the Forty-seventh Kilometer. One night a truck of NKVD officers arrived from Magadan. The next day prisoners were told they did not have to go to work. At roll call that morning, prisoners counted off by tens, and every tenth prisoner was separated and sent away to a barracks. When the entire group was assembled, a mock trial was held, and the segregated prisoners were accused of collective sabotage, subversive activity, and plotting to assassinate Stalin. All were shot. The corpses were left to rot in the woods. After two more roll calls, hundreds more corpses were dumped around the campsite. Garanin and his men shared the same fate as his predecessor; they were executed in 1939.

One morning I was awakened by the barked order, "Grab your belongings and get out!" Shock and fear propelled me off the bed board. I had no belongings except for the clothes on my body, but many of my comrades had accumulated various sorts of riffraff—a rag, a can, a wooden spoon, an extra shoelace or shirt, a sweater, a jacket, a hat. Anything was of value. They wore whatever belongings they could, and what they couldn't wear they strapped to themselves or tucked inside their shirts. Only newcomers had bags or suitcases.

It was still foggy when we were loaded onto trucks and left the Fourth Kilometer. Our truck ran on burned wood, something that quite amazed me. A guard continually fed the tall cylinder next to the cab with "wooden bricks," which he pulled out of burlap bags. As the fog dispersed, hills emerged on both sides of the road, covered with evergreens, thick and glistening in the morning sun.

The Kolyma Highway was not much of a highway. Paved with flat gray cobblestones, the two-lane road rarely had shoulders. Periodically, a driveway appeared at the side of the road where you could pull off and wander into the shrubs—the public latrine—but these were few and far between. I didn't see a single gas station or tavern on the highway. Traffic was heavy with trucks carrying prisoners, food, or supplies. We went through many mountain passes, the truck barely clinging to the cliff side, the road dropping a thousand meters into the valley below. On steep inclines the truck slowed to a crawl, and we were ordered to get off and hike, a welcome respite for my throbbing head and queasy stomach. As evening approached, the sunset, rich with reds and oranges and golds, spread across the hilly horizon. The northern sky appeared shallow, almost within reach. The last thing we saw before dark was a line of snowy mountain peaks in the distance.

The next day we headed toward the village of Maldyak and its associated gold mines. We got off the Kolyma Highway and turned onto a bumpy dirt road. As we wound higher and higher into the mountains, the pines thinned out, became more stunted, and were replaced by thick coniferous shrubs. Whitewater streams rushed down the mountains. At one point we descended to the bottom of a canyon and followed a crystal-clear river. I became mesmerized by the rapids. Deer and reindeer bounded across the land. Twice we came to unstable log bridges and were ordered off the truck. The logs, stapled loosely together with giant nails, were barely hinged, and the empty truck rattled precariously over them. I deeply inhaled the fresh, sharp mountain air and gazed at the virgin landscape, which reminded me of Zakopane, the mountain resort my family and I went to in Poland.

It was hard to believe that within this beautiful wilderness, thousands of innocent people were sent to work and die unnecessarily. I didn't feel defeated as I thought about the life ahead of me, but I was tense with anticipation, and I tried to tame my fears with one thought: I had to survive so I could go back to Poland and find my family. Having made it through Burepolom, having made it through so many days and nights of hunger and filth and terror, I knew I had the capacity to persist. But that capacity had its limits. I didn't want to test them.

The truck slowed down to make a sharp turn, and as the road straightened out, several one-story wooden houses appeared. Then I saw the zone, with its barbed wire, watchtowers, wooden gate, and red banners proclaiming Soviet virtue. The camp was new, so all prisoners were housed in gray-green military tents. There were only two barracks in the zone: one was the kitchen and mess hall; the other, the bathhouse and administration quarters. There was no electricity or running water. The tents were heated by wood fed into iron barrels.

My brigadier, Gromov, a former manager and financial officer for a large industrial company in Sverdlovsk, had been arrested for embezzling millions of rubles. His inclination for criminal activity led naturally to his transformation into a respected *urka* leader, complete with tattoos and obscene language. Gromov's skin sagged, and his long face drooped. He had two fierce lines between his eyebrows and deep creases running from his nose to the corners of his mouth. But his body was smooth and sinewy, like an athlete's. I told him my name, and he replied gruffly, "It doesn't sound Russian." I told him I was from Poland. He paid no attention. "Well, you don't look like you worked much. You probably had a good life over there. But here, you're going to work, and work hard, or you won't eat." He glared at me and spoke to his helper. "We'll start him with the wheelbarrow. Then we'll see how he's doing." He then turned to me and poked his finger into my chest. "You work, you eat. You stop working, you die. I take care of my people if they produce, but loafers don't stand a chance."

My brigade was assigned to clear a new area of boulders, stones, roots, and shrubs. Gromov divided the area into small squares measuring forty steps on a side and assigned a pair of prisoners to each one. The daily norm was to remove six to eight cubic meters of topsoil that, I was disappointed to find out, rarely contained gold. The gold appeared about ten to twenty meters down. Some of the older mines in Maldyak were nearly forty meters deep.

In the summer sun, my tunic quickly dampened as I ran the wheelbarrow full of dirt and stones across the latticework of boards. The concentration it took not to fall down into the holes made me sweat as much as the work itself. Staring at the planks all day long, watching for fallen rocks, maneuvering the single iron wheel over the boards, I was blind to the men struggling around me, deaf to their threats, curses, and moans. Everything disappeared except for the railway of boards.

Despite the warm weather, only the top meter of soil was thawed. This was relatively easy to dig out with a shovel, but digging into the permafrost required a pickax or chisel and hammer. Here the norm was lessened. The work sites were spaced regularly between the boards, which ran from each site to the edge of the large rectangular dumping area for dirt and stones. Running the heavy wheelbarrow on the bare bumpy ground was impossible; hence the boards. This system worked fairly well until the work site dropped about two meters below the surface; then the stones and dirt could no longer be heaved overhead and onto the wheelbarrow. At that point we had to load the wheelbarrow at the bottom of the pit and push it up a plank to ground level. This task usually required the efforts of both my partner and me—he pushed while I pulled the wheelbarrow up backward by the handles. The deeper the excavation went, the more intricate the system of boards became. They went from the ground level to a landing, where another board was placed going in the opposite direction. Sometimes it took a zigzag path of two or three landings to reach the surface. At depths of four or more meters, the excavated earth was placed in baskets and hauled up by a pulley. To break up large chunks of the frozen earth, deep holes were drilled and filled with dynamite. Gromov, an expert with explosives, personally placed the dynamite and lit the fuse.

For the most part I was assigned to newer sites where every aspect of the work was manual. The wheelbarrow runs were fairly simple at first: it took only forty-three steps to go from the work site to the dumping ground. But as my brigade cleared ground farther away from the dumping area, I found myself running the loaded wheelbarrow over greater distances, with more variation in the grade of the boards. Slight inclines, barely perceptible when walking, became mountainous when I was running a heavy load. The primitive iron wheel seemed more of a curse at these moments, as it would stick on almost anything, and if the wheelbarrow tipped even slightly to one side the whole load could turn over. With every run my calves, thighs, chest, and shoulders bulged to the point of bursting. As gravity pulled down on a full load, the wheelbarrow took on a life of its own, rolling faster and faster downhill, dragging me behind. You had to be shrewd and lucky to make it down the planks without smashing into anything. I dug my feet into the ground, reined the handles in, and hung on for dear life.

As if the bumps, sloping boards, shouting guards, and brigadiers weren't enough, we had to endure three additional curses: mosquitoes, gnats, and horseflies. I couldn't stop wondering how, with long winters and brief springs and summers, the insects could burgeon and thrive. But burgeon and thrive they did. After one week of warm weather, they were out in full force. The thawing snow and ice overfilled the streams and rivers and left swamps on the expansive floodplains. The mosquitoes were three or four times bigger than those in Poland. Their poison caused tremendous itching, which in turn caused the welts to get bigger and cause even more itching. I scratched my bites until they bled.

Dark clouds of gnats followed me wherever I went, swarming into my nose, ears, mouth, and eyes and down my shirt. But the worst were the horseflies—black, plump, shiny, and long-winged. Their stings could penetrate light clothing and left painful, plum-sized welts. Luckily for me, the bugs found my sweat and body odor less appealing than those of other prisoners, some of whom were stung and bitten to the point of becoming ill or infected.

My partner, Vadim Alekseyev, had been working in the mines for eight months. Before that he had constructed roads and worked as a lumberjack for three years. At first he was wary of having me as a partner—newcomers were usually a great hindrance. But when he saw how eager I was to work hard, he warmed up to me. Before his arrest, Vadim had been a mathematics professor at Leningrad University and a member-correspondent of the Academy of Sciences of the Soviet Union. He was not yet forty and must have been extremely talented to receive a position of such high distinction at such an early age. He had traveled abroad frequently as a lecturer, something only the most trusted Soviet citizens were allowed to do. We arranged to sleep next to each other in the tent so we could talk in the evenings.

Vadim's mother was from an old aristocratic family from St. Petersburg. Nearsighted, he squinted when he talked to me, his glasses having been stolen three years before in the first transit prison. His high forehead, rimmed by slick black hair, was wrinkled in an expression of concentration, and his gray-green eyes sparkled when he talked about his family and his work. I liked his gentle manner. When he explained the mystique of running the wheelbarrow, he stood close, spoke softly, and delicately moved his hand as though he were holding a piece of chalk at the blackboard. In the mine, however, he worked like an ox, breaking up boulders with grace and efficiency by expertly pinpointing the striking place and swinging the sledgehammer in multiple arcs until they broke.

His story poured out of him during the first few days we worked together. Vadim was arrested in the fall of 1937 and spent more than five months in the prison in Leningrad. He was accused of organizing a counterrevolutionary group of students and professors aimed at destroying the Soviet state and assassinating Stalin. At first he was deprived of sleep for eleven days and interrogated. When that didn't work, he was locked in a booth with two other prisoners for five days with only enough space to stand. His interrogators, young and zealous to prove themselves to their NKVD bosses, beat him with a rubber truncheon and twice staged mock executions—once, holding a pistol to his temple; the other time, placing the barrel of a gun in his mouth.

Vadim still held out. It wasn't until he was told that his parents, wife, and three children would be arrested and shot before his eyes that he broke down. He not only confessed to the preposterous accusations but implicated some of his colleagues and students as well. He was sentenced to ten years of hard labor plus five years in exile.

Vadim and I worked well together. I was amazed that after all he'd gone through, he could still have some feeling and interest in helping me, a total stranger. He taught me how to load and unload the wheelbarrow, how to run it safely on the boards, and how to crush the rocks most effectively. He was still capable of smiling on the rare occasions when I joked with him; he liked to tell me that for a bad joke you were given five years, but for a very good one you could get twenty-five. In defiance of the widespread principle, "You die today, I die tomorrow," I had found someone who cared about me, and this proved to me that you didn't have to become a beast to survive in this human wilderness.

Getting to know someone was usually a blunt, speedy process. You wanted to know the person's age, sentence, and occupation; where he was from; what had happened to his family; if he had been interrogated. Often I learned more from the way the person responded than from what he actually said. Some people were open; others were inhibited, fearing the presence of informers.

As quickly as acquaintances developed, they were broken. People were moved to other brigades, subdivisions, or camps; fell ill and were sent to the hospital; or died. Hunger made it difficult to share any food, and I often wondered what I would do if Vadim asked me for half of my *paika*. I didn't think I could give it to him.

Fortunately, neither one of us ever asked the other for food, nor did we offer it. We both knew that this sanctum could not be violated if we were to remain friends. Generosity between us was displayed mostly at work, where he made it easier for me to run the wheelbarrow and I made it easier for him to load. But most of all, generosity came in our evening talks. Camp friendships were about one thing: trust. You wanted to know who slept next to you and who ate from the same plate. You wanted to know on whom you could rely during the inevitable daily crises. You learned to judge people quickly, to size up those who appeared friendly and those who seemed likely to give you trouble. And on top of everything, you developed and maintained a sense of caution that sometimes bordered on paranoia. Political prisoners were usually much more cautious and introverted than criminals, who talked and talked, fabricating all sorts of stories to upgrade their status among their friends. Politicals were open only to a point and only when close ties were established. Then they might open their hearts to you. They were well aware that "friends" often harbored ulterior motives, as many prisoners who came from the Party and NKVD became informers in the camp.

The days were getting shorter, the sun barely hoisting itself above the horizon. On cloudy days the sun appeared silvery-orange and perfectly round, and I could almost follow it as it made its short course across the southern sky. Every now and then the sun and moon appeared together, which I interpreted as auspicious. The working hours remained the same; we left the zone in darkness and returned in darkness. I was still making my norm and getting my full seven hundred grams of bread every day. My palms were completely callused; my fingers, stiff and muscular; my body, slim but strengthened. I felt more and more hunger.

The only way to fend off despair and depression was not to think. I learned to shut out everything, to escape into the safety of my own space. Thoughts crawled into my mind like serpents, but I learned to sever them with the thrust of a shovel or pickax. I broke time down into hours, so that I only had to exercise my will for short periods—from waking up until noon, from noon until the evening meal, from the evening roll call until bedtime. I

forbade myself to think about the days ahead or about the length
of my sentence. I nearly banished thoughts of home because it
took only a moment of lost concentration to slow down, fall in a
hole, irritate somebody, not make the norm. Only mechanical
movements mattered: shoveling the earth, chopping up the permafrost, loading and unloading the wheelbarrow.

Fighting, quarreling, hunger, and thoughts of suicide broke
prisoners down, and I veered away from these hazards and kept
up my steady, relentless course. I never traded my ration to pro-
cure a smoke. I continuously searched for a better ax, a sharper
shovel, a heavier spike and hammer. Whenever I could, I snuck a
few pieces of gold and hid them in the ground, retrieving them on
days when I couldn't fulfill the norm. Between the hostile prisoners and guards and the workload, I was always aware of how easily I could break down, but until that happened I would do whatever it took to survive.

Volodia had been in prison since the age of nineteen. When I met
him he was twenty-four—closer to my age than any other prisoner—but we were about as different as two prisoners could be.
He had been raised in a deeply religious family near Ryazan, and
the five years in Kolyma hadn't changed his beliefs. In school he
was intimidated and harassed for not belonging to the Pioneers
or Komsomol. He ensured his rejection by the universities and
trade schools by writing that he was a believer on every application. When conscripted into the Red Army, he refused to bear
arms and was promptly arrested. Initially he was sentenced to
five years; ten more years were added because he insisted on practicing his faith in prison.

Volodia reminded me of a stork with his white skin, gangly
arms, and jittery movements. He rarely met anyone's eyes when
he talked, but he liked to talk to me about the religious practices
in Poland. From time to time I caught him crossing himself or
touching his thin lips in the sign of the cross. He'd been hanging
around the kitchen after meals with a group of *dokhodyagas*—
garbage eaters, the most degraded prisoners—and I wondered
what would happen first, whether he'd break down or give up.

It was late in the afternoon—I was running a heaping wheelbarrow on the icy boards—when out of the corner of my eye I saw Volodia running a load on a path parallel to mine. I thought he had slipped and stopped, but I was wrong. He and the wheelbarrow were tipping to one side. I heard a cry and the scraping of metal and rocks. I stopped immediately, then zigzagged around the boards to reach him. He lay motionless, about six meters down, partially covered with dirt, snow, and the overturned wheelbarrow. I shouted at the top of my lungs for help and jumped down into the pit. He was breathing, but his eyes were closed, and he didn't respond to my questions. I lifted the wheelbarrow and began to uncover him.

Gromov arrived and cursed at Volodia. "You scum! Saboteur! Enemy of the people! I've wanted to get rid of you for a long time." Volodia didn't respond. I lifted his eyelids and saw that his eyes were rolled back. I thought he was dying. "Bring him up!" Gromov shouted. Another prisoner and I tried to lift and carry him without twisting his spine, but it was impossible without a stretcher. Shishkov, Gromov's helper and bodyguard, lumbered up, his muscles bulging beneath his tunic; he threw Volodia's limp body over his shoulder and climbed the ladders. I followed them to the tent. Gromov told me stay with Volodia until the *feldsher* came from Maldyak.

Volodia remained unconscious and breathed laboriously. The brief medical training I'd had in Nakhodka had taught me to listen to his heart and take his pulse. I rolled him face-down on the stretcher to prevent him from swallowing his tongue or choking on mucus that collected in his throat, and his breathing improved. The *feldsher* arrived the next day and said Volodia had broken some ribs and possibly punctured a lung. One of Volodia's legs was fractured in two places, and he suspected other internal injuries. The *feldsher* and driver loaded Volodia onto the bed of the truck, covered him with blankets, and left for Maldyak. I never heard from him again.

The next day Gromov assigned me to work with Volodia's former partner, Ruchka, which meant "Little Hand" (he had been a pickpocket). It was a bad partnership from the beginning. His first words to me were, "First I worked with a religious freak. Now a Polish Jew. I don't know what's worse." He loved to mock and insult the politicals in the brigade, and he considered me one of them because of my friendship with Vadim.

I continued running the wheelbarrow; Ruchka was supposed to break down boulders and large rocks and load the wheelbarrow. After a few runs I became exasperated. He had broken only the smallest rocks and left the large ones for me.

"It takes two people to make the norm," I said. "I can't do it myself."

"Wrong, cocksucker. You make your own norm. I'm making mine." He glanced at the pile of small rocks.

Not only did he leave the large rocks for me to break, but he kept overloading the wheelbarrow. I asked him not to fill it so high, but he paid no attention. I didn't know how to deal with him, and in the evening I talked to Vadim about it as we lay next to each other on the bed board. It was such a small thing, Ruchka's harassment, but the unfairness of the situation got to me. The fact that I could neither defend myself nor complain to anyone made the personal attacks all the more irritating. Ruchka tried to trip me when I ran the wheelbarrow, he hit me whenever he passed me, and he left me to do the heaviest work. Twice I asked Gromov to change my partner, but he ignored my request.

Several weeks later, Ruchka and I found ourselves standing near each other by the stove. A pile of logs lay up against it, drying out. "Fucking Jew," he said, and jabbed me under the chin. The strike made me bite my tongue.

I spat on his feet and glared in his eyes. "Fuck your filthy mother," he growled. That sent me over the edge. I grabbed a log and swung. I wanted to hit his ugly face, break his teeth, bash his head. I would've killed him, but he moved to the side and the log struck his shoulder. He roared out of surprise and pain, holding his shoulder, not exactly sure what I had done.

"You're dead, fucker!"

I was on the floor, Gromov and Shishkov pinning down my arms and legs while Ruchka struck my face and stomach. Vadim tried to pull the men off. "Shut up, Contra," one of Gromov's criminal friends said, pushing Vadim. Ruchka tried to kick my head but missed and caught me in the jaw. My face went numb.

Gromov and Shishkov dragged me to the guards' quarters. Gromov reported the incident, stating that I was the instigator. Ruchka wasn't mentioned at all.

The head guard replied, "Five days in the isolator."

CHAPTER 12

The Isolator

The isolator was a windowless, gray concrete building with a flat tar roof. I passed it twice every day, going to and returning from the mines. The solitary building was outside the zone and encircled by a double row of barbed wire.

Every time I passed the building I felt disturbed and slightly frightened. I always feared that one day I, too, would be locked inside. The feeling was like a premonition; that in some unknowable way, my fate was connected to the isolator, and I superstitiously believed that by looking away from it when I walked by, I could escape the force it had over my life. The guard fiddled with the padlock and pushed open the iron door. We stepped into a small vestibule. A single encaged lightbulb burned through a film of dust, cobwebs, and dead insects. An unfinished bench sat against the left wall, and above it was a board with ten nails. Prison garb dangled from four of them, beneath which were four pairs of boots. On the opposite side were a table and chair.

"Take off your clothes," the guard ordered. "Keep only your underwear and undershirt."

A hallway led out from the vestibule. Through the murky light from another encaged lightbulb, I could see five doors on each side of the corridor. "Second on the left," the guard ordered. He never looked me in the eyes but gripped my arm tightly as he pushed open the door. The dim light from the hallway illuminated rippling water on the floor. I stepped inside. With a loud slam, the door closed. Everything became dark. The guard slid the bolt across the door and clicked the padlock.

The ice-cold water numbed my feet and sent spasms into my calves. I grabbed onto the bucket next to the door to catch my breath, then sloshed over to a wooden bench against the opposite wall. Light seeped through a slat in the door. The wall was slimy. The odor of mildew filled my nose. I lay down with my face away from the wall, brought my knees up to my chest, and huddled into a ball. Tucking each hand under the opposite armpit, I squeezed my arms close to my sides and tried to fall asleep.

The water was a permanent feature of the isolator; I could tell by the thickness of the slime on the walls and floor. It kept me confined not only to the cell but also to the bench, the effect obviously intended. At least this isolator had a roof—I'd heard of other isolation cells that had no roofs, leaving the prisoner at the mercy of the elements and insects. The most torturous cells were designed so that the prisoner had only enough room to stand. After three to five days in this cell, the prisoner's knees were badly strained, if not permanently injured.

Condensation dripped from the ceiling into the pool of water at a slow but steady rate. I counted the drops that landed on my hip. My underwear and undershirt were already damp, and I was shivering. My neck and shoulders got stiff and cramped. The soggy raw wood was decaying, especially on the edges of the bench, exposing soft but pointed splinters. I figured out the direction of the grain and moved with it to avoid getting stuck. The bench was so narrow I could not lie on my back, and when I lay on my side, my legs hung over the edge; I had to keep them bent all the time. It was difficult to decide which side to lie on—on one side my face was pressed up against the slimy wall; on the other, my back became damp. Pulling the bench away from the wall was out of the question—the legs were embedded in the cement floor. Sitting was difficult because there was no place to put my feet, and I didn't want to lean against the wall, so I hugged my knees to my chest, wedging my heels against the edge of the bench. The water on the floor was an ingenious touch. I pictured the NKVD architect who designed the cell discussing its features with his superiors: how to deprive the prisoner of rest, agonize him, maybe drive him insane—even kill him—all without leaving a mark on his body. I lay with my back to the wall, preferring a cold, wet back to a face full of mold and mildew.

My legs began to ache. I slowly sat up and lay down on the other side, protecting my face with my hands. I ran my finger along a thick, moist, jelly-like ridge on the wall that burst when I pressed too hard. The water's slow, hypnotic drip was the only sound in the cell. I shouted, wanting to fill the thick, stifling silence. "One! Two! Three! Four!" It didn't sound like my voice. I counted to twenty, then counted backward from one hundred. Suddenly I was screaming, "Ruchka! You fucking dog's prick! You bastard! I hope you die with an ax in your skull and your balls ripped out! You should be here. You were the instigator. You son of a whore!" My voice echoed off the cement walls, stirring me into a frenzy. I swore at Ruchka some more, then at Gromov, then at the whole fucking world. The guard didn't respond. He probably wasn't even in the building. Hearing my sharp, amplified voice comforted me, made me feel less isolated, less afraid. Calmer, I went back to thinking about Ruchka. I should have struck back the first few times he tripped and pushed me. But he was bigger and stronger, and if I started a fight no one would interfere. This was one of the codes of camp life: prisoners fought one on one to settle their own disputes. If I'd gotten entangled with Ruchka, he'd have beaten me badly for sure. But I was beginning to see that even if I'd been beaten, I'd have established myself among the *urkas* and gained the respect of the other prisoners—and I wouldn't have wound up in the isolator. I wasn't afraid of fighting back, but I wasn't born a street fighter. I could put up with being harassed verbally and physically, but I had a bottom line, and Ruchka crossed it when he insulted my mother. I needed to recognize that bottom line and defend it, fighting fiercely without becoming enraged and striking with an intent to kill. My violent outbursts would lead me nowhere except to the isolator, and that would turn me into a *dokhodyaga* faster than working in the gold mine.

Did I really intend to kill Ruchka? Certainly I wanted to hurt him badly, but I didn't really want to kill him. Many guards and prisoners looked for the opportunity to hurt, torture, and kill, but I didn't have a killer instinct. Rage could result in killing, but it was different from the desire to kill.

In the Red Army I once antagonized the master sergeant—a fat, stupid, ugly lout—by correcting him when he lectured about international affairs. I had no idea he was quoting from *The Agitator's Booklet*, the party's official instruction manual on how to present ideological issues to the population. His presentations were spotty and inaccurate; he knew nothing about international politics; he couldn't even locate Portugal on the map. He got back at me by making me do extra physical exercises after the rest of the battalion was sent home. I crawled through the mud, water, and snow, jumped over obstacles, and sprinted to the next course while he swore and shouted at me, saying he'd make me beg for forgiveness for my arrogant behavior.

One afternoon my classmates and I were cleaning our shotguns and bayonets. The sergeant casually inspected mine and glared at me. "Take it apart and clean it again." When he dismissed everyone else, he jeered in my face, "I'm going to run you down. I'll make you hang or shoot yourself just like the other soldiers who crossed me." I cleaned and reassembled the shotgun again, rage building inside. Without looking at it, he picked it up and slammed it down on the desk. "Do it again."

I grabbed the bayonet, forced him against the wall, and held the blade against his neck. I hissed two inches from his face, "One more word, and you'll never see your family again." I plunged the bayonet into a wooden desk.

He turned pale. "Quiet down," he mumbled nervously. "I'm just doing my job. I know you're a smart guy. Okay? It's over between us." I pulled the bayonet out of the desk and left.

That night I lay awake, certain to be arrested, but the military intelligence officers never came.

The damp cold air penetrated my body. It wasn't a cold that would leave me frostbitten, but it made it difficult to sleep, and I had to urinate frequently, which meant getting my feet wet again and again to get to the bucket. The darkness, cold, hunger, and silence put me in a state of semi-hibernation. My thoughts slowed and scattered. I didn't even think of bringing the bucket next to the bench so I wouldn't have to get my feet wet. I tried to settle and fall asleep but searched in vain for a comfortable position. The confinement of the bench was causing pain and agony. I counted thousands of water droplets, hoping to put myself in a trance and fall asleep. I used to be so irritated by a dripping faucet, especially when trying to fall asleep, but in the isolator it was comforting, entrancing, like the ticking of a grandfather clock.

The rattling and clicking of a lock pierced the heavy silence. A door opened. *"Podyom! Podyom!"** Pound, pound, pound. The footsteps, pounding, and shouting were repeated at other doors and, finally, at mine. "Get your ration," a voice said. I waded over to the door and found a diminished clump of bread and can of camp tea. I consumed the *paika* before I thought of leaving even a crumb for later hours. It was less than half of my normal bread ration, and there would be no soup or oatmeal served later in the day.

Another bang on the door was followed by the unlatching of the lock and the command, "Get your bucket." I waded over to the barrel, picked it up, and followed the guard to the end of the hallway, with the contents sloshing dangerously close to the rim. The guard ordered me to dump the contents in a hole through the cement floor. As I tipped the bucket, I overshot the target.

"Clean it up," the guard ordered angrily. I looked at him for a moment. "With your shirt. Wipe up the mess." I obeyed. Back in the cell I rinsed out the T-shirt in the water on the floor, wrung it out, and put it back on.

The next morning I woke up thirsty. With no drinking water in the cell, my mouth became parched. At first I could keep my lips

* "Wake up! Wake up!"

moist, but then my saliva began to dry up. My lips became chapped, my tongue stuck to the roof of my mouth, my throat became sticky. I could hardly swallow. I wanted to dip my fingers in the water or lick the moisture from the walls, but the thought of the billions of bacteria incubating there made my stomach lurch. I remembered reading about octogenarians in India and in the mountains of Georgia who drank their own urine to purify themselves. I'd never tasted my own, but if I became desperate it seemed preferable to the water on the floor.

The cell was as dark and quiet as a coffin. I didn't know if it was day or night. My cheek pressed against the damp wooden bench, my body contracted, I lay as though on a slow-moving river, on the surface of time, which I could no longer comprehend. I became weightless, suspended; my thoughts like clouds, whirling, changing shape, climbing on top of each other. I wanted to slow them down, to stop them, but could hardly focus on one thing. I was not only hungry, thirsty, and cold but also physically and mentally exhausted from the incessant shivering. Sensations and feelings waned. I became sluggish, dull, and drowsy. I dozed, came to, dozed again. There were no days, no hours, only minutes and seconds, millions of them, as heavy as the water droplets falling steadily to the floor.

Sleep, which had been so inconsequential before my arrest, was now a desperately needed harbor. I didn't care anymore that my bed was an unfinished board or that bedbugs fell on me from the ceiling, bloated with blood. Lice didn't bother me when I was asleep. Sleep was the only comfort I had known since my arrest. It took me away from the noise of the barracks, the filthy, dying prisoners around me, the stench thick in the air. Sleep was the only time I felt safe, not threatened by the guards or violent *urkas*. I developed a ritual: upon awakening, I would close my eyes again and count slowly to sixty, giving myself one more minute of comfort. The sound of the ringing rail early in the morning was the most bitter sound of all. If only I could fall asleep for these five days and wake up in another place, another time. But the hunger and cold kept me awake. My stomach growled. The knowledge that I was locked in the cell germinated fear, manageable at first but more difficult to conquer as time passed.

Muffled thumps sounded on the door across the hall. "Fascists! Fascists!" That was all I understood. The rest came out frenzied and in a language I couldn't understand. The thumping continued. No one responded. My heart raced. I wondered if I, too, would scream, pound my fists against the door, splash around the cell, howl into the murky silence. Escape was impossible, and no matter how much my neighbor and I might shout, no one would hear. What if I were to faint? choke? have a heart attack? go crazy? hang myself? Nothing. No one would care. I was a wild animal trapped in a cage. I wanted to thrash against the walls of the cell until I lost consciousness and died. Was my neighbor pounding the door with his fists or his head?

Agony screamed at me from all corners of the cell; searing pain exploded in my neck and temples. My muscles didn't obey as usual; some of them were quivering. My teeth chattered uncontrollably, and my tongue was dry and swollen. Out of saliva, unable to swallow, I feared I would choke. So much urine in the bucket—I didn't drink it. I still needed to urinate but could only spill a few painful drops. Diarrhea had taken away all my strength. I squeezed my belly hard to stop the pain, but it just went to a different place. Inhaling made it worse. I couldn't stop thinking about food—not ham, duck, or fried chicken but bread, oats, kasha.

I wanted to see or talk to someone, to know I hadn't been forgotten, wouldn't be left to die. The minutes felt like hours; the hours, like weeks and months. Is this unbearable, or is it something I can survive? I wondered. What is unbearable? How am I to decide where my limit is? How much can I bear? How much suffering must I take before I reach the point of self-destruction? No one can tell me where the edge is. Only I know how much physical and mental torture I can take. One day the cold, hunger, work, vicious guards, and *urkas* are bearable; the next day they could break me down. What is it like to break down?

I thought of the many pale, gaunt, death-like figures I had encountered in the prisons. Some confessed to crimes they had not committed, implicated their parents and children, and signed the most outrageous accusations after the first broken tooth or cigarette burn. Others survived months of interrogation, sleepless nights, pulled-out fingernails, and mutilated genitals but found the camps unbearable. Some people committed suicide within several days of their arrest. In Novosibirsk, two newly arrested Romanians, still wearing their fur coats, were both hanging by their scarves in the corner of the barracks at the end of the first day.

My arrest and trial on the front line had spared me from interrogation, and I wondered how I would react to it. I knew I could survive deprivation and vicious beatings, but what about torture?

The oppressive work regimen was a form of torture in itself. Sometimes I thought hacking the cement-hard soil with a wrought-iron crowbar was unbearable. I felt the limits of my endurance approaching when I couldn't fulfill the norm, when Gromov assigned me the most difficult jobs, when hunger made me weak and defenseless, when the wind blew in my face and through my clothes. I still wanted to live, but I thought about injuring myself as so many other prisoners had done, hoping to win several days in the hospital, to be assigned to a lighter job, to be transferred to another camp. But self-mutilation scared me. I didn't know if I'd be capable of cutting off a finger or toe. I once saw a man dragging a partially severed foot as he walked to the guards. He had tried to cut it off but couldn't finish the job. Blood gushed out and sank into the earth. I could probably cut off one finger, but that wouldn't be enough to get out of work. The thought of cutting into myself revolted me. I'd never do it. And inevitably the act would lead to another prison term, which scared me more than anything else.

The one thing I would never do, no matter how bad it got, was give myself an infection by forcing pus, saliva, or kerosene into my flesh. Prisoners used to inject a piece of straw or grass containing the substance under their skin or cut themselves and smear the substance in the wound. I'd witnessed many *mastirkas*,*

* *Urka* lingo for a self-inflicted infection.

and they always resulted in a blazing infection or septicemia. Sometimes limbs had to be amputated. Sometimes the infection spread throughout the body and the prisoner died—hardly the intended result.

It was becoming more and more difficult to make the norm. Would I reach the day, as so many others had, when I'd look for extra food in the garbage piles? It was the most common form of degradation. Rummaging through the garbage, eating rancid scraps of meat, chewing on fish skeletons—such behavior was so common that no one noticed. *Dokhodyagas* searched for food with half-human expressions and ate everything chewable. I was surprised by how quickly some prisoners fell into this state. Many men who seemed bigger and stronger than me rapidly deteriorated and began sifting frantically through fetid garbage. They ate decomposed material, stuffing it in their mouths and grabbing it out of each others' hands. Why some and not others? Why some and not all? The hard work, weather, rations, and living conditions were the same for everyone. The majority survived, but many gave up. At first I thought the *dokhodyagas* lacked inner strength, mental resistance, or faith in themselves or in God, but I was beginning to understand that they had simply lost hope and didn't want to be hungry anymore. The instinct for survival kept them from committing suicide. But I would rather kill myself than become a vermin-eater.

There were moments when I lost hope, when I felt as if I were hanging from a cliff and my hands were slipping. In the barracks in Buchta Nakhodka, I once caught an *urka* with his hand in my pocket trying to steal a wallet given to me by one of the political prisoners in Burepolom before he died. In it was a faded photo of his wife and daughter, and it had become very precious to me. As soon as I caught the *urka* trying to steal it, he began accusing me of stealing it from him. His buddies jumped me and took the wallet, but no one came to my aid. I was new. For the next few days they stole my bread, beat me, spat on me. More than the physical pain, it was the cruelty and hatred that drove me to despair.

After this incident I wanted to die, to kill myself, but I was too weak and injured to move. My plan was to go to the fence near a watchtower and start to climb. It would be over in a second. But these dark thoughts and feelings were foreign to me, and they passed after a brief time. Until the camps, I'd never thought of suicide. I believed in myself, in my luck, in my fate. Even now, after all I'd been through, hope circled back, though I didn't know how or why.

On the fourth day in the isolator, a curious thing happened—I began to miss the mine. I missed pushing the wheelbarrow. I missed the pickax, the shovel, the crowded barracks, the camp—everything I had hated. Even with the work, filth, violence, and senseless death, I wanted to go back to the camp, to tree-felling or mining. There, at least I was among people—some good, many bad, but a few who actually cared about me. The daily fight to survive—to make the norm, keep the full ration, prevent frostbite, remain strong in spite of the gnawing hunger, get along with the brigadier and his friends, avoid clashing with the *urkas* and being singled out by the guards—often made me think only of myself. There was no room left for human feelings such as friendship, compassion, generosity. This was why there were so many fights; why the weak were trodden upon—everyone was looking for someone on whom to take out his anger. In Burepolom I felt myself becoming a different person, isolated from others, less apt to give help to someone who needed it. I began losing what had been instilled in me since childhood—warmth, sensitivity, readiness to help. My humanity was slipping.

In Buchta Nakhodka, Dr. Semyonov and Dr. Popugajeva taught me how to defy this seemingly inevitable degradation. I was able to catch myself on the way down and reverse the process. If I hadn't been helped along the way, I probably would have become cold and devoid of any civil or human impulse. Perhaps it was my fate to meet people who not only saved my life but also showed me how to remain sensitive to those around them. Meeting them gave me something to strive for besides survival and gave me hope to keep on going. Kolyma had taught me that degradation was not merely a by-product of the conditions we lived in; it was part of the plan. The intent wasn't simply to extract as much labor as possible but also to force the prisoners to devolve into animals.

In the dark cell, hungry and shivering, I thought of all I had been through: the Red Army, the tank accident, the trial, Efim Polzun, Burepolom, the cattle car, Buchta Nakhodka, Kolyma, the isolator. Home. What lay ahead? Where was my fate taking me? I felt at peace. I would fight for my life. I would stay out of the isolator. It had brought me closer to the edge than I'd ever been before.

Late in the evening of the fifth day the guard released me. The night was bright, the full moon glowing in the deep blue sky. I was stunned by the cold air filling my lungs; it was only the middle of September. Such an early winter, I thought. I blew on my hands and wiggled my cold toes. At the gate, I checked through the guardhouse and entered the zone.

Alone in the isolator, I'd felt somewhat heroic. But going back to the tent, I felt scared. I was afraid Gromov and Ruchka would take advantage of my weakened condition. I wanted to make peace, but how could I make peace with people who despised me, who wanted to hurt me?

Gromov was sitting on a bed board next to the stove with some of his *urka* friends. He patted me on the shoulder as I walked by. "I see you're doing well. You're probably tired, though. Tomorrow, instead of running the wheelbarrow, you'll load the conveyor belt. That'll give you time to recuperate. Then we'll talk."

CHAPTER 13

Winter

A new work assigner arrived from Maldyak, a big shot who scared everyone, including Gromov. Every morning for two weeks he supervised the brigadiers as they led the prisoners to the work sites, and during the day he and his two aides randomly measured the outputs. In the evening he publicly chastised the brigadiers whose units didn't fulfill the norm. He and his men looked like thugs; their cockiness and pretension were typical of high-status *urkas;* rumor had it, however, that they had been high-ranking NKVD officers. High-ranking *urka* or *predurok*—there wasn't much difference between the two. But I had come to trust the *urka* far more than the *predurok*, who had been in the NKVD.

One morning we were assembled in front of the gate. It was bitterly cold, especially after standing an hour and a half for head count. We danced, hopped, patted our arms, rubbed our legs, blew on our hands. The work assigner appeared from the guardhouse wearing a sheepskin coat and high leather boots. Light snow gathered on the fancy fur covering his shoulders. He stepped up on a stump and gave a brief speech. "Attention all prisoners. Despite your heinous crimes, the Soviet state has awarded you the gift of life. So try with your honest and dedicated work to earn back the trust of your Motherland and your freedom. The Motherland is in peril." His metallic voice fell on me like the thrust of a hammer. "Every ounce of gold can be made into a bullet to kill the Nazis. The Soviet state, the Communist Party, and Comrade Stalin are leading us to new victories and to the glory of communism. We must do all we can to aid our courageous soldiers and officers fighting on the front.

"I must also deliver the following news." He paused a moment and looked gravely at the crowd. "Twenty-two people from the Maldyak mine were tried and executed last week for sabotage and counterrevolutionary activities. They failed to fulfill the norm. They never tried to pay for their crimes or to prove their devotion to the Motherland and to our Great Leader. Remember: work hard; fulfill the norm; and give gold to the country."

He scanned the prisoners to see the effect of his speech, his rigid expression and posture inviting a challenge. The way he commanded the brigadiers made me think he was used to giving orders and being obeyed. He seemed inclined to shoot twenty-two more prisoners.

Because he and his aides were in danger of being killed by the *urkas*, they served as each other's bodyguards. Poetic justice reigned in the camps. The waves of arrests in 1937–1939 turned yesterday's interrogators into today's prisoners, and victims of torture sometimes met their own torturers. You didn't have to be an *urka* to get revenge; if you were a political in good standing with the *urkas*, all you had to do was point out your former interrogator to them. I saw one former interrogator stabbed in the heart with a pickax, another smothered with a coat, another kicked and beaten to death in the barracks. In every case, the prisoners collaborated and claimed not to have seen a thing. Charges were rarely filed.

I was assigned to work in the steam shack crushing rocks and dirt and placing the broken pieces on a conveyor belt. From there the frozen dirt was thawed, rinsed, and sifted. Gold showed up in the residue. My new partner, Kyril Davidov, was a brawny, uneducated peasant. He'd been charged with group counterrevolutionary activity, counterrevolutionary agitation, terrorism, and sabotage. How he ended up as a political prisoner with a code four numbers long was beyond his—and my—comprehension. Kyril still hadn't gotten past the bewilderment of his arrest. All he talked about was his devotion to the state, his dedication to the *kolkhoz** he worked for, and his certainty that Stalin knew nothing about the arrests, camps, and executions. I felt sorry for him—his untarnished idealism would vex and torment him until the end of his days—but I loathed listening to him. His innocent, fervent belief in Stalin and communism was a painful reminder of how naive I had been not too long before.

However, Kyril was a superb work partner. He didn't mind when I took more breaks than he did or when I hid in the steam shack to get warm. He helped me fulfill my norm on many difficult days as I recovered from my stint in the isolator.

The winter was a curse in Kolyma. But before I suffered its effects, I was touched by its wild, desolate beauty. The first snow, at the end of September, caught me unexpectedly, as it did the few deciduous trees that hadn't shed their leaves. The next day it was gone—as were most of the insects—and the brief afternoons continued to feel warm. But by mid-October, full-fledged winter had set in. The mountains, valleys, and work quarries were white and peaceful. The hills appeared larger and closer, looming over the work site. The cold air smelled fragrant; the snow tasted clean and refreshing. I loved to let it melt in my mouth. The tents looked like temples with huge snow-covered domes. On cloudless days the sunlight turned the snow into sparkling prisms, the sky was cobalt blue, and the frozen snow crunched underfoot like glass. When fresh powder covered the earth, I trampled through a foot or more of it without making a sound, feeling light, unearthly, even happy.

Winter in Kolyma was much harsher than in Poland. At home winter followed the rainy days of fall. The first snow brought a joyous, refreshing change to ordinary life because of the way it transformed the trees, fields, streets, and buildings. My winter

---

* Collective farm.

pastimes included figure skating, ice hockey, and cross-country skiing. The welding of sky and land transformed the countryside I knew so well into a magical place. Skiing alone through the woods and fields was like writing in a secret diary, where every newly forged path and newly discovered place inspired day-dreams that were boundless and deeply personal.

Two events signaled the official beginning of winter in Kolyma: the distribution of winter clothing, and supplements added to the morning ration. The winter clothes were clean but previously used. Each of us received long underwear, a black tunic, quilted pants, a long quilted outer jacket, a felt hat with earflaps, rubber-soled boots, and fleece-lined mittens. These items were handed out indiscriminately, and it was up to us to find the right sizes. Everything I was given was much too big, and I spent hours trad-ing for a better fit. I began with boots about four sizes too large. On the first exchange, I traded them for one size smaller. Not per-fect, but better than what I had. This continued with every item of clothing. The atmosphere was like a flea market, intense but cooperative, with everyone seeking out someone else who might have something close to his size. I ended up with boots that were still too large, but I made them fit by stuffing a towel and extra foot rags inside. I held up the oversized pants and underwear with a piece of rope. The tunic and quilted jackets fit well. Un-fortunately, there were no scarves, and the sharp wind cut into my unprotected eyes, ears, and face. I had an additional under-shirt, which I'd stolen in the bathhouse, and wrapped it around my neck. It quickly became damp and icy, but it was better than nothing.

The black, stiff boots had no lining, and the soles were made from old tire treads. Mine had not worn all the way down, which I considered lucky, thinking I would have better traction in the snow. Felt boots were a luxury reserved for the brigadiers, *pre-durkis*, guards, and camp administrators. The camp commander and NKVD officers wore hats, boots, and coats made from rein-deer fur, the most stylish material in Kolyma.

I was happy to get the winter clothing but was less enthusias-tic about the supplements added to the morning ration. Grisha, a seasoned *urka* who managed the mess hall, greeted the prisoners with little cups, each containing a dark brown syrup. It stunk and tasted bitter. I wouldn't touch it. "Drink it," Grisha commanded. "Right here."

Yuri, my new work partner, goaded me further. "Don't smell it, drink it. It's an extraction of pine needles, *khvoya*. It contains vitamin C, the best prevention for scurvy." I closed my eyes and let it ooze down my throat. For the next two hours I drooled and spit the caustic residue.

At the next table a *predurok* gave each of us a tin cup half-filled with clear liquid. The smell of alcohol wafted around my nose. I'd heard we'd be given pure alcohol every morning to warm us up before going out, but I was afraid to drink it, not knowing what effect it would have on me. "Drink up," the *predurok* prodded. It went down like fire.

Gromov and his buddies were standing away from the table, hidden by a post. As I walked by, Gromov's friend kicked me in the butt. "Look, walrus's prick. You'd better learn the rules if you want to live in our brigade."

I couldn't imagine what I'd done that was so offensive. Gromov was aggravated. "The alcohol belongs to me. You take it in your mouth, and you spit it back out right here." He held out a tin pot. "Then I'll distribute it the way I see fit." Yuri spit his alcohol obediently into the pot. "Today you're forgiven," Gromov told me. "But watch it from now on."

As it got colder, swallowing the shot became more tempting, but I spat it obediently into Gromov's tin pot. He traded the alcohol for tobacco, bread, and clothing or bribed the guards with it. Gromov proved to be a decent brigadier, however, because he let me keep the relatively easy job of loading the conveyor belt. Even here, I grew weary and sore. The long hours of standing at the conveyor belt, crushing rocks and loading dirt, left me exhausted. Then there was the daily shoveling of snow, which in October was wet and heavy, and the daily gathering of wood, which had to be carried too far against the perpetual wind. Permanently tired, my back aching and my hands and legs becoming stiffer, I stopped my daily routine of early morning washing and exercising. I figured I had enough exercise in my day already.

As the temperature fell, the snow became dry and fluffy. The incessant high winds, like a potter's fingers, blew the snow into unusual patterns and places. Under the weight of successive snowfalls, the snow became pressed and packed together, often blocking the entrance to the tent; in the morning we often had to tunnel our way out before head count at six.

Yuri carried authority in his erect posture and stern facial expression, making him look taller and more serious than he really was. The *urkas* recognized his confidence and left him alone. He'd been an architect in Moscow. Well educated and widely traveled, he talked about the years he spent in France and Italy studying Byzantine architecture. He'd been a curator of the old churches in Moscow, and the new Soviet policy of tearing down the old churches or converting them into clubs, movie theaters, and warehouses upset him deeply. "They are world treasures, the only evidence we have of our ancient past," Yuri would say plaintively.

He had been in Kolyma for four years but had managed to maintain his physical strength. Although he was an architect, he had the body of a manual laborer, and he generously shared his strength with me. He had managed to avoid getting scurvy, which affected most prisoners who'd been in Kolyma for more than a year; hadn't lost any fingers or toes to frostbite; and had always received a first-category food ration, important for prisoners like us because no one back home was sending us food. The conveyor belt enhanced our friendship because it broke down often, especially during cold temperatures, giving us plenty of time to talk without being punished for not making the norm.

The conveyor belt was a new improvement in the mines. It ran on electricity fueled by burning wood, but not all the kinks had been worked out. The only nuisance to us was the noise—the incessant screeching, grinding, and thumping of the motor and dropping rocks made it impossible to hear one another. When it stopped, Yuri and I filled the silence with detailed, wide-ranging discussions about our lives. Yuri's colorful, gripping descriptions took me in my imagination to Italy, Greece, and Turkey, places I'd never been or even thought about visiting. In his enthusiastic descriptions I sensed his zest for life, beauty, and history. But then, with just as much fervor, he would smash a rock viciously and seethe through clenched teeth, "I would shoot the bastards who are destroying these cathedrals. Some of them are nearly a thousand years old and are so unique they can never be reconstructed. They aren't only Russian treasures but treasures of humanity. The Soviet government and the Communist Party have no right to do what they are doing to the buildings, or what they are doing to all of us, destroying the best people in the country. The Communists know only how to destroy—buildings and people. The best, the brightest, and the innocent."

I'd never really thought about the Soviet state's mission to desecrate or destroy the sacred buildings. I believed in Marx's proclamation that "religion is the opiate of the masses" and hadn't cared what happened to the churches, synagogues, and mosques. I didn't realize the buildings could be meaningful to people like Yuri, who wasn't religious.

I was growing perpetually tired, even upon awakening in the morning. One day, as we stole a break from our work, Yuri fixed his sad green eyes on me and said, "I'm worried about you. You don't look good."

"I don't think anything is really wrong," I said. "I'm still recovering from the isolator. It's my first winter here."

"Just tell me when you need more rest. I feel good. I can work a little harder." Yuri sighed and shook his head. "I'm worried about Yasha. We've been close friends since we were in school at the Institute of Architecture in Moscow."

I also liked Yasha. Although I didn't know him very well, I liked his unpretentiousness and outlook in life. "You don't compromise on right and wrong," he once said to me. "You fight for what you believe is right."

"What's wrong with Yasha?" I asked Yuri.

"He's so hardheaded. He's obsessed with finding out why the best people in this country, the most devoted Communists, are all in the prisons and camps. He can't accept that people falsely

signed confessions to the most heinous crimes. He won't accept
that people gave up. He thinks there must be another answer. So
he's gone on a hunger strike and refuses to go to work. He's suicidal. He wants to be tried and shot for sabotage. He's so self-
righteous—I can't talk to him anymore. Maybe you can try to
talk to him in the evening."

Yuri and I walked briskly back to the quarry, both to stay
warm and to avoid being prodded by the roaming guards and
brigadiers. You never knew who was watching you, but you always felt someone's eyes controlling your steps. The result was a
reflex of activity, of constantly doing something, even if it was
aimless. Most of us obeyed. Those who didn't paid for it with
smaller and smaller pieces of *paika*, then with the isolator, then
with death. The brigadiers were chummy with the guards, so it
was always them against us.

To create the illusion of activity, I pushed the empty wheelbarrow across the planks, and Yuri pushed it back. The only sounds
were our squeaking steps and a wailing northerly wind. Snow
swirled around our feet. The gusts blew away the dirty steam
coming from the steam shack, and the air smelled clean. Yuri
took a deep breath and said, "A blizzard is coming." Usually we
could tell when it was going to snow. The sky became gray and
heavy, drooping below the mountaintops, burying the horizon
far away—beyond the camps, beyond the hills, beyond everything. Snow started to fall—clumps of it, wet and heavy, slanting
sharply to the earth. The wind changed directions, fighting itself.
I looked straight up. The falling snow seemed to come from nowhere. I could barely see Yuri. I sat down on a stump and closed
my eyes.

"We've got to make it back to the zone," Yuri hollered.

Unable to see through the dense snow, we followed the conveyor belt to the steam shack. The mountains, watchtowers,
and mining pits had disappeared; the work sites and machinery
were quickly buried, and the snow drifted over the road and
transformed the shrubs into giant hills. We could barely step
forward, the wind was so sharp and strong. I squeezed my eyes
shut and buried my chin in my T-shirt, holding onto Yuri's coat
with one hand and the conveyor belt with the other. We reached

the steam shack and squeezed in between the other prisoners taking refuge there. Two guards and a German shepherd stood in the corridor, apart from us. The wind forced its way through the cracks in the building, crying like a wounded dog, then changed to a low, singular moan. For over two hours we remained in the steam shack, and it was getting dark. The guards ordered us back to the zone.

"I'm not leaving," I said to Yuri.

"Are you crazy? You'll freeze to death."

"How will we find our way back?" I was very weak and frightened.

"You won't get lost. I'll stay right next to you. We'll all hold on to a rope, and the dogs will lead us back. They can smell their way home."

I hung on to the rope with both hands and bent my knees to keep my balance as we felt our way over the terrain. Behind my closed eyes I envisioned a long string of prisoners, all tied to the same fate, cast into a frozen hell by a power we could not touch or see. Many of the same people who had ripped us from our lives were now holding on to the very same rope, the tormented and tormentors all thrown in together. I felt a twinge of justice. I wished the guards and *predurkis* would all die horrible deaths, that the whole system would eat itself alive, but I didn't waste my time or energy obsessing on it, as many prisoners did.

I couldn't see anything beyond Yuri's back and clung to the rope as though it were a life preserver. I inhaled cautiously, afraid the cold wind would burn my lungs. The swirling snow made me dizzy and kept pulling my head down. Short of breath, I became lightheaded. Every second I thought I'd fall or faint, but somehow I kept stumbling forward. With the familiar landmarks gone, I had no idea how much farther we had to go and was sure we'd never make it back. My foot fell upon something soft—a prisoner who had let go of the rope. "Stop!" I shouted. But there was no stopping. No one could hear my voice. I leaned down and pulled his arm toward the rope. "Here!" I tried to link his hand with the rope. "Hold on!" It was no use. The man's arm fell to the ground when I let go. Yuri's stern command to move on carried me forward.

Miraculously, we reached the camp. In the middle of the blizzard we stood for head count. Three prisoners were missing. I knew exactly where one of them was. Another missing prisoner, Dimitry Korotchenko, slept next to me. Physically he was strong, but spiritually he was broken. With his large brown eyes, he had the look of a dying deer. He'd become a *dokhodyaga*, and I guessed he'd picked his final moment.

Blizzards could last not just for hours but days. The bodies of prisoners who got lost weren't found until springtime, often within one hundred meters of the zone. As a storm dispossessed the camp of its landmarks and reminders of lost freedom—the watchtowers, the work sites, the barbed wire—it also obliterated our sense of being locked in. Sometimes I fantasized that the blizzard would free us, that its power would wipe away the zone, the camp, all of Kolyma, and that when it was over we would be free. Nature constantly surprised me, humbled me, reminded me again and again of how vulnerable we all were, prisoners and guards alike, in the harsh Arctic winter.

New dangers presented themselves in the cold. We were only released from work when the temperatures dropped below minus 50 degrees Fahrenheit, and the wind chill was never taken into account. Breathing became painful when the temperature plummeted to minus 25 or minus 30, piercingly so as it approached minus 40 or minus 50. It was dangerous to stop moving. During head count we jumped, ran in place, and slapped our bodies to keep warm. I perpetually kneaded my toes and curled my fingers into a fist. I paid most attention to the feeling in my toes, fingers, ears, and nose, as these areas were the most prone to frostbite. Yuri and I watched out for each other, calling out, "Rub your ears," "Rub your cheeks," or "Rub your nose" when we saw an area becoming white. I tried to keep my chin close to my chest and raised the collar of my jacket, covering the rest of my face with the shirt.

Touching a metal tool with a bare hand could tear off the skin, and going to the bathroom was extremely dangerous. A bout of diarrhea could land you in the snow forever. The safest place to relieve oneself at the work site was in a quarry, but the quarries were available only to those who worked in them. I trained myself to hold it all day long and relieve myself only in the shelter of the zone. The *dokhodyagas*, often racked with diarrhea, soiled their pants. Working next to them was unpleasant, and back in the tent, when we began to warm up, the stench was unbearable. Those who had soiled themselves were often beaten and thrown out.

Every phase of mining became more difficult in the cold, but the norms, working hours, and food rations remained the same. The lucky ones were able to retain the first category, but those who slipped into the second or third food categories began to starve and weaken daily. A difference of only three hundred grams of bread and an additional bowl of soup or oatmeal could mean the difference between life and death; the difference between getting up in the morning or staying on the bed board and being sent to the isolator. The isolator deterred loafers. No one remained in the tent to get extra rest or recover strength, because those who did were rarely seen again.

One day I noticed Fyodor Babinich walking unsteadily through the barracks. Babinich was a very frightened man, afraid of his own shadow and suspicious of everyone around him. His eyes darted around constantly, and he used to whisper to anyone close enough to hear, "I know the system very well. I once worked with my own interrogators. You know who I was?" Fyodor lowered his voice. "I was in command. I can't tell you anything more, but I was in a position of high command. Don't tell anyone." I pitied Fyodor but also despised him, certain he'd been an interrogator or NKVD chief.

Now, as he circled the barracks, he paused briefly to stare into everyone's eyes like a hungry dog begging silently for food. In return he was spit on, cursed at, and pushed. He fell down, and I helped him get up and led him to his place. He recognized me, but his eyes were empty. All he talked about was how hungry he was, and he asked repeatedly for something to eat. The sound of his voice came from deep in his stomach, together with a foul, bilious odor.

There were so many others just like him, transformed before my eyes from hardy workers into hollowed-out scavengers, licking empty bowls, rummaging through the garbage, begging with their eyes. I came to realize that it wasn't age, strength, health, education, religious belief, or upbringing that determined one's fate. The two things that separated those who went down from those who didn't were the two most difficult things to control, things having nothing to do with the prisoner's will to survive. One came from the person—strength; the other from somewhere in the universe—luck or fate.

In winter the bed of death lay close to everyone. Death sometimes occurred at the work sites, but for some reason more people died in the barracks at night. In the morning, at the first discovery that someone had died, the corpse was stripped by the other prisoners. Once, during roll call at the end of the day, a prisoner fell and didn't get up. I thought he had slipped and was pinned down by the wood he'd been carrying. A group formed around him.

"I get the hat," one man said. Others grabbed the victim's boots, foot rags, coat, and pants. A fight broke out over the undergarments.

No sooner had the fallen prisoner been stripped naked than he moved his head, raised his hand, and stated weakly but clearly, "It's so cold." But then his head flopped back into the snow, and a glazed look came over his eyes. The ring of scavengers turned away with whatever scraps they had, unaffected. In those few minutes after being stripped, he probably died of exposure.

The barracks orderlies, usually invalids or elderly criminals, reported the deaths and stacked the naked corpses in the woods until the soil thawed and a mass grave could be dug. An elevated wooden platform was built to keep the corpses off the snow and away from animals, but we saw many animal tracks leading toward the cadavers. The guards and *predurkis* had the pleasure of warning us that wolves were especially dangerous in winter, as was evidenced by the partially eaten bodies. Talking about the threat gave them a special delight.

Not only wild animals were desperate for food. The vermin-eaters huddled around the stove in the tent, boiling and eating meat that smelled rancid and foreign. I was told they'd gotten the meat from the cadaver pile, which was hard for me to believe and deeply disturbing. I hadn't yet realized what hunger could do to a person and had a hard time not passing judgment on these people.

I often reflected on my own behavior: would I ever be so hungry and desperate that I would do the same? At first I thought I would rather die from hunger than eat human flesh, but when I started to decline, I couldn't be so sure.

I wasn't in the best physical condition. I felt dizzy upon awakening, and my mind was foggy. It took more time and effort to pull myself together and go to the mess hall in the morning.

The first time I saw blood after biting into my *paika*, I thought it was accidental and didn't pay attention to it. But when I saw it again and again, I realized I was developing scurvy. Also, I felt hungry much earlier in the day. The first-category ration was no longer enough to sustain me through a day of work, and I was no longer able to fulfill the norm. Gromov, however, falsified the reports. When we dug soil, he reported that we were digging out heavy stones, which lessened the norm; when Yuri and I were able to crush only half the amount of soil required, Gromov reported that we had achieved the full norm.

He wasn't doing anything out of the ordinary. If a brigadier cared about his men and wanted to ensure they received their full rations, he falsified the reports. This maneuvering—presenting false reports with inflated data—was known as *tufta*, and the person doing this was known as a *tuftach*. *Tufta* occurred every day, as not everyone could fulfill the norm, and it looked bad if the brigadier didn't make his quota. No one challenged the false reports because bribery and camaraderie were the modus operandi all the way up the line. Each higher-up expected the person below him to pay for the oversight, the form of payment depending on what was available. Discrepancies between the amounts in the reports and the amounts actually shipped could be blamed on insufficient air transport and difficulties in transportation due to bad weather. From the mining camps and processing centers, across the desks of the regional administrators, and all the way to the headquarters of Dalstroy, *tufta* spread through the bureaucracy like a virus. Moscow demanded numbers and that's what they got—real or imaginary.

My old partner Vadim remained my closest friend. We slept next to each other and ate most meals together, which meant a great deal to me. We shared our suffering, thoughts about our families, our hopes and our fears. Although intellectually Vadim was much more advanced than I, mentally and emotionally we were quite similar. I worried a lot, mostly about my family, which made me prone to anguished obsessions. But I also knew it could be dangerous to dwell for too long on the people and life I'd left behind, to expend my energy worrying about them. I needed to focus on staying alive myself.

It was amazing how easy it was to forget things I didn't want to remember. I pushed out the bad memories about the deportations I'd witnessed, the anti-Semitism I'd experienced, the Red Army indoctrination, my arrest and mock trial—even Burepolom. I tried not to think about the fellow prisoners who were becoming ill and dying right in front of me. I didn't lose sleep over these horrors, but I hadn't become totally insensitive to the suffering of others; if I could bring a dying man water or spare him an additional spoon of oatmeal, I did it.

I came to feel very comfortable with the *urkas*. I never tried to be like them, but I understood them and shared my life and knowledge with them. Most of the politicals were afraid of the *urkas* or looked down on them. The *urkas* smelled their fear and despised their haughtiness. However, I also deeply admired the intellectuals in the camp and wondered if I would ever learn enough to become their equal. I didn't feel ashamed of my ignorance, just sad that time was passing and that I might never have the chance to attend the university. I identified with the political prisoners more than with the military men or *urkas*, but they hardly ever accepted me because I was much younger than they and a foreigner. From time to time my foreignness raised interest, and I was questioned about life in Poland. The *urkas* were mostly interested in the material life in Poland—the way we lived, dressed, ate—and I was forever having to answer questions about Polish women.

Conversations with the politicals took an entirely different turn. They were interested in fascism in Europe, political alliances, the influence of Soviet propaganda outside the country. Many of them asked if people in Poland were aware of the mass political arrests, trials, and executions of 1937–1939, and they always asked how much we knew about the conditions of the labor camps, which were far worse than those under the tsars.

One evening while going to the mess hall, I stepped off the path a couple of times and finally stumbled into a snow bank. I thought that, being very tired, I'd simply lost my concentration. But when this happened again and again I realized I was suffering from chicken blindness, the result of a lack of vitamins A and D. Hoping to get rid of it before it got worse, I started taking a double portion of the pine needle extraction every day. But my health continued to deteriorate. Several weeks later, small red dots appeared on my calves and arms—unquestionable signs that my blood vessels were weak and hemorrhaging and the scurvy was advancing. Once a week a doctor or *feldsher* came from Maldyak to examine sick prisoners, but it was difficult to get on the list to see him if you could still walk and were able to work, and I could do both. There was no one I could ask for help; no one who would or could do anything for me. Most prisoners had the capacity to work for up to one year before they became debilitated; then they were assigned to a lighter job, given a period of convalescence in a special camp, or sent to the hospital for treatment.

I was fast approaching that state. Unable to see in the dark, I held onto Yuri's arm walking to and from the work site. I couldn't be very productive before the sun had risen, and the sicker I became, the angrier and more ashamed I was. I worried that I was becoming a burden to my workmate. I became obsessed with fear that I would become a *dokhodyaga* but tried to keep these feelings to myself.

One day we were released from work two hours early due to severely cold weather. The clinic was still going on, and I was fortunate to be able to see the doctor. I didn't hesitate to lie and present myself as a third-year medical student from Warsaw University; I gave him the diagnosis and remedy in the same breath. The doctor, a middle-aged man with thick glasses and short gray hair, looked at me with interest.

"You should be working in the hospital. Why are you working as a general laborer? There's a shortage of doctors and *feldshers*." He said he'd recommend that I be transferred to a camp for convalescents so I could be treated, and he'd suggest to the authorities that I be transferred to work as a *feldsher*.

CHAPTER 14

Kolyma Highway

The head guard met us at the gate with a list in his hand. "Attention! The following prisoners, report after dinner with your belongings. *Etap* will depart at ten o'clock."

I was overjoyed to hear my own name called. I didn't know if I was going to a convalescent camp or a hospital, but I was going to be treated, just as Dr. Baranovich had promised. Once again, someone seemed to be watching over me, making sure I would survive.

As news of the *etap* spread, word got around the mess hall that the destination was Orotukan—another gold mine. I was shocked, certain I didn't belong to this *etap*. Vadim told me to go to the guardhouse and explain there had been a mistake. "Don't argue with them, just tell them to call Dr. Baranovich in Maldyak to confirm his recommendation. You're in no shape to be heading for another gold mine."

The head guard was gone, and I talked to the guard on duty. "I was called for *etap*, but I'm sure there's a mistake. Dr. Baranovich recommended I be transferred to a convalescent camp for treatment."

"Get out of here!" The guard pushed me in the chest. "Everybody thinks they need treatment. You people don't appreciate the fact that we're keeping you alive. Most of you should be shot. Load up."

I didn't want to give up. If I went to Orotukan, it would probably be my last destination. I grabbed his sheepskin coat and said, "Please, listen"—but before I could say more, the muscular Mongolian guard grabbed my arms and rammed me against the wall. "One more word and I'll break your bones. Now get on the truck or you'll go to the isolator. Then we'll deal with you for refusing orders."

I ran to get my undershirt, dry foot rags, a pair of mittens, and my wooden spoon. Who gave my name for this *etap*—Gromov? The norm setter? The commander? I stood fretting by the stove. I didn't want to leave. I'd made friends here. I knew the rules. I had a better chance of making it here, even in deteriorating health, than in another camp.

Gromov's voice startled me. He was standing behind a tent pole, surveying his men. "What are you doing here? You were called for *etap*. Get going."

Vadim gave me a pat on the shoulder. "Take care of yourself."

I was the last one to get on the truck, and the only place that remained was next to the open tarpaulin flaps—the coldest place to sit. On each side, a dozen prisoners sat hunched over on the benches, leaning toward the iron stove to keep warm. Two guards sat in the cab along with the driver. Another guard sat with us, leaning against the cab, his bayonet reflecting the orange flames in the stove. Every hour or so the truck stopped, and the guards traded places.

I fell asleep despite the cold wind whipping through the flaps. In a dream I felt as if I were being elevated, flying. It was a very common theme in my dreams. I'd be standing in the street, on the soccer field, in a large auditorium, and then, in front of everyone, I'd rise up to the ceiling or high into the sky, moving my arms as though swimming through the air. The admiring people down below watched me dip, circle, and soar. No one else could do it. The feeling that I possessed a special power always remained with me after I awoke.

This time I wasn't sure if I was awake or dreaming—the moment of flight seemed to last forever. Suddenly screaming, screeching, and bellowing awakened me. I'd been thrown into the air, and through the glowing light I saw the prisoners on one side hoisted into the air—I, too was elevated—while the prisoners on the other side remained strangely in place. I saw everything in slow motion—bodies flying, arms flailing, outstretched hands trying to grab onto something, the stovepipe ripping away and launching through the tarpaulin. The stove exploded. Red embers, sparks, and bits of metal and tarpaulin rained upon us. Screaming and shrieking filled the air. I grabbed onto one of the flaps. It ripped, and I tumbled out of the truck and crashed through a thin layer of ice. Snow got wedged in my nose and mouth. It went up my sleeves and under the collar of my jacket. I couldn't open my eyes.

Taubcia, Rachel, Julek, my parents—everyone I loved flashed vividly before my eyes. Was I dead or alive? My left hand was burning. I pulled it out of the snow and saw I'd lost my mitten. I thrashed around for it. Where was everyone? Where was the truck? Where was I? I brushed the snow from my face and struggled to stand. I'd been thrown into the middle of the embankment. At the bottom of the hill, the truck lay on its side, ablaze. Shouts and screams of agony filled the air. A full moon illuminated the snowy field. The sky was full of black stars. I could make out dark figures scattered in the snow.

Farther down the hill, a man struggled to walk. He stumbled forward, his legs stuck in the deep snow. He parted the snow in front of him with his arms, and as he steadied himself, I shouted to him, "Wait for me. I'm coming down."

He looked up, startled, and waved his arms frantically. "Come quickly. I don't think many are alive." It was a prisoner named Stepan, someone I knew from the camp.

Although I was cold, I had sustained no serious injuries. I hadn't broken a bone, hadn't been burned or even scratched—nothing was bleeding. I stepped forward and fell face down. My hat slipped off. My arms sank to the ground. I tried to pull each leg out of the snow to walk but couldn't clear the surface. I resorted to burrowing my way through, tucking my left hand inside my coat sleeve to keep it warm.

As I moved down the hill, the snow became more shallow. I'd been thrown into a deep snowdrift, but the lower part of the hill and the field below were wind-swept and barely covered. I anticipated finding many broken bones down there and badly burned bodies.

Stepan and I stood together and looked around us. I kept thinking how lucky it was that I'd had the last place on the truck, on the side that had been thrown up into the air. Stepan had been next to me. The two of us had been thrown through the back flaps; the rest of the prisoners went down the hill inside the truck, with the stove breaking up, tumbling, and burning.

Fire chewed rapidly through the tarpaulin, emitting long, orange-yellow flames that quickly died out. The wooden bed of the truck burned like a bonfire. As we got farther down the hill, we could hear screaming coming from the burning wreckage. We saw men lying in the snow; they moaned, wailed, and fell silent. A few of the victims hobbled a few feet, threw themselves down into the snow, rolled frantically, scrambled back up, and threw themselves down again. The heat from the fire kept us from getting too close to them. Around the truck the snow had melted, leaving a large puddle. The hot air reeked of combusting oil, rubber, wood, and cotton. Stepan and I got as close as we could and dragged some prisoners away from the smoke and flames, leaving trails discolored by ash, blood, and bits of tarpaulin. The bodies hissed and sizzled as snow gathered inside their jackets. The tangy odor of burned cotton mingled with the sharp, sweet smell of burned hair and flesh.

Stepan and I didn't rest for a second. As we grew tired, we paired up to haul the remaining bodies. Winter clothing had protected some of the prisoners' bodies, but nearly all of their faces were burned. One man's face appeared to have made contact with the iron barrel, and the skin had peeled off. I covered the hole in his face with snow. White teeth were all that remained of several victims' faces. The broken pipe smoldered with the material and flesh it had come into contact with.

As the fire in the truck began to subside, Stepan and I slowly approached it. Several charred bodies remained within the frame of the truck. The cab had collapsed, crushing the two guards and the driver underneath. All three were dead.

Surrounded by the smoldering bodies, dead and half-dead, I became more and more astonished at my survival. It seemed unreal. I wanted to disappear. We couldn't save anyone. The few survivors we'd pulled away from the fire were barely alive; if they didn't die of their burns, they'd probably freeze to death. I felt exhausted, and Stepan was moving slower and slower. "What are we going to do with them?" I asked. "We can't carry all of them up to the highway."

Stepan shook his head. His ash-smeared face appeared drained and defeated. "Let's sort out who's dead and who's alive."

Only a few prisoners moaned now. I bent down and talked to them so they'd know someone was looking after them. "They won't last long in the snow," I said.

"No," he agreed wearily. "We should wrap the survivors with the dead prisoners' jackets."

Together we removed the jackets from the corpses and tucked them around the survivors. We glanced at each other, thinking the same thing. He examined the jacket of one dead prisoner, removed it, and put it on over his own. I wandered from corpse to corpse looking for a scarf, hat, and a good pair of mittens. It was hard to find any that weren't burned, but I found a gray military scarf on one body and a good pair of mittens on another. A hat lay on the ground, which looked to be in much better condition than mine. We said nothing about the acquired clothing.

It was decided that Stepan would go up to the road to flag someone down. I remained in the field and sat down on a fallen tree, but the minute I quit moving, I felt the cold. I wanted to sleep but didn't dare close my eyes, afraid I might not reawaken. I paced a little to stay awake, then rested again. My head was pounding. I'd inhaled a lot of smoke. Tendrils of gray rose from the hissing wreckage. I walked along the edge of the woods, taking deep breaths of fresh air. The sky was getting lighter. My toes had stopped tingling long ago, and I shivered uncontrollably. Finally I walked up to the road to look for Stepan, worried that something had happened to him.

I found him angry and agitated. Many trucks had passed by, he said, but no one stopped. He doubted anyone would, because drivers were afraid of loners walking along the Kolyma Highway at night. Stories abounded about robberies and killings committed by escaped prisoners or ex-convicts. We waved at passing trucks for another half-hour but had no luck. When the sun had fully risen, a truck full of prisoners stopped.

A guard rolled down the window. "Who are you? What are you doing out here?" he asked. I told him about the accident. The guard talked to his partner for a moment. Seeing the ashes on my jacket, he asked to see the wreckage. I took him to the edge of the road. Under the blue sky, the skeleton of the truck lay on its side, surrounded by black figures. Everywhere the snow was sprinkled with ash.

"I'll get help in Myaket," the guard said. "We're heading to Strielka. Are there any survivors?"

"About half," I said. "But I don't know for how long."

The guard got back in the truck and disappeared down the road.

Two more men died before another truck arrived. The rescuers unloaded three stretchers and green military blankets. They established a route away from the snowdrift, down the flattest part of the hill. Stepan and I descended with the group and pointed out the most critically injured. In pairs, the rescuers slowly and gingerly stepped up the cleared path, walking sideways; two more rescuers helped to support the weight of the bodies. The steepness of the hill and slippery footing made the evacuation painstakingly slow.

I noticed one of the guards inspecting the cab of the truck. He climbed partway inside and reappeared carrying what I recognized as the box of documents. The tarpaulin case was slightly burned, but I could tell our files had survived the fire.

I helped two prisoners who could walk up to the road, then remained at the truck, resting. The rescuers packed the survivors tightly onto the bed of the truck, which had been covered with blankets. More blankets and sheepskins were thrown over them. The dead bodies remained at the bottom of the hill, to be picked up later. Covered with blankets, I fell into a deep sleep, despite the cries and moans around me.

I awakened when we reached Atka, a settlement four hundred kilometers south of Maldyak. Two doctors, several *feldshers*, and two NKVD officials were waiting for us. Stepan and I gave a report of the accident to the NKVD officials. "I'm not supposed to be part of this *etap*," I added. "I was supposed to be sent to a convalescent camp before starting a job as a *feldsher* at one of the camps near Sejmczan. There should be a letter by Dr. Baranovich in my file."

The NKVD official ignored me. "We'll deal with you later."

The doctors sorted out the victims and decided where to send them for treatment. Three prisoners with fractured limbs remained at the hospital in Atka. The rest, all severely burned, were to be sent to the Central Hospital of the Northeast Directorate of the Labor Camps on the Twenty-third Kilometer.

The two NKVD officials called Stepan and me again. One of them held the package of files bound with old shoelaces. We walked into the administration building. "We'd like you to help us identify the dead and injured." The officer dropped the heavy package on the table and started laying out files. I saw mine, casually picked it up, and leafed through it. The pages were stitched together with black and white thread. I turned to the last page to see what my next destination was. The answer stopped my breath: OROTUKAN. Then I saw the letter from Dr. Baranovich. He had suggested I be treated in a camp with light physical work and then employed as a *feldsher*, noting that I had studied in medical school for three years. The resolution appeared at the bottom of the letter, stamped in red: DENIED. POLITICALLY UNRELIABLE.

The NKVD officials decided to send Stepan and me with the burn victims to the Central Hospital. They lay on the floor of the truck, covered with blankets. There was plenty of space to sit near the stove, but I chose to remain at the back, next to the whipping flaps.

The next morning I stood in front of the gate to the Central Hospital complex surrounded by well-fed, rosy-cheeked guards wearing summer tunics and no coats. I peeled off both jackets. There wasn't a patch of snow on the ground. Spring was in full bloom; the whole trip had taken us from the dead of winter to the balmy climate near the Sea of Okhotsk.

A broad-shouldered guard approached Stepan and me. "Where are you coming from? Where is your referral? Who's in charge of this transport?"

"I am," I said with conviction. "I'm the *feldsher*. The doctors ordered me to accompany the injured prisoners. The *etap* from our camp in Maldyak had a horrible accident; half of our transport died at the scene—"

"You can tell the story later. The patients need to get to surgery, and you two must go through the guardhouse."

The search was standard—down to the underwear. Afterward, the guard told me to go to the surgery barracks to help identify the patients. "But tomorrow morning, report back here for *etap*. This isn't your destination."

Stepan was sent to a transition barracks. I'd be joining him later.

With heavy steps I walked down the dirt path, my eyes pulled toward the ground, knowing that the next morning I'd be sent back to the mines. I'd seen the bag in the cab with the dead guards, and I knew it contained the files. I could've changed my crime and sentence, created a new identity. But I hadn't thought of it. I would never have another chance like this one; I would only remember every grueling day how I lost it.

Inside the hospital zone, I caught myself staring at people. There were women here, well groomed, well clothed, their hair combed and nicely kept. Many wore white coats and nursing caps. The men, also neatly groomed and clothed, stood straight, walked slowly, and spoke to each other in calm, civil voices. No quarreling, fighting, cursing. Not a single guard in sight. Despite the barbed wire, watchtowers, body search, guardhouse, and isolator, I felt as if I were free. The fragrance of perfume wafted around my nose. It had been so long since I had smelled a woman. I couldn't stop watching them, as if seeing them for the first time.

I stopped a hunched-over old man in a white uniform and asked him about the patients with whom I had arrived. He stared at my unshaven face, my callused, gnarled hands, my clothing laced with ash, smoke, and filth. "Who are you?" he asked, bewildered. "You don't look like a *feldsher*."

"I'm coming from a terrible accident. Many of the victims are in surgery. I'm the *feldsher* who accompanied them here." I grabbed his hand. "Are you a *feldsher*?"

"No son, I'm an orderly."

"I know I don't look like a *feldsher*. I spent the last eight months in the mines. But I was a medical student in Poland, and I worked as a *feldsher* in the transit camp in Buchta Nakhodka. Can you introduce me to a doctor or someone who might help me get a job as a *feldsher*?"

He listened attentively, and after a long moment he said, "I'll see if I can talk to somebody."

He shuffled away and disappeared around the corner. I remained in the hallway waiting. The orderly returned with a tall, gray-haired man with deep-set eyes and bushy white eyebrows. He towered over me.

"You came here with the injured?"

"Yes, sir," I said, immediately sensing his authority. "I was a third-year medical student at Warsaw University. Then I worked in Buchta Nakhodka with Dr. Semyonov in the camp's polyclinic and in the hospital with Dr. Popugayeva. You can check with them." He looked with amazement at my tattered clothing, dirty face, winter boots, and prisoner's garb. "I was sent to the gold mines near Maldyak, where I spent eight months. I was being sent to another gold mine when the accident occurred. But as you can see, I'm in no shape for hard labor. I've got scurvy and chicken blindness."

"My name is Dr. Mayerson," he said. "I want to talk to you tomorrow. Come back in the morning.

"Trofim," he said to the orderly, "take this man and give him a good shower and clean clothes. Make sure he gets some food. Take him with you to the *feldshers'* barracks."

That night I slept in clean underwear in a real bed with clean sheets, a blanket, and a pillow, enveloped in luxury, too tired and too comfortable to worry about the next morning.

When I awakened, the other *feldshers* were gone. The room re-minded me of the army barracks—the white-washed wooden floor, lines of freshly made beds, the white pillowcases, and white sheets folded over green military blankets. Next to each bed stood a small wooden nightstand. Half-curtains hung over the windows, and pencil drawings hung on the walls.

I got dressed and went to the guardhouse. "We don't have a destination for you yet," I was told. "Come back in two days for *etap*." The guard gave me several ration cards for the mess hall and wrote something on a piece of paper. "This is a pass to your sleeping barracks."

As he talked, I felt as though I were falling from a high cliff into a bottomless gorge. I didn't need to come to this place, where women smelled of perfume, where everyone slept on a mattress with sheets, a pillow, and blanket, where prisoners walked freely in and out of buildings. I never dreamed that a place like this ex-isted in Kolyma, and this knowledge would make life that much more unbearable as I chopped the frozen earth with a pickax, hauled rocks on a wheelbarrow, or cut down trees in a forest.

The walls of the dining hall were decorated with scenic paint-ings of the snowy north, wood carvings, and artistic paper cutouts. Pinned to a large bulletin board were the pages of the day's newspaper, *Kolymskaya Pravda*. I caught the headlines: "Generalissimus Stalin Sends New Armies to Stalingrad"; "Stal-ingrad Defends Itself Against Nazi Tanks"; "Heroic Defenders of Leningrad Receive Help."

I exchanged the meal ticket for a large bowl of oatmeal mixed with meat. The tea smelled hot and sweet, not like tree bark. On the table I was shocked to find a basket of bread and two bowls of red caviar. I salivated uncontrollably. As I ate, I became aware of my hunched-over posture; my arms lying on the table, guard-ing my food; my head bent downward while my eyes darted sus-piciously around the room. There was no one else eating; the only person in the room was a woman cleaning the floor. She smiled briefly at me and, in a pleasant voice, said "Good day." Shocked, I said nothing. Although I was sitting in a straight-backed chair, at a clean table, eating from a wooden bowl with wooden utensils, my mind and manners were those of a *dokho-*

dyaga. All I could think of was how much bread and caviar I could eat without getting sick.

I waited all morning for Dr. Mayerson, sitting on the floor in the hallway of the surgery barracks. In mid-afternoon I walked around the hospital grounds and talked to patients sitting on benches. I discovered flower beds and a stream where people were fishing. I returned to the surgery barracks and resumed my place on the floor. At dusk Trofim came and took me to Dr. Mayerson's office.

"You look much better than yesterday," the doctor said. "Are you feeling better?"

"Yes. But I don't think I'll be here much longer. I'm scheduled to leave for *etap* the day after tomorrow."

Mayerson seemed to ignore this comment. "Tell me about yourself. What happened to you?"

His casualness threw me—had he forgotten what I'd told him? He leaned back in the chair and put his feet up on the desk. He still wore white surgery garb, his mask dangling from his neck, and he closed his eyes as if he was ready to fall asleep.

"I was in an accident—"

"Yes, I know. Tell me about your family."

Dr. Mayerson was very tired, and I tried to keep it short. But I took the opportunity to impress him with my family's medical connections, something I thought would make him remember me.

"My great uncle, Professor Juli Jakovlevich Bardach, was a microbiologist in Odessa. He also worked with Professor Roux at the Pasteur Institute. He established the first emergency service in Odessa, and it was named after him. His son, Eugeny, lives in Paris and works at the Pasteur Institute as a microbiologist." I also mentioned my mother's brother, Professor Marceli Nathanovich Neuding, a neurologist in Odessa.

Mayerson perked up with recognition at the names. "Impressive. I studied neurology from your uncle's textbook, and your great uncle is quite famous. His vaccinations are used throughout the world." He leaned on his desk and looked intently at me. "How long were you in Kolyma? What did you do there?"

"Eight months. I was in the gold mines in a subdivision of Maldyak."

"How did you fare?"

"I'm alive. I spent several days in the isolator, and now I think I've developed scurvy and chicken blindness."

"Let me see your gums. Any pain?"

I couldn't hold back any longer. "Can I stay here and work as a *feldsher?*"

"I can request that you be sent to a rehabilitation camp near here, which will give you time to recover, and while you're there, I'll try to find a place for you. If there are no *feldsher* positions, I'll try to make you an orderly."

Dr. Mayerson took a large glass flask from a cupboard. "Here's some cod liver oil. It'll cure your chicken blindness." He opened another cupboard and produced another smaller flask with a dark liquid. "This is a wild rose extract. It has the highest content of vitamin C. Take two spoonfuls from each flask once each day. You'll recover in no time. You're basically in good physical condition." Dr. Mayerson couldn't stifle his yawns. With a change in tone he moved to end the conversation. "Come see me when you get back." He got up, patted me warmly, and saw me to the door.

The rehabilitation camp was located across the river and upstream from the hospital, about ten kilometers away. The river cut through the bottom of a canyon. Although it was called a rehabilitation camp, the work was far from light: our job was to retrieve logs that had been sent down the river from a camp upstream.

I was issued thigh-high rubber boots and a long wooden pole with a large iron hook at the end. Four of us stood on a large raft tethered to two trees with cables and iron chains. Our raft floated next to the bank; another lay downstream, about fifty meters into the river. A small dam protruded from the opposite bank at an angle, funneling the logs in our direction, and we were able to cover the space between the rafts by grabbing the logs with the iron hooks. The raft had a wooden railing on one side, but it didn't prevent anyone from falling into the water. And when we needed it most—while trying to hook the log—we couldn't reach it. The rounded surface of the logs was slippery, making it difficult to balance on the raft even when not trying to catch a log. I tried to stabilize myself by planting my feet in the crevices between the logs.

The first log that came at me seemed to be traveling a hundred kilometers an hour; I thought it would impale me against the riverbank, and my impulse was to run out of the way. I wasn't sure how to handle the giant hook, and I was terrified of missing the log, afraid it would strike the raft with enough force to destroy it and knock us all into the ice-cold water. I watched my partners for guidance. They held their poles with the hooks over their heads and swung them like sledgehammers, trying to hook the log near one of the ends, as this made it easier to guide the log toward shore. I did the same, but the hook barely penetrated the bark. The log hit the raft, then turned and started to go downstream. I frantically swung the hook again, aiming for the other end, but missed because the log was too close and the pole was too long. I shortened my grip on the handle and swung again with all my force, this time spearing it. Another prisoner helped me direct the log around to the side of the raft.

After two hours my shoulders were numb, my precision was worsening, and I could barely raise the iron hook. The prisoner next to me noticed I was struggling. "Go and rest in the barracks. Just tell the brigadier. I only work four or five hours a day. I have a bad stomach ulcer that bleeds a lot. I might need surgery." A thin young man with white-blond hair, a sparse beard, and crystal blue eyes, he launched the pole like a javelin, his lithe body gathering force on the windup and unleashing it in one precise strike. He never missed a log. His Russian was broken. I sensed a Nordic lilt. "I'll come with you," he said. "I also need to rest." Paoli Nystrom was a Finn from Karelia, occupied by the Soviets in 1940.

We found Lenia Drapkin, the brigadier, sitting on a bench in front of the barracks with the cook and the guard. He paid no attention to the rafts but was engaged in an intense conversation with his comrades. "I need to rest," I said.

Lenia marked the time next to my name on the clipboard. "Go ahead. Send two people down to take your place. Make sure you go back to work in the afternoon."

The barracks was a large log cabin with moss stuck in the cracks for insulation; it had two windows, wooden bed boards, straw mattresses, blankets, and pillows. A large iron stove and two long tables stood in the middle. Prisoners drank tea and talked at the wooden tables. Compared to the conditions in the gold mines, the cabin looked like a holiday resort. There were no *dokhodyagas* here, which surprised me.

Paoli shouted, "We need two people on the raft." After some commotion, two prisoners got up and went outside. He turned to me. "Ask the cook if there's anything to eat. Usually there are some leftovers."

I couldn't believe what he was saying. Even though I'd eaten well the previous few days, the gnawing hunger was still with me. It never went away. I went outside to ask the cook for leftovers, feeling like a beggar. "You're new here?" he asked. I nodded. The cook's right hand was deformed; three fingers had been severed at the knuckles. He noticed I was looking at him and said, "I lost, but I got away with my thumb and little finger." He wiggled them in my face. He was a handsome, dark-complected man with an easy smile, very much an *urka*. I realized he'd lost his fingers in a card game. Sometimes the *urkas* played for fingers, eyes, and ears instead of food or clothing. "Anytime you're hungry, come and see me. I'll be here. I'm never going back to the gold mines." He waved his stubby fingers again.

I ate two bowls of clumpy oatmeal and fell asleep until late in the afternoon, when someone shook me and told me to go back down to the river.

Lenia, the cook, and the guard had been joined by two other prisoners, probably Lenia's *urka* friends. The guard looked laughably out of place. He didn't say much, just guffawed at the *urkas'* vulgar humor. As I walked by, Lenia waved me over.

"The chief," he said, referring to the bedraggled guard, "and I are in charge here. You know what the job is. You have to work six hours a day—three in the morning and three in the afternoon.

The job must get done, but you have plenty of time to rest. If you're hungry, talk to me or to Zviad. All of you are expected to get well and go back to the mines. This is no camp for *dokhodyagas*."

I joined three other men to help them roll the captured logs up onto the bank. They stood in the river with heavy poles, water splashing up over their boots. Two parallel logs protruded from the riverbank and angled into the water, forming a primitive ramp. The goal was to roll the logs up it and onto land. The men thrust their poles into the mud under each log and inched it up the ramp. These actions were orchestrated by shouts and grunts from the man in the middle, as it was extremely important to keep the log well balanced. Two prisoners held the log in place while the other repositioned his pole.

I relieved the person at the far end of the line. "Make sure it doesn't slip," he warned me in the gravest tone. "The log slips and it'll pin you in the river."

After my shift, my back ached more than ever, and I felt every bit as exhausted as I had after a day in the mine. After dinner I lay down on the mattress with a pillow under my head and fell into a deep, luxurious sleep.

With rest and food I was getting stronger, and experience made me better at retrieving and rolling logs. Dr. Mayerson's concoctions cleared up the bleeding gums and chicken blindness in two weeks, but I tried to hide the improvement of my health by complaining of fatigue and blurred vision, and I made sure no one knew what I was drinking from the flasks.

One day I went fishing with Paoli. He made a fishing rod for me out of a thin stick of hazelwood and some braided strings taken from a mattress. The hook was made from a pin, brought in from the hospital. The fishing rod even had a bobber, made from a piece of bark with a hole in the middle. Paoli asked if I'd ever fished for trout. I hadn't. There were no trout in the streams near my home, and in Poland it was considered a delicacy and appropriately called "royal trout." Paoli had me built up for a great fishing expedition.

We walked down to the bridge about two hundred meters from the barracks. Several other prisoners were already fishing. I was disappointed and didn't think we'd catch anything. "Be alert," Paoli said. "The trout bites as quick as a viper. The bobber doesn't stay down for more than a second. You must pull sharply when that bobber disappears to hook the fish, then bring it gently to shore. Keep the line tight all the time." Paoli produced a little jar of red caviar and showed me how to bait the hook with several eggs. I lost the bait about twenty times before catching my first fish. I was too slow, didn't see the bobber go down, and looked around too much, especially at Paoli, who was catching one after another. He strung the caught fish on twigs embedded into the ground next to the shore.

I was surprised when I caught my first fish. It was completely unintentional. I thought I'd lost the bobber, and as I retrieved the string, I found a fish flopping on the end. At the end of the evening I had nine fish. Paoli had caught close to thirty.

Red caviar proved to be an incredible bait; the trout couldn't stay away from it. At first I wondered if it wouldn't be better to eat the bait rather than waste it fishing, but the nine trout were well worth it. With the cook's permission, we returned to the kitchen, skinned and gutted the fish, and cut off the heads. Then we put all the fish into a large kettle, boiled them until the bones could be easily chewed, and added a little salt. It was the freshest meal I'd ever had in the camps.

After six weeks in the rehabilitation camp my pants were tight, I was stronger than I'd been since before my arrest, and I sported a deep tan. I wasn't the only one who noticed my improvement; I was called for *etap* and transferred to a camp deep in the taiga to fell trees.

The logging camp, about thirty kilometers upstream, brought back memories of Burepolom. Not even the vibrant wildflowers, new grass, fresh air, and cold streams filled with trout could lift my spirits; I'd fallen another step away from the hospital. Now it would be difficult, if not impossible, to get in touch with Dr. Mayerson; and the logging camp was only a transit camp—from here we'd be sent to the mines. Dr. Mayerson probably had hundreds of prisoners asking him for help. He probably didn't even remember me.

My partner, Nikolai, was a master *tuftach*. He'd been an administrator in a tool manufacturing company before his arrest and had spent most of his career making up numbers and filing false reports. He'd been arrested not for this, however, but for counterrevolutionary activity and sabotage: the factory had failed to fulfill the plan assigned for it, and as a result the administrators were sentenced to ten or fifteen years in the camps. His real crime, manipulating reports and raking in millions of rubles for non-plant activities, never came up in court. He taught me how to make the norm in only four or five hours a day.

Our job was to cut down trees, clean off the branches, cut the logs into segments of equal length, and stack them for hauling. But instead of performing this exhausting work, Nikolai's mission was to find stacks left over from last year, of which there were plenty, and claim them. "All we need to do," Nikolai confidently explained, "is cut off the ends of the logs so they look freshly cut and bring the brigadier to measure them."

The butt end of each log was notched with a distinctive mark to identify the worker who had stacked it, and one of the logs had the date carved on it. But since the taiga was so immense, many of the stacks were never found by the workers doing the hauling, and thus they remained year after year, until Nikolai or some other *tuftach* discovered them. This eliminated the most exhausting work, allowing Nikolai and me to concentrate on what he called "cleaning the stacks"—cutting an inch off each end of the log so it looked freshly prepared. We put our signatures on the fresh ends, buried the scraps we'd sawed off, and covered the hole with moss and branches.

We were allowed to foray into the taiga unaccompanied by guards—escape was unthinkable—and because the forest provided excellent cover, we could perform our clandestine activity and enjoy the free time we had gained without being caught. Anyone's approach was announced by the snapping of twigs and crunching of dry needles, shrubs, and leaves.

The taiga had been undisturbed by man for thousands of years. The vines, pine trees, and prickly bushes and plants that bloomed tiny but spectacular flowers had achieved a harmonious community, a hierarchy based on how much sunlight each plant was able to obtain. Unlike the north European forests, with their towering canopies and carpets of moss, fallen leaves, and small plants, the taiga discouraged interlopers. Only secluded areas of tall trees could be penetrated on foot. The thick, rope-like vines were its guardians, entangling the sap trees, shrubs, and short, thorny bushes. The thorns could shred clothing and flesh, making the taiga hazardous for human travel. The lithe mink and burrowing marmots could make it through the treacherous foliage, but a man could fall through holes, get trapped in the vines, and never be found again.

Wandering with Nikolai, I felt happy and proud that I had learned how to cheat efficiently. We spent the sunny afternoons foraging for mushrooms the likes of which I'd never seen in Poland. There I used to awaken just before dawn and go to the forest near my home to look for mushrooms, searching for the small heads as they emerged from the dark. The white mushrooms were the best, with their soft fleshy bodies. The young ones were small and sturdy—my mother used to pickle them—and they sprouted plate-sized caps that were a foot tall and mostly unscavenged by worms. The caps varied in color from yellow-brown to deep reddish-brown or white bordering on yellow. All varieties of the *boletus* mushroom were edible, but there were poisonous kinds, usually the most colorful, and I was amazed that something so beautiful could be so deadly.

Every day Nikolai and I ate handful after handful of berries— blueberries, black mulberries, and bright red cowberries. Sated and sleepy, we rested on gigantic boulders, which were everywhere, left during the last Ice Age. Sometimes, if we lay very still, a deer leaped over the brush right past us. If it saw us it sometimes stopped to get a better look, and its beautiful brown eyes appeared ready to cry. I saw so much innocence in their steady gaze; they were totally defenseless, so easily hurt. I couldn't understand how anyone could shoot or trap trusting animals. Many red fox and hares scampered by, ever alert for any rustling sound.

Late on one warm, sunny afternoon, I was picking mulberries and stuffing them by the handful in my mouth when I looked up and saw a brown bear looking at me. He was as startled as I was and stopped to raise his nose in the air, sniffing the breeze that carried my scent. Then he wagged his head slowly while staring at me. Forgetting everything I had ever heard about how to act when encountering a bear, I froze in the middle of a thorny mulberry patch. We looked at each other. He remained standing on all fours and sniffed the ground. He looked around. I didn't move. Minutes passed. The bear finally lost interest and walked away.

Every morning before leaving for work and every evening before dinner, we had a head count. In the morning the brigadier gave us the orders for the day; in the evening he summarized the performances. The two guards were oblivious to what was going on. The community was small, only about fifty prisoners in all, and gossip, arguing, and fighting were rampant. Card games provided the main source of entertainment. The cook had a rotating work force of two prisoners every day. The only other permanent job was the job assigner, who was also the brigadier's helper.

One evening I was told not to go to work the next day. I said goodbye to Nikolai, knowing it was the end of my good life. A full *etap* had been assembled; I'd be going back north.

The truck arrived in the morning and took us to the Central Hospital. The guard told me to go to the Registration and Distribution Office to get further instructions.

CHAPTER 15

Central Hospital

My hand trembled as I filled out the form in the Office of Registration and Distribution. PROFESSION: *"Feldsher,"* I wrote. EXPERIENCE: "Warsaw, Poland—three years of medical school; two years as an emergency room assistant; ambulance paramedic. Buchta Nakhodka—six months as a *feldsher.*" Except for the latter, everything was a lie. Anyone who added up the years would realize that, according to this statement, I would have begun medical school at the age of sixteen.

The secretary's red lipstick and splotchy rouge looked theatrical on her stern, wrinkled face. She spoke to each prisoner who came through the door as briefly as possible, then resumed sighing, shuffling papers, and opening and closing the heavy wooden desk drawers. Her impatience bore down upon me as I filled out the form. When I finished, she took it without looking up and waved me away. I sat down with about a dozen other prisoners, all of us hunched over, eyes on the floor, wearing prisoner's garb and worried expressions.

The director's door opened, and an NKVD lieutenant appeared. He called my name in the monotone voice of a bored bureaucrat. I followed him back to an office. Sitting behind his desk, he said disdainfully, "So you've had some medical experience in Poland."

"Yes, sir."

"Well, I don't know what they taught you in Poland. I'm sure you didn't receive the same quality of education our students receive in our medical schools. But I'll give you a chance to show what you know. If you prove to be honest and dependable—and if Dr. Piasetsky is pleased with your work—you'll have a job in the hospital. Any complaints and you'll be sent on the first *etap* back to the mines." He slid a piece of paper across the desk. "This is your new assignment. You'll be working under Dr. Piasetsky. He's the chief of the TB ward." In the same dull voice he assigned me to a barracks and gave me enough ration cards for a week. "After these run out, you'll receive others at your work place."

As I closed the door to the director's office, I tried to hide my smile from the other prisoners. Good luck and happiness were so scarce in Kolyma that another person's gaining of it always felt like your own personal loss. I asked the secretary for directions to the tuberculosis ward and emerged from the log building feeling like a prince. Blooming rose bushes lined the path. Flower beds bordered by whitewashed cobblestones decorated the other entrances. The hard-packed dirt glistened with fresh sand.

No sooner had I left the building than I began worrying about being exposed as a liar and cheater and expelled from paradise. Had I done something wrong by interfering with my fate? Should I have followed it and gone on another *etap*, as planned? Or had my fate been served by the truck accident, which landed me at the hospital and put me in touch with Dr. Mayerson? A collective fate, designed by Stalin and the regime, governed all the prisoners sent to Kolyma: to work more than humanly possible until we got sick, got injured, or died. If someone happened to survive his term, it was just good luck. But I felt I had an individual fate, one that defied again and again the bleak destiny of the Soviet prisons. Why me? I wasn't any better or smarter or stronger than the thousands of other men in the mines. Was it fate or luck that was giving me this opportunity to become a *feldsher*? Or was good luck the same thing as fate?

Hospital personnel walked by briskly. I was struck by their neat, clean attire, straight posture, and sturdy gait. How did they get selected to be here? Fate or luck? Did they lie or cheat?

I passed the mess hall and the surgery department, turned left, crossed onto another packed-dirt road, and found barracks 15. The yellowish-clay exterior was crumbling off, baring bamboo slats and vertical beams underneath. To the right of the entrance was a little footpath lined with green bushes and flowers.

I knocked on the door. A tall, slender, gray-haired woman wearing a white gown and cap greeted me. Her yellow front teeth jutted out from her face and rested on her bottom lip. Wire-framed glasses magnified her gray eyes. I introduced myself as the new *feldsher*. She brightened, extended her hand, and offered me a wooden chair. Everything in the room was painted white—the two chairs, a taboret, the walls and cabinets. The wooden floor had been meticulously scrubbed.

"I'm Maria Ivanovna. I've been working with Dr. Piasetsky for three years. We're quite shorthanded. I'm glad you came. What's your code and sentence?" I gave her my legend and started telling her where I was from, but she cut me off tersely, turning toward the charts on her desk. This preliminary encounter was not at all what I was used to. In the mines, we'd tell each other our whole life stories, or as much of them as we could during the first meeting, knowing there might not be another chance. I didn't know whether Maria Ivanovna was a cold person or if people were more reserved in the hospital. But I knew not to drag out my story and above all not to ask her any personal questions.

We sat next to a small white desk, the patients' charts and colored files neatly assembled on top. A spoon, a ceramic cup, and a little bowl of sugar sat off to the side. The desk was also equipped with a lamp; the lampshade was made out of sheets of newspaper that had been glued together, dyed, and pleated. A medicine cabinet hung above the desk. Half of the chest was labeled "Group A," the other "Group B."

Upon seeing my puzzlement, Maria Ivanovna reached into her gown pocket and said, "You know what's inside." She glanced at the cabinets. "Always keep these keys with you." I had no idea what she meant. I felt I was sinking very quickly into my pile of lies.

"In Poland, we had a different labeling system for medications," I said. "Would you mind explaining the system here?"

She didn't blink. "Group A drugs are narcotics. Every night you'll be pestered by patients asking for sleeping pills or codeine to stop coughing. They want opium most of all. You must be careful with it. On the other side are poisonous drugs. Always keep the keys with you," she repeated, patting her pocket.

As she talked, she moved deftly between the desk and burning stove. Inside the white wooden cabinets were glass bottles and instruments. A small metal sterilizer sat on a stove in the middle of the room, with small logs neatly stacked in front of it. The water was boiling.

She opened a drawer. "We've only got four syringes—please be careful with them." I'd never given an intravenous injection, although I'd learned to give intramuscular and subcutaneous injections in Buchta Nakhodka. I put on the white gown she gave me. Maria Ivanovna looked me over and smiled broadly. "Let's introduce you to Dr. Piasetsky." She opened a door in the thin partition and ushered me in. "Nikolai Rafaelovich, this is our new *feldsher*."

The shelves of books rivaled the man for my attention. On two walls, books and papers, well organized and obviously well used, were stacked from the floor to the ceiling. A man wearing a white coat with a black tunic underneath sat at his desk leaning on his elbow, legs crossed, sporting tall black leather boots and smiling with full, protruding lips. "Sit down," the doctor said.

Maria Ivanovna asked if we'd like hot tea. "How many teaspoons of sugar would you like?" She looked at me. I was stunned to be offered sugar with my tea. "Two," I said, just as I had at home.

She went back to her office while I sat, as though on burning coals, waiting for the inquisition. Dr. Piasetsky's first question was about my code and sentence. Then he said, "Tell me about your home, your parents, your education. How old are you?" he looked at me with genuine curiosity. His cherubic face, topped by wavy brown hair, emanated warmth and peace. His hands were soft and pale, his fingers plump. It was hard to believe he was a prisoner, just like me.

I was proud to tell Dr. Piasetsky about my mother's and father's families. I told him I was twenty-four and repeated the experiences I'd written on the application.

"Who did you work with in Buchta Nakhodka?"

"Dr. Semyonov in the ambulatory clinic and Dr. Popugayeva in the hospital."

"What kind of patients did you work with?"

"Terminal and chronic patients suffering from scurvy, pellagra, and tuberculosis. Their sentences had been cut, and they were being shipped back to the mainland."

Dr. Piasetsky seemed satisfied with my answers. "In our ward, all the patients have open tuberculosis. As you know, it's highly contagious. Be careful. Watch Maria Ivanovna. Learn everything she does. Learn the routine. You'll be working nights, and you'll be in charge. In case of an emergency, you can summon the doctor on duty in either surgery or internal medicine, whomever seems most appropriate. Keep the doors closed at night. Sometimes guards and *predurkis* make night visits. Don't panic, just let them in. They may conduct a search, go through the charts, ask you questions. They may be rough with you. If they should come, send Kurban, the night orderly, to get me."

Maria Ivanovna showed me around the ward. The nurse's room was set apart by a heavy red curtain that emitted a tangy odor. It reminded me of the velvet curtains in my grandfather's bedroom, which smelled of stale tobacco smoke and medicinal vapors. Before leading me into the ward, Maria Ivanovna placed her hand on my arm and looked straight in my eyes. "The patients on the right side are extremely sick. They won't make it. The patients on the left have a chance to recover." She pulled aside the curtain, revealing a large hall with sixteen beds on each side. A large wood-burning stove stood in the middle of the room. Patients wearing gray pajamas or long gray gowns were clustered around two long tables. They slapped it hard with dominoes, sliding them forcefully into place and cursing and teasing each other in garrulous but raspy voices.

"Everyone back to bed," she said with a clap of her hands. The noise died down. The figures shuffled to their beds. Standing in the middle of the room, Maria Ivanovna introduced me to the patients. "This is our new *feldsher*. As of today, he'll be on night duty. Don't give him any trouble. I've told him about every one of you."

The majority of patients looked at me with curiosity, but a few stared with contempt and resentment. Dominoes were splayed across the tables. Dashes of red from the three checker boards were the only color in the room. At the end of each table was a large metal water dispenser with only one drinking cup dangling from a chain. Next to each bed was a nightstand and a metal spittoon on the floor. The wooden floor was scrubbed nearly white.

Maria Ivanovna introduced me to the patients. Alibey Makhmutov resembled a venerable patriarch, with a crown of silver hair and a short silver beard and mustache. His olive skin nearly glowed in contrast. "Are you doing better today, Alibey?" she asked.

Gasping for air, his chest heaving, the man pulled himself up and leaned against the head of the bed, which made him breathe easier. "I think so," he answered in a strained voice. Dark crescents underlined his round black eyes.

Maria Ivanovna turned to me, "It would be good to give him a third pillow. The patients usually breathe easier when they're propped up. If he's really struggling to breathe, you can give him oxygen. We've got three bags in the nurse's room."

Maria Ivanovna raised his pajama top to listen to his heart and lungs. Alibey's ribcage stuck out like the bones of an emaciated ox, and his skin was whitish-blue. In a low, labored voice, Alibey murmured, "I'm coughing less. There's no blood in the sputum. Do you think I'm ready for commission?"

"No doubt about it, Alibey." Maria Ivanovna responded gently. "I'm sure Dr. Piasetsky has submitted your papers. You'll be out of here before you know it." She took his hand and squeezed it lightly. "Try to stay awake during the day. Then you'll sleep better at night. And eat everything on your plate. Don't exchange food for tobacco. You need to eat as much as you can."

Coughing, hacking, and spitting came from all directions, the gray-clad bodies heaving forward in their beds. It never stopped.

The young man at the next bed struggled to sit up as we approached, but he had a hard time moving his legs. Maria Ivanovna put her arm around him and helped him dangle his legs over the edge of the bed. Protruding from his gown were two pale sticks, not a scrap of muscle left on them. "Radion was just transferred here from the hospital in Sejmczan. He's already commissioned to be shipped to the mainland. We're waiting for him to get stronger." I glanced at his chart and saw the diagnosis—bilateral tuberculosis and alimentary dystrophy. The latter was a medical term for starvation.

"Have you tried to get up today?" she asked while taking his pulse.

He shook his head. "I don't think I can walk yet."

"You must exercise your legs several times a day, even while lying in bed," she replied. A deep rattling cough shook his body. He tried to stifle it, grabbing the rag sitting on the nightstand. Maria Ivanovna placed one hand on his forehead and the other on the back of his head and held him tightly to stop the coughing. A gurgling sound came from his throat. He spit a reddish-brown clot of blood into the spittoon and took a deep breath.

"It's bothered me since morning. I felt there was something in my throat."

"Have a good rest. I'll give you a double dose of cough medicine."

An orderly came from the other end of the ward. Maria Ivanovna waved him in. She whispered, "Could you please take care of Radion." Blood was spattered on the bed sheet and spittoon. The orderly fetched a pail of water and began to clean up.

It didn't look to me as if Radion was going to make it out of the ward the next day. His sunken eyes were glazed over from fever; his freckled cheeks and lips were rosy and hot. On his chart I saw that he'd been spiking a high temperature.

Genia Gerasimov was dozing when Maria Ivanovna felt his forehead and took his pulse. His hair was white, but his face didn't look old or emaciated. I wondered why he was in the row on the right, with the extremely ill patients. The wooden wedge-shaped back support was elevated as high as it would go. "How's your breathing?" Maria Ivanovna asked.

He didn't open his eyes but whispered, "So much pressure. I can hardly breathe."

She raised his gown to listen to his chest. Genia's stomach was round and distended, his legs thick as an elephant's. Maria Ivanovna pushed her fingers into his calves and feet. A deep impression remained at each site. "We'll remove the fluid today," she reassured him.

I was impressed by the swiftness and precision of Maria Ivanovna's movements. Her touch was so gentle, her words so reassuring; I could feel how much she cared about each patient. I was growing fond of her. She commanded respect, yet she also inspired fondness and devotion.

I could already pick out the patients who had only a short time left; after living in the prisons and camps, it didn't take long to recognize the dying. Their facial features became sharper—the eyes deeper-set, the nose more protruding, the cheeks sunken. The glazed-over eyes no longer focused, making me wonder if the person could still see. The patient usually didn't move much, remaining in one position for extended periods of time. Injections, painful for most patients, caused no or little reaction in the dying.

One patient amazed me by his presence. He stood next to the bed, composed and dignified. His pale, drawn face remained unmarked by pain or fear. When Maria Ivanovna asked how he felt, he complained of nothing. "Everything is fine," he said weakly, looking from Maria Ivanovna to me with glassy blue eyes. "I don't want any more injections or procedures." I wanted to get to know this man who accepted his fate so calmly. As much as I wanted to learn about life, I wanted better to understand death. Not believing in heaven or hell, I found dying a frightening mystery.

As we moved over to the left side of the room, several patients got out of bed to greet us. A short, dark-haired man grinned widely, his black eyes darting in all directions. "I see you feel good," Maria Ivanovna said. "You must be winning at checkers."

"I'm working on becoming a national champion," he said with a broad smile, then quickly covered his mouth and turned away from us, racked with deep coughing. When the spell subsided, he asked if I knew how to play checkers. "I don't sleep well, so maybe we can play at night." He turned to Maria Ivanovna, pulled up the sleeve on his gown, and flexed his muscle. "Look. I'm getting stronger. I think the injections are helping. Do you think Dr. Piasetsky will qualify me for pneumothorax?"

"I'm going to talk it over with him. Khaciek has been with us only two weeks," she said to me. "We're still conducting tests, but he seems to be improving. We'll have his X rays at the end of the week."

The two standing patients appeared more vivacious than the others. Maria Ivanovna praised them both and told them they were fit enough to help the orderlies in light chores—scrubbing the floors, keeping the fire going, and helping the very sick patients on the night shift. This was happy news to them, as it meant they were healthier than the rest.

After completing the rounds, Maria Ivanovna told me to get settled in my sleeping quarters and rest before coming back at six to relieve her. She reached into her desk, pulled out an extra ration of *paika*, and offered it to me. Still very hungry, I accepted it with more enthusiasm than I could control.

The sleeping barracks for the hospital staff stood near the entrance to the camp, between the administration building and the bakery. I was assigned to the barracks for lower-level staff—orderlies, janitors, and kitchen help. There were also separate barracks for doctors, *feldshers*, hospital administrators, and camp administrators. The women were housed in a separate zone next to the gate, protected by a fifteen-foot-high wooden fence with contiguous boards and coils of barbed wire at the top.

The barracks was clean—no dirt, no stains, no stench. It looked like a military barracks, with each bed neatly made, the rows of bunk beds straight, and the wooden floor swept clean. The barracks attendant greeted me kindly. He was an older man, tall and slender, with a shuffling walk. He asked if I was working the night shift and what time I wanted to be awakened. "Don't leave anything valuable at your bed," he warned. "You won't see it again. My name is Sienia, in case you need anything."

I took off my pants, shoes, and tunic, pulled back the sheets, and crawled in. But I was too excited to sleep. I soaked up the fresh smell of the sheets, the wool blanket, and the feeling of my bones sinking into the soft mattress. But as the hour approached for me to return to the ward, I became nervous. At six o'clock I walked to my new job with a pit in the center of my stomach.

The first several weeks were stressful and upsetting. Despite the audacity with which I'd assumed the position, I was in no way prepared to care for thirty-two patients. I didn't know what kind of damage tuberculosis did to the lungs or why the patients spit up blood. I didn't understand night sweats, the spiking of body temperature in the evening, or the lowering of temperature in the morning. The symptoms and treatment of the disease remained obscure and impenetrable.

At first I thought tuberculosis only affected the lungs. Then I learned it could affect all the organs, but I didn't know why or how. I thought many times that I should tell Dr. Piasetsky how ignorant I was so I could learn something, but I couldn't be sure of his response. Instead I took down a few of his books every night and tried to study them, but the language of anatomy and physiology was far over my head. My confusion came to a painful crescendo whenever I had to make a decision, which was often. I was rarely sure of myself, and the fact that the person's life depended on what I did made me feel very nervous and guilty.

When I came on duty in the evening, Maria Ivanovna and I went over the patients' charts. She explained their prognosis, showed me X rays, and discussed treatment plans. I couldn't understand much—the X rays were particularly foreign—but I nodded in agreement, and she took my seriousness as a sign that I was deeply involved in the work. I asked her to go over some of the X rays again, since I was unable to distinguish normal from diseased tissue—I couldn't even identify the heart. I watched nervously for her reaction to my questions, but she didn't seem particularly alarmed. She told me which patients could die at any time, emphasizing that they needed to be carefully watched, and gave me a list of patients who required either caffeine or subcutaneous camphor injections—caffeine to stimulate the heartbeat, camphor to facilitate breathing. "Every patient is given codeine to suppress dry coughs or codeine with terpine hydrate to facilitate productive coughing. If the heartbeat stops, you can give the patient a shot of adrenaline in the heart." No further explanation.

I didn't know how to interpret heartbeat, pulse, or blood pressure readings and worried that I might miss an important change in a patient, resulting in his swift decline or even death. The only thing I could do was carefully read the notes Maria Ivanovna and Dr. Piasetsky had made during the day and write a report that closely followed theirs. The only changes I noted were changes in behavior: for example, "Tonight the patient was more active. He walked for half an hour without feeling short of breath." "Patient needed a third pillow for elevation to aid in breathing." "Patient coughed all night and spit up blood. I increased his dose of codeine to stop the coughing."

My first intravenous injections were disastrous. The patients yelped and writhed; I sweated and grew frustrated. The poor men's arms grew bloodied and bruised. With no training or experience, I usually needed several tries to find the vein, and the dull needles didn't make it any easier. I was most afraid of giving injections of 10 percent calcium chlorate—if I missed, the solution went into the surrounding tissue and caused intense burning and necrosis. But it was one of the only drugs to fight tuberculosis, and every patient needed an injection every other day. I also gave injections of 40 percent glucose solution, but here the consequences of my ineptitude were not as painful or serious.

The patients who had worked physically for a long time developed large veins, which looked like they could be easily penetrated, but often they were hard and slippery, requiring me to pin down the vein with two fingers. Puncturing the skin always made me nervous. When I gave injections, the patient was always tense with fear, grimacing and hissing, making me feel the pain of the injection myself.

The veins of patients who'd had many injections were thin and difficult to find. It was easy to go all the way through the vessel, causing intense burning at the injection site. In such cases I immediately retracted the needle, but it didn't make the patient feel any better, especially when he saw me looking for another place to stab. I had to learn to move the needle very carefully, slowly entering the vein and waiting to see blood appear inside the syringe. As long as blood continued to appear, the needle was appropriately placed. Then the plunger could be slowly depressed. Success was achieved when the patient began to feel hot, as if melted metal were coursing through his veins.

One day I was giving an injection to a severely emaciated elderly patient named Oleg Vatulin, a high Party official before his arrest. He cursed angrily when I missed the first time. "Stop practicing on us, you butcher. You're not going to practice on me anymore. You have a long way to go to do it right."

I was crushed and told Maria Ivanovna about the incident, knowing Oleg would tell her for sure.

"Be patient," she said. "It takes practice. I don't think it's so much your fault as the needles. With a dull needle, you need more strength to get through the skin, and then it's easy to tear or puncture the vein. It's happened to me many times."

I felt reassured but was still hesitant, especially when confronting Oleg. I was even afraid to greet him.

One evening I arrived just as Maria Ivanovna was taking out a trocar, a hollow tube with a long needle inside used to drain fluid from the abdominal cavity. The end of the needle looked like a miniature bayonet. The needle could be pulled out of the skin while the hollow tube was left inside the body. I'd seen it done in Buchta Nakhodka but had never done it myself.

Genia, his stomach twice as large as the week before, sat on a chair, holding his swollen belly. "Why don't you do the puncture today?" Maria Ivanovna said to me, using the same encouraging tone she used with the patients. I couldn't believe she hadn't caught on to my ignorance—her complacence was beginning to unnerve me. She knew I couldn't do intravenous injections, so why would she ask me to insert a trocar? Perhaps she was trying to expose me, to gather evidence against me and have me expelled.

She removed the trocar from the sterilizer and placed a large metal basin between Genia's feet. She took my finger and placed it in the midline of his belly, between the umbilicus and the beginning of his pubic hair. "Puncture here, but be careful not to go too deep."

Genia's body squished beneath my hands. I felt sick to my stomach. Having no notion of abdominal anatomy, I was terrified of what I might hit—his liver, his bladder, his intestines. I was afraid of hurting him badly, maybe even killing him.

"Maria Ivanovna, after working in the mines and cutting down trees, I'm afraid my hands are stiff. I'm not sure of my precision."

"I'm glad you're cautious, but I think you should try anyway. I'll help you." She gave Genia a wooden spatula. "Bite on it as hard as you can and hold onto the chair. It'll take just a second."

Trying to conceal my trembling, I stretched the skin with my thumb and forefinger. With the other hand I gently pushed in the needle. Genia whimpered, which made me more hesitant.

"Push harder," Maria Ivanovna commanded, taking my hand and pushing in the trocar. I felt the needle puncture the skin. "A little farther. Now, hold the tube in place and remove the needle."

As I pulled out the needle, a stream of dark brown odorless liquid arched up and splashed all over my gown.

"Raise the basin," Maria Ivanovna ordered.

Genia groaned.

"Breathe deeply," Maria Ivanovna insisted. She put her hand on the upper portion of his abdomen and gently pushed. Yuri, the daytime orderly, measured the liquid. At five liters, the force of the stream tapered off. Maria Ivanovna pressed harder on Genia's abdomen. The stream picked up. "How do you feel?" she asked Genia. "Is it easier to breathe?"

Genia sighed. "It's such a relief. I wish you'd put a tight bandage on my stomach so the liquid would never come back."

I changed my gown and sat next to Genia on his bed. "You have a light touch," he said. "It wasn't that painful." In a paroxysm of relief and gratitude, I took his hand and squeezed it tightly.

I adjusted easily to the reverse order of my life—staying awake and alert all night, sleeping during the day. I thrived sleeping on a mattress with sheets, a blanket, and a pillow, wearing only my T-shirt and underwear. I kept bread underneath my pillow and held it while I slept, nibbling a few pieces if I awakened. The comforts of my new assignment made the fear of being caught and sent back to the mines more intense than any fear I'd experienced in the mines. It lurked as another death sentence. If I were sent back, in six months I'd be lying in a bed on the right-hand side of a hospital barracks—or on top of a pile of corpses.

I began to dream again. In the mines, exhausted after a day of work, I never dreamed. I fell asleep immediately and reawakened only to the hostile order *"Podyom!"* I felt terror but not anxiety; I slept hard but never dreamed. But in the safety of the hospital, I dreamed of being sent to the isolator or buried deep in a mine pit. Sometimes I choked in my sleep, unable to breath, as though buried by falling dirt. I dreamed about *urkas*, each with the face of Ruchka, tying my arms and legs behind my back and hoisting me into the air.

The terrors of my waking life were less graphic but just as intense. A few times a week, Dr. Piasetsky was still working in his office when I came on duty. What if he saw me at work and concluded I had lied about my medical training? I wanted to ask so many questions but never did. Although I tried my best to take care of the patients, I was never sure if I was meeting Dr. Piasetsky's expectations. When he made rounds in the evening, I accompanied him, pencil and notebook in hand, taking his orders and writing down his every word. He addressed very few patients by their first names. With all but the very young, he used the formal rather than familiar address. He always wore a mask and turned the patient's face away from him with a light nudge of the finger.

Although Dr. Piasetsky was kind and friendly with patients, he was distant, an invisible partition separating him from the infected person. He showed no emotion, just concern as a doctor over the patient's condition. I wondered what he felt toward the patients, for whom he represented the only hope for survival. He conducted rounds quickly, exchanging a few words with each patient but examining only the very sick or those who had undergone the pneumothorax procedure.

From time to time Dr. Piasetsky offered me some rudimentary instruction. On one occasion he took out his wooden stethoscope, listened to a patient's heart and lungs, and then handed the instrument to me. "Here, Janusz, listen. The upper lobe is filled with whistles and crepitations. Compare it with the other side." I heard whistling and crunching and gurgling, but didn't know what any of it meant. The other lung roared like whitewater rapids. Dr. Piasetsky tapped softly on the lungs and margins of the heart. When he listened to the heart, he told the patient to hold his breath. When listening to the lungs, he asked the patient to cough lightly or intermittently.

One evening following rounds, I came up with the courage to ask Dr. Piasetsky to give me something to read about tuberculosis so I could learn more about the disease. He pulled a book from his shelf, *The Manual of Internal Diseases*, and pointed out several chapters. Removing his white coat, he looked at me with his brown eyes wide open, smiling. "Would you like to join me for tea?"

One night after midnight, when I was feeling most keenly the seductive fingers of sleep, there was a harsh thumping on the front door. I bolted out of my chair and opened it. A guard stood in the doorway. "Why did you open the door without asking who it was?" he barked. The guard was accompanied by a *predurok*, who swished his flashlight around the nurse's office. Each carried a crowbar.

"Never open the door without finding out who's there," the guard continued in a threatening voice. "What's your name, code, and sentence?" I recited it the way I had a thousand times. "How many patients are on ward?"

"Thirty-four."

"Where are the charts?" asked the *predurok*. He was well built and well dressed, wearing leather boots, riding breeches, and a three-quarter-length gabardine coat. He sat down at Maria Ivan-ovna's desk, unbuttoned his coat, and made himself at home. The guard snooped around the cabinets and drawers. I asked if I could help him find anything.

"Give me the keys to the drugs." A clump of hair dangled down on his forehead, nearly covering his eyes.

"I'm not supposed to open the cabinets."

"Who said?"

"My boss. We don't have enough medication for all the pa-tients. I'm supposed to keep the cabinets locked at all times." I didn't know what to do. The patients needed the medication. Maria Ivanovna would be very upset if any was taken.

"Do you know who I am?" The guard swung the crowbar in an arc. "I'm the camp commandant. Ask anyone if they know Pruchno. This here is my partner, Philipov." Philipov was taking notes on the patient's files. "You'll find out who I am, and the next time I come here, I expect you to offer me the keys."

I didn't know who these guys were. They could be patients; they could be thieves. Maybe Maria Ivanovna would think I took the drugs.

"Do you want codeine? I can give you some codeine," I blurted out.

"You got it." Pruchno smiled. "And alcohol." He found the two bottles of alcohol we used as disinfectants. Both men pulled glasses out of their coats, sprinkled the codeine powder in them, and filled them with alcohol. After several glasses each, they left.

"Say hello to Dr. Piasetsky. He's a good man—and so are you," Pruchno said.

The next morning I told Dr. Piasetsky. "You did the right thing," he said, looking to see if we had anymore alcohol. "They usually come by when I'm on duty. They think they rule the camp, and sometimes they act like it. Don't ever cross them."

I was glad not to be the only one awake at night. Kurban, the nighttime orderly, was close to my age—four years older—and we quickly became friends.

An Uzbek from Tashkent, Kurban was stunningly handsome. His dark hair was slicked back, he kept his clothes clean and well mended, and he scraped the dirt from beneath his fingernails. His teeth were white and healthy, his downturned black eyes soulful and languishing. Kurban had studied philosophy at the university and was filled with philosophical thoughts and poetic expressions. But just as expertly he got down on his hands and knees and scrubbed the floors, wiped the dust off of every bed and nightstand, and polished every window.

Kurban cared for the patients in the most delicate manner, protecting them with both his strength and gentleness, and he assumed a protective relationship with me, too. He considered himself an old-timer in the camps and me a novice and foreigner. Kurban gave out advice like a worried parent: "When you are on the edge, don't give up. But when you are well, help others who are on the edge." "Never take advantage of those who are weaker than you. And never kneel down to those who are stronger." "Never dig in the garbage pile. It will never fill you up."

His advice wasn't focused as much on survival as on ethical and moral principles. It had been a long time since I'd come in contact with this kind of thinking. Kurban was rich with compassion and caring, cleaning the patients, helping them eat, holding their feverish hands. Compassion seemed to be a part of his nature, but he'd had no previous experience working with the sick or disabled.

Spending night after night together, we fell into a routine that reinforced our friendship. We distributed the evening's medications, remade the beds, and settled the patients down for the night. When all was quiet we ate dinner at the desk in the nurse's room, our shoes off, feet up, and talked about our lives before our arrests. Kurban's parents were religious and nationalistic, and he grew up believing in the greatness of Tashkent and despising the Russification of his country. After we'd become quite close, I raised a question I'd been hesitant to ask but had been wondering about for a long time.

"Kurban, how did you, so strong and healthy, get out of working in the mines?"

His dark eyes grew wide. "I wanted to know the same thing about you—you don't have any more experience as a *feldsher* than I have as an orderly." He continued, "I spent two years in the gold mines. Twice I was sent to punishment camps that had very tight discipline and vicious guards. One day a friend began coughing and spitting up blood, and I took his sputum in a tin can to the camp clinic. I faked a cough and told the doctor about pain in my chest. I was nearly a *dokhodyaga*, thinking constantly about suicide, emaciated and run down.

"The test was positive for tuberculosis, and the next thing I knew, I was sent to the Central Hospital. Dr. Piasetsky knew right away I was faking but didn't say a word. He simply called me to his office and told me I was to start cleaning the ward and helping with the patients. He keeps me on the list of chronic patients to keep me from *etap*. So what about you?"

I told him about the truck accident and how I'd claimed to be a *feldsher* when filling out forms.

Kurban rolled another cigarette, lit it, and leaned in close to me. "I don't think lying and cheating are always wrong. I was taught to be honest. But my parents also taught me to be smart when dealing with the Soviet officials, and sometimes that means you can't be honest." Across the dim light his dark eyes gazed deeply into mine. "Do you think we are honorable, decent people? My job cleaning the floors, changing beds, and bringing bedpans to the patients doesn't hurt anyone. But your work directly affects the lives of the patients. Do you ever feel guilty?"

His question struck like a dagger. "Sometimes, yes," I said. "I cheated to get in. I cheated to save my life. But I never intended to hurt anyone. You're right, my work does affect the lives of the patients, but if you were me, what would you do?"

"I'd spend every minute learning as much as I can. And I'd talk to Dr. Piasetsky and ask him to teach me."

"So what do you think of me?"

He thought seriously for a moment. "I didn't like you at first. I thought you wanted to get as far as you could, no matter what. I thought you were arrogant. But over the weeks I've seen another side of you. You work hard. I know you care about the patients. But I think it's time you talked to Dr. Piasetsky."

With every passing day I felt less secure. *Etap* went regularly from the hospital, and the fear of being exposed as a fraud peaked every morning at roll call. I stood in line shaking with trepidation, expecting my name to be called. Dr. Piasetsky had given no indication that he was unhappy with me, but he took his job seriously, and he could easily inform the Office of Registration and Distribution that I wasn't up to standard for a *feldsher*. Doctors caught trying to protect prisoners by listing them as patients or keeping them as orderlies and *feldshers* were sent to the mines themselves. Patients whom the officials decided were not really sick were yanked out of bed and sent on *etap*. I didn't know if Dr. Piasetsky was protecting me or if he hadn't caught on yet. The unexpected *shmons** kept me on edge. I had nothing to hide, but I didn't doubt that they could find something that could drastically change my fate.

I became more confident working with the patients. Aside from caring for them, I was frequently required to referee arguments between them. Tuberculosis, if it hadn't depleted the patient's energy, made him feisty and irritable. The patients argued and fought over differences in opinion and over the veracity of the stories they told each other. In one instance, a tall, blond, pearly skinned Finnish patient named Gustav started an argument with seemingly innocent reminiscences about his life back home. "My father and I lived on a lake about twenty kilometers from Helsinki, where we worked in the port as docksmen. We fished and hunted together every weekend. There were so many

* Thorough searches.

deer, jackrabbits, wild geese, and ducks that you could simply pull the trigger and you'd hit something. My two dogs chased those deer and carried the birds from the water without leaving a mark on them. We owned the lake and the surrounding woods, so it was only my father and I—"

"Who owned the lake?" Oleg Vatulin shot back with hostility.

Gustav was puzzled. I knew that for him, the notion of owning land was perfectly natural. His father and grandfather had owned it before him. Now it was his. But for Soviet citizens, owning a lake and a forest was unthinkable, and the patients thought Gustav was boasting to humiliate them.

Horochko, always ready for a fight, pushed Gustav. "Stop telling us lies. You think we're stupid? No one can own a lake, especially not a simpleton like you. Maybe a millionaire in other capitalist countries, but not you." Gustav, however, insisted that every word was true.

I talked privately with Gustav in the evenings. I liked his honesty and openness. He completely lacked the ability to lie, and this caused him trouble over and over. I tried to explain why his stories about Finland were so infuriating to the Soviet patients, but he just looked at me quizzically, unable to pretend to be someone he wasn't.

He was very sick. The tuberculosis had taken over the lobes of both lungs, and he was going down quickly. The pneumothorax had been performed on him several times, making it very difficult for him to breathe. Despite his large frame he was easy prey, and Horochko, small but wiry, frequently picked fights with him.

Inevitably, I became wrapped up in the lives of the patients, forming individual relationships with each. I would spend a moment with each man during my evening rounds, peering cautiously into each pale emaciated face. The prevalent sounds in the ward were of coughing and hacking, but I didn't wear a mask. Neither Maria Ivanovna nor Kurban wore masks, and I didn't want the patients to feel I was repulsed by or afraid of them. To the contrary, I sat next to them, held their wet hands, lifted them up while Kurban was changing the bed. I believed that touching the patients, hugging them, and smoothing their hair was as important as the calcium injections and pneumothorax procedure.

As I spent more time with them and learned more about tuberculosis, I felt increasingly compelled to get close to them, not only as a *feldsher* but as a friend. My heart opened when I was with them.

One evening Dr. Piasetsky invited me to his office. I'd been working for over three months, and I had no idea if Dr. Piasetsky was satisfied with my performance. He asked Kurban to bring us tea and offered me his chair while he lay down on the cot. He removed his boots and folded his arms across his chest.

"How do you feel working here?" he asked.

"I'm very happy."

"Maria Ivanovna tells me you work hard and that the patients like you. I understand you're trying to do your best, but I think you need to learn more."

Kurban knocked on the door and delivered the tea. Dr. Piasetsky sat up. He looked into the cup, took a sip, and bit on a piece of sugar.

"Tell me, Janusz, how much did you really learn in medical school? How many years did you attend? What courses did you complete?" His voice was pleasant, his face relaxed. But my heart was thumping like that of a racehorse on the last curve of the track.

My face turned bright red, and I lowered it to hide my burning cheeks. Dr. Piasetsky knew I couldn't read X rays or perform basic procedures. But would he fire me for this? My medical knowledge was based on the eight years I studied Latin, the vials of medication I'd seen in my father's office, and my work in Buchta Nakhodka as a night watchman and orderly. I sipped my tea slowly, my thoughts racing. Finally I said, "Nikolai Rafaelovich, I never went to medical school."

A broad smile lit his face. "Finally, the truth comes out. For a long time Maria Ivanovna and I knew you didn't know anything about medicine. But she was impressed by your determination and rapport with the patients, and I like your wit, intelligence, and enthusiasm. I'd like you to stay on here, and I'd like to begin tutoring you. But don't forget, we are prisoners. Any day, you or I could be shipped away. I just hope that as a skilled *feldsher*, you'll be able to survive wherever an *etap* may take you. But I'm glad you'll be with us for a while."

CHAPTER 16

Tuberculosis Patients

Dr. Piasetsky opened the faded gray tome on his desk, *Diagnosis and Treatment of Internal Diseases*, to the chapter on the lungs. "Tell me what you don't understand, and then I'll explain how tuberculosis infects the body."

I'd been studying with Dr. Piasetsky for two months. We started with the anatomy and physiology of the heart, lungs, and circulatory system, and now I was learning about the effects of tuberculosis. I had never tried so hard to be a good student. At school I had been very good in the subjects I liked—geography, history, and languages—but I failed mathematics twice, got very poor grades in physics and chemistry, and repeated a grade in the gymnasium. Because of my aptitude for geography, I thought of the body as a map: the blood surged through the heart, went to the lungs to pick up oxygen, and then nourished every cell. As I took notes and turned the pages of the medical books, I clenched my callused hands and flexed the bridge of muscles across my neck and shoulders, wondering again and again how I ever landed in Nikolai Rafaelovich Piasetsky's ward.

My experiences in the mines frequently impinged on my studies. I thought of the number of men I had seen die. It always boiled down to one thing: the heart stopping its pumping. It seemed like nothing else mattered—the brain, body, and soul. All of these things depended on the heart.

Since I'd begun working on the TB ward, I regretted that I would never attend a university; ex-convicts were prohibited from obtaining higher education. In any case, I'd be too old to go when I was released; I would have forgotten all my schooling and would never pass any entrance exams. But my studies with Dr. Piasetsky, his close attention and tutoring, filled this void and took away some of the anguished sense that I was wasting my life.

"The bacillus thrives in a patient's sputum," Dr. Piasetsky explained. He let me sit in the big chair at his desk and pulled up a wooden chair next to me. As he talked, he looked in my eyes to see if I understood. His soft, learned gaze held me gently as I struggled to make the connections between the destruction of the lungs and the effect on the rest of the body. "Every time a patient coughs or sneezes, bacilli are spewed into the air, where they are inhaled by someone else. This is why the lungs are the most common site of infection. When the bacillus eats away the lung tissue, it leaves cavities. When it destroys the blood vessels of the lungs, the patient coughs up blood."

Although I knew tuberculosis was highly contagious, I never worried about becoming infected. Once I'd secured my position on the ward, I felt invincible. I'd inhaled millions of bacilli but hadn't gotten sick. I believed my youth and fate protected me.

Dr. Piasetsky's love of teaching was evident from the start. Sometimes Maria Ivanovna or Hela Borisovna, a new daytime nurse, attended the sessions, and I imagined Dr. Piasetsky standing at the podium in a large auditorium, lecturing to hundreds of students and doctors.

"The treatment of tuberculosis requires prolonged rest in a dry climate—preferably in a pine forest, the high mountains, or in a desert—and a diet high in calories and fat, none of which we have in Kolyma. Nor has a medication been found to treat tuberculosis. Given these limitations, all we can do is contain the destruction, heal the cavities, and suppress coughing."

Although our patients could rest twenty-four hours a day, the atmosphere in the barracks was not therapeutic: the men rarely exercised; the beauty of nature was not available for contemplation; and, most detrimental of all, they couldn't make plans for what they would do once they had recovered. The patients did receive "enriched" diets in the form of a pat of butter every day and an additional portion of oatmeal, which was more than the other hospital patients were given, but it was hardly enough to reverse the process of consumption. As the patients wasted away, they had obsessive cravings for lard and bacon, as well as dog, seal, walrus, and bear fat. The legendary remedy for fighting tuberculosis was a mixture of lard, butter, honey, and hot milk, but our patients did not receive it.

Injections of calcium chlorate were aimed at encapsulating the cavity, which, theoretically, would prevent the spread of the bacilli. The pneumothorax procedure compressed and immobilized the affected lung, thereby closing the cavity and allowing the lung to heal. But not all patients qualified for the procedure. Those who had cavities in both lungs or whose hearts were infected could not withstand the distress of immobilizing a lung.

My education proceeded in two directions—the lessons from the books, where I learned anatomy, physiology, the symptoms of the disease and its treatment; and the lessons on the ward, where I learned how the disease affected the patient and how to care for another human being. When I worked during the days, I followed in Dr. Piasetsky's steps. We went to the X-ray department, where I was tutored not only by Dr. Piasetsky but also by a charming radiologist, the purported daughter-in-law of Zinoviev.

Sofia Leontevna, slim and elegant even in prison garb, was known throughout the hospital for her meticulous readings of X rays. She'd been a professor of radiology in Leningrad. Though kind and soft-spoken, she stated her opinion firmly and precisely when reading X rays. Her memory was superb; she knew many of Dr. Piasetsky's patients by their X rays alone. Discussing X rays in her small office, Sofia Leontevna addressed Dr. Piasetsky but paid no attention to me. She had no patience for my ignorance nor any interest in talking to me about other things. But I listened intently to her conversations with Dr. Piasetsky, trying to absorb all I could.

With every page I read, every patient I examined, and every lesson with Dr. Piasetsky, I found the disease less abstract. Tapping on and listening to the patient's heart and lungs began to yield meaningful information. The wheezing, gurgling, and crepitation coming through the wooden stethoscope told me where and to what degree the lungs were damaged, and after looking at hundreds of X rays I began to see the contours of the lungs and heart, like figures emerging through murky water.

From the day he arrived, Kolia was one of my favorite patients. He came from a family of schoolteachers in Smolensk, he was my age, and, like me, he had been drafted into the Red Army. The Nazis had captured his unit, but Kolia and a few others escaped the POW camp, made it through the front line, and returned to the Soviet Union. Like thousands of others who'd been captured by the Germans and returned home, Kolia was suspected of being a German spy and was interrogated. These absurd accusations did not apply to Kolia or his escape, but that did not matter. He was sentenced to fifteen years of labor and five years of exile.

Kolia was the first patient on whom I performed the pneumothorax procedure. He lay on his side with his arm over his head, and I ran my fingers down his ribcage until I found the intercostal space between the fourth and fifth ribs. I then inserted a long needle through the skin, muscle, and outer wall of the pleural cavity. This space, situated between the two membranes lining the outside of the lung and the chest cavity, was no more than a few millimeters wide, and we relied on a manometer, which registered negative air pressure, to tell us when we had reached our target. As soon as I saw the silver rise, I stopped pushing the needle and held it in place. Dr. Piasetsky steadied my hand with his, and together we injected air into the pleural cavity. The aim was to create enough pressure between the lung and the chest wall to stop the lung's movement, thereby closing the cavity. Kolia's cavity was on the left side, which meant that not only the lung but also the heart was compressed, a situation that created great discomfort.

I concentrated hard, trying to do exactly as Dr. Piasetsky told me. My back and forehead were sweating, but my hand was steady. Kolia strained to inhale. His face grimaced under the increased pressure. "Fifty, one-hundred, one-hundred-fifty. That's enough," Dr. Piasetsky said. I extracted the needle and carried Kolia back to bed. He'd wasted away so quickly in the hospital that he only weighed about a hundred pounds. His bright pink cheeks and shining blue eyes resembled a child's, exuding innocence and trust.

Kolia looked frightened as he tried to breathe. "Is this really going to help me, or am I going to die? There's so much pressure. Are you sure it's okay?" He could barely speak, the pressure in his chest was so great. I laid him down and propped him up high in bed. I couldn't leave him. His fever was so high that his cheeks nearly glowed in the dusky room.

Before I learned the rudiments of treating tuberculosis patients, I could only help them by easing their fears and comforting their souls. As I gained medical knowledge, this sensitivity helped me to see the whole patient, not only his lungs; to care about the whole person, not only his disease. Many patients couldn't sleep at night, and I was touched when they called me over to talk. The more I learned about medical procedures, the more convinced I became that sitting with Kolia, holding his hand, and making plans for him to do some artwork for me was as important to his recovery as the medical treatment.

Tending to the sick and dying patients day after day, I thought about how the disease erased all distinction between the young and old, the half-literate and university educated, the *urkas* and Party or state officials. Everyone coughed and bled in the same way, and everyone was afraid to die. The prognosis for most of the patients was not good; the mortality rate on the ward was the highest in the hospital. The diagnosis of TB was a second sentence for every patient, and every bit as lethal as the first one.

As new patients came, I'd grow attached to them, then follow them to the morgue. With every death I witnessed, the calcium chlorate injections and pneumothorax treatments seemed more futile. More often than not, Dr. Piasetsky and Sofia Leontevna expressed despair when viewing a patient's X rays, but Dr. Piasetsky still prescribed treatment. I questioned why we were

treating patients who had no chance for recovery—was prolong-
ing life for a day, a week, or a month more humane than letting a
person die without interference? Did that dignify death? Or was
death simply death, no matter how a person died? I thought
about what I would want if I were a patient. I was terrified of dying; I would want the doctor to try to save me no matter how
hopeless my condition. I wouldn't want to be abandoned to my
fate. But was this the best way to treat the patients? I finally realized that patients died in different ways and had different needs.
Some wanted to be lied to until the last moment. Others were
calm and accepting of the truth, viewing death as an escape from
the illness and the mines.

Losha Alekseyev was dying. His eye sockets had become too
large for his glassy eyes; his gasping and wheezing resembled
something between a cry and a howl. When I gave him the
mouthpiece and squeezed the bag of oxygen to fill his lungs, his
cheeks changed color from gray to pale pink. The gasping diminished. "Am I dying?" he asked. "Please, help me. I don't want to
die. I'm too young."

"Losha, I'm with you. I'm not going to let you die. Tell me
what you need. Would you like more oxygen? Another pillow?"
I put one hand on his forehead, and with the other I took his
hand and squeezed it. He squeezed back. I sensed his anxiety
ease. Holding his hand wasn't enough to save his life, but it did
heal the aloneness that made dying so terrifying. Losha held my
hand tightly and whispered, "Can you give me an injection to
make me breathe easier?" In his condition, an injection would be
of minimal help. "I think an injection will help me get through
the night," he said thoughtfully, "and I always feel better in the
morning."

Every patient had strong beliefs about what would make him
feel better. Sometimes a request for more medication or a certain
pillow or fresh air worked; sometimes it was merely an expression of hope. For the terminal patients, there was virtually no escape from slow suffocation. But doing something—like giving
them an injection—took their minds off their pain and impend-
ing death for at least a short while.

"I'll go and get a syringe," I told Losha.

When I came back, his eyes were staring straight ahead, his pupils enlarged, his mouth taut in an expression of surprise. At least he died peacefully, believing he'd feel better in the morning.

Leaving the TB ward after a twelve-hour day was like emerging from a cave into sunlight. I went to the barbershop and heard new gossip or stopped by the kitchen to see the chief cook, One-Eyed Ivan, an *urka* elevated to *predurok* who was my best chess partner. Sometimes I wandered around in the sunshine or sat on a bench.

I made a daily foray onto the hospital grounds, going to the pharmacy at the other end of camp to pick up drugs for the ward. I volunteered to go because the load was often heavy and I got to know other *feldshers* and nurses, as well as the pharmacy director, a Pole and free worker, Wanda Pienkovska. We spoke Polish, but since Wanda was a free worker, and free workers were forbidden to interact with prisoners, we stopped talking when anyone else was around.

The first time I met Wanda, she was celebrating her sixtieth birthday and engagement to the chief of the guards, a twenty-seven-year old Mongolian. She took great pride in her appearance, dying her hair blond with peroxide, curling it, wearing rouge and lipstick, and swinging her corpulent breasts and hips as she walked. Her white coat was spotless. I enjoyed watching her small pink fingers move as she mixed liquids from different flasks, weighed the powdered medication, and scraped the dosages onto small pieces of paper. At the same time, with her cold blue eyes, she watched every worker around her. Nothing escaped her attention.

Among the people I met was a blond nurse from the ophthalmology department whom I'd seen several times passing our barracks on the way to the morgue. One day after receiving the medical supplies, I waited for her. When she emerged from the building, I offered to carry her basket. She looked surprised, smiled, and looked straight in my eyes. I hadn't been smiled at by a beautiful young woman since I'd left Taubcia. For over three years, I hadn't thought about women. My erotic fantasies, if they occurred at all, were limited to the past.

She walked lightly by my side while I babbled about myself, trying to keep her attention. The feelings welling up within me—of love, mystery, attraction—were so strong I thought they would overflow and overpower me. I couldn't look at her for more than a moment without averting my eyes. Half-turned, she directed her gray-green, deep-set eyes at me with apparent interest.

"You know, I've been going to the pharmacy every day hoping I'd meet you," I said. She squeezed my arm lightly, her wavy blond hair blowing across her face. Her eyebrows and lashes were dark, making her eyes look even greener and more expressive. The only thing that kept me from taking her arm were the baskets in each of my hands.

At the end of the path she took her basket and said, "I enjoyed meeting you, but I have to go." She walked away without looking back, and I watched her, rooted in my steps and transformed by her presence. The feeling of being a prisoner disappeared, and I felt as if I were on Farna Street with my friends in Wlodzimierz-Wolynski, singled out and smiled at by a beautiful woman. I tried to imprint her face in my mind and ran my hand over the place where she had touched me. Her playful squeeze had sent a thousand signals, all of them warm and gentle, and I couldn't stop thinking about her for days and nights to come.

One rainy afternoon while sitting with Maria Ivanovna and Kurban in the nurse's room, I heard a gentle knock at the door, followed by a familiar voice. "May I come in?" I felt like I'd been immersed in boiling water, but I jumped up to get the door. A navy stocking cap covered her blond hair, and a gray prisoner's coat was draped over her shoulders. "I wanted to see where you worked," she said. She greeted Maria Ivanovna by name.

Maria Ivanovna responded with more affection than usual. "Come in, Zina. It's so nice of you to visit. Sit with us and have some tea." She offered Zina a chair. "This is Janusz, our new *feldsher*."

"We've already met." She extended her hand, which was soft and warm. I kissed it. Butterflies danced through my heart.

Maria Ivanovna introduced Zina to Kurban, who gazed at her. She whispered something to Maria Ivanovna at the desk, and I excused myself from the room, feeling she hadn't come to visit with me. Kurban followed.

We walked across the ward and went into the storage room, where Kurban rested at night.

"So you've met Zina before?" Kurban inquired.

"I met her once. She seems to be pleasant."

"I'm sure she's very pleasant. There's a big romance between her and Viktor, the guy who works in the morgue. You know him—he's from Vladivostock."

I saw Viktor nearly every day, but we didn't talk much. He was busy in the morgue as the chief assistant to Dr. Umansky, the pathologist. Dr. Piasetsky and I went there frequently to watch the autopsies performed on our patients. The results helped Dr. Piasetsky confirm his diagnosis, and looking at the organs helped me better understand anatomy.

Dr. Piasetsky highly respected Dr. Umansky. In addition to being a competent pathologist and well-rounded intellectual, he protected the doctors whose diagnoses did not match the autopsy results. He didn't denounce a single doctor in his daily reports to the camp and hospital director. Instead he tailored the report so it was consistent with the doctor's clinical findings. Discrepancies between the autopsy results and the doctor's diagnosis could get the doctor into serious trouble. The hospital director, also a doctor, prided himself on running a first-class hospital. Dr. Umansky protected the doctors indiscriminately, believing they were under so much stress and had experienced so much tragedy that they were bound to make mistakes. He didn't want to give them any more trouble.

I, too, admired Dr. Umansky. Deep creases, etched across his forehead by years of thought, crept all the way up to his receding hairline. He did everything slowly and precisely, whether reading a report or examining a piece of tissue. He had practiced in Odessa before and after the revolution, and he knew my relatives there. He was a man of few words, so when he told me stories about Odessa and his life there, I felt honored.

The first several sessions in the morgue made me sick to my stomach. In the middle of the prosectorium was a large cement table that gently sloped inward toward a drain, which emptied into a hole in the floor. The cadaver lay on top of the hole. This allowed Viktor to rinse off the specimens before putting them on the examining table.

He was extremely skilled with a handsaw, able to cut through the cranium without grazing the brain underneath. With a gloved hand, he reached into the skull and scooped out the brain, gave it a tug to release it from its nerve and vessel attachments, and plopped it on the table, where he weighed it and sliced it into several sections for Dr. Umansky to examine. With the same acumen, he sliced into the chest and abdomen, making one incision from the neck to the pubic hair. He broke through the sternum with a rotating saw and made additional openings with a chisel and hammer. With a final thrust, he wrenched apart the ribcage.

Viktor removed the lungs and heart and sliced them into sections. The sick lungs oozed a whitish substance resembling cottage cheese. Viktor then cut out the liver, spleen, pancreas, and kidneys, sectioned them all, and laid them on the table. He left the bowels in place but opened them, releasing a stench so concentrated I could hardly breathe. After the examination was complete, Viktor dumped all the organs back into the abdominal cavity and stitched it up.

With no drainage system in the morgue, the blood and tissue accumulated in the hole below the examination table. At night Viktor covered the hole with a wooden lid, but sometimes the contents were carried off anyway. The drain in the floor and the underground creatures figured prominently in my dreams.

I had become used to the senseless deaths in the camps. I had come to expect the shooting of a prisoner because he was too weak to march to work. I had become oblivious to the heap of cadavers that lay outside the mining camp; their bones picked clean the very next day by scavengers—animal and human. The hospitals proved to be the exception to the rule of death and degradation. With the millions of people dying in the camps, why bother to heal the sick? Why bother to perform autopsies? No families were going to be informed of the results. Why bother to stitch up the corpses when they all were going to be buried in mass graves anyway? Why bother with all the doctors, tests, and treatments? Most of the patients sent to the hospital were already half-dead, too far gone for any treatment to work.

As with all my troubling thoughts, I went to Dr. Piasetsky. He explained that our hospital, the main facility for the entire Kolyma labor camp system, served as a showcase for the authorities who came from Moscow to inspect the camps. The hospital director wanted it run as a university hospital would be. As usual, Dr. Piasetsky left me to ponder the contradictions myself; he had pondered them long ago, and now he was too weary and troubled to discuss them with me.

The news that Viktor and Zina were lovers came as a shock. Zina had told me she had someone in her life, but it was hard for me to imagine Viktor—who made the same joke every time he sliced open a brain: "With a couple of eggs, this would make a good meal"—holding and touching the warm, beautiful, delicate Zina. I found the whole thing distressing.

Kurban added matter-of-factly, "Viktor's sentence ends next month. He'll go back to Vladivostock. What kind of sentence was that—three years in the hospital? The family probably paid off some officials. He didn't spend a day doing hard work. He went straight from being an orderly in the surgery barracks to working in the morgue—not that I would want his job."

I was barely listening. All I could think of was Viktor slicing apart dead organs and Zina visiting him in Dr. Umansky's office. But he was leaving next month, and Zina had many more years left in the camps. Would she continue her relationship with Viktor? Would he stay in the vicinity to visit her? I had no idea what was to happen, and the uncertainty made me irritable and impatient.

Zina and I met several times on the street and in the pharmacy, but she never said anything about Viktor's leaving. I felt a thread of warm feeling between us, but not a word had been said about it. Then one day she invited me to have supper with her when she was on evening duty. I found myself becoming more and more attracted to her. With all the years ahead of us in the camps, I thought that having a romance or even a close friendship would enrich our lives, if only for a short while. I felt safe, rested, and well fed, and longing pierced my heart. Zina stirred in me a long-relinquished need for female love, warmth, and touch. Surrounded my whole life by women whom I loved and who loved me—my mother, younger sister, and, most of all, Taubcia—I felt lonely and orphaned without them. I missed the intimate talks with Taubcia, the new meanings we found in the word *love* as we explored each other's thoughts, feelings, and bodies. I missed our walks along the riverbank, evenings in the garden sitting on the bench holding hands, the times we were all alone and the rest of the world forgotten.

One morning Viktor came by, all dressed up, to say goodbye. His papers had gone through, and he was heading home. A week later I had my dinner date with Zina.

I knocked on the door of her cubicle, and Zina appeared in a clean white blouse, white coat, and white nurse's cap. Illuminated by a dim lamp, her hair looked as golden as an autumn field. I sat quietly, unable to find the right words as Zina put a bowl of soup in front of me and sliced bread with a handmade stiletto. "That's quite a knife," I said. The double blade had been filed to a sharp point, and the handle was inlaid with colored strips of plastic.

"It's a present from a patient. You know how they like to give presents."

The soup was thick and hot, with chunks of meat and mushrooms. "I got a letter from Viktor. He's moving to Kiev," Zina said. "The last six months between Viktor and me were not so good. He was looking forward to being released, he hated his job, and sometimes he got really ugly. But what I hated most was his jealousy."

The door opened and we were interrupted by Zina's boss, Dr. Loskutov. "I didn't know you had company. When you finish, could you stop in my office?"

Zina introduced us. Everyone adored Dr. Loskutov. He possessed dashing good looks—blond hair, green eyes, and a warm smile—and a perceptive, personal way of dealing with people.

You always felt he could read your soul just by looking in your eyes. He could make people feel very good or very bad with a few words. Many people took advantage of him, but only because he let them. Zina and I both assumed he was aware that people manipulated him but that he let them do it because he pitied every prisoner. If he could give them some relief, he gave it freely. The women envied his camp wife and worshiped him, but he didn't seem aware of his allure. He didn't distinguish between people— urkas or politicals, the young or old, the contagious or noncontagious. All suffered. All had hearts and souls.

As we ate I watched Zina's face. I sensed so much life and warmth in her. I wanted to embrace her, hold her close to me, tell her I was falling in love with her. Her hand felt so good in mine. It was so new. Before coming to the hospital, I felt that good emotions had been washed out of me. I didn't think I'd ever be able to love again. But sitting in the nursing office, with only a flimsy wall separating us from the patients, I felt immersed in love and happiness.

As the evening came to a close, I kissed Zina's hand and held it tightly. "I hope we can see each other more frequently."

Zina's joyful face turned serious. "Let's wait and see what develops. I'm tired of relationships for convenience and protection." She patted me on the arm, and I left not feeling the ground under my feet.

Winter arrived. Although we were close to the Sea of Okhotsk, the snow and windstorms were as strong as those in Maldyak. Some snowfalls accumulated so quickly that we had to dig tunnels to get to the barracks, and all men working in the hospital were called to shovel the road to the highway, a distance of six kilometers. If the snowstorm lasted long enough, the road became impassable, resulting in one of the few crises at the hospital. Our food supplies depended on that road.

Nevertheless, I loved the snowstorms. Even when the visibility was no more than five to ten meters and snow swirled around my head, I loved to walk outside. Outfitted in warm felt boots, padded pants and jacket, a scarf, and a hat with earflaps, I felt safe from the violent elements. I loved the smell, like newly washed linen, and the anarchy of it. The whirling snow and cold air were the opposite of the stifling heat of the prisons, stench of the barracks, tyranny of the guards, and frequent *shmons*, which badly rattled my nerves.

Winter didn't make life any easier inside the ward, however. The TB patients roiled about the barracks, their lips and cheeks rosy, their flailing arms deathly white, their eyes bright with fever. Although the boisterous activity seemed to enliven the drab gray room, the patients became more aggressive and difficult to control as the long winter wore on.

One night I heard Sierioga, a young pickpocket, crying out and shrieking in pain. His lungs were like sieves, but he was perpetually optimistic and helped with the other patients, as if willing himself back to health. Before I'd parted the curtain, Vova, a night orderly, came rushing in. "Come quickly. Something very bad is happening."

The patients were alert, their eyes following me as I followed Vova back to the storage room. The door was locked from the inside; Sierioga was crying out wildly. "I'm calling the *predurkis* and guards if you don't open the door!" I said. Nobody answered.

I glanced around the room. Three patients were missing—two *urkas* and one military man, a captain who bragged continually about his heroism in the war. I was enraged. The patients lying in their beds told me repeatedly, as if I didn't understand, that they were raping Sierioga. I grabbed an ice pick and shouted through the locked door, "Open up now or I'll break through and turn you all in to the guards." The onlookers followed my every move, waiting to see what would happen. When I got no response, I drove the ice pick through the door and kicked in the wood.

The three patients stood against the wall with a bench between me and them. Sierioga lay on the floor, his gown ripped off, bleeding and moaning. I shoved two of the men against the wall, took Sierioga in my arms, and carried him to bed. Then I went back to the storage room, still carrying the ice pick. "I'll deal with you later," I said to the three rapists. I sent Vova to the emergency room to summon *feldshers* to take Sierioga to surgery. I had no experience to know how badly he was injured.

After Sierioga had left, I thought about how to deal with the perpetrators. I decided not to be both judge and executioner and to wait for Dr. Piasetsky. Although I wanted to beat each of them, I was too aware of my position in the barracks and the effect beatings would have on the other patients.

In the morning Dr. Piasetsky tried to explain the harsh reality of the situation. "The patients know they're going to die, and they don't care what happens to them. They have a strong sex drive, and they know they can get away with whatever they want. If I report this incident to the guards, all three of them will be sent to the isolator. Then they'll come back and they'll be more sick. I've faced this problem before, and I don't want to start a war. You did the right thing in stepping in to save Sierioga from further injury, but we aren't going to look for justice. These patients don't care if they die today or tomorrow. They got what they wanted."

Zina and I had been friends for two months, but I still didn't know her very well. I had revealed nearly everything about myself, but she held back a great deal, and I didn't know how to take it. Sitting in the nurse's room one day, I told her I had fallen in love with her.

She clutched her arms around herself protectively. "What are you talking about?"

Shocked by her sudden change of mood, I repeated, "I love you."

"I don't think this is a place for love and commitment," she said. "Today we're together, but who knows about tomorrow? You're lucky. Your sentence is not a political one. I've got nearly every code under Article 58. I may never get out of here."

Zina had never indicated she'd been sentenced under such severe indictments. I couldn't believe it and asked how she'd gotten into such trouble. She held her face in her hands and began to sob, and I felt guilty for stirring up memories I had no right to inquire about. But she began to talk anyway, a steely voice emerging through her tears.

"My father was the first secretary of the Party in Yoshkar-Ola, the capital of the Bashkir Autonomous Republic. My mother was an instructor at the university, and my relatives were well respected professionals and Party members. One night the NKVD pounded on the door. I had just finished high school, and my brother was attending the university in Kazan. My parents and I were ordered to sit in the dining room with a guard while the others ransacked the place. They went through every book in the house, read every scrap of paper, and emptied every drawer. They repeatedly asked my father for the names of his co-conspirators, and my father repeatedly answered that there were no co-conspirators—he didn't know what they were talking about.

"I lost my head. I cried and held onto my mother. She tried to calm me, telling me it was a mistake and that everything would be fixed in the morning. She'd call the first secretary of the republic, and everything would be straightened out. But my father gave us no words of encouragement. The NKVD officials began beating him in front of us. They made him kneel and lick their boots. They threatened to rape me and my mother. He was crying and begged them to leave us alone. The air reeked with their alcoholic breath. They broke my father right there. They spit in his soul. I never saw him again."

Zina got up and began walking around the table, her eyes locked with the floor, her arms still folded tightly against her chest.

"Zina, stop. You don't have to tell me. I'm sorry I asked—"

"No, I want you to know." Her voice burst through the tears. "I want you to know. I want you to listen." For the first time she looked into my eyes. She sat back down and gripped my arm tightly.

"In prison I learned that my father's friend, the first secretary of the republic, and their associates were arrested the same night in a big sweep conducted by the NKVD sent from Moscow."

"But why did they arrest you? You were only seventeen. Did you say something?"

"You didn't live in this country in 1937. Thousands and thousands of innocent people were arrested. The accusations were all lies. It was all to prove how effective the Organy were. The irony is that the highest-ranking members of the local NKVD were arrested, too.

"I was in prison for over four months. I met so many family friends there, some as prisoners, some as interrogators. Then the interrogators became prisoners—the whole city was mixed up. I had no trial, only interrogation after interrogation. 'Name the friends who conspired with your father.' 'With whom did you plan terrorist activities?' 'Who are your mother's friends?' 'Who frequently visited your home?' As the insanity went on, the interrogators became more bestial. They were no longer men, no longer human. I don't know how I survived what they did to me. The beatings I could take, but being ordered to sit naked—being raped—I just wanted to die. I slashed my wrists so many times." She pushed up her sleeve and showed me her arms. Thick pink scars, like the claw marks of a wild animal, ran across her wrists. "But they wouldn't let me. They sent me to the infirmary, and there I met this lady who knew my mother. She took care of me like her own child. She told me that the best way to survive in the camps was to become a nurse."

Zina's story brought me down, hard, to reality. I felt again my own weightlessness, like a grain of sand floating in a sea of terror and brutality. No one would care if we lived or died. No one was interested in who we were, we who lived torturous lives and were buried without names or markers.

Zina lay on her arm on the desk and sobbed quietly. I wrapped my arms around her to soothe her shaking body. She clung to me in return.

"I wasn't in love with Viktor. I stayed with him because it isn't safe for a woman to be alone, even in the hospital."

She pressed her head against my chest and wrapped her arms tightly around my waist. I held her closely but gave up any illusion of taking away her pain and sorrow. As with the TB patients, Zina's suffering lay beyond my power to heal.

One night a loud shriek woke me up in the nurse's room. It came from the ward. I parted the curtains and saw the patients crowded around one bed. I forced my way through and found Leonid, a middle-aged man, lying with a knife in his heart. The guy who killed him, Sviet, sat listlessly on the next bed.

Both men were Georgians. They had been lying next to each other for three months. I could see the hostility growing between them but had no idea it would result in murder. Sviet had been taunting Leonid with various epithets—"bloodsucker," "torturer," "murderer." "How many did you kill?" The insults and accusations were shouted loudly and were meant to turn the other patients against him. Leonid rarely responded, but when he did he called Sviet a traitor and fascist. His retorts did little to dispel the growing opinion that Leonid had been an interrogator. I had even come to that conclusion. But Leonid was still one of my patients, and I was responsible for him. When the hostilities first threatened to get out of hand, I had called Sviet into the office and told him to stop the abuse. Leonid had been hemorrhaging badly, and I thought he was in the last stage of the disease. Sviet's eyes were like little stones. "You have no idea what he did to hundreds of innocent people. He's a sadistic bastard. I know. He interrogated my father and uncle. He gets what he deserves."

After the murder, Dr. Piasetsky took the same stance as he had on the rape. "They have their own accounts to settle. You don't know what's gone on between them, and you definitely don't want to get involved. Let justice work itself out."

Predurkis and guards paraded in and out of the barracks all morning. The patients were as agitated as ever. I had to write a report and answer a lot of questions. Sviet was taken away to stand another trial, but he didn't care. He knew he was going down. When he saw me he said, "It's over. I can die in peace. My only wish was to see him go down first."

The murder of Leonid made me think about the power of hatred toward the people who torture us; how deeply it must penetrate the heart to inspire an otherwise peace-loving person to kill in cold blood. Maybe this is how we should treat our oppressors for all the tortures of the soul and pains of the flesh. Maybe we are entitled to be judges and executioners should we ever meet our oppressors on equal ground.

I'd been hurt and betrayed more than a few times, starting with Nikitin, my tank mate who denounced me. I despised all of them, but I didn't want to murder any of them. To beat them, punish them, see them sentenced to the same harsh labor, yes; but I wouldn't stick a knife in their hearts or pull a trigger and blow their brains out. But I did feel murderous rage toward Zina's rapist-interrogator. Slapping her, hitting her, and spitting in her face wasn't enough. This man had to degrade and humiliate her, crush her soul. I would stab him repeatedly, make him feel pain, and watch him die slowly, making sure he knew what he had done.

I wasn't capable of judging Sviet. His pre-terminal condition put him in a different predicament. But I wondered if Leonid really had interrogated Sviet's father or if Sviet had killed him simply because Leonid had been a member of the NKVD.

I no longer believed in symbolic protests. I wouldn't become a martyr for the cause. I wouldn't kill someone just because he represented the oppressive power of the state. This kind of revolutionary heroism was long in my past. I'd grown up believing that the cause of socialism was more important than the individual; that I would sacrifice my life to defend my people and the honor of my country. But seeing the thousands of political prisoners and knowing that millions of innocent people had been arrested, tortured, and shot made me aware that fighting the state was futile. I hated the system more than any particular person representing it.

Zina and I saw each other every day. We thought we were hiding the relationship well, but Dr. Piasetsky pulled me aside and told me to cool it. Liaisons between prisoners were strictly forbidden. If the partners were caught, they'd be sent to different camps after punishment in the isolator. Despite the threat, a good number of prisoners in the hospital were in relationships, known as having a "camp husband" or "camp wife." Zina explained that for women, having a "camp husband" protected them from being pursued and raped, which was why she had stayed with Viktor even though she didn't love him. As for myself, my love for Taubcia remained as strong as it was the day we parted, and I maintained hope that I would be reunited with her and my family. But as I read in the newspaper about the ghettos and mass executions of Jews, I doubted more and more that this would happen.

We limited our visits to the workplace, meeting under the pretense that we were discussing patients, bringing supplies from the pharmacy, exchanging syringes or needles. Since there was no safe place for intimacy, we usually had to be satisfied with holding hands, stealing kisses in the nurse's office, and giving brief embraces. Strangely, we didn't become frustrated with the lack of privacy. Simply being together for a short period dramatically changed the remaining hours of the day. When we did take the risk of closing a door, it was well calculated, brief, and blustery, with both of us keeping an eye on the door knob and listening intently for sounds. Aside from the fear of being caught, the fear of a pregnancy curbed our lovemaking. Upon discovery, pregnant women were immediately shipped to Elgen, a camp seven hundred miles away. The babies were kept in an orphanage; the mothers allowed to see them only for feedings. I asked Zina one day if she thought our love could last under these constrained circumstances.

"If I've learned anything during my five years in the camps, it's never to think about the future," she said. "Be happy with the day you are living, and hope the next day is as good or better than the one that passed."

I wasn't used to such calm calculations in matters of the heart. "But we love each other. I can't believe it will ever end. I love you, and I want you always next to me."

"I love you too," she said. "But love in this place, where I still have five years ahead of me and you have seven, is not easy. Who knows what can happen over these years? Who knows how we will feel about each other?"

I was stunned. She took my hand. "It's a great comfort to have you in my life, and I hope I provide the same for you. But you're trying to force me to make promises I cannot make. Please try to understand my reasoning. It isn't time for us to be making commitments."

More than anything, I was saddened by the thought that she was right. This way of thinking was so contrary to my nature that it hurt me deeply and took a great deal of effort to understand. I could not help feeling rejected.

One morning Dr. Piasetsky arrived later than usual and sought me out to talk. I felt that we were becoming real friends, despite the differences between us in status, age, and education. Our lessons in his office usually lapsed into an hour or more of idle talk, each conversation becoming more and more personal. In ordinary life such diversions would be condemned at the workplace, but in Piasetsky's little office our budding friendship was a gift from heaven, transcending the impersonalization the camps were designed to enforce.

He pulled a letter out of his pocket and gave it to me. "Read it. It's from my sister."

The envelope was stamped with a brown circle and the word "CENSORED." The flap was worn and tattered. It had obviously been opened and glued back together more than once.

The letter was only half a page. Four sentences. His sister wrote that their parents were in good health and that their father was still working despite his old age and frequent bouts of rheumatism. She and her son were also in good health. She was still at her previous job and her son was attending school. The last sentence read, "Yevgenia Fedorovna got married in December."

"She used to be my wife," Piasetsky said sadly, staring at the letter. "She was also the first person to denounce me when I was arrested. In front of the staff of the Institute of Endocrinology, she got up and said that she had sensed for a long time that I had been involved in counterrevolutionary activity, and she called for my expulsion from the Party and the institute. She used to be my assistant. I had helped her with her doctorate—I wrote it for her. I promoted her. We'd been married for seven years. Everyone in my family liked her except for my mother, who said before we married, 'Don't cuddle a snake to your chest.' To this day I haven't gotten over the shock.

"We confided in each other about everything. She was my refuge from the terror of arrests that surrounded us. I don't understand how from one day to the next, a person whom you thought—whom you *knew* loved you more than anyone else could turn against you just to preserve her position and good standing in the Party. I never sensed a false note in our relationship. She was so warm and loving.

"The investigator showed me the written statement in which she denounced me and asked for a divorce. I didn't want to live after that. It hurt me more than the nightly interrogations and beatings."

"Did you try to kill yourself?"

"I thought about it constantly. It occupied my thoughts for months. I had always loved life, people, my work. Ultimately, I wanted to live."

"What about in the mines—did you think of suicide then?"

"Yes, more than once. And what about you?"

"I got to the point of deciding how I would end my life if things got too unbearable. It was a comfort to know I could do it. But things turned around. I came here."

Nikolai Rafaelovich got up and stretched, cracking his bones. His eyes glistened. "Suicide is multifaceted. It can be done out of courage or cowardice. It can be an escape or an act of protest. There is no ethical standard by which to judge suicide. It always depends on the individual and the circumstances. I think everyone has the right to make his own choice. When I was faced with the decision, I realized I had to come up with some way of deciding what my life was worth and whether killing myself was justified. The moment hasn't come yet."

CHAPTER 17

Antechamber to the Morgue

In the spring Dr. Piasetsky told me we'd be relocating to the surgery barracks, where we'd both have our own office and a large nursing station. Two new nurses were joining our staff, which meant I'd be able to alternate day and night shifts. The news elated me. The surgery department was next to ophthalmology, which meant I'd be able to see Zina every day.

Elation had been a frequent visitor in my life. Ever since I was a child, any happy event filled me with a joy I couldn't contain, and I had to tell everyone how happy I was. Conversely, rejection and criticism filled me with shame and anger that took me years to learn how to contain. But the ability to feel elated by the smallest things was the best defense I had against the spirit-killing force of the camps. Eating *paika* and oatmeal in the mornings made me intensely happy, even though I was still hungry afterward. I attached meaning to all good events—food was an omen that I'd live another day; finding a wooden spoon or procuring additional rags to wrap around my feet was evidence that I had the luck or skill to survive; meeting someone carrying full buckets was a sign that something good was coming my way. An unsolicited smile from a fellow prisoner was a personal message:

"We are in this together; I know what you're thinking; I understand you; don't lose hope."

Those of a darker temperament, such as Nikolai Rafaelovich, had it harder. Every blow seemed to accumulate inside him, and nothing could lessen his suffering and hardship. In the privacy of his office he told me he had received another letter from his sister. "My father is in bad health. It's his heart. My sister asked my ex-wife to admit my father to the hospital, but she refused. She lived with me in my parents' flat for seven years."

Nikolai Rafaelovich stared blankly into space. "I have no friends I can call on, even though I lived in the same flat for thirty-eight years. Some of my close friends are in prison, and those who are free don't want to have anything to do with me. I can understand their fear, and I know some of them are ashamed by their behavior."

Nikolai Rafaelovich got up, walked the four steps across his cubicle, pivoted, and gestured pleadingly at the floor. "What happens to people? Is trust and loyalty gone? Is friendship gone? What's happening to us? How can my ex-wife refuse to help my sick father? He's not a criminal. He's not in prison. He's just a sick old man. We've known our neighbors for years, but they've stopped talking to my parents. Have their hearts turned to stone?"

Dr. Piasetsky kept his word. In the new barracks I got my own room with a bed, nightstand, desk, and chair. Like a monk's cell, it was long and narrow and had a window at the end that ran from the floor to the high ceiling. And, like a monk, I had few personal items to put in the room. I had only one set of clothing—a black tunic and pants, underwear, footrags, and short boots—and my personal belongings included a shaving kit (which I'd gotten in Buchta Nakhodka), a towel, a comb, and a wooden spoon. I had no reminders of where I'd been and was glad of it. I shielded myself from despair by shutting out the worrisome thoughts of my family and immersing myself in the patients and Zina.

The door to my room had two locks and opened to the main corridor. Next to my room was the nursing room and then Nikolai Rafaelovich's office. The latter was huge. It had two large windows, one facing the backyard trees and the other facing the road. Looking out the window, I could see the entrance to the ophthalmology clinic as well as the mess hall. Dr. Piasetsky's bookshelves lined two walls. He brought his large desk from the old office and acquired a new wingback chair, which looked impressive behind his large desk. Two armchairs, new additions to his office, faced the desk, and on the opposite wall stood a cot, freshly made with white linen and a pillow. A screen in one corner of the room concealed a sink with running water and a dressing area. The office was also equipped with a rack for X rays and an X ray viewer. It looked like a doctor's office in any large city.

In the evenings, before going to the woman's zone to sleep, Zina would sneak into my room. Under the glow of the kerosene lamp she often talked about her parents. We'd sit on the edge of the bed holding hands and hugging, or she would lay her head against my shoulder. "I have a hard time remembering my mother's face," she told me once. "I can no longer picture her laughing, talking, singing. The only memory I have of her is holding me while the NKVD officer held a pistol to her head. That's all I can see of her face—that terrified look. And my father, his face only appears as it did when he was arrested. I remember things we did as a family, my childhood, but I can't picture their faces. My mother had beautiful blue eyes, but I can't recall the shade of blue anymore. Can you understand this? I think about my brother. I remember him so well, but I can't recall the happy years we spent together. My recollections are always tragic. My mother crying, my father begging. They don't look like my parents. They are strangers. Either my memory fails me or my imagination plays tricks on me. What's happened to them?"

Not many people were able to shut out the past—Zina couldn't, Nikolai Rafaelovich couldn't—but I had to or it would eat me alive. The only reminder I had of home was a tree outside my window. A branch had grown out so it was just touching my window, and it reminded me of the tree outside of our house that had a branch growing up to the attic hatch. I used to climb the tree and crawl into the attic to see my pigeons. I spent hours petting, feeding, and watching them. While one partner sat on the eggs, the other left the nest to forage. I loved the sound of the pigeons warbling to each other. I cared for over one hundred of them and loved them all. I could recognize each of them by their colors, feathers, beaks, legs, and tail feathers. The pigeons differed in their abilities. Some could turn somersaults in the air; others could fly a hundred miles to deliver a letter and come straight back; others had a huge bag, like a second throat, where they stored food. Some male pigeons had beautiful colors with which to attract female pigeons. They fanned their wings, swept their tails across the floor, and strutted around, warbling for the females' attention. Once coupled, the male pigeons attacked anyone who dared approach their partners.

In the spring and fall I built boxes against the walls so each couple would have a private nest. I filled them with hay, feathers, and sticks, then watched as the couples wove the most intricate nests. I monitored the nests daily so I wouldn't miss the baby pigeons pecking out of their shells, and I spent hours watching the parents teach the babies to fly.

When the days lengthened and the earth warmed up, when the insects hatched and the flowers bloomed, Sunday became a work day. The entire hospital staff, except for those on duty and the department chiefs, was led outside the zone to pan for gold in the creeks, cut down trees, gather firewood, and pick berries and mushrooms. From time to time Zina and I were delegated to the same crew. The guards didn't accompany us into the forests, since there was no where to escape to, and Zina and I found hiding places where we could spend an hour or more alone.

The more involved Zina and I became, the more I thought about our future. Since my arrest, my only thoughts about the future had concerned the next day; I had banished the idea of longterm plans. But now I wanted some kind of commitment. I never again wanted to be as lonely as I had been before I met Zina.

"I hope we'll always be together," I said one day. We had climbed on top of a boulder and lay in the warm sun, feeling the cool stone beneath our backs. "I dream about our future all the time. When we're free, we can be the happiest couple." I tried to look in her eyes, but she avoided me. "Zina, there is no past for either of us. Stop thinking about your parents. It's tearing you apart. If they're alive, you'll find them. If they're gone, they're gone. But you are alive, and you must live your life."

I jumped down off the boulder and threw a rock as far as I could. Birds flapped away in the distance. I shouted up to her, "How do you feel about me, about us? Do you love me?"

She rolled onto her stomach and was quiet for a while. "I feel empty inside. I can't feel deeply, like I used to. You want me to tell you I love you. I think I do, but I also know that I could love you much more if I knew my parents were alive. You ask me about our future. I would love to be with you always. It would be the greatest thing in the world. I really feel this. But I don't trust the feeling. I'm not sure of myself. I'm not sure of anything. How can you be sure when your life can be ruined so easily? I'm hollow inside. Empty."

I didn't know how to react. I was so angry and agitated that I wanted to run. But I could feel her suffering as she lay on the boulder.

"You're not empty inside," I shouted back. "I can feel your warmth and love. You can't be making up your feelings. I know your love is true and sincere. I trust you. No matter what happens to us, I'll wait for you if I get out earlier, and if you get out first, I hope that you'll wait for me. We may still have several years together here, but if one of us is sent away, I'd like to know I'm waiting for someone, and that someone is waiting for me."

"Janusz, don't make me promise something I may not be able to keep. There would be nothing more wonderful than believing everything you've said, but the reality is different."

I lay awake that night unable to stop my thoughts. I had to have a commitment. I paced up and down the corridor. I felt hot. I went back to bed and dozed off, only to awaken with my shirt drenched. I opened the window. The dark night was slipping away. I put my clothes on and went from patient to patient on the ward, looking for something to do.

One morning not long after the talk with Zina, I felt a strange tickling in my throat. I'd just finished rounds and was on my way to Nikolai Rafaelovich's office when I coughed and spit something up. Bright red drops of blood appeared on the floor. Everything whirled inside me. "No!" I howled. I leaned against the wall, holding my handkerchief to my mouth. When I stopped coughing, I ran into Dr. Piasetsky's office and showed him the handkerchief. "It's me."

His face paled. His brown eyes widened. I steadied myself against a chair. Another cough racked my body. Blood gushed into my throat. I felt weak and needed to sit down. So many times I'd dreamed this dream—saw myself spit up blood, felt myself choke on it. Maria Ivanovna reassured me; she had had the same dream, but she believed it was a sign we'd never get sick. "It's good to see blood in your dream. It means you're alive and well." I was ready to wake up now, ready to greet the morning again, fresh and healthy. I hadn't had any symptoms. I'd felt a little more tired than usual, but I could still work. I hadn't been coughing or losing weight. Maybe it was just a blood vessel in my throat or esophagus. Maybe it had nothing to do with my lungs.

Dr. Piasetsky reached around my waist and helped me into the nursing room. Maria Ivanovna was bent over her desk looking at something in a patient's chart. She didn't hear us enter the room.

"Maria Ivanovna, please get Janusz a double dose of codeine." Piasetsky's voice was barely audible. Maria Ivanovna looked up and stared at me in disbelief.

"No, not Janusz." She put her arm around my shoulder and held my hand. Both she and Nikolai Rafaelovich led me to my room. I undressed and crawled under the sheets, trying hard to suppress the coughing.

Hela, the day nurse, came with a double dose of codeine and a glass of water. "It will make you sleepy, but it's good for you to rest."

I pulled the blanket over my head and curled into a ball. I closed my eyes, wanting to disappear in the dark. I didn't want to see anyone, didn't want anyone to know what had happened to me. I didn't even want to see Zina. What if I'd infected her? I would never kiss her again or share glasses and spoons with Nikolai Rafaelovich. All of the sudden it struck me that I was contaminated; I was filled with bacilli. They were in my breath, in my spit, on my handkerchief, on my sheets and pillow. Anyone who came into contact with me could become infected, too.

I'd been very sick before, twice with pneumonia, and I'd contracted rabies as an adolescent. The illnesses had made me feel weak and vulnerable but not ashamed, not an outcast. But now I was contagious; I didn't want anyone to come near me and believed no one would want to come to close to me, either.

I fell asleep with these thoughts and awakened with them two hours later. Hela brought more codeine, and I dozed again. I felt someone's presence before I opened my eyes; someone holding my hand and stroking my hair. It reminded me of my mother sitting next to my bed, stroking my hair when I was sick. It was Zina. It couldn't be anyone else, with such a gentle stroke and light squeeze that expressed more than words.

"It's all right," she repeated quietly. "Don't open your eyes. Just sleep. I'll be sitting here next to you." I didn't want to open my eyes or talk. What could I say? The only thing I could say was for her to stay away. Enough terrible things had happened to her. She didn't need to get sick, too.

Zina bent over and kissed me lightly on the cheek. I felt her hair sweep across my face. I loved the smell of her hair and skin. I wanted to shout loudly for her to go away, but couldn't say a word. I felt the same lump in my throat, the same urge to cough, but held back.

The next morning both Maria Ivanovna and Nikolai Rafaelovich wheeled me to the X-ray barracks. Sofia Leontevna greeted me with a wide, surprised stare. As she helped me into the X-ray room, I turned my face away from her. How many times I had seen Nikolai Rafaelovich turn a patient's head away with one extended finger.

Sofia Leontevna emerged from the lab with two developed films. Her office was dark except for the light from the viewer.

She put the films into the viewer and pointed with a pencil to the left upper lobe.

"You have a cavity right here, between the first and second rib. Looks like the size of a cherry, but the lymph nodes aren't enlarged. That's a good sign, and I don't see any other destruction."

I stared at the image. The hole was unmistakable—a light gray patch surrounded by a dark gray rim.

Sofia Leontevna continued. "You need two things: food and rest. Nikolai Rafaelovich will take good care of you, and I'll help as much as I can."

The words of encouragement and hope for recovery didn't sound convincing. The younger the patients were, the more rapidly the disease progressed. Kolia had died in my arms after being ill for only two months. The pneumothorax procedure had done nothing for him.

The next day the results of the sputum analysis arrived. Maria Ivanovna let me read the description: "A great number of bacilli Koch are present in the viewing field. The patient is highly contagious."

Something new emanated from Maria Ivanovna. She put her hand on my forehead and cheek and held it there for a while, saying quietly, "Why you and not me?" The most caring, sorrowful eyes glistened when I asked her to sit with me. Her distance was gone. For as long as I had known Maria Ivanovna, she remained detached from the other nurses and workers. She liked other people and respected them, but she never opened the door to become an intimate friend.

Now, as her patient, I began to learn about her and to understand why she didn't talk about herself or show her emotions freely. Maria Ivanovna had been born into a wealthy family. At the age of eighteen she volunteered as a nurse in the Red Army, and she married a Civil War hero who later became an army general, the commander of the military district in Belarus. In 1938 he was arrested along with a group of other high-ranking commanders while attending a meeting at the Ministry of Defense in Moscow. Maria Ivanovna and her two sons, eighteen and twenty years old, were living in Minsk. All three of them were arrested the same night. For months Maria Ivanovna was kept in an isolated cell on death row. Each day she was interrogated and tortured, but she never signed the accusations against her husband. She was sentenced to ten years as a family member of an enemy of the people and was denied the right to correspond. The verdict was read to her in the cell. She never had a trial.

I asked Maria Ivanovna to talk to Zina and explain to her that she must stay away from me so she wouldn't get infected. "Don't say such things," Maria Ivanovna responded. "She loves you. Let her do what she wants. She's not a child."

At the end of the week all the test results were in, and Dr. Piasetsky invited me to his office. I put on pants and a shirt, which exhausted me. He started right in. "I think we should begin treatment right away. Injections of calcium combined with pneumothorax, lots of rest, and large portions of fat will heal you. You must rest as much as possible. You can walk around for half an hour in the morning and half an hour in the afternoon, but the rest of the time you must be in bed. I know it's boring, but it's important. I've talked to the kitchen and had the cooks double your portion of butter and give you two servings of meat and oatmeal. I wish I could get you more fat, bacon or lard, but we just don't have it here. I'll try to use my connections with the free doctors to get something from outside the zone. So how about starting the calcium injections today and pneumothorax on Monday?" He tried to sound upbeat.

"Do I have any choice?"

"This is my recommendation, but you don't have to decide today."

Dr. Piasetsky had taught me that the disease develops more rapidly in anyone under the age of forty. At twenty-four the disease would gallop through me so quickly that I'd be dead in a matter of months, even with the pneumothorax procedure. Could I refuse the treatment? Could I tell Nikolai Rafaelovich that I didn't want it because I was afraid of the pain, afraid of feeling my heart being squeezed like a frightened bird in a clenched fist?

I couldn't sleep. In the evening my fever climbed well above one hundred degrees, and I ached and sweated through the sheets. I was restless. I thought obsessively about the pneumothorax procedure, picturing the patients who'd gone through it, who had suffered the unnatural stopping of the lung. I didn't want to offend Nikolai Rafaelovich—he wanted the best for me—but I didn't know how I could breathe with one lung. I was already short of breath. For the past three months I'd gotten short of breath when walking fast—only now did I realize it. How could I have missed the symptom? The cavity was on the left side. The squeezed lung would press on my heart. Patients with this condition suffered the most.

I got up and went into the nursing room to look at the clock and found Hela sleeping on the crook of her arm at the desk. It was one A.M. I reached out and touched her. She started awake.

"I need to talk to you."

Hela was the complete opposite of Maria Ivanovna. Plump and nearsighted, squinting even through her glasses, she did everything quickly. She'd learned about nursing in the camps and was innately caring and joyful, sharing her compassion with everyone in need. She gave away portions of her own bread ration to the patients, saying, "Take it! I'm so fat! I'm forty-eight now; I'll look like a barrel when I'm fifty."

I needed her compassion now. "Hela, I've thought about everything Nikolai Rafaelovich told me today," I said. "I'm afraid to have pneumothorax. He strongly believes it's the only cure, but I don't want to put myself through it. It doesn't always work."

"I can understand your fear," she said. "The pressure and shortness of breath is uncomfortable. But you need to look at what's available. There isn't anything else we can do. We don't have enough fat here to give you a high-calorie diet."

"What would you do?" I asked.

"I'd talk to Igor," she replied definitively.

Igor Kuprejanov, a former biochemist and researcher from the University of Moscow, was Hela's camp husband. He worked as a locksmith and had his own workshop, where Hela visited him frequently. They'd been together for two years. "I advise you to talk to Zina. She's an intelligent girl, and it's only fair to ask her opinion." Her eyes, magnified through her glasses, were filled with pity. I felt as though I'd been sentenced to death, and the treatment hadn't even started.

I awakened in the morning to One-Eyed Ivan, the chief cook, standing in the doorway. He wore a black eye patch and resembled a Viking with his big bones and red hair and beard. He was a high-ranking *urka* in the camp and had also been designated a *pre-durok*. We met playing chess.

"What kind of joke is this, you lying in bed?" Ivan said. He put a large package on the nightstand and pulled up a chair. "I've got some goodies for you. Don't be shy to ask for more." I tore off the newspaper. There were three small packages of white waxed paper. The first one contained a large chunk of butter; the second, a cube of bacon; the last and heaviest, lard—pure and salted. It was enough to feed me for a month.

Ivan fixed his sparkling blue eye on me, an oasis in the expanse of his red hair and face.

"How did you know I was sick?"

"A good friend always knows when you're in trouble. I hope you won't be in bed for long, but while you're there we can play chess every day."

He pulled out his handmade chessboard and pieces. "I'll leave this here with you in case you want to play with anyone else."

With the abundance of fat in my possession and a promise to receive more, I decided not to undergo the pneumothorax procedure. Dr. Piasetsky didn't argue with me, and Zina took the decision in stride.

The question of whether or not I would get well occupied me constantly. Every time I coughed, I checked the handkerchief for blood. I analyzed every mark and estimated from it whether the cavity was getting bigger or smaller or if more cavities were forming. The other symptoms didn't bother me so much, but I became fixated on the blood because it came directly from the inside.

Zina came to visit me one day with her boss, Dr. Loskutov. I'd known him for over a year, but we'd never had a chance to talk. I was surprised and honored and hoped he'd stay for a while. Dr. Loskutov was a busy man. He was called frequently to Magadan for consultation on the eye disorders of high-ranking officials of Dalstroy and the NKVD. A limousine with NKVD officers picked him up and dropped him off. He returned with bottles of wine or vodka or boxes of chocolate, all of which he shared with his nurses and *feldshers*. Zina often invited me to these parties, which took place in his office and lasted as long as it took to drink a shot of vodka and take a few pieces of chocolate. He earned the highest respect from the prisoners by never reporting a prisoner who faked an illness. "Everyone is sick in this place," he said. "No one needs to fake anything. If they aren't sick in the eyes, they are sick in their souls."

Dr. Loskutov sat at the foot of my bed and pulled from his coat pocket three small glasses and a little flask. He didn't go anywhere empty-handed. Vitamins, alcohol, tobacco, sugar, tea—all these things he gave away freely.

Now, sitting at the edge of my sickbed, he filled three shot glasses with vodka and said, "It's good for your appetite. If I were in charge, I'd give a shot of vodka to all the prisoners, patients, doctors, and nurses. The administration is mistaken in their practice of only giving it to prisoners digging for gold in the winter. I think the patients need it more." Dr. Loskutov raised his glass and pointed it toward me. "To your recovery."

I held up my glass. "To you."

Zina was still holding her glass. Dr. Loskutov prodded her with his smile. "Come on Zina, to Janusz's health. And I want you to be sure he gets a little vodka every day. It's good for the soul. A little alcohol never hurt anyone. But only a little. I know this from personal experience. When I was a doctor in the army, I never had any trouble with a little drink. But once when I had too much I made a little joke about Stalin—and you're both here to witness the consequences."

As word of my illness spread, visitors streamed in to see me. Many of them were patients for whom I'd cared. They filled me

in on the other patients, two of whom had been commissioned
for the mainland, several others who had died. They told me in
detail the circumstances of their friends' deaths. Finally I understood the dark, inner world of illness—the anger, despair, and bit-
terness; the physiological changes that ebbed and flowed; the
turns in thought and feeling that made the patients animated or
irritable; the effects of being hospitalized and bedridden. I developed a deep bond with the patients who came to visit me, a bond
that never could have existed before. Their sincere desire to see
me recover and their gratitude for what I'd done for them
touched me deeply. It was often expressed in an offer of food, tobacco, sugar, or pressed tea. My nightstand was loaded with
goods, and as my appetite declined, I circulated the gifts to the
people who came to visit me.

I coughed much less, but the sputum tests showed that I was
still infected. The size of the cavity was shrinking. In the afternoons and evenings I felt excitable; in the mornings I was tired
and sleepy. The temperature spikes in the evenings caused me to
sweat profusely, and I changed my gown and sheets two or three
times a night. Kurban kept me well stocked. After a month, I
asked Nikolai Rafaelovich if my condition was what he'd expected.

"Believe me, you're doing well," he said. "It's only been one
month since we began treatment and there are no signs of further
damage. You're stable."

But during the sleepless nights the worst thoughts overwhelmed me. I wanted to run to Nikolai Rafaelovich's office to
hear again and again his reassuring words. I was getting more
tired. The only visitors I still wanted to see were Zina and Dr.
Loskutov; One-Eyed Ivan, because he played chess with me when
I felt well; Maria Ivanovna, because she sat next to me and listened with compassion; and Hela, because she talked so much I
didn't need to say a word.

Every time Dr. Loskutov opened the door, he pulled vodka and
glasses from his coat and said, "Janusz, you look better. Are you
ready for a shooter?"

"It's been over a month that I've been ill. What's going on?"

"You've survived here for over three years. Did you ever think about how many of your comrades in the battalion are still alive? About how many prisoners with you in the mines are still alive?"

"I'd rather die on the battlefield, not here with TB."

"As long as you're alive, you never want to die. You have to be sick in the head or very depressed to want to die. You have every chance to recover if you keep your hopes high and your willpower strong. Tell me the truth, do you want to die?"

"No. I never wanted to die, although in the mines, sometimes I didn't think I could bear life anymore."

Dr. Loskutov's blue eyes pierced through my mine. "Don't let this thought cross your mind again. Even a hard life is better than death."

"But when I think of Burepolom or the gold mines, or when I hear about what Maria Ivanovna, Zina, and her parents went through, I think I would rather die if I were them."

"Janusz, you have no idea what a human being can live through. A horse would die, an elephant would die, but a human being can survive so many hardships, so many tortures, so much pain that it defies understanding. Don't think about dying anymore. If you do think about it, I want you to talk to me."

It was amazing how Dr. Loskutov's short, heated discussions could get to me. He was the only one capable of stirring me from my growing depression. Nikolai Rafaelovich was my closest friend, but he couldn't make me feel better. Quite the opposite, sometimes I felt I needed a second opinion after his visit. He was my doctor, the specialist, the one who knew the most about tuberculosis, but I couldn't trust him. I felt he was sparing me from upsetting news or too frightened of losing a friend. Maybe his warmth and pity got in the way. Dr. Loskutov, however, could make me feel better for a whole day, and I asked Zina to bring him frequently.

But I continued to get weaker. During the solitary hours I thought of Taubcia, my family, and friends more frequently and more vividly. The long-suppressed feeling of loss and longing for them became wrenching. I closed my eyes and saw their faces, heard their voices, felt their touch, closeness, and love. Depression gripped me more strongly every day. I envisioned myself in a month or two, emaciated, perhaps bloated from edema, with burning cheeks and glowing eyes. I dreamed of being a corpse in the morgue, Viktor approaching me with his knife. I screamed at him not to cut, but he couldn't hear me. I awakened shivering, my teeth chattering, soaked in cold sweat; time to change the sheets and gown again. Another time I dreamed of lying next to Kolia and Horochko. They called for me to go fishing with them, but I couldn't go because I didn't have shoes and didn't want to walk barefooted on the stones.

Zina was the only person I was really happy to see, but I felt guilty for letting her spend time in the contaminated room. I didn't even want to talk to Dr. Loskutov anymore. I lay on my right side and faced the wall, pretending to be asleep when he came in. Maria Ivanovna and Hela began to irritate me with their mothering. I was sick of seeing their long, worried faces. The repeated phrases of encouragement as they poked into my veins—"This one will help you for sure. It's like adding another brick to close the wall of the cavity"—sounded fraudulent. I was angry, filled with bitter questions about how I could've gotten sick, what it meant about my ability to survive, and whether I would ever recuperate. The chorus of voices that I was getting better and looking better, that my symptoms were not progressing, became fainter. The outside voices were no match for the images I had of my own deterioration. I'd seen the destruction on X rays and during autopsies. I coughed up the blood that was hemorrhaging from the cavity. I sensed the tiny bacilli eating through my body. I'd seen the patients slowly die. It was happening to me.

But why me? Why did I have to die? Lying with my head under the sheet, I searched for answers, reasons, meaning. One day it came to me with certainty that my family was gone. I tried to ignore the thought, but while contemplating my illness and the inevitable end, which I felt was coming quickly, I became convinced that I was joining my family. I had left them when they needed me most—it didn't matter that I was forced. Now I must join them. There was no reason for me to stay alive. There was no hope for them; and now there was no hope for me.

This conviction both comforted and revolted me. I wanted to join them but worried that perhaps I was burying them too soon. Perhaps it was bad luck to assume they were dead. Perhaps they would survive and I'd be the one to die. I could feel death entering my body—not the death I'd seen on the battlefield, which was swift but terrifying, but the death I saw on the ward: peaceful, quiet, like disappearing into a fog. The eyes became fixed; the body stopped struggling.

My mind became overwhelmed with the unfathomable, the unknowable. What happens when you die? Is there anything left after the flesh is cut open with a sharp knife, examined, hastily put back together, and burned or buried? What happens to the soul—our emotions and feelings? Does everything vanish as if it had never existed? I had thought I was doing something good for the patients. I was happy helping them. I thought that I made their lives and deaths easier and more comfortable; that I protected them during their last minutes with my strength and warmth. Was this work of no importance? Didn't it matter? What if I were an evil person, full of hate, not loving and not loved, a person whose life was a chain of heinous acts? Would I die then? Is death different depending on what a person did in his life? Or is it callous and undiscriminating, striking some with wrath and others with a gentle touch?

I didn't think I was a bad person. I never stole anyone's bread or tried to hurt another person. No one could convince me that the lives of a sadistic murderer and missionary could be judged the same. But death comes to everyone, and the only thing that will be left of me will be memory, which will fade as quickly as summer. I came into someone's life; I left. I thought that meeting Zina and being happy had changed my life, had freed me from imprisonment. I thought that loving and being loved would protect me. Being safe from the mines, helping and caring for sick people, and loving Zina had filled me with such joy and happiness.

But now the end was coming, and nothing could stop it. Neither the injections nor the fat I forced myself to eat were helping. Nikolai Rafaelovich said that in the first two months I could ex-

pect a break. He told me I would do well, but he was lying. I
knew it. I could feel it. He was trying to protect me like a child,
keeping me ignorant and hopeful.

"Lose hope," Loskutov once said, "and you lose your life.
Don't ever lose hope, no matter what happens to you. Let me tell
you my story." I hadn't been in the mood to hear anyone's stories,
but there was no way to stop Loskutov when he wanted to say
something he thought was important. And I chewed on his story
quite a bit during the days I lay in my monk's cell. It wove in and
out of the despairing thoughts, the obsessive checking of the
handkerchief, the fear of dying, the self-pity.

"Who'd ever think that a joke, inspired by too much vodka,
could screw up a life so badly?" He always smirked when he said
this. "I mined lead and gold for two years and became a
dokhodyaga. I chewed on anything chewable—sticks, bones,
leaves, grass. Once I even killed a rat and ate it raw. I was losing
my mind. The only thing that kept me alive was knowing I could
get killed any second. I could run at the fence, attack a guard. I
didn't want to kill myself; I wanted to be killed. For some reason,
toying with this thought kept me going day after day. At the same
time, other *dokhodyagas* came to me for medical advice. They
were worse off than I was, and they needed me. That's when I began to pull myself out.

"So stop your silly thoughts. I know what kind of thoughts are
trampling in your head. You are sick. I know it. You know it. But
I also know that if you fall into despair, you'll die like the rest of
them. But if you take control, you can pull yourself out. Get up.
Stop lying in bed. You're not a corpse yet, and you won't be for
the next fifty years. Heal yourself. Stop waiting for someone else
to heal you. And smile when I come to see you. I'm sick of seeing
your back. I want to see your face."

No one talked to me the way Loskutov did. I believed what he
was saying was true, but it took more than his encouragement to
unshroud the dark thoughts. I needed to find meaning in what
was happening. Just as I had believed fate protected me, the
thought occurred to me that perhaps my illness was a punishment, the ultimate lesson to teach me that my place was with my

family. Since they are dead, my reasoning went, I have to die. Or maybe God was punishing me because I never believed in Him. I never invoked His help, His mercy. I saw too many terrible things to believe that God existed. If God were just and merciful, if He punished evil and rewarded good, why did he punish me? Why punish my parents? My beloved Taubcia? My sister?

As I felt life escaping from me, I felt lost and abandoned. There was nothing in this world that could save me, and no one at home waiting for me. When I am buried, there will be no stone with my name, no one to come and put a flower on my grave. I wanted to stop the injections and stop stuffing myself with lard, bacon, and meat. Any effort to cure me was futile. As grateful as I felt for all the help I received, being ill for such an extended period of time made me feel pitiful and ashamed. I wanted it to stop. I thought about killing myself, bringing the end faster, not feeling any more grief, guilt, shame. I didn't really want to die. I loved life. I loved people. I wanted to live. But was that enough to keep the disease from killing me?

Hela came one day to visit me. Her eyes were red. She sat on my bed and told me that in the early morning, Igor had gone on *etap*. She had stopped by his workshop on the way to the hospital and found out from the other prisoners that eighty men had been shipped to the mines in the early morning. She sobbed quietly, wiping her eyes with a handkerchief and then with her sleeve.

"I'm sure he'll contact you as soon as he gets established," I said. "I'm sure you'll be able to communicate with him, maybe even send him parcels. Perhaps it's only for the summer, and then he'll be sent back here."

She stopped crying and squeezed my hand. "I needed to hear these words. I'm so afraid for him in the mines. But maybe you're right. He will come back at the end of the summer."

Soon after Hela's bad news, Zina found out, through a letter from her grandmother, that her father had died of a heart attack. There was no news of her mother.

"There's nothing we can do but live our lives," I said. "I'm feeling better." A lie. "I hope to be up and out of bed soon."

That night I lay looking at the cracks on the high ceiling, picturing Zina's father and wondering exactly what had happened to him. The news had broken Zina again. She said I was the closest person to her in the world. I couldn't continue to lie in bed. Dr. Loskutov had said that the bed was sucking out all the juices from me. "Get up. Move around." This was contrary to Dr. Piasetsky's advice, but Piasetsky was an academician, and Loskutov had worked all his life on the battlefield and in the camps with soldiers and prisoners. I longed for fresh air, sunlight, and greenery. I put on my black prison pants and tunic and walked out of the building without telling anyone. The fresh spring air still carried the sharp cold of winter. I inhaled deeply through my nose, which stung my lungs like hundreds of tiny needles. My head spun. My legs felt like cotton. I hadn't walked in eight weeks. The air was saturated with pine, flowers, melting ice, the awakening forest. I leaned against the wall of the barracks and smelled everything—the blossoming bushes, the petal of a white rose. I didn't know if I could make it back to my room. Every step made me pant. My legs threatened to crumble. But I made it.

That evening I got up again and walked the length of the corridor. One lap, two laps. The corridor was twenty-eight steps long. I breathed slowly. I repeated this morning and evening routine for three or four days, increasing the length of my walk each day.

As I gained strength, I walked slowly between the buildings. I walked down the alley that led to the old barracks 15, which now housed patients with chronic scurvy, pellagra, and alimentary dystrophy. Dizzy and tired, I sat on the bench just outside the old familiar door. I didn't want to go in the barracks, but I knocked to see if any of the nurses I knew were working.

Nadja Kopylova, a former ballerina, threw her arms up and hugged me. "I'm so happy to see you. You look good!" My pants and shirt hung on me as if I were a coat hanger. I didn't look good. "I've been thinking of you but didn't want to bother you. Congratulations on your recuperation." I smiled bashfully. We sat on the bench and talked with great excitement about the possibility of an amnesty for prisoners. The war had taken a turn, and the Soviet army was pushing the Germans back into their own territory. Nadja was cautiously optimistic. "I doubt politicals will be released. I'll have to wait for our Great Leader to die. But with a war victory, who knows what will happen?"

After this outing I could barely walk back to the barracks, I was so tired. Maria Ivanovna was waiting for me with my morning injection and a reprimand. "It's not smart to be walking around without any coat. Did you clear this with Dr. Piasetsky? Are you short of breath?" She grabbed my wrist and took my pulse. I forced myself to eat a hefty snack and fell into a deep sleep.

I continued to walk laps down the corridor and walked outside for a few minutes each day. I reassured Nikolai Rafaelovich that I felt better, but my temperature spikes and X rays hadn't changed. I was still sweating, coughing, and short of breath. But my mood was much better. Best of all, there wasn't a sign of blood on my handkerchief. Dr. Piasetsky advised me not to overdo the walking but otherwise left the exercise regimen up to me. He complemented me on my willpower but warned me over and over not to do too much.

One afternoon I was feeling particularly strong and did what I'd intended to do since I'd begun to heal myself: I strode in to the ophthalmology department and found Zina. I took her hand and squeezed it strongly. The joy on her face made all my efforts worthwhile. We went to see Dr. Loskutov, and he jumped up from his chair and hugged me. "I knew you could do it. You're on your way out of the hospital."

My next goal was a visit to the general TB ward. Cheers and raspy voices followed me as I walked into the room. A few of the patients got up and greeted me; the others begged for me to come and sit by their bed. Some of the faces I had hoped to see were missing. I sat at one of the tables in the middle of the room and listened to the jokes and warm wishes for recovery, happily enveloped by the people who had become my family.

I had lost so much weight that the muscles strung across my body were like rubber bands. When I rested after a walk, I broke out in a sweat, and my head felt like cotton. But the visits made me feel strong inside, optimistic, and happy.

Many weeks after I'd begun my regimen, Nikolai Rafaelovich and I went to see Sofia Leontevna. She smiled as she pinned the

X rays onto the viewer. "The cavity is about half the original size. I'd say you're well on your way to recovery."

Back in the ward, Nikolai Rafaelovich invited me to his office and closed the door. "I wanted to tell you how happy I am about your recovery. Your will to live pulled you out of it. The injections, food, and rest helped, but you healed yourself more than anything."

He sat at his desk with his arms folded across his chest, his lower lip pouting. He was quiet for a moment, then looked at me more seriously than he had in a long time.

"We need to decide what to do with you next. I'm concerned that if I sign a discharge, they'll send you back to the mines. I think I should keep you on the list of sick patients but transfer you from the open to the chronic ward. At the same time I've been looking around for a job for you in another department. I hate giving you up as a *feldsher*, but I don't want to risk reinfection. There's a job in the Department of Psychiatry. I'm going to meet with Dr. Sitkin to see if the job suits you. He and his staff are very good people."

This news hit me hard. "If I heal completely, why can't I continue working here? I don't want to work any place else. You're my real family, the only family I have now. All of you and Zina. This was what made me get better."

"Janusz, I'm more saddened by the thought of having you leave than anyone else. But you must. You don't realize how fragile you are now, how vulnerable you became after enduring such an episode. It will take at least another six months or a year or more before you'll be completely healed. Reinfection could be fatal. I don't want to scare you, but I don't want to see you back as a patient.

"For six or eight weeks I'll keep you here. Then for another three months I can keep you on the chronic ward. You'll be listed as a patient, but you may be able to begin working sooner."

Dr. Piasetsky rose from his chair. "We're set, then." We sat in silence, sipping tea and gnawing on sugar cubes.

Things were looking up. The Soviet army was pushing the Germans back on all fronts; a newly organized Polish army was fighting alongside the Soviets; and more than half of Poland had been liberated, including Wlodzimierz-Wolynski.

My thoughts and emotions were turbulent—my family, my future with Zina, my new job at the hospital. For the first time since my imprisonment, I thought about trying to contact some relatives living in the Soviet Union. I hadn't wanted to contact anyone before because I believed it was shameful to have a criminal in the family, and I didn't want to spoil our good name. But with the news that my hometown had been freed, I felt compelled to contact someone.

I knew the address of my uncle who lived in Odessa, but I thought the family had probably been evacuated when the Germans invaded and I didn't know whether they had returned or were even alive. I had another uncle and three cousins in Moscow. I remembered the name of the street one of my cousins lived on, but the apartment number was vague. I made a great effort to recall the exact address, and after a few days I thought I had come up with something close.

In Poland my mother had diligently kept in touch with her relatives and enjoyed reading their letters aloud to us. In this way I felt that I knew something of my relatives, although I'd never met them. One night in the dusky quiet of my room, I lit the lamp and picked up a pen. I remember every word I scrawled slowly on the paper:

Dear Katia,

I am in Kolyma but am alive and well. I still have some time to spend here but am eager to find out what has happened to my family in Wlodzimierz-Wolynski. If you know anything about them, please write. My address is:

Central Hospital of the Northeastern Directorate of the NKVD
23rd Kilometer
Kolyma.

Nikolai Rafaelovich obtained an envelope for me, and in my calligraphic handwriting I wrote the address. I wasn't sure if it was correct, but there was nothing else to do. I took the letter to Dr. Loskutov and asked him to mail it from Magadan in order to avoid censorship. He promised he would.

CHAPTER 18

Psychiatric Ward

One warm summer afternoon Dr. Piasetsky and I went to see Dr. Sitkin, the chief of the psychiatric ward. An armed guard and *predurok* stood at the gate and checked us in. Dr. Piasetsky signed our names and the time of our arrival.

The psychiatric ward occupied two barracks, both enclosed by a tall wooden fence. Like the isolator and the women's barracks, the ward was a zone within the zone. Between the barracks was a large yard with several trees, green bushes, and benches. Only the patients spoiled the tranquil scene—a dozen or so gray-gowned men, their hair matted in swirls, pursuing their errant courses. The animated patients argued sharply with themselves or each other—their gestures flamboyant, their eyes wide as an owl's, their faces pale and set like putty. Others sat frozen on a bench or on the ground, staring into the air like statues.

The scene made me nervous. As a child I had been frightened by the ghoulish expressions, loud muttering, and penetrating stares of the mentally disturbed people who walked the streets of Wlodzimierz-Wolynski. My nanny, Marynia, used to threaten to give me away to one of them if I didn't eat my dinner or behave well. Later, when I joined the army, there was an officer who ordered us to stand at attention, and then he himself stood at attention, saluting the wall for up to an hour. Once he announced in class, "We're all going hunting, but we need a dog." He then got on all fours and began barking at the top of his lungs. Orderlies from the hospital came to take him away in a straitjacket. He kicked so fiercely that we all had to overpower him. I'd seen plenty of other people in the camps do insane things—hurt themselves, attack the guards, or fall into psychosis—but I never had to deal with them. I looked upon my new position as a chance to further my understanding of human behavior.

Dr. Piasetsky rang the bell, and an orderly, a burly man dressed in white, unlocked the door. The darkened corridor echoed with our footsteps. Every door was closed and locked. Near the end of the hall the orderly stopped, plucked a key from a massive metal ring dangling from his belt loop, and unlocked a door.

"Welcome," said a bald man barricaded behind a huge desk piled with papers. He reached over, shook our hands, and offered Dr. Piasetsky and me chairs. His face was like a horse's, twice as long as it was wide, with a protruding chin and large square teeth. His round black glasses added to his freakish appearance.

"This is quite a change from the TB ward. You'll have to get used to our patients." His deep voice carried a note of concern. He tapped his fingertips together and looked thoughtfully at me. "As you saw when you came in, we live inside a zone. We further separate ourselves from the patients with two locked doors. The patients' rooms are double-locked, and the doors to each office are also locked. We've always got two men, like Siemion here, patrolling the corridor to deal with breakouts. We live in a double prison, and for good reason." He pouted his thin lips and nodded seriously. "Most of the patients are further imprisoned inside themselves. It isn't easy to get them out."

I liked Dr. Sitkin's directness, but I wasn't sure if he was merely warning me or trying to scare me.

A woman wearing a white coat entered the room. She introduced herself as Sofa Lerner, a psychologist and the head nurse. Her black hair was pinned loosely on her head, a few wavy wisps clinging to her powdery white neck. Her brown eyes were outlined in black, and she had wide, rosy lips. Her open coat hardly concealed her large breasts and swinging hips.

Dr. Sitkin looked at me through his round black frames and said seriously, "The job here can be stressful. Let me know if you're feeling drained. But I think, and I believe Sofa would agree, the work is quite interesting. The mind is endlessly fascinating and complex."

Those words were my only introduction to the psychiatric ward. I had no apprenticeship; no Maria Ivanovna to explain things; no Dr. Piasetsky to instruct me. From the moment I started, I handled patients, and I quickly learned that the job had less to do with caregiving than with freestyle wrestling.

Each morning we drank tea in Dr. Sitkin's office while Stepan Trofimovich, the night *feldsher*, updated us on the night's events. Gravity seemed to exert an extra force on Stepan's body—his head drooped forward, his shoulders curved in, his back bent toward the ground. Still, he was a large man, big-boned and strong despite his haggard appearance. His soft, slow voice carried the same oppressive weight. When we had a moment alone, he confided, "I like to work nights here. It's the only ward where you can sleep undisturbed—the patients are sedated, and the doors are all locked in case they wake up."

One morning when everything was still new and disorienting to me, Piotr, a daytime orderly, pounded on Dr. Sitkin's door. Stepan let him in. Short of breath and red-faced, Piotr announced, "Come quickly to room number three. Siemion and Vanya are trying to quiet the patients down, but we need your help." Sitkin jumped over the desk and strode out the door and down the hall. Sofa bustled after him. I trailed behind.

Siemion and Vanya stood at the threshold like lion tamers, protecting themselves from the patients with chairs and not letting anyone out into the corridor. The howls and screeching inside resembled sounds from a jungle. The patients were jumping up and down on the beds, tearing apart pillows, flailing their arms, and attacking one another. One man swung from the bars of the window. Another picked up the end of a bed and slammed it repeatedly against the floor. Still another tore at his hair, wailing and chastising himself. Maniacal laughter, crying, and shrieking filled the room, a chain reaction activating all the patients' inner demons. The uncontrolled activity and emotions, all chaotic and undirected, made it seem as if we were dealing with a different species.

After surveying the situation, Dr. Sitkin pushed the orderlies aside and separated two patients who were beating each other with pieces of wood from a broken nightstand. He wrapped his long arms around the most violent man and ordered, "Straitjacket!" The patient kicked furiously, landing his heels on Sitkin's feet and shins. "Grab his legs!" Sitkin roared. Stepan took a blanket and cautiously approached the man's feet. The patient kicked and knocked Stepan to the ground. "Get up!" Sitkin barked breathlessly. "Vanya, help us!"

Stepan and Vanya immobilized the man's legs with the blanket. While Vanya held them still, Stepan opened the gray-padded jacket. Within a minute the patient was wrapped like a mummy and lying on the bed.

As Sitkin turned his attention to the remaining patients, high-pitched chirps and whimpers replaced the frenzied noise. The patients grew wide-eyed and clung to the bedposts as Sitkin approached them, terrified as trapped monkeys. Sitkin, Vanya, Stepan, and Siemion subdued them systematically while I guarded the door.

Once the aggressive patients were under control, I noticed a young man sitting in a corner with his eyes closed, rocking back and forth. He seemed not to be aware of anything around him. Whenever he bent forward, he pounded the floor three times and shouted, "Attention! All radio stations in the Soviet Union be on alert. In five minutes I will start the transmission. All stations get ready. An important message is coming. I repeat, all stations get ready." He continued pounding the floor.

I walked up to him and asked, "Where's the radio?"

He looked at me strangely. "Under this board. I have to hide my radio station." He pounded the floor again, this time harder and faster. He then turned accusatory and shouted, "You're interfering! My transmission is out! It's gone! Get away from here! You ruined it!"

"He's okay," Dr. Sitkin told me. "Leave him alone."

"They were quiet all night," Stepan explained, half-bewildered. "I don't know how it happened."

"It's probably Ivan," Sofa said, referring to the man Dr. Sitkin had first put in the straitjacket.

"We're trying to mix the acute patients with the chronic ones," Dr. Sitkin told me. "Sometimes the chronic patients help calm down the acute ones. For example, our radio commentator can be quite helpful when he's not trying to transmit messages. He hallucinates frequently, thinking he's establishing a direct line with Stalin to complain about the way he's being treated, but he's never violent. He's been this way since he came here." Dr. Sitkin walked up to the patient. "Good luck, Fedia. I'm sure you'll get through today."

Fedia put his finger to his lips and whispered to Dr. Sitkin. "Shhh. It's a state secret. No one else should hear. It's a state secret."

My job was to take notes on the patients while making the morning rounds with Dr. Sitkin and Sofa. We made quite a procession, with Dr. Sitkin striding down the corridor, Sofa half a step behind, myself trailing attentively, and three orderlies behind us. One orderly turned the key, while the two others stood on either side of the door to protect Dr. Sitkin as he walked in. The doors opened to the outside so no one could hide behind them, but sometimes we still were surprised. Once, two patients attacked our party with the dismantled iron legs of a bed. Dr. Sitkin was struck on the arm and nearly suffered a broken bone. We then changed our protocol. The door was opened; an orderly stood on the threshold and made sure everyone was in bed; and then we proceeded into the room. If someone wasn't in bed, one of the orderlies went into the room armed with a wooden baton. He usually found the patient hiding under someone's bed, playing hide and seek.

Three rooms housed acute schizophrenics; one held ten patients, and the other two each held six. There were two isolation

cells for the most violent patients, who were additionally confined by straitjackets. The remaining rooms were for chronic
schizophrenics and manic depressives. The barracks next to ours
was designated for chronic psychiatric patients only, but in reality it included patients with other chronic disorders. One room in
the barracks was reserved exclusively for Japanese prisoners of
war, who were attended by Japanese doctors. I had no idea what
they were doing in our camp instead of a prisoner-of-war camp.
Except for the Japanese patients, Dr. Sitkin took care of all the
patients in the chronic ward, even those without a psychiatric illness.

In the afternoons I made rounds with the orderlies. We
checked on the isolation cells first. I was especially concerned
about the patients kept in straitjackets, as they were often ne-
glected. Sometimes they smelled bad or had gone unfed. I made
sure the orderlies took good care of them, taking them to the
bathroom regularly and cleaning or bathing them. Lydia and
Anya, nurses from the barracks for chronic patients, told me that
the orderlies in our barracks had been known to steal food from
the schizophrenic patients, especially those in straitjackets, leaving them to waste away in the solitary cells. The orderlies would
then sell the food for tobacco, clothing, and other goods.

When I told Sofa about the situation and asked her what she
thought we should do, she bristled. "Why are you nagging me all
the time? You must realize that the psychiatric ward is not run
like other wards. We have different sets of problems here. You try
to feed the patients yourself and clean up after them."

Although Sofa was a psychologist, I never saw her talking to
patients. She was very good at writing; in fact, she wrote most of
the reports for Dr. Sitkin, which he signed and sent to the authorities. I had mixed feelings about her. I was impressed by her
intelligence and knowledge of the arts, but she spent no time in-
structing the orderlies on how to take care of the patients. Dr.
Sitkin and Sofa seemed not to be aware of the conditions in
which the patients were kept; their main concern was each other.
I almost never saw Sofa alone on the ward. The orderlies were
left unsupervised, acting professionally only on rounds with Dr.

Sitkin or in emergencies. I decided to try to organize things myself.

Dr. Sitkin's main order to me was to take scrupulous notes on
every patient's physical and verbal behavior. Conversations I had
with patients had to be written down verbatim, as well as conversations I overheard between patients. With the utmost seriousness, Sitkin told me, "Our job is to expose fakers. You won't
believe how many prisoners try to get out of work by faking mental disorders. People think it's easier to fake a mental illness than
to fake a physical one, and for the most part it's true. When a
prisoner acts strangely—fakes a seizure, speaks incoherently,
bites another prisoner—he is shipped here. Even if he is later exposed, he still gets out of the mines for several weeks. But some
are never exposed. Sometimes they are commissioned and released."

Patients who loudly announced at the entrance that they were
Jesus Christ, Napoleon, Karl Marx, or Lenin were immediately
suspected of faking. Sitkin was on to them as soon as he heard
the proclamation, which was usually accompanied by theatrics
such as beating the head against the wall, hiding under the cov-
ers, lying motionless for hours, refusing food, trying to hurt a
neighbor, tearing off the gown, or throwing food across the room.
I was never able to tell the difference between a well-studied
faker and a true schizophrenic, and I doubt Dr. Sitkin could either. But he boasted of his skill to pick them out as though he had
a sixth sense for the task.

Sitkin sounded more like a camp official than a doctor. "Faking any illness in the camps is a crime. The prisoner is cheating
not only the government and the camp commander but also me
personally. We must all diligently look out for suspicious behavior and record everything we observe about each patient."

I went to see Nikolai Rafaelovich about my distress over the way
Dr. Sitkin and Sofa treated the patients. He was lying on the small
sofa in his office reading a book. His tall black boots and white
coat were off, his tunic unbuttoned, his brown hair ruffled. A
plate of kasha mixed with meat sat on the table next to him, un-

touched. He sat up when he saw me. "How about some dinner—
or a hot, sweet tea? But first, let me examine you." He took a
thermometer from his drawer and gave it to me, then listened to
my heart and lungs. "You're still running a temperature in the
evenings. Don't overdo it. You need lots of rest."

Hela brought tea, and the three of us sat and talked as in the
old days. After she left, I got straight to the point. "I'm having a
hard time understanding Dr. Sitkin. He doesn't seem interested in
treating the patients. Instead, he's obsessed with exposing fakers.
What do you think of him? You've known him longer than I."

Nikolai Rafaelovich sat forward, leaning on his elbows, thinking seriously about my complaint. "Yes, I know a little about Dr.
Sitkin. Maybe if I fill you in, it will help you understand him a bit.
Sitkin was a young star at the Krasnushkin Mental Hospital—the
largest psychiatric hospital in Moscow. Like most psychiatrists in
the Soviet Union, he worked very closely with the NKVD."

"What do you mean?" I interrupted. "He was a doctor at the
hospital, or he worked for the NKVD?"

"Both. Psychiatry is different from other medical fields. Here
on the TB ward, I'm in charge. No one looks over my shoulder. I
decide how to treat the patients. But in psychiatry, Sitkin's work
is closely monitored by the hospital director and the NKVD commander of the camp. Every psychiatric patient must be reported
to these men and carefully evaluated. Therefore, Sitkin is under
much more pressure than other department chiefs."

"But you said he worked with the NKVD in Moscow."

"In Moscow, recalcitrant prisoners were sent to the Krasnushkin Mental Hospital. Dr. Sitkin was one of the psychiatrists
who extracted confessions. He performed procedures on the most
prominent Soviet and Party government officials. Electroshock,
induced seizures, and lobotomies were all at Dr. Sitkin's disposal,
in addition to numerous drugs."

"Then why was he arrested? It sounds like he was one of
them."

"Yes. He was one of them. And half of the NKVD officers who
worked with him were also arrested. They all got swept up and
were accused of counterrevolutionary anti-Soviet activity, espi-

onage, and group sabotage. He went through the standard interrogations, just as the rest of us did. Even his family was arrested.
I've known him for six years. He's a bright, capable doctor, but
he's deeply frightened. For years he worked for the NKVD, just
as he does here. Sitkin's under more pressure from the authorities
than I am. He's just trying to survive, as we all are."

"What bothers me," I said, "is that beneath his imperious behavior, he's so frightened that he's willing to do anything to
please the camp authorities. Whenever an NKVD official strides
into his office, Sitkin jumps to attention, all nerves and polite-
ness, a conciliatory smile across his face. Anyone present in the
office has to leave immediately, and the door is locked. You
should see him talk on the phone to the authorities. He immediately stands up and waves frantically at everyone to leave the
room."

Nikolai Rafaelovich laughed at my imitation but had no more
advice.

Sitkin's primary test for exposing fakers was to put them in the
same room with the acute schizophrenics. "Works like flushing
rabbits out of their holes," he said proudly. It was true that within
hours, many prisoners, even the most determined, knocked on the
door to be let out, overwhelmed by the gibberish and antics of
the truly insane.

A new patient, Kapitonov, was brought into the ward in a
straitjacket. Despite the orderlies' efforts to control him, he
broke out of their grip, banged his head against the wall, and
jumped up and down with terrific force, muttering incoherently
and foaming at the mouth. His eyes were rolled back. I had no
doubt about his insanity and assigned him to one of the isolation
cells. But when I described the patient to Dr. Sitkin, he told me to
move Kapitonov to room two with the other schizophrenics and
watch to see how he behaved.

That afternoon Kapitonov lay in bed with a blanket and pillow
over his head. I approached him cautiously and flipped over the
blanket. For a second I thought I saw a perfectly sane person
peering back at me; he was frightened and perplexed by the situ-

ation, and his eyes locked with mine, as if searching for information. But then he rolled from the bed onto the floor and repeated his previous head-banging, foaming, and writhing. I thought perhaps he was faking, but I couldn't be sure. I didn't report the incident to Dr. Sitkin.

A few mornings later, Kapitonov lay again silently with the sheet pulled over his head. When Dr. Sitkin went up to him, Kapitonov mumbled and writhed. Within earshot of Kapitonov, Dr. Sitkin said, "Bring him to the procedure room at eleven. Keep him in the straitjacket." This announcement was Sitkin's second line of attack in exposing fakers. He believed that the loud command to bring the patient to the procedure room would separate the lucid from the insane: those in the midst of an acute schizophrenic episode would show no apprehension, whereas the fakers would become visibly nervous, often calling everything to a halt as the straps were applied. If the patient still hadn't exposed himself as a fake, Sitkin went ahead and administered a camphor injection, which induced a seizure. He relished the procedure, certain that no one could maintain his pose in its hazy aftermath.

After rounds I sterilized a syringe and thick needle—the camphor oil was viscous—and checked the six white leather straps on the table: two for the arms, two for the legs, one across the chest, and one across the pelvis. At eleven two orderlies brought Kapitonov to the room and strapped him down. Kapitonov howled and twisted his wrists.

"Kapitonov, can you hear me?" Sitkin barked.

No sign of comprehension.

"Kapitonov, can you stop moving?"

Garbled shouting was his answer.

I tied a tourniquet tightly around Kapitonov's arm. A blue vein popped to the surface, and I plunged in the needle.

"Wood in the mouth!" Sitkin commanded. An orderly shoved a wooden block in Kapitonov's mouth and tied it around his head with a strip of cloth. I depressed the plunger. The thick yellow oil oozed slowly into Kapitonov's bloodstream. "Slower." Dr. Sitkin advised. "Not too much at once. You know what can happen."

Sweat streamed down my back, and my stomach was queasy. The oil could create an embolism in the brain, causing a massive stroke and sudden death.

Kapitonov's fingers twitched. His legs trembled. His body began to shake and convulse. He threw his head backward, his chin pointing to the ceiling, and his torso arched rigidly, then collapsed. White froth seeped from his mouth. The whites of his eyes shone. His throat gurgled loudly. Seconds later, a full-blown seizure racked his body. He chomped into the wood, his fingers clenched the air, his body shook the table like an earthquake.

"Hold the head. Don't let him injure himself," Sitkin ordered. "Janusz, give him a little more." The syringe became slippery in my wet hands.

The seizure continued for another five minutes; then Sitkin touched my arm and said, "Give him the rest."

I depressed the plunger, feeling the resistance as the oil mixed into the bloodstream.

The convulsions returned with renewed force. As they began to subside, Sitkin began his interrogation.

"Kapitonov, can you hear me? Nod if you can. Kapitonov, give me a sign that you can hear me."

A finger raised. Sitkin asked again if Kapitonov could hear him. After a moment a relaxed hand raised, but Kapitonov's head had slumped to the side. Vanya removed the wooden block and wiped the foam off his mouth.

"Can you hear me?" Sitkin shouted again, sounding like an NKVD interrogator. Kapitonov responded with a barely perceptible nod. "Are you listening to me? Yes? Yes?"

I thought I saw his head nod but couldn't be sure.

"I want to make sure you understand what I'm saying." The same drugged nod came from Kapitonov.

"Can you open your eyes?"

No response.

"Let me look at you." Sitkin lifted Kapitonov's eyelids. The eyes rolled back.

"Are you faking your insanity?"

I waited breathlessly for a response.

"Kapitonov, are you faking your insanity? Answer me now."

All eyes were fixed on the pale, flaccid, sweat-streaked face. No answer.

"Take him to the isolation cell. I'll talk to him when he wakes up."

Two hours later the orderlies returned Kapitonov to the procedure room. Kapitonov was propped up by an orderly on each side. His eyes were still closed; saliva drooled from his mouth. His head rolled backward, and he mumbled quietly to himself.

Sitkin announced, "This is a crucial period. One and a half to two hours after the seizure, the patient is still in aftershock. His cognitive ability is still scrambled; he's still trying to find his way out of the maze created by the seizure. Now is the time to find out the truth. If nothing comes of it, we'll repeat the shock in two days."

I watched Kapitonov for a reaction to the threat of another shock, but nothing registered.

"Kapitonov, listen to me," Sitkin barked, trying to commandeer the unconscious patient. "Are you sick? Answer yes or no." No answer could be found in Kapitonov's uncontrollable head-rolling. Sitkin, squelching his frustration, said to the orderlies, "Take him back to the room, strap him into bed, and watch him. When he starts coming out of it, let me know."

The orderlies left, carrying Kapitonov under the arms.

Sitkin took off his glasses and leaned back in his chair, hands clenched behind his head. "A tough case. He could be one of those con artists who makes it out of the camps by endurance and cunning. But with another shock, I should be able to find out the truth."

I checked on Kapitonov frequently the rest of the day. He remained listless and drooling. I kept seeing his violently shaking body on the table. The next day, as I led Kapitonov to the procedure room, I looked for signs of nervousness. There was nothing. I became convinced that Kapitonov was sick; no one in his right mind would willingly go through another injection.

I administered another injection of camphor oil, feeling as if I were in Frankenstein's laboratory, and again Kapitonov tremored, foamed, and chomped on the wood. Once again he was unresponsive during the interrogation, and finally Sitkin gave up. "Well, there's nothing else we can do. We'll have to declare him insane."

But what came next was even more distressing: Sitkin announced that we'd be treating Kapitonov's schizophrenia with further convulsive therapy, although it would produce relatively mild effects. "I don't like performing these procedures," he said. "But we don't have any other treatment. We can sedate the acute patients, but we need to bring the chronic patients under control. Convulsive therapy is the only way to do it. Sometimes, in the aftermath, lost connections in the brain are reestablished and the patient improves. It's painful to watch patients sink deeper and deeper into the abyss of insanity. Look at Rybakov. He's been cutting himself for three years; he'll never fully recover. It's a hard lesson, but one you must accept, or you'll drive yourself crazy."

Sitkin's explanation sounded like a confession. I believed him, but in the back of my mind was the knowledge of Sitkin's connection with the NKVD. I considered him an intelligent man, but his zeal in exposing fakers upset me. It didn't seem to fit him; at least, I didn't want it to. He seemed to care about people such as Sofa, myself, and the orderlies, but not about the patients.

Leaving the psychiatric ward after work each day, I almost felt that I was returning to the free world. The job was becoming harder and harder to accept. Kapitonov was not the first patient I'd injected with camphor oil, and it was getting to me. The injection could cause severe brain damage or even death; at the very least it produced violent effects that were painful to watch. The patient lost control of himself, became dehumanized, took days to recover. That was the purpose; it was torture. And with Sitkin's questions afterward, I felt like part of the interrogation team. "You're the one who can stop it," part of me said to myself. The right thing to do would have been to confront Sitkin, to refuse to do the job. But I couldn't. I kept trying to shake the feeling of responsibility by telling myself that I had no choice, that these were the camps; someone else would do it if I didn't. Sitkin had ordered me to perform the injection; didn't that absolve me of committing any crime? I couldn't help but think of the analogy with the Nazis—they had commanders who gave the orders and executioners who performed them. I was the executioner; I obeyed. But if I didn't obey, I might as well walk to the *vakhta** and get on the next *etap* for the mines. I was recovering from my illness, had a good job, was well fed, and worked indoors. I should have been helping other people, giving something back to the patients. But instead I had crossed the line onto the side of the oppressor, and I wasn't doing a damn thing about it.

Every evening I met with Zina in her office or in Nikolai Rafaelovich's office. I had moved out of the TB ward and slept in the *feldshers'* barracks. I talked to Zina about what went on in the psychiatric ward but not in detail, especially not about the convulsive therapy. She was so happy that I was out of the TB ward and that my health continued to improve that I didn't want to worry her with new problems. But I couldn't hide my turmoil for long.

One evening I told Nikolai Rafaelovich and Zina what I was doing in my job. Zina looked aghast with my descriptions of the camphor injections. "What really bothers me is that Sitkin has no conscience," I said, "yet I must obey his orders. I manipulate people's minds and torture their bodies. I feel responsible. Sitkin is like two different people. Sometimes he's witty and knowledgeable, but when he treats patients he's a totally different person. He doesn't care about them. He doesn't talk to them. They are like objects to him."

Zina held my hand tightly. "Why didn't you tell us about this earlier?" Her voice was chastising. "Why did you hide this from me? It makes me feel that you don't trust me."

"It took me a long time to figure out if the procedures were helping the patients, what kind of person Sitkin is, and how responsible I am. I don't know what to do. Should I quit?"

"How can you stay?" Zina asked. Agony twisted her face. Her nails burrowed into my skin, but I didn't move my hand.

---

* Guard shack.

"You want me to leave? You want me out of here?" I shouted back. "You know I'll be on the first *etap*, and we won't see each other for the rest of our days."

"No, I don't want you to leave. Maybe you can get a job on another ward or in the kitchen. But look what it's doing to you. You've become a stranger, half-human since you've been working there. It's poisoning your soul. Keep doing it and you'll become one of them."

Nikolai Rafaelovich put one hand on mine and one hand on Zina's. He said calmly to Zina, "Janusz isn't as healthy as he thinks he is." He looked at me softly. "You're improving, but you're still running a fever in the evenings. You aren't well yet. The mines would destroy you."

He looked at Zina, who was listening intently but with fire in her eyes. "Zina, Janusz needs to take care of himself. If he quits, I doubt he'll be assigned another job in the hospital. It's very likely he'll be sent on *etap*. You've helped him recover this far. Please support him in this difficult job, too."

Zina hugged me and nodded her head, trying to accept what Nikolai Rafaelovich was saying.

"Janusz, the psychiatric ward is a safe haven for you. It's the safest. You're not going to get infected with schizophrenia or manic depression. You've established a place for yourself as a *feldsher* in psychiatry—no one's going to send you on *etap*. Sitkin has enough clout with the NKVD to protect you. I saw him recently, and he's pleased with you. My advice is to stop feeling guilty. Stop torturing yourself. You don't have a choice in what you do as a prisoner. Even when free, we have very little choice in what we do in this country. You are not responsible. If you don't do it, someone else will. Do your best to care for the patients, but don't worry about what you cannot control. You've got good friends here. Look at the good things."

Nikolai Rafaelovich stood up. "I'm going to check on the nurses. I'll be here if you need me."

Rybakov had been transferred from a camp for chronic patients. Most of them were sent back to the mainland; the others went on to work light jobs as janitors or night watchmen. Rybakov was sent to us.

It was his sixth trip to our ward. All he wanted was to cut himself and bleed. He had slashed both wrists countless times, and his abdomen and chest were streaked with scars. The worst were the scars from glass, which he'd use to cut himself and then stick under his skin. I'd pulled many pieces out of his scalp and face. This time he came in with a gash from the side of his mouth to his ear.

Rybakov could cut himself with anything, and so we had to keep him strapped down when he was actively hallucinating. We couldn't even let him eat by himself because he'd cut himself with the spoon. The worst scars were on his lips and around his mouth; he'd caused them by chewing and biting on the fragile labile flesh. Teeth imprints extended up to his nose and down to his chin.

When he wasn't having an acute attack, he was warm and charming, despite his grotesquely exposed teeth. His shy smile and shame for the way he looked made me feel sorry for him. When I greeted him, he took my hand with both hands and held it for a moment, as though giving me his trust and devotion. Between attacks he'd work on the ward cleaning up dishes, washing the floors, and dusting the beds. During these periods he had the delusion that his wounds came from the NKVD interrogators. He confided in me that the interrogations were still going on, but instead of sending him to prison, the interrogators were talking to him through the wireless phone. Only he could hear the voices. Every day he had to report to them, and every day they asked him a question he could never quite understand through the mix of voices. When I offered to answer for him, he was visibly relieved.

I could never find out from him what he had done before his arrest. His sentence was for counterrevolutionary agitation, which could mean that he'd read a forbidden book or told a joke. I only heard him talk about his family once, when he said his parents were coming to visit him. He was most responsive when talking about sports. Sometimes in the yard he made a ball out of cloth and kicked it, imagining he was playing soccer.

He also liked to talk about the books he'd written. He believed he was a famous, prolific writer, and every day he promised to give me a new book to read. He greeted me with identical words each day, uttered in the same excited tone of voice: "I'm glad you came! I just finished a philosophical study. It's called *From Here to There*. You would like it. You'll learn a lot about Greek philosophy. It's not a very thick book. If you want, I'll tell you about it. I left everything at home. You know, I have a beautiful house close by. Come visit me one day."

I'd steer him back on track. "I'd love to read your new book. Your philosophical findings are of great interest to me. Exactly what does the title mean?"

"It means the beginning and end; life and death; the period of our life when we know what we are doing. The period of my life when I am writing books. From now when I start until the time when I end." He gestured emphatically to make sure I understood his concept. "The whole life is from here to there."

With such conviction and excitement in his voice, Rybakov sometimes sounded quite logical. But then he'd go off, inevitably, on a tangent, like a squirrel jumping from branch to branch.

"The horses in my stable always ran away. I didn't know how to keep them. I had so many horses."

"I know about the horses," I interrupted.

"No," he said with irritation, "I'm not talking about horses. I'm talking about my brother. He was a bad boy. He always stole sugar and jam from the kitchen."

Other titles were *Jumping on One Leg, Looking up the Chimney, Crossing the Bridge*. They all had to do with space and movement, reflecting his meandering thoughts. He was happiest when I asked him about his books. He rattled off the stories, which made no sense, but he was deeply animated when telling them.

I spent a lot of time with Rybakov, hoping to reach him and perhaps bring him out of his delusional world. The orderlies informed Sitkin that I was spending a lot of time with Rybakov, and Sitkin pulled me aside one day and said I was wasting my effort. I saw his point, but I had to try my own form of psychotherapy. It seemed to make his days go better, and I continued to hope that I might be able to keep him from slipping so far away that he'd begin to cut himself again. I kept him occupied with various tasks and reserved time every day to talk to him on his bed.

There were so many things I couldn't understand in psychiatry that from time to time I asked Sitkin questions. Once I asked him what caused mental illnesses.

"There may be some predisposition. Or perhaps severe trauma activates certain conditions. The harsh conditions of the labor camps will worsen the illness. It's as if the mind tries to help the body by offering an escape through a mental disorder."

"You mean that the patients escape into the disease and remain sick?"

"I wish I could answer that question. We'd like to know how the patients become ill, but the more difficult question is how to get them better. The schizophrenics live in a different world, but we don't have the key to this world. The greatest tragedy is that the patients don't have the key either. We've dissected the brain. We know how it is built. But its mechanisms are invisible. We can glean nothing about why, when, and how the gray and white matter goes awry."

I thought of Viktor's dissection table and how easily Viktor sliced through the soft, spongy tissue of the brain. It was one thing to understand how a muscle contracts when looking at the striated tissue; it was quite another to understand where thoughts came from or how they worked when looking at the cheesy matter of the brain.

Although I learned how to deal with the acute schizophrenic patients, the illness continued to frighten me. Convulsive therapy seemed to put some patients in a chronic state. But I still wondered if the transition from an acute to chronic state was the result of the therapy or a normal course of the disease.

When the weather was mild, the chronic schizophrenics and manic depressives were allowed to spend most of the day in the yard. I used the time to talk to the patients. I wanted to learn more about their illnesses, but most of all I wanted to penetrate their thoughts, to find out what had happened to their minds, and to see if I could help some of them feel better. I wanted to understand how psychosis could overtake a person; how people could completely lose contact with the world around them and with other human beings. I wanted to know how the depressed patients could become so lost inside themselves, unable to escape their moods and feelings, but still remain lucid and logical. These patients weren't insane but permanently sad and hopeless. Sometimes I worried whether my curiosity impinged on my compassion. I didn't want to become a cold observer like Sitkin and Sofa.

In the yard I picked out the patients who seemed most responsive that day and talked to them. Neither Sitkin nor Sofa told me to do this or trained me in it. Rather, it was a calling within myself; I felt I had the ability to talk to, listen to, understand, and persuade the patients. Ultimately, I thought I could make them feel better.

When talking to some of the chronic schizophrenic patients, I discovered that certain topics—such as their arrest, imprisonment, or family—made them retreat like startled birds. I was amazed by how quickly they could turn off and frustrated by the fact that nothing could bring them back. I never knew when I'd press the button that would shut them down, but when it happened I'd continue talking, thinking that perhaps I could alleviate their suffering and help them deal with their traumas. Some of the patients behaved perfectly normally after an attack of acute schizophrenia had passed; others continued to have delusions and hallucinations.

One of our patients, Misha Perlman, had been a well-known poet in the twenties and early thirties, but in 1934 his poetry was banned, and he was arrested along with several other poets and writers in 1937. He often recited his lyrical poems to me. He wrote about the beauty of nature, love, and friendship. He once commented bitterly, "I didn't write about Stalin, the heroic workers, or the great achievements of socialism. Journal editors and colleagues suggested that I write about these social themes, but nothing ever came to me."

Severely depressed, he didn't leave his bed at all on some days. Even when I sat next to him, he lay with his back turned to me, unresponsive. He refused to talk, asked me to leave, said it was too painful to utter a word. He couldn't eat, didn't want to look out the window, and kept his eyes shut when I spoke to him. All he could say was, "Please, leave me alone. I don't want anything. I don't bother anyone. I just need to be left alone." Every word throbbed with pain. I often remained with him but said nothing. I put my hand on his shoulder so he knew I was there. Like every other prisoner, Misha suffered from the pain of his arrest, imprisonment, and ruined life, but he carried an ache that lay beyond those circumstances. I could see it in his dull stare and slow walk; hear it in his monotone voice. He looked and sounded ill, but the cause lay not in the body but in the mind. I'd seen the same look in my mother after her surgery. She, too, slowed down, stared at the wall for hours, and didn't laugh or talk. I didn't know what to do or how to react. She'd become a different person.

I tried not to abandon Misha. Once, sitting on the bench under a tree, he put his hand on my knee very gently and said, "I know you want to help me, but I can't get better. Something keeps me locked inside a loneliness and fear of the world. Even you become alien when I feel like this. Then I think that maybe you are the only person who cares about me. It doesn't matter to anyone else if I live or die, if I'm sane or insane. I don't think I'm insane, but I'm definitely very down. I don't know how to pull myself out. I've never heard voices or seen devils dancing before my eyes. Sitkin insists that I'm manic, but I've never experienced what I see in the other manic depressives. I just can't function. All I can do is lie in bed, letting time pass, wishing I were dead. I feel as though I'm suffocating with these hopeless feelings and fatigue, but I can't bring myself out of it."

We both sat staring at the ground, troubled and disturbed. I felt so close to Misha, and this made the incurability of his illness even more difficult to take. The only thing that seemed to help him was writing phrases and poems. "They keep tumbling through my head," he said one day, pleased and encouraged. "I must be insane—I can write. I couldn't write when I was sane, but now I can't stop the images from flowing. Can you get me a pencil?" I obliged, even though it was against the rules—a patient might hurt himself or others with the pencil.

I tried to convince Sitkin that Perlman never had manic attacks, that he was only depressed. Sitkin shot back, "What do you mean 'depressed?' Depressed people don't belong in the hospital. In the aristocracy it's known as hypochondria. In the nineteenth century it was known as melancholia. All the rich people who had nothing to do suffered from depression. They were depressed, hysterical. They didn't know what to do with themselves. It's like Perlman. He thinks of himself as a great poet, but his writing is worthless. If you want to become his personal caretaker, I don't care. I want to get him in better shape and send him back to the mines."

One day the guards brought in a prisoner in shackles and handcuffs. Sitkin ordered Vanya and me to put him in an isolation cell, with the warning that he might be rambunctious. "And don't ask him his name. This patient is to remain incognito." The man's chart was confidential, and his name wasn't revealed to anyone. Sitkin kept a safe in his office for confidential charts and reports.

When the patient realized he was in the psychiatric ward, he exploded in anger. "I'm not crazy! Why did they bring me here?" We put him in a straitjacket as soon as the handcuffs and shackles were removed, just as Sitkin had ordered. The man's sharp, frightened eyes and protests gave me the sickening feeling that he was perfectly sane. I tried to calm him down by telling him that if he wasn't sick, he'd be released. "I hope you're right," he replied. But his voice sounded defeated and filled with despair.

For two days we kept him in a straitjacket in the isolation room. On the third morning Sofa asked me to get ready with a camphor injection. The nameless patient was brought in. I'd talked to him several times, and he told me he constructed airplane engines. Arrested in 1938, he'd been sentenced to five years for telling a political joke. Two months ago his sentence had expired, and now he was accused of revealing secret information while in the camps. He was under investigation, terrified of what might happen to him.

He spoke so articulately that I was convinced he wasn't mentally disturbed. I shared my impressions with Sofa. She thought for a moment and said, "Sitkin has special information on the patient. He may seem lucid at times, but we've been told that he's delusional, imagining himself to be a different person. I wouldn't mention this to anyone else. You know his case is top secret."

Sofa seemed to know what she was talking about, but when it came time to inject the patient with camphor, the old guilt burned my stomach and made my hands shake. The seizure was especially strong and extended. After several hours Sitkin decided to interrogate him, and I had to leave the room. Late in the afternoon Sitkin asked Sofa and me to come to his office. We sat down, but Sitkin remained deeply preoccupied. He finally said, "I got the impression from Dr. Rutko that this patient may be an exceptionally severe case. He's very stubborn. His delusions are unshakable."

Sitkin paused and reread the man's chart. "Janusz, you reported that he seemed lucid before the seizure?"

"Correct."

"After the seizure his thoughts were muddled up and his identity even more confused. We'll know in a day or two if he gets better. But his condition may arise from brain damage, and further treatment might be necessary. We may perform a lobotomy."

Patients who remained in the acute stage of schizophrenia and had only very short, partial remissions were lobotomized. But this man didn't complain of auditory or visual hallucinations, and he seemed different from the acute patients. I didn't feel I had the experience to challenge Sitkin's conclusions, and waited for the next two days to see how he recovered.

I never again had the chance to talk to him. He remained semiconscious, uncommunicative, and exhausted. At the end of two days he was transferred to the hospital in Magadan, where he would undergo a lobotomy.

The patient vanished as though he'd never come. I once asked Sitkin what had happened to him, and he replied, "How do I know? No one reports back to me on the patients who go through here. And to tell you the truth, I don't want to know. I'm not interested."

CHAPTER 19

Letters

The winter of 1944 arrived early. The temperature hovered at minus forty. The whipping winds bit at my face. My eyes teared, my nose dripped, and the cold air pierced my weak lung. I sweated profusely and quickly became short of breath. Snowstorms closed the road to the highway and caused severe drifting inside the hospital grounds. Nearly all the men working in the hospital were called to shovel snow. I worked on a brigade digging out the road. The fresh air and physical effort offered a reprieve from the schizophrenics' shouting and head-banging, the brutish orderlies, and Sitkin's shock treatments. But I tired easily and leaned frequently on the shovel until one of the guards came along and kicked it out from under me.

The division of NKVD guards had been exchanged for a fresh contingent. Nikolai Rafaelovich said this was typically done every two or three years to cut down on fraternization between the guards and prisoners. Many *predurkis* had also been exchanged. One-Eyed Ivan was transferred to the transit camp in Magadan to work in the cafeteria for free workers, an upgrade he'd arranged through *urka* connections. I heard he'd been given a pass to leave the zone during the day.

The change in guards and *predurkis* was upsetting and dangerous. Even in the hospital, the NKVD commanders and guards wielded absolute power, and the *predurkis* were given free reign. The doctors were fairly safe from being sent on *etap*, but *feldshers*, nurses, and orderlies were at risk. As usual, the new guards were Asians. The NKVD planned it that way, counting on racial and ethnic differences to increase the hostility between the guards and us. The new guards didn't speak Russian very well, which made them unpredictable and excessively brutal. With the old liaisons broken, communication was badly hampered. I knew Sitkin wouldn't stick his neck out for me. The only person I could count on was Nikolai Rafaelovich.

Even before I'd been assigned to the shoveling brigade, I had lost weight and was feeling weak. Nikolai Rafaelovich insisted on readmitting me to the hospital and doing tests, not sure whether or not this was a flare-up of the old illness. The sputum analysis was negative, which meant I wasn't contagious, and the X rays also came back negative; the cavity in my lung was gone. However, Nikolai Rafaelovich requested that I be commissioned out of heavy labor, meaning that if I were sent on *etap*, I'd be assigned to work in a greenhouse, to clean off fallen trees, to level land for a road, or to work as a janitor or night watchman. He presented my case at the monthly meeting of the Medical Commission, and the change in my work status was approved and a note was written in my file. I was safe from the mines for another year.

The margin of safety freed my thoughts, and they scattered in many directions. In another year the war might be over; then I could be released by a general amnesty, return to Poland, and look for my family. The hope of reuniting with Taubcia gradually reemerged. Although I tried to control my fantasies and expectations, hope simmered.

Shmons had been taking place frequently. The day and hour were unexpected—no announcements were made, no rumors leaked. They were conducted by a specially trained brigade brought in from Magadan. The moment the *shmon* began, the hospital came to a halt: everyone had to stay right where he or she was. The wards, sleeping barracks, workshops, bakeries, tool sheds, and administration offices were thoroughly searched. Desk drawers were turned upside-down, shelves were emptied, and every piece of paper, including Misha's poems, was confiscated. I watched as one officer examined every book in Dr. Sitkin's office and shook it to make sure nothing was hidden inside. The patients' charts were carefully inspected, and Sitkin was questioned about the diagnosis and prognosis of each patient. Patients who had been hospitalized longer than three months were scrutinized especially closely, as were political prisoners. The NKVD officials double-checked to make sure the politicals weren't faking and had all undergone shock treatment.

Word got out that they were searching for testimonies written by a group of political prisoners. Apparently, a group was conspiring to ship testimonies about the labor camps to the mainland and from there to foreign countries to be published. In the evening Nikolai Rafaelovich told me that many of his professional notes had been confiscated and were to be examined in Magadan. "This whole thing could be a setup. These officers don't understand medical language. They'll think I've written counterrevolutionary material in code. They're just looking for people to ship out."

Indeed, with each *shmon* several arrests were made, sending fear into every corner of the hospital. The hospital director and NKVD officials pressured the department chiefs to discharge more patients, and a group of free doctors went from barracks to barracks talking to personnel, looking through charts, and evaluating patients. More gold was needed for victory. More workers were needed in the mines. The number of *etaps* increased. But I was safe for one year.

Every day the *Kolymskaya Pravda*, pinned up on the cafeteria wall, announced that some new country had been liberated—Estonia, Latvia, Lithuania, Poland, Czechoslovakia, Romania, Austria. There were twenty-four-gun salutes in Moscow for the liberation of a capital and twelve-gun salutes for the liberation of major cities. Colonels were promoted to generals; generals to marshals. Eight thousand miles away, in the camps, the only interest in the victories revolved around the question of whether or not there would be amnesty for prisoners. For us, the defeat of Nazi Germany meant nothing. Camp rules were still enforced; food was still scarce; the guards were still brutal; the sentences still long. The NKVD still searched and interrogated us.

The only change we noticed was an increase in the prison population. As the Soviet army liberated the Nazi-occupied countries, the NKVD swept through and arrested suspected Nazi collaborators as well as the local bourgeoisie. They were sent to the camps, and many of them ended up in the hospital. The barracks reserved for chronic psychiatric patients began to burgeon with prisoners suffering from all types of chronic disorders—syphilis, emphysema, ulcers, pellagra.

Two nurses and a *feldsher* working in the chronic psychiatric barracks had left the hospital during the previous two months. Dr. Sitkin asked me to take charge of the barracks and said he'd look for another *feldsher* or nurse to help me. In the meantime, two orderlies and two housekeepers were my only help. I slept in a cubicle next to the nurses' room, which meant I was on duty twenty-four hours.

I continued to spend most of my time with the chronic schizophrenics, the manic depressives, and the severely depressed. The latter would lay for hours facing the wall, curled up in a fetal position, pain emanating from their listless bodies. I thought that my presence and kind words might draw them out of their state, in which nothing meant anything. Their inner worlds were closed shut, and they did not welcome communication with the outside world. I was guided only by my intuition and by the silent howl for help that I read in their eyes and saw on their faces. Even if they couldn't respond, I told them I cared about them and that they would get better. I held their hands, brushed back their hair, put my arm around their shoulders.

If the mentally ill patients were sent back to the work camps, they would most certainly suffer another breakdown and/or be devoured by the predatory guards and *urkas*. I thought they all should be commissioned back to the mainland, as other patients with chronic diseases were, but very few received this blessing. Sitkin and the Medical Commission made the selections. I never figured out their rationale, although it was clear that politicals were seldom commissioned.

Dr. Sitkin found a young Polish medical student named Zaslawsky to replace me in the acute barracks (I continued to work alone with the chronic patients). He was everything I was not: tall, blond, blue-eyed, a real medical student, and a real Pole—he was Catholic. He had been a fourth-year medical student when the war started and had belonged to a group of Polish partisans near Brest. He was arrested when the Red Army took over the area. Zaslawsky irritated me with his hand kissing, heel clicking, and deference to Sitkin. He was constantly smoothing back his blond locks and spoke aristocratic Polish, frequently mixing in French words. His heavily accented Russian charmed Sofa and Dr. Sitkin but left me cold. The partisan group he belonged to— *Wolnosc i Niepodleglosc*, or WIN (Freedom and Independence)— was well known for its anti-Semitism.

Zaslawsky and I circled each other carefully, not wanting to get into a discussion that could be unpleasant for both of us, but after several weeks I needed to talk. I invited him to my room and closed the door. "I have a problem I need to discuss with you," I said uneasily. "We work with each other very closely and see each other every day. I need to know if it's true that your group exposed Jews to the Nazis or killed them in the forests. I need to know how you feel toward Jews."

Zaslawsky blushed deeply. "You go straight to the heart. What do you want, a confession?"

"No. Just the truth."

"The truth is not very pleasant, but if you want to hear it, I'll tell you. When the war started, young Poles were either enlisted into the support services of the German army or sent to work in Germany in the factories. Polish men were rounded up in the streets and sent to concentration camps. I went into hiding with my cousin at my parents' estate near Lida on the Belarussian border. But the Nazis as well as the collaborating Ukrainian and Lithuanian police were scouring the area for Poles, Jews, and partisans who'd gone into hiding. It so happened that WIN was operating near my parents' estate, and to protect myself I joined up with them."

"Did you know the group was anti-Semitic?"

"Yes." Zaslawsky began to pace. I was afraid he'd walk out, but instead he picked up the chair and slammed it down hard. "You really want to know what we did to Jews? You think it will clarify things between you and me?"

"Yes," I said calmly. My aim wasn't to provoke Zaslawsky but to clear the air between us.

Zaslawsky clutched the hair that flopped down on his forehead and held it in place. "I witnessed some killings. Many members of the group hated the Nazis, Soviets, and Jews. When they had the chance, they were violent. Jews were the easiest targets."

"How could you witness this? How could you remain with these people?" The anger I'd always felt toward these groups converged on Zaslawsky. I wanted to hit him or spit on him. All I could think of were the Jews hiding in the forests and these people hunting them down and killing them.

Despite my rising hostility, which showed in my loud voice and trembling hands, Zaslawsky didn't lose his composure. He looked me dead in the eye. "When I went to medical school in Lvov, anti-Semitism was rampant. I fell into it blindly and stupidly. I'm ashamed of many things I did, of hurting many decent people. In the forests while fighting with the partisans, I tried to stay away from killings. I even warned several Jews of our presence and gave them directions where to hide. I'm not trying to make excuses. I did some bad things to Jews. I'm not innocent." Zaslawsky pulled some tobacco and a rectangular piece of paper from his pocket and rolled a cigarette. He lit it and took a drag. "If you don't want to talk to me anymore, I understand."

Listening to Zaslawsky made me sick. Even before the war he had belonged to a fascist organization. Many of my close friends were badly hurt by these groups while attending the university. I doubted that he had joined WIN by chance. Zaslawsky and I belonged to two different worlds. Our paths had diverged long ago. Nothing he could say could undo his past or my feelings.

The relaxed atmosphere in the chronic psychiatric barracks was exploited the most by our kitchen worker, Marieta. She was a gorgeous Georgian with raven-black hair; thick, arched eyebrows; and flirtatious black eyes. A procession of hopeful men came to the barracks every day—mostly high-ranking *predurkis* from the administration. She smiled at me without saying a word as they came and went.

Marieta and I became close friends, spending the days talking and laughing about her string of suitors. "Men are like dogs. I make eyes at them, give them a promising smile, and they follow me anywhere." She puffed on a cigarette, threw her head back, and laughed in a husky voice. One of them brought her alcohol; another, food; another, beautiful fabric and clothing. She dropped them as soon as she had enough goods and had found another man who brought more useful presents.

I was struck by her beauty but was too afraid to be anything but friends. She'd killed her first husband with a stiletto after he had hit her. The second one she killed with an ax after an argument. Both murders were committed in cold blood. For me, the best thing about Marieta was that she arranged with the guards to let Zina come and go whenever she wanted. Marieta treated Zina like a younger sister, dressing her up in her fancy clothes. Zaslawsky came over in the afternoons and Marieta played hostess, offering him a cigarette, a drink, and probably something more.

On New Year's Eve 1945, Marieta and I hosted a party. Marieta talked the guards at the gate of the psychiatric complex into letting our friends enter. Marieta and Zina planned the event and made out the guest list. We decided to have the party in the kitchen, a large room in our barracks with a big table, wooden benches, and a large stove. The guest list included Dr. Sitkin, Sofa, and the night *feldsher*, Trofim; Nikolai Rafaelovich, Maria Ivanovna, and Hela Borisovna; Dr. Loskutov and his camp wife, Nina, a surgical nurse; and Dr. Mayerson and his recent girlfriend, Sofia Leontevna, the radiologist. Zina and Marieta insisted on inviting Zaslawsky.

The air was filled with joyful anticipation. The Red Army was in Poland and Czechoslovakia, and the camp was full of rumors that the greatest amnesty of the century would occur to celebrate the great victory. Everyone hoped freedom was just around the corner. We drank alcohol from the pharmacy, which we'd been stockpiling by filling out prescriptions in advance. Loskutov brought a big box of chocolates and two bottles of wine. Nikolai Rafaelovich surprised all of us with cans of pork and beans. Marieta's two boyfriends, Marik and Lova, both high-status *urkas*, brought an abundance of food: sweet rolls with raisins, fresh-smelling white bread, red caviar, ham, sausage, cheese, chocolate cake, and, rarest of all, pickles and mustard. Marik and Lova brought three other well-known criminals and three young women.

The kitchen seemed like a banquet hall; the wooden plates, like china; the aluminum utensils, like silver. Zina and Marieta decorated the kitchen with evergreen branches. The table was heaped with food. Marieta invited me to make the first toast. "Dear friends," I began, embarrassed. "Let's drink to the hope that our lives will change this year when victory is won. I toast our good luck, happiness, and freedom in the New Year. I dream that we all will meet somewhere as free citizens and share our new lives with each other."

The toasts followed one after another. Glasses clinked; alcohol drained from the flasks. "Let's get to know each other better," Marieta slurred. "No titles, no patronymics." She turned to Dr. Mayerson and kissed him warmly on the mouth. Then she grabbed Marik and kissed him passionately, her whole body clinging to him.

Two young girls sitting on each side of Nikolai Rafaelovich announced that they wanted to dance on the table. "I want to take off my clothes. It's hot in here," one of them said.

Everyone stood and clapped rhythmically. *"Davay! Davay!"* Marik sang "Ochi Tchernyje" in his beautiful voice while the two girls and two *urkas* performed a gypsy dance.

Marieta and her two boyfriends drank from the same bottle and cuddled together. Lova, with his shirt unbuttoned to the navel and the hairs on his chest hanging out, pulled Marieta on his lap and put his hand up her skirt.

"Stop it, you idiot!" hissed Marik.

Marieta jumped to her feet. "There's enough for both of you, and some left over for somebody else." She pulled Zaslawsky away from Zina and hugged him.

Dr. Sitkin and Sofa left first. Sofa's white blouse was stained red with caviar; her stockings sliding down. They looked like two school kids, proud that their love affair was finally in the open. I spent most of the evening with Zina but had long talks with Nikolai Rafaelovich and Dr. Mayerson. We sat in a small group and planned what we would do when we were released. Zina and I planned to go to her home first to look for relatives and then go to Poland. Toward the end of the evening everyone except Zaslawsky and me began singing Russian songs—we Poles didn't know the lyrics.

Before the ten o'clock curfew, everyone had gone. I lay on my cot, unable to close my eyes without the room spinning. I kept one foot on the floor to steady myself and thought about being released and about all the places and people I had known. I could see them all, as though looking at the sand and pebbles on the bottom of a crystal-clear stream. I had so many pasts now. Such a long string of people, vastly different kinds of people, had entered my life.

One cold morning in late January, a messenger came from the administration building. "You've got a letter in the mailroom. You can come and get it in the afternoon when the mail is sorted." I went immediately.

Eugenia, a young Jewish woman and good friend, was working. I told her I'd received a letter and asked if she could get it. She went to the "B" section and pulled an envelope from the stack. The letter was addressed to me, but I didn't know the sender—B. F. Anchipolovsky. The letter had been stamped in the city of Omsk. My heart sank. Perhaps there had been a mistake.

I nearly tore the envelope in half with my shaking fingers. Inside I found two neatly folded pieces of paper—one letter was written in Polish, the other in Russian. With my heart nearly bursting, I read the Polish one first.

Dear Beloved Brother,

I'm happy to have finally found you. I'm a Captain in the Polish Army and am doing everything possible to obtain your release. I hope you can join me. I'm sending you three hundred rubles to help you buy necessary things. You will hear from me again soon.

Kiss you,
Julek

The other letter, written in Russian, was a great surprise. It was from a cousin I'd never met.

Dear Cousin,

We're happy you sent news about yourself and that you are well. My family and I now live in Omsk. We moved here from Karkhov in 1941. Although we've never met, I've heard a lot about you and would like to hear more. Please write to me at the following address. I'll be in touch with your brother.

Affectionately yours,
Bella

I read the letters again and again. My brother's handwriting was the most precious thing I'd ever seen. I kissed his signature. I kissed the envelope and held it against my heart. I no longer touched the earth. My brother was alive and well; maybe the rest of my family was safe, too. I wondered how Bella had found out about me, how either of them had found out where I was. It had been five months since I'd sent the letter to Katia; it seemed unlikely she had ever received it.

I ran to the ophthalmology barracks and shared the letters with Zina, then went to find Nikolai Rafaelovich. I waited at the TB barracks for over an hour, but he had gone on a consultation somewhere. I went to share my good news with Dr. Mayerson, whom I seldom ever saw. As chief of the surgery department, he was extremely busy, spending most of his time in the operating room. When we met he was friendly and asked how I was doing, but at the same time I felt a distance between us. It could have been age, education, or status. Although I owed him so much, I didn't feel comfortable in his presence and therefore never sought him out. But I considered him a dear person, although not a close friend like Nikolai Rafaelovich or Dr. Loskutov. I caught Dr. Mayerson between surgeries and briefly shared my news with him. He seemed pleased that I had chosen to tell him and seemed genuinely happy for me.

Back in my room, I read the letters again. I badly wanted to get in touch with my brother, but he didn't give me an address. He was probably still on the front line, changing locations frequently. That evening I sat down to write to Bella. It came to me that my father had a younger brother in Kharkov, Ukraine, who had two daughters, Bella and Zina, both close to my age. I'd completely forgotten that two of my father's siblings, Uncle Fischel and Aunt Charna, had never returned to Poland after World War I but lived permanently in Ukraine. I'd never met any of these relatives.

It was strange to write to a person I'd never met or even seen in a photograph. I tried to imagine her when I sat down to write, picturing her with my father's dark eyes and hair. Not having written a letter for so long, and exercising the utmost caution, I wrote a terse response, mentioning only my health and longing to see my family.

I admired Bella's courage in writing to me. But I worried that she might be questioned about corresponding with a prisoner who wasn't part of her close family. I was also concerned about her last name—she was born Bella Bardach. Was she married? Had she changed her name to sound Russian? Not knowing the circumstances of her life, I sent only the briefest note to deflect any suspicion our correspondence might raise.

At the end of February I received another letter from Bella and a short letter from Julek. He didn't disclose his exact location but said he was still on the front line in Poland and that he'd been promoted to major. His superior had written a letter to the Society of Polish Patriots in Moscow requesting my release.

So much changed inside me with these letters. The love conveyed by my brother, to whom I'd never felt close, was fresh and deeply touching. When we parted we were living in very different worlds and were unable to bridge the gap. All these years I'd tried not to think too much about him, but I sensed through his brief, hastily written notes that he had thought continually about me.

Julek was five years older than me, and we inhabited different worlds. I was always curious about what was happening behind the closed doors of his room when his friends, boys and girls, were visiting. I couldn't keep from looking through the peephole and felt hurt and angry to be so ignored and excluded. When Julek was sixteen and I was eleven, his first girlfriend, Niunia, visited him frequently. He'd lock his door, and I'd spend hours circling his windows outside the house and climbing trees to get a glimpse into his room. "What are they doing in there? Why does he lock his door?" I asked my parents. They never gave me a satisfying answer, and my spying continued. Julek never knew how interested I was in his life. I never had a chance to tell him.

His room was filled with books in Polish, Russian, and French. He was always reading, and I envied his knowledge. At twelve, I was less interested in reading than in playing with my dog, Billy. I was very impressed when Julek began receiving literary and political magazines from Warsaw. My mother and aunt also read one of them, *Wiadomosci Literackie*, from cover to cover. Julek and his friend Antoni Gronowicz, a published poet at the age of sixteen, carried on heated discussions about the articles with my mother and aunt.

Julek brushed me off anytime I asked him a question, most of which I had carefully prepared ahead of time and considered to be quite intelligent. "What a childish question," he'd scoff. "You're too young to discuss such things. Go play with your pigeons/play soccer/ride your horse/play with your friends." His condescension made me feel not only insignificant but also rejected, reminding me over and over that I didn't belong to his and my mother's circle. He was always serious, concentrated, and deep in his thoughts; reading, writing, debating. He couldn't dance, never attended parties, didn't like sports or outdoor games, and never came on a picnic to the riverbank. The only thing he liked was kayaking with Niunia, disappearing upstream for the entire day. I thought he was a bore.

When I was thirteen, Julek went to Vilno to go to law school. After that I saw him only during the summers. If we had little in common at home as children, we had nothing in common when he was away at the university. Julek started writing his master's thesis during his second year and had become the editor of *The Worker*, the local edition of the Polish Socialist Party newspaper. His thesis was so good that it was published in book form. My mother gloated over every one of Julek's achievements.

But the most surprising news came before Julek's final year at law school—he and Niunia had broken up, and Julek was getting married to his new girlfriend, Fruma, also a law student. The wedding was secular. Julek once again was the center of attention, while I wandered among the strangers, just another youngster whom no one knew. After four years at Vilno, with all his achievements, Julek was untouchable—worldly, highly educated, famous—while I felt stuck in the rut of mundane, provincial life.

The invasion of Poland one year later by the Soviets and Nazis not only divided Poland but also separated Julek and Fruma from us. We became part of the Soviet Union, whereas Vilno was incorporated into Lithuania and had its name changed to Vilnius. The separation greatly worried my parents and inspired long talks about how to bring them home. When I volunteered to get them and bring them back through the "green border" (i.e., illegally), my parents were hesitant. But there was no other way to get them home—their requests for a visa to enter Soviet territory had been denied. My parents finally agreed to the plan after Chaim Ochs, a strong, experienced street fighter and good friend, promised to accompany me. We succeeded in our mission, and for the first time Julek acknowledged my competence.

Since that time Julek had risen to the rank of major in the Polish army, while I had spent four years in the camps. Although we'd never been so far apart, I felt closer to him than ever before. I believed in him and trusted he would secure my release.

Along with his brief letters, Julek sent money, which I saved in the camp depository, anticipating I would need the money when I got out. I had never thought I might be released before my term had expired; even rumors about the amnesty failed to raise my hopes. But now that the high command of the Polish army was working to get me out, long-buried thoughts and images of home surged forth. I imagined my reunion with my parents, sister, and, most of all, Taubcia. I daydreamed about what I would do with my life. I wondered how my mother's health was, how Taubcia and Rachel had changed, if various friends were still alive. I looked forward to seeing my father's joyful face. I had no doubts that Taubcia was waiting for me and that our feelings for each other would be as fresh and strong as the day I'd left for the army five years before.

But thoughts of Taubcia inevitably led to thoughts of Zina— and to guilt and turmoil. When I was released, I would fly home. Zina would stay here. But if there were an amnesty, and Zina were released with me, then what? What about our plans, our future? Could it be that I might have to choose between two futures, when for so long I thought I had none?

Taubcia was my first and greatest love. But I was also in love with Zina. What if I had to make a choice? Which one would I betray? Neither Taubcia nor Zina had parents, a family, a home. One was probably in the ghetto; the other was a prisoner. I couldn't bear the thought that either of them might suffer more because of me.

I quit sharing the letters with Zina, quit talking to her about my release. I didn't want her to know my dilemma.

The news came that the Soviet flag was hanging from the Reichstag. Victory was at hand. We read in the Kolyma newspaper of Hitler's and Goebbels' suicides. Unconditional surrender was only hours or days away.

On May 9 victory was declared. The camp commander ordered a day free of work and a camp-wide dinner in the mess hall. And on the mornings that followed, crowds gathered around the bulletin board in the cafeteria to see if the amnesty had been announced.

But days turned to weeks. Our hopes were not fulfilled by the powers in Moscow; our prayers were not answered. The crowd stopped forming in the morning, and everyone became bitter. Nikolai Rafaelovich was taking the disappointment very hard. His free patients had built his expectations too high. I felt terrible for my friends and guilty to be the only one left with hope.

My correspondence with Bella flourished. I wrote to her about my family, school years, and love for Taubcia. Julek wrote that he had been promoted to colonel and was going to remain in the military. I shared every letter with Nikolai Rafaelovich but kept my hopes sealed off from Zina, just as she'd been sealing off parts of herself from me. As spring blossomed, Zina became more and more distant. She didn't smile easily, nor look deeply in my eyes, nor squeeze my hand so lovingly. The higher my hopes soared, the greater the distance between us grew.

One day in July, an orderly from the TB barracks came to my office. "Janusz, hurry up. Nikolai Rafaelovich wants to see you."

I went to his quarters and found him packed and dressed in civilian clothing. He had been released and fully rehabilitated, with back pay for the years he'd spent in the camps. It was two years before his term was up. The news took my breath away. He said he was going to work at the Dalstroy Clinics in Magadan while arranging for a flight back to Moscow. A flat was already prepared for him. I was so happy for him and so sure that my release would follow that I didn't even think about our parting. I didn't think for a second that my brother might fail in his mission.

As the car waited Nikolai Rafaelovich repeated that he would never forget me and that if I ever needed him, I was to contact him right away.

During the previous two summers, Zina and I had spent Sundays gathering mushrooms and berries in the woods. It had been the best time for Zina and me, since we could meet at our secret places far from camp and be totally alone. But when I asked her to meet me again, she refused.

"Janusz," she said, "I don't think we should see each other anymore."

I'd felt it coming for a long time, but the words cut me deeply.

"It's become unbearable to listen to your joyful announcements," she explained, "to hear again and again what your brother is going to do for you, to plan our phantasmagoric future in Poland. I've still got three years of my sentence, and I don't have a brother in the Polish army. I have to take care of myself, and I've met someone else to share the remaining time with me. I wish you luck. I've enjoyed our friendship, and I loved you. But you spoiled it."

She began to cry and walked off.

I couldn't move, couldn't talk, could only watch her walk away, feeling my life change as drastically as the day I met her.

Over the next few days I learned that Zina had a new boyfriend—Zaslawsky. And I was given tips that made me think they'd been interested in each other for quite some time. At first I felt betrayed, but as these initial feelings lessened, I felt relieved not to have to chose between Zina and Taubcia. I didn't even condemn Zina and Zaslawsky. I couldn't judge them as I would if we were free. Zina had to take care of herself. And I was sure I'd be leaving, convinced my brother would succeed in his efforts to get me out.

The empty days of July dragged on with nothing to distinguish one from the other. I no longer had to run to see Zina; I didn't have comradely discussions with Nikolai Rafaelovich. Dr. Loskutov was my closest remaining friend. Doubts crept in about my release. For three weeks I didn't hear from Bella or Julek. On July 28 I turned twenty-six. I was still a prisoner. My spirits plummeted.

In August a messenger came from the Office of Registration and Distribution and told me to report there right away.

Vorobyev, the same officer who'd assigned me to Dr. Piasetsky, stood at his desk with his hand outstretched. "Congratulations," he said. "I'm pleased to announce that a decision has been made by the Collegiate of the Supreme Military Court to shorten the term of your punishment. You are to be released under the condition that you sign the following statements."

Two papers lay on his desk. He gave me both of them to read and sign. The first paper was a statement that I would not reveal to anyone by word of mouth or in writing anything I witnessed from the day of my arrest to the day of my release. If I broke the condition, I'd be imprisoned without trial for a minimum of five years depending on the type of information I had given.

"Sign here," he said. He then took the thumb of my right hand, pushed it onto an ink pad, and rolled my thumb beneath my signature. "This paper will stay with us." He shuffled through other papers on his desk. "This one is for you." He rolled my thumb at the bottom of the form as well.

The paper was my official release form. It had been signed and dated three months before. I wondered about the discrepancy but was too stunned to speak.

Vorobyev's voice brought me out of my trance. "Take these papers, go to bookkeeping, and they will write an order for the money you received from your brother. I see you've got nearly two thousand rubles. It's probably enough to buy a plane ticket to Moscow. You are free to go to your barracks, gather your things, and go the *vakhta*. Show the guards your release form, and they'll let you out.

"One last thing, I have a message from Dr. Doctor, the hospital director. He wants to see you at four o'clock in his office."

CHAPTER 20

Free, But Not Home

With the release document and two thousand rubles in my pocket, I went to say goodbye to my friends. The release document, containing my photograph and thumbprint below it, served as a temporary passport and traveling document. This little piece of paper represented not only my freedom but also my ticket home to Wlodzimierz-Wolynski. I no longer yearned for adventure. I no longer cared to see the big world. I'd had enough. Nothing was more precious than peace and home.

I wished I could tell Nikolai Rafaelovich the good news, but that would have to wait until I went to Magadan. I went to the TB ward and found Maria Ivanovna and Hela in the nurse's room. I showed them the release document, unable to repress my smile. Maria Ivanovna hugged me with her strong arms, too stunned to say anything. Hela kissed me and squeezed my hands. My release had inspired fresh hope in her. "When you're in Moscow, please give my name to the people at the Association for Polish Patriots. I'm sure someone there will remember me and my husband from the years we worked in Warsaw. Tell them everything about me and the circumstances of my arrest. Please let me know what they say."

I'd read in the newspapers and heard from Polish prisoners coming from Magadan that the Association for Polish Patriots had been formed in Moscow to search for and repatriate Polish citizens scattered throughout the Soviet Union during the war, people who had been exiled from the Soviet occupied territories, were arrested and sent to the prisons and camps, or fled voluntarily to escape Nazi occupation. I planned to find the association's office, give the names of the Polish prisoners I knew, and seek their help in getting back to Poland.

I said goodbye to Dr. Mayerson and Dr. Loskutov and then went to find Zina. She had been avoiding me, and I hadn't bothered to seek her out. But now I wanted to talk to her. I had only warm feelings toward her, memories of closeness and love. I wanted to leave as friends.

I cracked open the door to her cubicle and peeked in. Her blond hair was tied with a red ribbon. She was sitting at her desk. It was the first time since we had parted that I'd seen her so close.

I waited for her to feel my presence. She turned toward me slowly. Her eyes widened with surprise; a smile brightened her face. She hugged me warmly.

"I'm glad to see you." I kissed her deeply.

"Janusz, I'm sorry if I hurt you." She held my hands tightly. "I still care about you. I don't know if I did the right thing by breaking up. But you were so preoccupied with yourself, so sure your brother would get you out. I felt you didn't care about me anymore."

The knot was growing in my throat.

"Zina." I took her hand and kissed it. "I came to say goodbye. I was released an hour ago." My voice had faded to a whisper.

Tears welled up in her eyes. "I'm happy for you. Really, I am. I hope you find the rest of your family alive and well."

"Zina, I'll never forget you." It sounded hollow but it was true. "I hope we meet again."

"Good luck, Janusz." She hugged me one last time. "Now go."

Back in my cubicle, I looked for things to take with me. I had acquired a small wooden suitcase and put my shaving kit, towel, comb, mirror, and winter hat and mittens inside. I put on the beige tunic that a patient, who was a professional tailor, had made for me out of a blanket; I packed my black one in the suit-case.

Now it was time to say goodbye to my patients. I worried about what would happen to them, since Dr. Sitkin still hadn't found anyone to help me on the chronic ward. It had never occurred to me that I might leave so suddenly. Who was going to take care of them, especially the severely depressed? I thought the process of being released took time, that I would be able to train my succes-sor, that I would have time to plan where to go and what to do.

I found Dr. Sitkin in his office. My announcement astonished and annoyed him. "What are you saying? How can you be re-leased so suddenly?" But then, in his typically detached way, he came around from the side of his desk and shook my hand. "You did a very good job. The patients liked you, and you were very pleasant to work with." I thanked him for giving me the job and asked who would be taking care of the patients, adding that the depressed patients needed special care. Sitkin was perfunctory. "It's not for you to worry about."

I walked quietly into the ward and pulled a chair up to Misha. He lay in the corner with his back to the door. When I told him I was leaving, he turned to me and for a moment looked deeply in my eyes. He said nothing. He retreated into his cocoon. I went from bed to bed. Many patients cried openly when I said good-bye. Behind their good wishes was an unmistakable look of ap-prehension. I would miss them deeply.

I went back to my cubicle and sat at my desk, not sure of where to go or what to do. I had the paper to leave the camp, but then what? I couldn't get a ride to Magadan until the next day, and at four o'clock I had to be in the office of the hospital direc-tor, who had the ironic name of Dr. Doctor. I couldn't imagine why he wanted to see me. I wanted to leave the camp immedi-ately, before anything could go wrong. But skipping the appoint-ment was unthinkable. I'd been molded to obey and be afraid. The hospital director was also the camp commander, and his power gripped me more tightly than the notion that I was free.

I was hungry. There was a cafeteria for free workers outside the zone, and I decided to go there and buy my first meal. I went to the *vakhta*. Trembling with joy and fear, I pulled out my release document. The guard in charge read it and unlocked the door, expressionless. Walking through the corridor, I glanced through the window to the rooms where the body searches took place. I had an urge to spit on the floor. Another guard held open the door at the other end. I walked out onto the dirt road.

Luba, a former Polish Communist, was in charge of the cafeteria. I ordered bread, a bowl of stew, and tea with sugar. I took out the wad of rubles from my breast pocket and examined them closely to give the correct amount. Luba slid the money back. "It's on me," she said. "You're the first Pole to come through here. Poland is a free country again. Maybe we'll all be released soon." She asked me to give her name to the Association of Polish Patriots.

Luba told me of a house a few doors down where I could rent a room, and I made arrangements with the owner, an agronomist, telling him I didn't know if I'd be staying one night or ten. The question of what to do next—the next hour, the next day, the next month—overwhelmed me. My past had not prepared me to be on my own. My only wish was to go home and find my family.

At five minutes before four o'clock, I went to see the hospital director. A long conference table covered with a fancy green cloth dominated his office. He settled into a wingback chair, which looked like a throne. I remained standing.

"Now that you're free, I'm sure you'd like to go home," Dr. Doctor began. "Where is your home?"

"Poland. I'd like to leave as soon as possible. I intend to catch a ride to Magadan tomorrow and buy a ticket on the earliest ship to Vladivostock. Then I'll take the train or fly to Moscow. I have relatives there. From Moscow I'll find a way to go back to Poland."

"Don't be in such a hurry," he sneered. "Sit down. Everyone who gets out wants to leave immediately, but the wait to get on the ship can be long. As far as I know, you don't stand a chance to get a ticket any time soon. You've got to get on a waiting list."

"But navigation is open for at least another three months—"

"Don't be naive. I'm telling you, you'll never get a ticket to leave during the next three months. You've got to wait like everyone else. Go to Magadan if you want and find out for yourself."

"I plan to go to Magadan to see Dr. Piasetsky. I'm sure he knows what the situation is."

"Dr. Piasetsky is a big man now in Magadan. In fact, he asked me to find a job for you."

"What kind of job?"

Dr. Doctor's tone changed from irritated to businesslike. "Dalstroy is building a new road to the airport and to the outposts in the taiga. It's a big operation. There will be a much larger work force. We're starting an ambulatory clinic for the prisoners working outside the zone. I've got three doctors and two *feldshers* working there, but they are prisoners. I need a free doctor or *feldsher* to sign the patients' work releases, validate hospital admissions, and write daily reports on the clinic's activities. I've heard good things about you from Dr. Piasetsky and Dr. Sitkin. I'm sure you can do the job. Let me know if you want it when you get back from Magadan."

Meeting Nikolai Rafaelovich in Magadan was like reuniting with a long-lost family member. He treated me to dinner at a luxury restaurant and invited me to stay with him. Despite his prestigious position as director of the Dalstroy-NKVD ambulatory clinic, he had only a single room in a four-bedroom apartment that housed three other families. They all shared the kitchen and bathroom. His large room was divided in two by a screen: one side had a bed and couch, the other a dining room table, living room sofa, and buffet.

We went shopping the next day because, as Nikolai Rafaelovich remarked, I looked like a "poor relative getting out of prison." He had a permit to shop at a special clothing store open to Dalstroy officials and to the NKVD. I bought a pair of pants, a shirt, and tall leather boots. Nikolai Rafaelovich bought me a short fur-lined jacket. I felt like a millionaire and invited him to a restaurant.

"Save your money," he said. "You'll need it to get out of here." Nikolai Rafaelovich confirmed Dr. Doctor's grim prediction.

"Tickets are scarce, Janusz. You probably won't get one until next season, and it will cost you a bundle. I'll try to get you on the waiting list or look for some other means of transportation." My spirits were lower than ever. I didn't want to remain in Kolyma working at the hospital, but Nikolai Rafaelovich thought it was the smartest thing to do. "Consider the job with Dr. Doctor temporary. I'll try to find you a job here so we can be together, but you need to have a job so you can get food stamps and make some money."

The job in the ambulatory clinic was odious. My primary duty was to keep the daily work releases below 5 percent of the total number of workers, a formula that was supposed to keep cheating and bribery down to a minimum. I felt ridiculous supervising the three doctors and, to limit my presence in the examining room, spent most of the time hiding out in my office, signing work releases and writing reports.

In September two *urkas* demanded drugs and a work release. Both had been patients in ophthalmology, and I knew them fairly well. They appeared when I was closing the clinic for the day.

"We're sick," Scorpion said. "We need codeine and a week off work."

I said I'd give them one day off but that a week was impossible.

"What do you mean, a day?" Scorpion snarled. He parted his tunic to reveal the blade of an ax. We settled on ten packages of codeine apiece and three days off. The decision cost me many sleepless nights. Giving out drugs to *urkas* was a major camp infraction for which I could be rearrested. I was in great danger of being blackmailed.

The situation worsened in the fall and winter. More prisoners got sick, and more *dokhodyagas* appeared at the doorsteps. I didn't have the heart to turn them away. The releases rose to over 10 percent, and finally I was inspected by two free doctors and an NKVD officer. They ordered me to explain every work release I'd signed that day. "Don't be so soft-hearted," the younger doctor said with a congenial smile. "Look out for the interests of the camp, not the enemies of the people."

The *urkas* made more frequent visits. They liked opium, alcohol, and codeine. The ax tucked in the tunic accompanied every visit, and I complied with every request.

On a cold, snowy day in November a patient whom I knew well arrived. Siemion Ogurcov, a chemist, worked in the hospital laboratory. He had bronchitis, and I signed a three-day release following the doctor's recommendation and invited him to my office for a talk. I told him about my troubles and shared with him an idea that I'd been thinking about for a long time.

The idea had come to me after witnessing an incident on the surgery ward three months before. Dr. Mayerson was gone for the day, and a new prisoner from Budapest, Janos Zader, was in charge. Zader looked like a gypsy, with wiry black hair, bushy brows, olive skin, a radiant smile, and debonair clothing and manners. He was the camp darling. In addition, he was an excellent surgeon and the only ear, nose, and throat specialist in the hospital.

A large amount of donated blood had gotten too old to use for transfusions, and the head nurse asked Zader what to do with it. His answer was quick and, in my opinion, brilliant. "Add some sugar to it for taste and serve it to the patients as a protein supplement." The nurse did as she was told, dispensing the blood from a teapot into little cups at dinner.

Dr. Doctor fired Zader, accusing him of instituting cannibalism, and rumors spread that Zader might even stand another trial. He went to work as a lumberjack for three months, but then Dr. Doctor became desperate for an ear, nose, and throat specialist and requested that he be sent back.

The need for a protein supplement in the hospital had been on my mind for quite a while. Blood is very high in protein and makes an excellent supplement for patients suffering from malnutrition. Zader's pitfall was using human blood for this purpose. But what about reindeer blood?

The more desperate I became to get out of the ambulatory clinic, the more I thought about creating an enterprise for collecting and distributing reindeer blood. I remembered an old Eskimo prisoner, a TB patient, telling me about the semiannual thinning-out of the reindeer herds up north. During a week-long celebration, the Eskimos slaughtered the old and infirm animals to keep the population healthy, and I envisioned the reindeer blood spilling out into the snow. Perhaps I could find some way to collect it.

I talked to Siemion several times about the idea, and he thought it had great potential. He said it was chemically possible to preserve blood with citric acid and to enrich it with alcohol and sugar. Siemion helped me write a proposal outlining the idea. I requested one truck with a driver; six wooden barrels to collect the blood; and two gallons of pure alcohol, twenty packages of pressed tea, and fifty packages of *makhorka* to be used as gifts for the Eskimos. With the final proposal in hand, I went to see Dr. Doctor. My aim was to get a trial period so I could get the enterprise off the ground. I was well aware, however, that the idea was so bizarre that Dr. Doctor would never go for it. In that case, I would resign, move to Magadan, and find a job there. I could no longer take the fear of being blackmailed or murdered by the *urkas*.

I handed Dr. Doctor the proposal. "We have a great need for a high-caloric protein supplement in the camps and in the hospital, and I've designed an enterprise to produce such a product." To my surprise he became quite interested in the proposal, asking if I'd witnessed the reindeer kill and if I knew how the blood could be preserved. "We'll only collect the blood in winter, so it will remain frozen during the long transport," I explained. After detailing the process of preservation and enrichment, I asked him for his approval, adding that I wanted Ogurcov as my associate and chief chemist.

Dr. Doctor fell for it.

The reindeer blood collecting enterprise far surpassed Siemion and my expectations. In two months' time I had established good connections with several Eskimo tribes, and I was given two additional trucks and eight prisoners to perform the work. Siemion got his own lab and had three women working under him to sterilize the bottles and package the enriched blood, which we called hematogen.

In January Dr. Doctor granted me permission to sell the product outside the hospital, something I'd already been doing on the black market in Magadan. I no longer went on the expeditions up north but delegated the collection to the prisoners and spent all my time marketing the product and counting out the money. I was better off financially than I had ever imagined possible. Dr. Doctor created a new position for me, with the title Senior Inspector for Furnishing Animal Blood. I was paid nine hundred rubles a month, which wasn't much to live on, but I made twice as much on the black market.

Whenever I was in Magadan I saw Nikolai Rafaelovich. He said he was taking the steps necessary to get me on the first ship to Vladivostock and added that he was looking for other means of travel as a backup. I had no idea what he meant, but trusted he wouldn't let me down.

In the meantime, I adopted a stray dog—half-husky, half-German shepherd. He had an injured leg; I nursed him back to health, and he stuck close to me thereafter. I named him Yantar, the Russian word for "amber." There were so many dogs running wild that I accumulated seven of them very quickly—Atlas, Romeo, Jack, Billy, Nana, and Jana. Then I bought a sled. Early on Sunday mornings, I hitched up the team and hit the road. Flying through the woods and on the rivers, I inhaled the open air, absorbed the sunlight and freshness of the snow, and felt like the Prince of the North. Sometimes I invited one of the other free workers living in the settlement to come with me, but they almost always declined. They usually preferred to spend Sundays with their families at Luba's cafeteria, where they ate a big dinner and drank excessively. On rare occasions I went to this "family" dinner. The highlight of the day was the drinking competition between the men. A full glass of pure alcohol was poured, and the drinker was goaded into drinking the entire glass in one gulp. Insults were hurled at those who couldn't keep up. There was great drunkenness, vulgarity, and vomiting at the table.

I spent the evenings reading books borrowed from my landlord and answering letters from Julek and Bella. The agronomist and his wife were very kind, but we had little in common. They were wealthy—free workers in Kolyma were paid a double salary and were given a six-month vacation every other year—and conversations with them centered on money and travel, subjects on which I had nothing to say. The only thing we had in common was our love for the dogs; they took care of them whenever I went to Magadan.

At night I lay awake for hours in the large but spartan room. I luxuriated in the silence and fresh air, the absence of snoring, hacking, talking, and fighting.

It had been nearly a year since I'd begun corresponding with my brother, but in all his letters he never mentioned Wlodzimierz-Wolynski or our family. I wondered what he knew about their fate. Sometimes I thought his failure to mention the family was a good sign, that he probably hadn't located them yet. But in the depth of night, the dark message in his silence came through too clearly.

I wrote several letters to Julek demanding to know what he knew, but he never answered my questions. The letter writing was becoming unbearable. I wanted to talk to Julek, hear his voice, ask questions, get answers. It became an obsession, and one day I went to the post office in Magadan and asked if I could get a telephone connection to Poland. It was crazy—I didn't have Julek's phone number—but I had to do something. The clerk turned me away, saying it was impossible to get a line outside of the country from Kolyma.

At the end of March I received a call from Nikolai Rafaelovich: "I've got a plane ticket for you from Magadan to Khabarovsk. It's a cargo flight scheduled to leave on April 4 at seven o'clock in the morning." I resigned that day and left the blood-collecting enterprise in the hands of Ogurcov and the dogs in the hands of the agronomist and his wife, with money to take care of them. I promised Nikolai Rafaelovich I would visit his parents and sister in Moscow and write to him about their welfare. He hoped to be in Moscow the following year, and we left it that I would send him my address, whether I was still in Moscow or in Poland. I left him on the airport runway, a lonely figure standing tall with his hands clasped behind his back.

The cabin was loaded with crates and boxes; I was the only passenger on the plane. The pilot pointed to a metal bench and told me to sit. Not another word was spoken between us during the flight, even though the cabin temperature plummeted far below zero and I banged on the door of the cockpit to let him know I was freezing to death. During the four hours in the air, I rubbed my face, hands, and toes constantly, staving off frostbite once again. When we landed, the pilot promptly told me to get lost.

The airport in Khabarovsk was twenty kilometers from the city, and after an hour-long bus ride I arrived at the train station. The plaza was swarming with people waiting to buy train tickets. Some said it took two or three days. I wasn't about to waste more time standing in line and left to look for a place to spend the night.

In the late afternoon I overheard a man speaking Polish with a hint of a Yiddish accent. Henryk was from Vilnius. He'd gone to the same university as my brother and had been a philosophy student when the war started. He and his family were deported to a village in Siberia when the Soviets occupied the city. Then he moved to Khabarovsk and learned to be a cobbler. He had a small shop in the room where he lived, and he invited me to stay with him.

Henryk treated me like an old friend. He lived in a huge room separated into three areas by screens. One corner held his workshop, another his cot; the third corner was occupied by two women friends. They started work in the evening and continued all night, bringing their clients back to the room. When they woke up late in the day, the four of us went to a restaurant together, for which the ladies insisted on paying. They were also Polish and were well educated and cultured. They and their families had also been deported to Siberia under Soviet occupation, and the two women were saving money to go back to Poland and resume legitimate lives.

I went to the train station every day with the hopes of finding a shorter line, and every day after several hours I went back to Henryk's flat, frustrated and angry. It was hopeless for a single person to keep his place in line. I shared my frustration with Henryk, and he came up with the idea of buying a plane ticket: the tickets were more expensive but probably more available. He offered to go with me to the airport to wait in line.

For two and a half days we took turns standing in line. The queues disbanded for the night, but at seven o'clock the next morning everyone was back. Each person made a list of the ten people ahead and behind as proof of his or her place in line.

On the fourth day I boarded the plane. I sat next to the window and peered out at the clouds, feeling as if the whole world were mine. I found myself daydreaming like I used to, imagining what the world was like in the valleys and hills, the forests and steppes. It was so wonderful to see the whole landscape, not just a patch of land through the grated window of the Stolypin car; to wonder about the world, not fear it. I could feel myself becoming civilized and sensitized again. This way of thinking was so strange. The camps, the Twenty-third Kilometer, the zone, the guards, and the patients had become my reference points. All these things seemed familiar, whereas the airplane, Moscow, and the world below seemed foreign. With a joyful thrill I kept closing my eyes and opening them, awakening every time to the fact that I was free and heading home.

Since the airplane didn't fly at night, the plane stopped overnight in Omsk and Sverdlovsk. As I lay with four other passengers in the crowded airport sleeping quarters, essentially a dormitory room, I thought about the prisons in the two towns, the prisoners sleeping pressed against each other. I felt an intimacy with the cities that no one else around me had.

On the afternoon of the third day, the plane landed at the Vnukovo Airport in Moscow. It was spring. Still chilly, but budding, blossoming spring. With my cousin Katia's address in hand, I asked passers-by how to get to Yaroslavskoye Chaussee 148. I was told to take busses, trolleys, and trams, but I was so afraid of not getting off at the right stop and missing a connection that I walked. After two hours I reached Yaroslavskoye Chaussee, which began at the Yaroslavskoye train station. From there I counted the street numbers up to 148.

I found the building but couldn't believe Katia lived there. It was a massive gray structure—a work of social realism—two blocks long. Finding her apartment took another hour. I had to walk through each separate wing and check the names on the doors. I found it in the third wing on the sixth floor. Panting, sweating, my heart pounding, I knocked.

A white-haired woman answered. Without a moment's hesitation, she cried out my name and hugged and kissed me. She then held me at arm's length to study my face. "It's you! We've been waiting for you. Look, Sioma, it's Janusz."

Her husband, a tall, well-built man in his fifties, stepped forward and gave me a big hug. He picked up my suitcase and asked if I had any other luggage.

I felt both joyful and sheepish, unable to take my eyes off the relatives I had never seen in my life. They were genuinely happy to see me, to have me, an ex-convict, in their home. How much fear they must have overcome to take me in.

Every day they had set an extra place at the dinner table in the hope that I or their son would show up. Their son, Shurik, had been fighting on the front line, and although he was declared missing in action, they still hoped he was alive and would appear one day soon.

We sat in the dining room and interrupted each other with questions—nearly every sentence uttered begot another question. Katia patted my hand during the meal and held it when Sioma got up to serve the next course.

A short while later the doorbell rang, and a young woman with the figure of a lanky girl appeared. Katia introduced me, and the woman kissed me on both cheeks. She said, "Janusz, we've been waiting for you for so long. Katia has been so anxious. It's so good to have you here." Confused, I hugged the stranger aimlessly. Finally Sioma stepped in to quell the chatter and excitement.

"This is Sonja, our mail carrier. She also took care of Shurik when he was young. We consider her a member of the family. Over a year ago Sonja came with a letter addressed to E. D. Weinstock, but the address was wrong. Since only the initials were given, Katia and I figured it belonged to a different Weinstock and we refused to open it. We gave it back to Sonja to find the right owner."

"I had a feeling about the letter," Sonja jumped in, "and carried it around for several weeks. I checked for other E. D. Weinstocks, but no one else had the same first initials. There was no return address, so what was I to do?

"One day I brought the letter back to Katia and said, 'Either we open the letter now or we burn it.' We waited until Sioma got home and opened it. Inside was your brief note. We celebrated until one o'clock in the morning for having found you."

Katia began to cry. "The war was still going on. Sioma was working at a secret chemical factory for the military. We were frightened of receiving mail from a prisoner. Sioma could lose his job; he could be arrested for having such contact. We didn't know what kind of sentence you had—we thought you were a political prisoner—and so we asked Bella to write to you. We thought it would be safer, since she is your first cousin and isn't associated with any secret work."

Sonja disappeared into the kitchen and came out with a bottle of vodka and four short glasses. "We've been saving this bottle ever since Katia received news from Bella that you'd been released and were coming to Moscow. Let's toast to your good health and happiness, and to those who aren't here but are on their way."

Sioma filled my glass again and said, "This is for your brother."

"Where is he?" I asked.

"Just a minute." Sioma picked up the telephone and dialed. "He's here," he said into the receiver and handed it to me.

Julek spoke my name. I hardly recognized the voice, but the slight nasal tone was unmistakable.

"Where are you?" I shouted into the receiver.

"I'm in Moscow. I'll be there in half an hour to pick you up."

Julek appeared in a Polish officer's uniform. At least twenty colored bars decorated the left breast pocket of his tunic. His face looked the same, but he was bald, square-shouldered, and less stooped. He kept looking at me as we ate dinner.

In his slow, deliberate style of speaking, he said, "When I first got news of your letter, I had just been offered the position of military attaché in Mexico City. I turned it down, still hoping I'd find you or someone else from the family. You don't know how happy I am to see you."

"And our parents, Rachel, Taubcia—"

Julek's glance was brief and sorrowful. "They're gone."

"All of them?" As the words left my lips, something in me collapsed, drowned, was lost forever. The thing that had kept me alive in Kolyma had begun to unravel in the silence of Julek's letters, and as I asked the question and saw the answer in his eyes, the unraveling came to an end. The contents of my heart spilled out; the coldest water rushed in.

Julek nodded.

After dinner we left in a black limousine with little Polish flags mounted above the headlights. "I have a guest room arranged for you," Julek said, interrupting the uncomfortable silence in the car. This struck me as strange, but I was so shocked with everything that I didn't know what to say. Julek seemed more distant than ever before.

Julek continued talking in the same placid tone, explaining as we drove past the Mayakovsky metro station that we were close to the embassy and that Molotov's and Beria's mansions were nearby. "The embassy is in a building of one of the wealthiest Moscow merchants. You'll see," he said. "I hope you don't mind staying in the guest room—my wife and baby are sleeping."

Two policemen opened the iron gate, and we drove into the courtyard of a U-shaped building. As Julek unlocked the door to my room, he asked, "Do you have pajamas?"

"No," I replied.

"I'll give you a pair of mine."

"It's not necessary." We glanced awkwardly at each other and disappeared into our separate quarters.

The next morning Julek introduced me to his new wife, Halina, a former streetcar conductor he'd met in Lodz after the liberation. She got pregnant; they got married. Their three-month-old daughter, Christina, lay in a bassinet. Halina was ten years younger than Julek and attractive, with a pretty face and simple manners. We liked each other. I wanted to know what had happened to Julek's first wife, Fruma, but that question would have to wait until a more appropriate time.

Julek's apartment was furnished with Louis XVI furniture, chandeliers, red brocade curtains, tapestries, mahogany paneling, thick Persian carpets, gold and silver goblets. After breakfast Julek took me to meet the Polish consul, Mr. Motruk. I'd become a Soviet citizen during the occupation, and in less than an hour Mr. Motruk changed my citizenship back to Polish and issued me a passport.

"It's better if you don't tell anyone where you've been," Mr. Motruk informed me. "You are now a foreigner, and foreigners are highly esteemed in the Soviet Union. You won't have any problems with the local police if you stay out of trouble." He said to Julek, "Get Janusz a Polish officer's uniform. He can pose as a Polish officer discharged from the army. This will make a good impression."

We went to Julek's tailor, a man assigned to work for the diplomats. Julek had me fitted for a Polish officer's uniform and an elegant suit—navy with white pinstripes—which he'd already picked out. Then we went to another special shop, where he bought me shoes, socks, a long coat, and a felt hat.

The next day Julek introduced me to the Polish ambassador, Professor Raabe, and his wife. They were exceptionally warm and invited Julek and me to dinner at their home. They wanted to know everything I had experienced in the camps, but I found it extremely difficult to talk openly. I couldn't put out of my mind the paper I'd signed when I was released, and I was afraid the ambassador's apartment was bugged.

For four days Julek left me completely alone. He didn't talk to me, didn't ask what I'd been through, showed no interest in my life. He said he was busy processing the repatriation papers of Polish deportees and prisoners. During the days I went to visit Katia and Sioma and wandered around the city. Four days later he asked me to go for a walk in a nearby park.

We sat on a bench and watched ducks swimming in a pond. "We can talk safely now," Julek said. "I want to know everything that happened to you—how you got arrested, how you lived over there, how you are now."

As I told Julek the main events, I watched for his reaction. It was strange to be telling my brother, this stranger whose life had followed such a different course, how I had been arrested, how I'd worked in the gold mines, how I'd landed the job at the Central Hospital. I'd never seen such sorrow in Julek's eyes and couldn't bear adding to it. I left out many painful details. When I finished, I asked him to tell me what had happened to our family.

"Yes, you should know," he said, indicating that he'd thought the matter over carefully. He spoke quietly and methodically, making sure every event was given in the right order. With every sentence I felt as if a pool of water were growing around me.

"In May 1944," he began, "I went to Wlodzimierz-Wolynski with my unit. We arrived the third day after the town was liberated. I walked down Farna Street. I looked for our friends and found Professor Filarsky. He invited me to his home. Papa had given him many items from the house, and he gave them back to me.

"Under Nazi occupation the doctors and their families were not forced into the ghetto, and for a short while the family remained together in the flat. But the Gestapo was entering the houses robbing, raping, and sometimes killing, and it became very dangerous for Taubcia, Rachel, and Fruma to remain at home. They went voluntarily to the ghetto because it was safer.

"I found Chaim Cukier, Papa's dental technician, and he had seen the family being taken from the flat in July of 1942. The Gestapo forced everyone into the yard. When Chaim heard them coming, he jumped out the window and hid in the outhouse. He saw Papa suddenly fall to the ground. Papa always carried cyanide with him, saying the Nazis would never take him alive. The family, except for Rachel, Taubcia, and Fruma, who were in the ghetto, were taken to the forest and shot. The ghetto was liquidated the same week."

Julek and I sat in silence, two ghosts. When we got back to the embassy, he moved me into his personal quarters.

"Why did you keep me in the guest house?" I asked, no longer able to conceal my hurt. He replied that after four and a half years in the prisons and camps, he didn't know what kind of person I had become.

"What do you want to do with your life?" he asked.

"Drive a taxi. If I could borrow money from you, I'd like to buy a car." Julek made no comment.

From then on, every hour we had alone, we talked. Julek tried to convince me that being a taxi driver wasn't the best idea. He suggested that I study at the university, but I was certain I couldn't pass any entrance exams. He dropped the idea for a while, but I could tell he thought continually about what I would do with my life. One day he said he had found an opportunity for me to study: through his connections he could get me into the Medical Stomatological Institute in Moscow without taking the entrance exams, and he could arrange for me to get a stipend from the Polish government. He told me I could study medicine or dentistry, whatever I wanted. I didn't know if I'd make it at the institute but decided to try.

Not a day passed that I didn't think about my family. Although I reconnected with Julek and my newfound relatives, I found it very difficult to think about my life ahead without dealing with the life I had left behind. I needed to expunge the persistent but lunatic hope of finding someone alive—the thought that perhaps Taubcia or Rachel had escaped the ghetto liquidation and was living somewhere in Poland. I felt an urge to face my hometown, my home, my room, my school, my streets, my river, all the places of my worry-free years, when everyone I loved was alive and happy. I needed to know why I had been spared, why I survived, why I deserved better than everyone who was killed or died by their own hand.

During the summer I went to Wlodzimierz-Wolynski. The city, now part of Ukraine, was in a restricted zone, and as a foreigner I had to apply for a special permit to visit the town. The officials granted me a three-day visit, and I was required to report my arrival and departure at the local NKVD office.

I took a train from Moscow to Lvov, stayed overnight, and resumed the journey in the morning. Pulling into the train station, I saw that the name of the city had changed. It was now written in Cyrillic—Vladimir Volynski. Half of the train station had been destroyed and was being repaired, but the other half looked just as I had remembered.

Taubcia's house was still standing, still painted red, with the large, wrap-around veranda. I knocked at the door. A middle-aged Russian woman answered, and I asked if she knew what had happened to the family who had lived there before the war, hoping that Taubcia's parents and brother had returned. She knew nothing. The house had been vacant when the city council designated it to her and her family three months earlier.

I looked for the stores and shopkeepers I had known so well on Farna Street—nearly all of them Jewish—but the stores had changed and the people in them were foreign. On Farna Street I ran into a former Polish classmate, Yevgeny Karkuszewsky. He'd become a major in the Polish army and was living in Warsaw but was visiting his parents who still lived in town.

"You're alive. We heard from so many people that you'd been captured by Germans at the beginning of the war. Several locals came to your father with news of what had happened to you and promised to arrange for your escape for a lot of money." He told me the names of the extortionists, young Ukrainians or Poles I knew well, a few of whom had been schoolmates in the Polish gymnasium. Yevgeny also gave me the names and addresses of townspeople who had looted the house after my parents were killed.

I knew one of the Ukrainian families and went to their home. I was invited in, and for several awkward minutes I looked at my father's rocking chair, the small Roman statue my mother had loved, the dining room credenza displaying my mother's china, a painting that had hung in the waiting room of my father's office. Overwhelmed with despair, I couldn't make any small talk and left.

The Jewish gymnasium had been burned to the ground, and Dr. Schechter's home had been turned into a military office building. It was heavily guarded. A few empty buildings remained in the Jewish quarter, which was the site of the ghetto. I stood on the empty lot overgrown with weeds and imagined the ghetto filled with my dear friends and with Rachel, Taubcia, and Fruma. I wondered where they had lived. I pictured their faces, imagined their voices, and stared at the stones in the sidewalk, the same stones on which they had walked. A few stubborn fenceposts remained, outlining the boundaries of the ghetto. With unnamable feelings welled up within me, I walked back down Farna Street and went to my home.

The building was still standing. The restaurant on the ground floor had been turned into a rundown bar, and my family's flats had been turned into offices. I double-jumped the stairs up to our flat, just as I'd always done, and was overcome with the expectation of running into my father on the steps as he went to buy cigarettes and the morning newspaper, or my mother as she set the table for breakfast.

What I found instead was the office of the local education agency. Desks and smug Soviet workers occupied my parents' bedroom, my bedroom, and the dining room. Typing clattered in the background. The bored clerks stared as I walked through the rooms.

"May I help you?" a woman asked tersely.

I said no and looked out the window to the backyard. The posts that connected Billy's wire were still there, and in the orchard I discerned the trees that concealed the entrance to Spielberg's shelter.

Feeling empty and aimless, I wandered around town looking for Jews I had known. I found several. Polish families had hidden them in the surrounding villages, and one of them told me that several of my close friends and a few distant relatives had been hidden together by a Ukrainian family and that all of them had survived.

I went to the Piatydnie forest six kilometers away to look for the spot where my grandparents, mother, sister, and wife had been executed. There was no marker, no memorial, no evidence. I went back to town and spent the rest of the day sitting alone on the riverbank. It, too, was abandoned, and the weeds and cattails had grown so dense that in some places they stretched all the way across the river. It was a strange and empty place, without boats or fishermen or young people swimming and kayaking. I stayed until daybreak, alone with my grief, watching the slow-moving water. With the first rays of sunlight I went to the train station and said goodbye to Wlodzimierz-Wolynski, knowing I would never return or forget the happy days of my youth.

Epilogue

During the years I lived in Moscow, I searched for Efim Polzun—
the NKVD captain who had commuted my death sentence—and
found a few of his relatives in Odessa. They told me he had disappeared during the war and was never heard from again. For
many years I had the feeling that perhaps he had been arrested
and shot for helping me.

One late afternoon in 1948, Nikolai Rafaelovich Piasetsky reappeared in my life. I was a second-year medical student returning
from my classes at the hospital Sokolinaya Gora when we ran
into each other at the metro station at Izmajlovsky Park. Since
my arrival in Moscow, I'd written him several letters, but he
never responded, and I thought we had lost contact for good.

He'd moved to Moscow with his wife and two children, and I
went to dinner at his cramped apartment several times. He told
me he hadn't responded to my letters because I'd given him the
Polish embassy for my return address, and it was too dangerous
for Soviet citizens to correspond with foreigners. The letters were
always censored, and often the sender was put under surveillance
and/or arrested.

He looked nothing like the ebullient, optimistic man I'd left behind in Magadan, newly rehabilitated and enjoying his position as director of the medical clinic of Dalstroy. The hostile atmosphere toward Jews, now labeled "cosmopolitans," was growing, perpetuated by the state through the newspapers and radio. Nikolai Rafaelovich was worn out with worry and terrified of being arrested again. He had expected to return to the life he had left behind, to his career in academic medicine, but the world had changed, and he couldn't find a place for himself.

Frightened by the growing campaign against Jews in 1949, he decided to leave Moscow and return to the Far East, hoping to find a life of peace and obscurity. He found a position in a hospital in Yakutsk, a remote corner of Siberia.

Only two people saw him off at the train station—his sister and me. It was not a happy departure, and I thought how strange it was that, having been released only four years earlier, he was returning, essentially exiling himself, in anticipation of being re-arrested. I never heard from him again.

In 1956 a dear friend from my past showed up at my doorstep in Lodz. Wladek Cukierman, the friend with whom I had fled to the Soviet Union when the Nazis invaded Poland, had just been released from a Siberian labor camp, having survived a ten-year term. He was on his way to Israel, wanting to get as far away from Eastern Europe as possible. His family, including an aunt, had perished during Nazi occupation. He had married a Polish woman who had also been a prisoner in the labor camps.

Among the many stories we exchanged about our experiences in the prisons and camps, one stood out. Wladek told me that one day while loading supplies onto a horse-driven cart, the driver looked over at him and said, "Where's your friend with the motorcycle?" Wladek looked at him, puzzled. "In 1939, you and your friend were heading for the Soviet border on a motorcycle, and my unit took it away and gave it back." The man went on to tell Wladek that he had spent the war on the front line as a highly decorated officer. He had ascended to the rank of colonel when he returned home, but after praising the quality of life he had seen in other countries, he was arrested and sentenced to ten years in the labor camps.

My brother, Julek, left his position in the Polish embassy in 1948. He remained in the army for another year and then began his academic career at Warsaw University. Today he is Professor Emeritus of the History of Law and a member of the Polish Academy of Sciences. He has received several honorary degrees from Polish and European universities, and his books on the history of law in Poland and Lithuania have served as the basic textbooks for several generations of scholars.

In 1950 I graduated from the Medical Stomatological Institute in Moscow and spent the next four years there as a resident in plastic and reconstructive maxillofacial surgery. In 1953 I married a Russian classmate, Elena Laniejeva, and in 1954 we moved to Lodz, Poland, where I began my academic career. I developed a special interest in the treatment of congenital facial deformities, especially cleft lip and palate.

In 1972 I was invited to join the Department of Otolaryngology—Head and Neck Surgery at the University of Iowa in Iowa City. I became chairman of the Division of Plastic and Reconstructive Surgery of the Head and Neck. I could not return to Poland without the threat of being arrested by the Communist government, so fifteen years passed before Julek and I saw each other again. In 1987 Julek was granted permission to visit the United States. After the fall of communism I went back to Poland and have returned frequently to visit Julek ever since.

In 1995 I went to Israel with my daughter, Ewa, and spent a day with Wladek, now a retired aviation technician and grandfather, and his wife. While in Tel Aviv, I met another Jewish friend from Wlodzimierz-Wolynski. He told me that a monument had been erected in the Piatydnie forest in honor of those who were killed by the Nazis in 1942.

Glossary

avoska. Maybe. Just in case. The term for a net bag used for carrying groceries.

bezprizornik. A homeless child.

ChSIR (*Chlen semyi izmennika rodiny*). A member of a traitor's family.

chelovek. Man.

chelovek cheloveku volk. Man is wolf to man. This phrase comes from the Latin proverb *homo homini lupus est* and is a popular Russian idiom expressing the cruelty people are capable of inflicting on each other.

che-pe (*Cherezvichainoye proishestvye*). Extraordinary incident.

chorny voron. Black Raven. A black truck specially constructed for the transport of prisoners.

Davay! Let's go!

dokhodilovka. A killer camp.

dokhodyaga. A goner. A degraded prisoner on his last legs.

etap. Transport; shipment of prisoners.

feldsher. Medical assistant.

Gotovsya k vikhodu. Get ready to leave.

KRD (*Kontrrevolutsionnaya deyatelnost*). Counterrevolutionary activity.

KRTD (*Kontrrevolutsionnaya troskistskaya deyatelnost*). Counterrevolutionary Trotskyite Activity.

khvoya. Extract of pine needles.

kipyatok. Boiled water.

kolkhoz. Collective farm.

komandirovka. Temporary duty assignment.

kulak. A well-to-do peasant who was persecuted during Stalin's collectivization of the farms.

lapty. Leather, canvas, wood, or tire tread bound to the foot with string.

mastirka. Self-inflicted infection.

makhorka. Tobacco.

NKVD (*Narodny Kommissariat Vnutrennikh Dyel*). People's Commissariat for Internal Affairs; later known as the KGB.

Ne tron! Don't touch!

Organy. The popular name for the NKVD.

paika. The bread ration.

pakhan. Ringleader of a group of criminals. The term often used by prisoners to refer to Stalin.

perekur. A smoke break.

Podtyanis! Catch up!

Podyom! Wake up!

politruk. Political leader.

ponyatoy. A civilian required by law to assist in and witness searches and arrests, legitimizing the activities of the NKVD.

poverka. Roll call. Head count.

predurok. A prisoner of high status who worked for the administration.

Sadis! Sit down!

Shevelis! Move!

shmon. A frisk or thorough search.

stukach. A squealer. An informer.

TFT (*Tyazoly fezichesky trud*). Heavy physical work assigned to healthy prisoners.

Trotskyite. Follower of Trotsky.

tufta. Chiseling. Padding, falsifying, or inflating the data used in work reports to obtain a better percentage and hence a better ration.

tuftach. A chiseler, swindler, or cheat.

urka. A professional criminal.

vakhta. Guard shack.

volk. Wolf.

V peryod! Move forward!

vrag naroda. "Enemy of the people." A term applied to political prisoners.

zapadnik. A Westerner. Ukrainian, Polish, and Jewish prisoners who had lived in former Polish territories of Western Ukraine and Belarus before 1939.

ze-ka. A prisoner. The word is shorthand for *zakluchoney* but is the official form of address to prisoners.

Map and Photo Credits

Designer: Steve Renick
Compositor: Impressions Book and Journal Services, Inc.
Text: 10/13 Sabon
Display: Sabon
Printer: Edwards Bros.
Binder: Edwards Bros.